Measurement in Economics

הָיָה אִישׁ – וּרְאוּ: אֵינֶנּוּ עוֹד
וְשִׁירַת חַיָּיו בְּאֶמְצַע נִפְסְקָה;
עוֹד שִׁיר מִזְמוֹר אֶחָד הָיָה־לוֹ,
וְהִנֵּה, אָבַד הַמִּזְמוֹר לָעַד,
אָבַד לָעַד !

ח. נ. ביאליק, "אחרי מותי"

There was a man — and lo: he is no more;
the song of his life, unfinished ceased;
another song, another psalm, he had,
and now that song is lost for aye,
is lost for aye!

Ch. N. Bialik, "When I Am Dead"
(translated by Sholom J. Kahn)

Stanford University Press
Stanford, California

© 1963 by the Board of Trustees of the
Leland Stanford Junior University

Library of Congress Catalog Card Number: 63-11863
Printed in the United States of America

Contents

Yehuda Grunfeld: In Memoriam

Yehuda Grunfeld's death by drowning on July 16, 1960, brought to an abrupt and tragic ending, at the age of thirty, the life of one who had already shown abundant promise of a brilliant career.

Born in Berlin on March 11, 1930, Yehuda Grunfeld was brought by his family in 1935 to what was then Palestine. During most of his early life, the family lived in Petach Tikva, on the outskirts of Tel Aviv. Upon his graduation from high school in 1947, Yehuda Grunfeld—like other young people of his generation—volunteered for the Palmach, the *sub rosa* combat unit of the Jewish community in Palestine. In Israel's 1948 War of Independence he fought with the Yiftach Brigade in the battles of the Galilee, the Jerusalem Corridor, and the Negev.

Upon his release from the army in 1949, Grunfeld enrolled in the Department of Economics at the Hebrew University of Jerusalem, where he was awarded the B. A. (1953) and M. A. (1955) degrees. His further graduate work was completed at the University of Chicago, where he was awarded the Ph.D. in 1958. In 1954 he married Dvora Shakeyd; a son, Gilad, was born in 1956.

At the time of his death, Grunfeld was Lecturer in Economics and Statistics at the Eliezer Kaplan School of Economics and Social Sciences, the Hebrew University of Jerusalem. He was also a Senior Economist at the Falk Project for Economic Research in Israel. Earlier (1957–58) he served as Assistant Professor of Economics at the University of Chicago. He also served as an economist in the Fuel Division of the Israel Finance Ministry (1953–54) and as Project Leader and Advisor to the Transportation Center, Evanston, Illinois (summers, 1957–59).

Grunfeld's first serious research in economics was his unpublished master's thesis, "Optimal Planning of the Import of Petroleum and Its Refining at the Haifa Refineries," which grew out of his work at the Finance Ministry. This contains an original and independently formulated linear-programming type of solution to a refinery-scheduling and gasoline-blending problem. His main completed work was his doctoral dissertation, "The Determinants of Corporate Investment," published in a revised and shortened version in *The Demand for Durable Goods* (A. C. Harberger, ed., Chicago, 1960). In it he gave an operational meaning to the hypothesis that a firm's investment depends on its profit expectations; this he did by measuring these expectations in terms of the over-all value of the firm's securities in the market. Most of this study is devoted to a detailed empirical testing of this and related hypotheses. His work at the Transportation Center dealt with resource allocation problems in the railroad industry, with the effect of government subsidies on capital–labor substitution in the maritime industry and on the maximum speed of newly built ships, and with the effect of the differences between countries in income and terrain on their respective transportation systems. His interest in various aspects of econometric methodology resulted in papers on the aggregation problem, on nonparametric tests of association between time series, and on the relationship between time-series and cross-section estimates of the same equation. The full list of Grunfeld's publications is given in the accompanying Bibliography. It is a mark of the breadth of his interests that these publications constitute contributions to three of the four fields represented in this book.

At the time of his death, Grunfeld was carrying on a study of the economic aspects of education in Israel. His intention here was first to construct an annual time series of the stock of "educational capital" in Israel, as represented by the money value of the formal education of the population. This he estimated by the cost (inclusive of income foregone) of reaching the respective educational levels in the designated base year. He then began to use this estimated stock as an explanatory variable in an empirically fitted production function. Grunfeld was also beginning to investigate the role of education in the general process of economic growth, and in particular the possibility of its being one of the most important sources of external economies. He had already accepted an invitation from the University of Chicago to spend the academic year 1960–61 there, working on an expansion of his study and the application of its methodology to the data of other countries as well.

What one will always remember about Yehuda Grunfeld is the spark and ebullience with which he approached everything he did, whether in private life, teaching, or research. He excelled particularly in empirical work in economics, the effective pursuit of which depends on a rare mixture of art and science. It was here that his remarkable sense of what was important played so vital a role. Equally vital was his basically optimistic outlook. As a matter of principle he would refuse to accept the contention that it was impossible to measure a certain economic phenomenon—and would insist instead that it was a question of finding the proper approach. He had little patience with idle speculation and scholastic debates, or with the equivocation that sometimes tends to empty economic analysis of real content; for him proper analysis had to conclude with testable hypotheses. And he was not afraid to suggest hypotheses that did not conform to accepted notions.

Yehuda Grunfeld thrived best in an atmosphere of mutual exchange of ideas. But he gave to the creation of this atmosphere much more than he took from it. This was particularly evident at staff and faculty seminars, where Grunfeld's role was invaluable. His queries were always designed to bring the researcher to set out precisely the purpose of his study: the nature of the questions to be answered and the reasons they were important. In discussions, Yehuda Grunfeld would rapidly cut his way through to the essentials of the argument, point out its hidden implications, and more than once bring his colleague to reconsider his entire position. But he knew how to do this with a smile and good spirits—and with an attempt not only to criticize, but also to make constructive suggestions.

He was cut down brimming with ideas and plans: for an extension of his study of education, for a book on econometrics, for a series of essays in price theory. He did not live long enough to make the mark that he seemed destined to make on the profession as a whole. But even in the short time that was granted to him, he did leave a deep and indelible mark on teaching and research in Israel—and on all who knew him personally or professionally.

Bibliography of Yehuda Grunfeld

Published Writings

1. The Effect of the Per Diem Rate on the Efficiency and Size of the American Railroad Freight Car Fleet, *Journal of Business*, **32** (1959), 52–73.[1]

2. Review of J. R. Meyer and E. Kuh, *The Investment Decision: An Empirical Study* (Cambridge, Mass.: Harvard Univ. Press, 1957), in *Journal of Political Economy*, **66** (1958), 450–52.

3. The Determinants of Corporate Investment, in *The Demand For Durable Goods*, ed. Arnold C. Harberger. Chicago: Univ. Chicago Press, 1960, pp. 211–66.

4. (With Zvi Griliches), Is Aggregation Necessarily Bad? *Review of Economics and Statistics*, **42** (1960), 1–13.

5. (With Leo Goodman), Some Nonparametric Tests for Comovements Between Time Series, *Journal of the American Statistical Association*, **56** (1961), 11–26.

6. The Interpretation of Cross Section Estimates in a Dynamic Model, *Econometrica*, **29** (1961), 397–404.

Work in Progress at Time of Death

"Human Capital in Israel"

> [Grunfeld described the plan and objectives of this study in Falk Project for Economic Research in Israel, "Fourth Report: 1957 and 1958" (Jerusalem, 1959), pp. 177–78. The later developments of the study are described in the Falk Project's "Fifth Report: 1959 and 1960" (Jerusalem, 1961), pp. 146–50].

---

[1] Awarded the McKinsey Prize for the best eligible article that appeared in the journal that year.

Unpublished Writings

1. "Optimal Planning of the Import of Petroleum and its Refining at the Haifa Refineries," M. A. thesis (Hebrew), The Hebrew University of Jerusalem, 1955 (on file at the University library).[2]

2. "The Determinants of Corporate Investment in the U.S.," Ph. D. thesis, University of Chicago, 1958 (on file at the University library).

3. (With Yoram Barzel), "The Structure of the Transportation System— A Cross-Country Comparison," in *The Transportation Geography Study: An Exploratory Study of Surface Transportation Development*, The Transportation Center, Northwestern University, 1960, pp. 1-59 (duplicated).

4. (With Nissan Liviatan and Don Patinkin), "*Lectures on Price Theory*" (Hebrew), the Hebrew University Student Organization, Jerusalem, 1961 (duplicated).[3]

---

[2] Awarded the Koenig Prize for the best M. A. thesis in economics written that year.

[3] It is planned to publish these lectures in a revised form in English.

I. Theory and Measurement of Consumption

1

Windfalls, the "Horizon," and Related Concepts in the Permanent-Income Hypothesis

MILTON FRIEDMAN, *University of Chicago and the National Bureau of Economic Research*

In the analysis of consumer behavior, one question that arises is how a consumer unit reacts to an unanticipated change in circumstances. According to the permanent-income hypothesis, the answer depends on how the change affects the consumer unit's evaluation of its longer-term income prospects, as summarized in its estimated permanent income. The effect on permanent income, in its turn, depends on the "horizon" of the consumer unit. A unit that in some sense looks far ahead and gives relatively heavy weight to the longer-term future will alter its permanent income less in response to unanticipated changes in circumstances that affect mainly current receipts than a unit that is short-sighted and will alter its permanent income more in response to changes that affect mainly distant receipts.

The mathematical model I suggested [3], for converting the rather commonplace observation that consumer units adjust consumption to longer-term income prospects into an operationally meaningful theory capable of being contradicted by observation, has two major elements and one important supplement. The elements are a model of income structure and a relation between consumption and income derived from the pure theory of consumer behavior. The supplement is an expectations model applied to aggregate time-series data in order to estimate permanent income. In the model of income structure, the concept of "horizon" is given a precise meaning that is highly relevant to the effect of an unanticipated change in circumstances: the "horizon" is a period of time used to dichotomize factors affecting income into "transitory" factors, all of whose effects on income are over within this time period, and "permanent" factors, whose effects last beyond this time period.[1] In the discussion of the pure theory of consumer behavior, the word "horizon" is used in a very different sense and one that turns out not to be relevant to the effect of an unanticipated change in circumstances: the "horizon" refers to the length of the period being analyzed; it betokens an end point, not a dividing line between

---

[1] The model of income structure was taken over from an earlier analysis of professional incomes [3, pp. 21-25], [4, pp. 325-28, 352-64].

shorter and longer periods [3, pp. 11, 14]. Moreover, no concept is singled
out in the theoretical discussion as playing a role corresponding to that
of "horizon" in the model of income structure. In the supplementary
expectations model, one parameter is said to be related to the income
structure "horizon." However, the relationship is not made explicit, and
I now believe that the one implied is wrong [3, p. 150].

This initial confusion of terms is not rectified in the rest of the book.
The term is mostly used in the income structure sense: several pieces of
empirical evidence are assembled suggesting that the "horizon" in that
sense is approximately three years for consumer units in the United States
for consumption as a whole, and the concept is used to predict the effect
on consumption of unanticipated changes in circumstances. I have always
been dissatisfied with these attempts to bridge the gap between the income
structure model and the pure theory of consumer behavior. They are
vague and indefinite in language, which simply reflected the vagueness
and indefiniteness in my own understanding of the concept. And I am
now persuaded that they led me into error and have misled others as well.
I may not have found even now a fully satisfactory economic interpretation
of the mathematical construct of the horizon, but I believe I can give a
better and less ambiguous formulation than that contained in my book.

This paper presents the improved formulation. The occasion for my
rethinking the issues and writing this paper is twofold: (1) In an interchange on the permanent-income hypothesis, Robert Eisner and Hendrik
Houthakker exchanged comments that exhibit particularly clearly the
misleading character of my earlier formulation.[2] (2) In a paper on "Windfall
Income and Consumption" prepared for a conference on consumption at
the Wharton School, Ronald Bodkin presented the results of a test of the
permanent-income hypothesis along the lines of one that I suggested in
my book. In this connection he was troubled by what seemed to him,
and rightly so, ambiguities in my discussion of how to determine the
effects of windfall receipts on consumption [1].

The Eisner-Houthakker interchange and the Bodkin paper raise three
sets of issues with which this paper deals: (1) the economic meaning of
"horizon" and its use to predict the effect of unanticipated changes in
circumstances—the particular change dealt with by both is a windfall in
the form of an unanticipated cash receipt; (2) the effect of windfalls, and
more generally any unanticipated change, on permanent and transitory
components of income; (3) the effect of windfalls on the lack of correlation

[2] See [2, esp. fn. 3] and [5, esp. fn. 2].

I am greatly indebted to Armen Alchian and William Meckling for calling my attention
to the difficulties raised by these footnotes. The reformulation that follows was largely
stimulated by their comments and owes much to their suggestions.

This note, which was first drafted in 1959, has benefited greatly also from comments on
the initial draft by Hendrik Houthakker and Arnold Zellner.

between transitory and permanent components of income that is assumed in the permanent-income hypothesis. In addition, the paper considers (4) the relation between the supplementary model applied to time-series data and the horizon.

1. The Meaning of Horizon

It is easier to say what the horizon is not than what it is. My estimate that the horizon is about three years does *not* mean that permanent income is to be defined as a three-year moving average of measured income. This is perhaps the most egregious error that has been made in interpreting the permanent-income hypothesis and the concept of horizon, and one for which my own loose use of the term deserves much blame despite my explicit *caveats* against such an interpretation [3, pp. 23, 213]. The error has two components. First, permanent income is of the nature of the mean of a hypothetical probability distribution, not the mean of a sample, so it cannot be calculated from actually experienced measured incomes, although these may of course be used to construct an estimate of permanent income (see Section 4). Second, a three-year horizon does not mean that consumers plan for only three years and seek to balance their books over that interval. On the contrary, it requires that consumers look beyond three years. It is of the nature of a mean length of time, not of total duration.

Economically, "permanent income" is significant as an index of wealth, where wealth is to be regarded as including not only the nonhuman assets we ordinarily designate by that term but also human capacities. The permanent-income hypothesis regards the consumer unit as having at any moment of time some estimate of his wealth, presumably in the form not of a single value but of a probability distribution of alternative values, and as adjusting his flow of consumption to an estimate of wealth formed from the probability distribution (in the simplest case, its expected value). If W stands for this estimate of wealth, then the permanent-income hypothesis in its most general form asserts that

$$(1) \qquad c_p = f(W),$$

where c_p is permanent consumption or "planned" consumption expressed as a rate of flow per some unit of time, and the function $f(W)$ may of course include variables other than W. The specific variant of the hypothesis that I have proposed gives a particularly simple form to the function $f(W)$. It asserts that

$$(2) \qquad c_p = qW,$$

where q is a number that is independent of W—though it does, of course, depend on other variables (such as market rates of interest, the fraction of W consisting of nonhuman assets, and so on).

On this level, it is clear conceptually how to handle some windfalls, but not others. A windfall is an unanticipated favorable change in circumstances, which is to say, a change that promises additional receipts not previously allowed for by the consumer unit in his estimate of W.[3] These additional receipts may be wholly coincident in time with the occurrence of the windfall, as, for example, when an individual unexpectedly finds on the street a packet with no identification containing $1000 which he gets to keep because no valid claim is made for it. Such a windfall raises W dollar-for-dollar. The $1000 the individual finds is indistinguishable from the rest of his wealth, except that it is of a particular form (nonhuman wealth), and so may change the fraction of his total wealth that is of that general form, even after he has made the feasible alterations desired by him in its specific form. The change in form of wealth may in turn change q. This qualification aside, the consumer unit can be expected to increase consumption by q times $1000.

The additional receipts need not, however, be coincident with the occurrence of a windfall. For example, an individual may receive word that he has come into a wholly unanticipated inheritance to be paid to him at some specified future point in time, or he may learn to his surprise that he has been named a beneficiary in the will of a living person, so that the receipt will be at some indefinite future time, or he may find himself possessed of hitherto unsuspected talents that will enable him to earn larger sums in the future than he had allowed for in estimating W. Such windfalls raise W by an amount that depends not only on the dollar value of the additional future receipts but also on their dating and on how the individual forms his estimate of W from his estimated future receipts.

To analyze such windfalls, we must go beyond the formulation given in (2). Moreover, (2) is not very useful for the interpretation of available data. These data do not give estimates of W. They typically tell something about receipts and payments, little about the value of nonhuman assets, and even less about the value of human capacities.[4] To convert (2) into a more useful form, we may proceed, as I did in my book, to replace q by the product of two factors: one expressing the permanent income flow as a fraction of the stock of wealth, the other expressing consumption as a fraction of income.

---

[3] A precise statement would have to be more elaborate, particularly when W is regarded as the mean of a probability distribution. The problem is suggested by a lottery ticket. In advance of the drawing, the ticket enters into W at its expected value; after the drawing, W goes up by the excess of the prize over the expected value if the individual wins a prize or goes down by the expected value if he loses. The notion of "windfall" is therefore logically identical with that of positive "profit" in the uncertainty theory of profit.

[4] It is worth recording that we do have some relevant data on human capacities—age, occupation, education, etc. One interesting direction of research would be to try to estimate human wealth from such indexes thereof and to use such estimates in analyzing consumption.

Symbolically, let

(3)
$$q = kr,$$

so that

(4)
$$c_p = krW = ky_p,$$

where k is the average propensity to consume, r is an undefined term having the dimensions of an interest rate, and $y_p = rW =$ permanent income.

If we require that rW on the average (over people or dates) approximate in size the magnitude we ordinarily term "income," the observed average propensity to consume will give an estimate of k (with the usual qualifications about group transitory effects), and the problem reduces to estimating the size of r. The size of r is in turn related to the estimation of W in view of the requirement that rW approximate average measured income. It is at this stage that the concept of horizon enters.

To simplify matters, consider first consumer units that own no non-human assets except some balancing resource, which might be the possibility of borrowing, to carry them from one pay period to the next, and expect all of their future receipts other than the yield from this resource to be from human capacities, these capacities themselves being regarded as homogeneous. We can then regard W as the discounted value of anticipated future receipts plus the amount of the balancing resource, where the discount rate is a "subjective" rate that need bear little or no relation to any market rate of interest, since human capacities cannot be bought or sold, though they can of course be improved through training. A short-sighted unit (equivalent to short horizon) will weight receipts in the near future more heavily compared to distant receipts than a long-sighted unit (equivalent to long horizon). We can interpret this as meaning that the former uses a higher discount rate than the latter in converting future receipts into present wealth. Let r be this subjective discount rate. The horizon can then be defined as $1/r$, or "the number of years purchase" implied by the discount rate. On this definition, my estimate that the horizon is on the average something like three years implies a subjective discount rate of 0.333. A unit with a shorter horizon would use a still higher discount rate, a unit with a longer horizon, a lower discount rate. For simplicity, I speak—and shall continue to do so—of a single discount rate as applicable to all future receipts, regardless of their timing. A completely general analysis would allow for the possibility that the discount rate may be a function of the time that elapses until the receipt occurs.

To avoid misunderstanding, it is perhaps worth noting explicitly that the level of the discount rate does not imply anything about whether wealth is being consumed, maintained, or increased. That is determined by k. If k is above unity, wealth is being consumed; if k is equal to unity,

being maintained; and if k is less than unity, being increased. The use
of different discount rates has offsetting effects on y_p. The higher the
value used for r, the lower will be the value assigned to W, and conversely.
Whether the product rW is higher or lower depends on the time shape
of expected future receipts. It is perhaps worth noting explicitly also that
the relevant magnitudes are expected "real" receipts, not nominal money
receipts, and hence that r is to be interpreted as a "real" discount rate.
To avoid complications introduced by expectations of changing price
levels, we shall suppose that the price level is expected to remain constant,
or what is equivalent, that all magnitudes are adjusted for expected changes
in prices.

To state these relations more formally, let $R(\tau)$ be anticipated receipts
(which may be positive or negative) at time τ. Since these receipts occur
at particular points in time—when the pay envelope, or the dividend
check, or the rent is received—$R(\tau)$ is zero almost everywhere, nonzero
at only a denumerable number of points in time. Let $r(T)$ be the discount
rate applicable at time T, assuming continuous discounting, and let
$D(T)$ be the accumulated balancing resource (depreciation reserve if
positive or net borrowing if negative) that enables the consumer unit
to bridge the gap from one receipt to the next or to adjust for variations
in the size of successive receipts. Then wealth at time T is given by

$$(5) \qquad W(T) = \sum_{(\tau_1)} e^{-r(T)(\tau-T)} R(\tau) + D(T),$$

where (τ_1) stands for the set of values of τ which are greater than T and
for which $R(T) \neq 0$. For simplicity, assume that $D(T)$ yields interest
continuously at a rate of $r(T)$ if positive or requires the payment of interest
at the rate of $r(T)$ if negative. Permanent income is then given by

$$(6) \qquad y_p(T) = r(T)W(T).$$

Note that expressing the rate of discount as a function of the date for which
the wealth estimate is constructed does not conflict with the assumption
that the rate of discount is the same whatever the elapsed time until a
receipt of a particular category occurs. At any point in time T a single
rate is used for all future receipts whatever may be the elapsed time
$(\tau - T)$, but this single rate can vary with T.

If all anticipations were realized and if r were to remain constant, then—
in the absence of consumption expenditures—wealth would grow at a
rate equal to permanent income. If in addition $k = 1$, so that consumption
equals permanent income, then wealth would remain constant. True,
over time intervals for which $R(T)$ is zero, the financing of consumption
involves a drain upon depreciation reserves or borrowing. But this is
just balanced by the increase in the present value of subsequent receipts

as a result of their coming closer in time.[5] Similarly, at points where $R(T) \neq 0$, the first term on the right-hand side of (5) takes a sudden drop as a receipt occurs, but this is just matched by the addition of the whole of the receipt to $D(T)$ to replenish the depreciation reserve or to repay borrowing, so again wealth remains intact.[6]

The situation is complicated if the assets are of more than one type, such as different kinds of human capacities, or different kinds of non-human wealth, or both human and nonhuman wealth. Suppose, temporarily, that the markets for the different assets are perfect, in the sense that the assets can be exchanged for one another at prices that are the same regardless of the direction of exchange. There would then be one subjective rate for each consumer unit for all assets, since if subjective rates differed, the consumer unit would have an incentive to shift the composition of its assets away from those with low subjective yield to those with high subjective yield. This subjective rate cannot, however, be identified in principle with any market rate and need not be the same for different consumer units. Different types of assets could have different market rates, so there would be no such thing as "a" market rate, whereas there is "a" subjective rate for each consumer unit. The reconciliation is that the subjective rate includes not only pecuniary returns but also nonpecuniary returns. Under the circumstances envisaged, each consumer unit would adjust the structure of its assets so that these nonpecuniary returns differed by just enough to equalize total returns. For example, currency generally yields a zero market rate of interest. If the subjective rate is r per year and a consumer unit holds currency, this implies that it values the services

---

[5] Proof: Suppose $R(\tau)$ is zero and r a constant for $\tau = T$ to $\tau = T + \Delta T$, and no consumption takes place, so that the depreciation reserve changes only by virtue of interest received on it if positive or paid on it if negative. By definition,

$$W(T + \Delta T) = \sum_{(\tau_2)} e^{-r[\tau-(T+\Delta T)]} R(\tau) + D(T + \Delta T)$$

$$= e^{r\Delta T} \sum_{(\tau_1)} e^{-r(\tau-T)} R(\tau) + e^{r\Delta T} D(T)$$

$$= e^{r\Delta T} W(T),$$

where (τ_2) is the set of values of $\tau > T + \Delta T$ for which $R(\tau) \neq 0$, since by assumption no terms are added to the sum by extending the range of summation from (τ_2) to (τ_1). Replace $e^{r\Delta T}$ with the first two terms of its Taylor expansion around $\Delta T = 0$. This gives

$$W(T + \Delta T) = W(T) + rW(T) \cdot \Delta T,$$

an approximation that approaches an equality as ΔT approaches zero. The second term on the right-hand side is precisely permanent income accrued during period ΔT. If it is wholly spent on consumption, wealth remains unchanged.

[6] Whatever the *rate* of consumption so long as it is finite, the amount at a point in time is zero, which is why the whole of the receipt is available to add to $D(T)$. That is, the value of any finite multiple of the $rW(T) \Delta T$ of the preceding footnote approaches zero as ΔT approaches zero.

rendered by currency as worth r cents per year per dollar held. To keep the books straight, the value of services rendered by currency (and similarly the difference between r times the values attached to other assets and the money yield on them) must in principle be included in consumption.[7]

Although the value of r cannot in principle be identified with any particular market rate of interest, its level for any consumer unit will be affected by and related to the level and structure of market rates. Moreover, in practice, there might be some asset or assets which typically yielded little or no nonpecuniary returns to most consumer units, and whose yield might therefore serve as an empirical estimate of r.

The typical situation is intermediate between the two just considered. Some assets, particularly human capacities, are not directly bought and sold at all. They can be exchanged for other assets only to a limited extent or at a temporal rate fixed by conditions largely outside the control of the individual consumer unit. Other assets, such as currency, deposits, and government bonds are traded in essentially perfect markets. Still others, such as small owner-operated businesses, are traded in highly imperfect markets involving wide differences between buying and selling prices. Still others, such as future earning capacity, can be converted into property only through transactions (e.g., personal loans) involving large differences between rates of interest paid and received, equivalent to a wide difference in the buying and selling price of an asset. Under these circumstances, there may be different subjective rates for different assets, though it remains true that none need be identified with any particular market rate.[8] The general rate r is a weighted average of these specific rates, its precise level determined by the rate used for each type of asset and the relative importance of the different assets. The horizon $1/r$ is likewise a weighted horizon. The existence of several specific rates is an additional reason why the average rate, $r(T)$, might vary over time. Even though each rate stays the same, the weights may change.

It is perhaps worth reiterating that the relevant horizon need not be identical for all consumer units or even for one consumer unit for different categories of consumption. For example, it seems plausible that consumer units who receive their income primarily from human capital may have a different, presumably shorter, horizon than units who receive their income

---

[7] This is essentially what is done in the national income statistics for bank deposits and similar items when banks are treated as "associations of individuals." It is not done in consumer budget data, except to a limited extent for owner-occupied housing. It might be highly desirable to include a similar allowance for "imputed income" for a wider class of assets.

[8] Note that there need not be different subjective rates. For example, the phenomenon of the individual who holds savings deposits yielding, say, 3 per cent and at the same time buys on an installment contract involving paying, say, 18 per cent for a loan, need not involve different subjective rates. Because of the liquidity value attached to the savings deposits, the subjective rate on the deposits may match the 18 per cent rate paid on the loan.

from property.[9] Similarly, it seems plausible that a unit may adopt one horizon for determining housing expenditures and another for food expenditures because the types of expenditures involve different time structures of future commitments. The use of different horizons by a single consumer unit for different types of expenditures is equivalent to the use of different discount rates for different categories of assets. Presumably, neither situation would arise if all assets could be exchanged in perfect markets.

In terms of this conceptual framework, it is clear how to handle all windfalls that take the form of anticipated additional receipts at particular dates.[10] The consumer unit discounts the additional receipts to the present at a rate that may depend on the form of the additions to future receipts. The result is added to W. In addition, the rate r may be revised to allow for the different composition of assets. The product of the revised rate and the revised estimate of wealth is the revised permanent income. The average propensity to consume, k, may also be revised to allow for the different composition of assets. The product of the revised k and the revised permanent income is the new level of consumption. If, for simplicity and because it will often be plausible to do so, we neglect any revisions in r and k, the increment to permanent income as a result of the windfall is r times the present value of the additional receipts, and the increment to consumption is k times the increment to permanent income.

2. Windfalls and Transitory Income

According to the view just expressed, a windfall raises both wealth and permanent income, the increment in wealth being indeed a measure of the size of the windfall. What effect does the windfall have on the transitory component of measured income? This question has been raised and discussed explicitly primarily for windfalls for which all of the additional receipts come at the same time as the windfall itself. It is tempting to say that such a windfall raises transitory income by the excess of the windfall over the increase in permanent income, that the windfall is,

---

[9] If this were so, it would imply a life cycle in permanent income even for a consumer unit for which k is unity throughout and for which anticipations are realized throughout (a concept that itself raises some difficult issues), since the ratio of human to nonhuman wealth would change steadily as human wealth was transformed into nonhuman wealth. Of course, a life cycle would also be produced—and this seems a clearly important factor whether the preceding is present or not—by a dependence between the value of k and the age of the consumer unit [3, pp. 23-25].

[10] The qualification is to avoid explicit consideration of the problems raised by uncertainty and multi-valued anticipations. These problems, though certainly important, are not directly relevant to the issues considered in this paper, except when the existence of uncertainty or perhaps the degree of uncertainty is an important factor making for imperfection of asset markets and thereby affecting the horizon as defined above.

as it were, to be regarded as divided into two parts, an increase in permanent income and an increase in transitory income, the division depending on the horizon, so that if the horizon is three years, one-third of the windfall is permanent income and two-thirds is transitory income. It is but another small step to regard the windfall as distributed over three years, one-third becoming permanent income in each year. The initial step therefore easily leads to the erroneous concept of permanent income as a moving average of measured income.

I fell into this trap, at least to the extent of the first step, and Eisner followed me.[11] The stated conclusions are wrong, deriving indirectly from a confusion of stocks and flows. Though a cash windfall raises permanent income, it can nonetheless also be true, paradoxical though it may seem, that the whole of the windfall is a transitory receipt, and raises the transitory component of income by the time rate of flow that corresponds to the whole of the windfall. And windfalls that give rise to future receipts can give rise to negative transitory components of income.

The transitory component of income (y_t) is defined as the difference between measured income and permanent income. Measured income, in turn, corresponds to the concept labeled "income" in budget studies and other statistical records. Its precise definition varies from one study to another. Always defined for a particular accounting period, usually a year, it is equal to the sum of specified (positive or negative) cash and imputed receipts during that period with occasional adjustments that are designed to go part way from a "cash" to an "accrual" concept. For present purposes, we may regard the items to be included in measured income as corresponding to those included in $R(\tau)$, the series of receipts from which wealth is estimated, plus, for logical completeness, the (positive or negative) receipts from interest on what we have called the depreciation reserve, $D(T)$.

Although the receipts to be included in measured income may correspond to those included in $R(\tau)$, we cannot take $R(\tau)$ itself as defining measured income. The reason is that we want measured income to be a rate of flow, to have the dimensions of dollars per unit time, like permanent income or permanent consumption, so that we can write

$$(7) \qquad\qquad y_m(T) = y_p(T) + y_t(T),$$

where $y_m(T)$ and $y_t(T)$ are measured and transitory income at time T.

---

[11] "The transitory component is only the excess of the windfall over this element of permanent income" [3, p. 29].

"For a man who wins $100 at the races should, with the three-year horizon that Friedman postulates and a modest rate of interest, reckon that his permanent income is up by about $35. It would be only the remaining $65 that would constitute transitory income. . . . However, this consideration of the nature of the income components does suggest a problem as to the consistency of Friedman's definitions with his assumption of zero correlation of permanent and transitory components" [2].

However, $R(\tau)$ is not a flow; its units are simply dollars, like $W(T)$, which is a stock at a point of time. One formal solution would be to define $y_m(T)$ as the time rate of receipt corresponding to the payments $R(\tau)$,[12] but this is operationally useless since it would yield an infinite time rate of receipt at the points in time when $R(\tau) \neq 0$, and a zero rate elsewhere.[13]

I can see no way to get a meaningful concept of measured income to fit into an equation like (7) except by explicitly introducing an accounting period and defining measured income in terms of receipts during that period. We can still express measured income as a time rate of flow at a point in time, like permanent income, but the rate of flow will have to be computed from receipts during a specified period rather than being the limit of the ratio of receipts during a period to the length of the period as the length of the period approaches zero. Since the accounting period could, of course, be chronologically short, the difference will be of no practical importance for many purposes and it may appear pure pedantry for me to insist on the difference, yet I believe it is conceptually basic for the present problem.

One possible definition along these lines of measured income at a point in time is the annual rate of flow corresponding to the week (or month, or year, or decade) of which that point in time is the center. Formally, let A be the length of the accounting period. Define measured income at time T for an accounting period A as

$$(8) \qquad y_m(T, A) = \frac{1}{A}\left[\sum_{(\tau_A)} R(\tau) + \int_{T-A/2}^{T+A/2} r(T')D(T')\,dT' \right].$$

where (τ_A) is the set of values of τ for which $T - A/2 \leq \tau < T + A/2$ and for which $R(\tau) \neq 0$, and T' is simply a variable of integration. The final term is included for logical completeness and consistency with our previous treatment.[14] Except for the final term, measured income so defined is of course a step function, having the same value over any time

---

[12] That is, as the derivative of the step function obtained by cumulating successive receipts.

[13] Or, if account is taken of the depreciation reserve, a positive or negative rate equal to $rD(T)$.

[14] A yield r of $33\frac{1}{3}$ per cent per year implied by a horizon of three years may seem radically out of line with market yields and hence inconsistent not only with the general theoretical interpretation presented in this paper but even more with the supplementary assumption that the depreciation reserve yields a continuous yield at the rate r. However, it should be kept in mind that we are treating the value of nonpecuniary returns from particular assets as an addition to permanent income, consumption, and measured income. For this reason, r is to be taken as the market yield only on assets yielding no nonpecuniary returns. Rates paid on installment contracts, small loans, etc., are not strikingly out of line with an estimated subjective rate of $33\frac{1}{3}$ per cent. Note also that the depreciation reserve in the general case where there are many assets may be held in the form of assets such as durable consumer goods, the imputed value of whose services would then be included in permanent income, consumption, and measured income.

period for which the shifting boundaries of the accounting period neither drop out nor add a nonzero receipt.[15] For example, for A equal to one month and a unit whose only receipt is a paycheck at the end of each month, y_m would be constant from the midpoint of one month to the midpoint of the next except for interest received or paid on the depreciation reserve.

Transitory income at time T could now be defined simply by substituting (8) and (6) into (7). But if this were done, it would implicitly involve different time references for y_m and y_p: y_m as defined for time period T is an average over the interval $T - A/2$ to $T + A/2$, whereas y_p is an instantaneous rate at time point T. To make the time reference of the several terms the same, we can replace $y_p(T)$ by its average value over the same time interval. Designate this average by $\bar{y}_p(T, A)$, the second argument denoting the length of the accounting period, and introduce a second argument similarly into y_t. This gives

$$(9) \quad y_t(T, A) = y_m(T, A) - \bar{y}_p(T, A)$$

$$= \frac{1}{A} \sum_{(\tau_A)} R(\tau) + \frac{1}{A} \int_{T-A/2}^{T+A/2} r(T')D(T')\, dT'$$

$$- \frac{1}{A} \int_{T-A/2}^{T+A/2} r(T')W(T')\, dT' \, .$$

For simplicity, assume that calculations are made retrospectively as of $T + A/2$, so that actual depreciation reserves and those that enter into the calculation of W are the same over the interval $T - A/2$ to $T + A/2$, and assume further that r is constant over the same interval. If we now replace $W(T')$ by its value as given by (5), the terms in (9) involving the depreciation reserve will cancel, leaving

$$(10) \quad y_t(T, A) = \frac{1}{A} \sum_{(\tau_A)} R(\tau) - \frac{r(T)}{A} \int_{T-A/2}^{T+A/2} \left[\sum_{(\tau_1)} e^{-r(T)(\tau-T')} R(\tau) \right] dT'.$$

Transitory income so defined is precisely the average rate at which depreciation reserves must be added to or subtracted from during the accounting period over and above interest on the reserve in order to keep wealth intact. Note that because we assume the calculation to be made retrospectively at the end of the accounting period, the elements of $R(\tau)$ that enter into

---

[15] Note that two time units are involved: (1) the accounting period equal to A; (2) the period in terms of which the rate of flow is expressed, implicit in the units in which T is expressed. For example, A could be a month and T could be expressed in years. Then $y_m(T, A)$ would give the annual rate of monthly receipts. The first unit is substantively important. The second is purely conventional and arbitrary; it requires only a transformation of variables to go from any one unit to any other.

the first term of the right-hand side of (10), are the same as those for the corresponding period which enter into the second term; in addition, anticipated receipts after the accounting period enter into the second term. Without this assumption, we cannot use the same symbol $R(\tau)$ in both terms. We would have to distinguish actual from anticipated receipts.

Let us consider now the effect of a windfall that occurs during the accounting period. Suppose the windfall consists of the discovery that a cash receipt of U (for unanticipated) dollars will occur at time T_0, and let $R^*(\tau)$ be the new stream of receipts, so that

$$(11) \qquad R^*(\tau) = \begin{cases} R(T_0) + U & \text{for } \tau = T_0 , \\ R(\tau) & \text{for } \tau \neq T_0 . \end{cases}$$

Similarly, let an asterisk attached to any other variable convert it to its new value after the windfall.

2.1. T_0 Is Within Accounting Period. Suppose first that not only the windfall but also the cash receipt occurs between $T - A/2$ and $T + A/2$. Then

$$(12) \qquad y_t^*(T, A) - y_t(T, A) = \frac{U}{A} e^{-rfA} ,$$

where f is the fraction of the accounting period elapsed before receipt of the windfall and where, to simplify the expression, I have written r for $r(T)$.[16]

If the windfall is received at the very beginning of the accounting period, so that $f = 0$, then transitory income is raised by U/A, which is to say by the whole of the windfall converted into an annual rate by treating it as received during an accounting period. For example, if time is expressed in years, A is a month, and the windfall is the finding of $1000, the transitory component during the month subsequent to the windfall is at the

---

[16] Proof.

(i)
$$\sum_{\tau A} R^*(\tau) = \sum_{\tau A} R(\tau) + U ,$$

(ii)
$$\sum_{\tau_1} \exp\left[-r(\tau - T')\right] R^*(\tau) = \begin{cases} \sum_{\tau_1} \exp\left[-r(\tau - T')\right] R(\tau) + \exp\left[-r(T_0 - T')\right] U \\ \qquad\qquad\qquad\qquad\qquad\qquad\qquad \text{for } T' < T_0 , \\ \sum_{\tau_1} \exp\left[-r(\tau - T')\right] R(\tau) \qquad\qquad \text{for } T' \geqq T_0 . \end{cases}$$

Substitute these expressions in (10) to get $y^*(T, A)$ and subtract $y_t(T, A)$. The result is

(iii)
$$y^*(T, A) - y_t(T, A) = \frac{U}{A} - \frac{U}{A} \int_{T-A/2}^{T_0} \exp\left[-r(T_0 - T')\right](rdT')$$

$$= \frac{U}{A}\left[1 - \left(1 - \exp\left\{-r\left[T_0 - \left(T - \frac{A}{2}\right)\right]\right\}\right)\right] .$$

Replace $[T_0 - (T - A/2)]$ with fA and combine terms, and we have equation (12). Q.E.D.

annual rate of \$12,000. If A equals a year, we can say that the transitory component is equal to the whole of the windfall. But this is really an erroneous and inaccurate statement because the transitory component is a rate of flow and has the units of dollars per unit of time, while the windfall is an amount and has the units simply of dollars; the numbers come out the same because of the accident that A happens to be unity; but the equality is not invariant to an arbitrary change in the time dimension; the statement is analogous to one asserting that the rate of speed of a car equals the distance covered.

To continue for a moment with the special case $f = 0$, wealth at the outset of the accounting period is raised by U, the amount of the windfall, and hence permanent income is raised by rU. This is the amount by which the rate of consumption can be increased while keeping wealth intact. On our assumption that the depreciation reserve to which U is added in the first instance has a continuous yield at the rate of r, the interest on the addition to the depreciation reserve is just enough to pay for the additional consumption, hence the transitory component is—as noted earlier—the average rate at which the depreciation reserve is added to from receipts during the accounting period to keep wealth intact.[17]

These comments may help to explain why transitory income rises by less than U/A when the windfall comes after the beginning of the accounting period. Our assumption that wealth is calculated throughout the accounting period as if the unit foresaw the events of that period (i.e., the assumption that actual and expected receipts are equal during the accounting period) means that a windfall anytime during the period raises wealth at the outset of the period by its discounted value or by $U \cdot e^{-rfA}$. But this means that permanent income is also raised at the outset of the period. Now, however, there is for a time no interest on a raised depreciation reserve to finance the higher level of spending possible while keeping wealth intact; it would have to be financed by drawing down the depreciation reserve. Part of the windfall would have to be used, as it were, to make good this drain, leaving only the rest as a net addition to depreciation reserves. Hence transitory income is smaller when $f > 0$ than when $f = 0$.[18]

---

[17] To put it differently, receipts during the accounting period go up by the windfall plus interest on the windfall for that period; permanent income accrued during the period is higher by an amount equal to interest on the windfall for the period; the difference, which is transitory receipts, equals the windfall.

[18] To put it differently, receipts during the period go up by (a) the windfall, plus (b) interest after the windfall receipt on that part of the receipt which does not make good the earlier drain on the depreciation reserve, minus (c) interest lost during the period prior to the windfall on the lowered depreciation reserve; permanent income accrued during the period is higher by an amount equal to (d) interest on the discounted value of the windfall during the whole period. Item (d) is at the same rate as item (b) but for a longer period, hence exceeds (b) and *a fortiori* (b) minus (c). Hence transitory receipts are less than the windfall. See Appendix A.

If we suppose $k = 1$, which is to say consumption equal to permanent income, then wealth is in fact maintained intact and we can readily write down the effect of the windfall on wealth, permanent income, and measured income:[19]

(13)
$$\bar{W}^*(T, A) - \bar{W}(T, A) = Ue^{-rfA},$$

(14)
$$\bar{y}_p^*(T, A) - \bar{y}_p(T, A) = rUe^{-rfA},$$

(15)
$$y_m^*(T, A) - \bar{y}_m(T, A) = Ue^{-rfA}\left(\frac{1}{A} + r\right).$$

If $k < 1$, there will be, through saving, a greater increase in wealth during the accounting period than otherwise, so the increase in average wealth will be greater than that shown by (13). Permanent income and measured income will likewise rise by more than they would have otherwise by virtue of the yield on the greater wealth. If $k > 1$, so that there is dissaving, the converse of each of these statements holds. But on our assumption that the depreciation reserve yields income at a rate of r, none of these effects will alter the increase in transitory income. It is given by (12) whatever the value of k.

2.2. T_0 Is Subsequent to the Accounting Period. Suppose that although the windfall occurs during the accounting period, the associated cash receipt does not occur until some date after the end of the accounting period. Then, from (10, and (11),

(16)
$$y_t^*(T, A) - y_t(T, A) = \frac{-U}{A} e^{-rL}(e^{rA} - 1).$$

where L is the length of time between the beginning of the accounting period and the cash receipt of U.[20] The increment to transitory income is

---

[19] Equations (13) and (14) come directly from the fact the Ue^{-rfA} is the discounted value of the windfall at $T - A/2$, hence the increase in wealth at that date, hence the increase in wealth at every date during the accounting period if wealth is in fact maintained. Equation (15) can be derived most easily by substituting (12) and (14) into (7). But it can also be derived directly from (8) by evaluating (a), (b), and (c) of the preceding footnote. See Appendix A.

[20] Proof:

(i)
$$\sum_{\tau A} R^*(\tau) = \sum_{\tau A} R(\tau).$$

Equation (ii) of footnote 16 holds for this case as well, but this time $T_0 > T + A/2$. Consequently, when (i) of this footnote and (ii) of footnote 16 are substituted in (10) to get $y^*(T, A)$ and $y(T, A)$ is subtracted, the result is

(ii)
$$y_t^*(T, A) - y_t(T, A) = -\frac{U}{A} \int_{T-A/2}^{T+A/2} \exp\left[-r(T_0 - T')\right] (rdT')$$

$$= -\frac{U}{A} \exp\left\{-r\left[T_0 - \left(T - \frac{A}{2}\right)\right]\right\} [\exp(rA) - 1].$$

Replace $[T_0 - (T - A/2)]$ with L and we have equation (16). Q.E.D.

negative because the windfall raises wealth, and therefore also permanent income, but provides no additional receipts to enter into measured income. Why this magnitude? Ue^{-rL} is the discounted value of the unanticipated receipt and is therefore the increment to wealth at the beginning of the accounting period as a result of the windfall; i.e., it is the size of the windfall. Then rUe^{-rL} is the amount by which permanent income is raised. This is the additional rate at which the depreciation reserve can be depleted with wealth kept intact. To a first approximation, therefore, this is the negative transitory component as a result of the windfall, as can be seen by replacing e^{rA} with the first two terms of its Taylor's expansion around $rA = 0$, that is, $(1 + rA)$, in which case the right-hand side of (16) reduces to simply $-rUe^{-rL}$. The actual transitory component is larger in absolute value because it allows in addition for the decline of interest receipts on the depreciation reserve as a result of the larger drain on it that would be required to finance spending equal to the higher permanent income. That is, not only does permanent income rise but also measured income declines. Needless to say, the shorter the accounting period, the less the latter effect, and the closer the fall into transitory income approaches to the rise in permanent income.

If we suppose that $k = 1$, the increments to wealth, permanent income, and measured income for this case are[21]

$$(17) \qquad \bar{W}^*(T, A) - \bar{W}(T, A) = Ue^{-rL},$$

$$(18) \qquad \bar{y}_p^*(T, A) - y_p(T, A) = rUe^{-rL},$$

$$(19) \qquad \bar{y}_m^*(T, A) - \bar{y}_m(T, A) = -\frac{U}{A}e^{-rL}(e^{rA} - 1 - rA).$$

2.3. Effects of Restrictive Assumptions. The specific assumptions made above have enabled us to get rather simple and definite answers but, so far as I can see, have not distorted the answers. If the calculations were not made retrospectively as of the end of the accounting period, it would be necessary to introduce a distinction between actual and anticipated receipts and actual and anticipated depreciation reserves, and this would introduce other possible transitory components and effects on permanent and measured income; but the ones we have isolated would still be there. Similarly, if the depreciation reserve did not earn interest continuously at the rate used in discounting future receipts, it would be necessary to examine explicitly how an unanticipated receipt during the accounting period was invested and how this affected measured income, and it might

---

[21] Equations (17) and (18) can be written down directly. Equation (19) can be derived by substituting (16) and (18) into (7). It can also be derived directly as (15) was by evaluating the reduction in interest receipts on the depreciation reserve. (See Appendix B.)

then be that the form which the windfall initially takes is important.[22] Similarly, it would be necessary to examine the form of additional drains on the depreciation reserves as a result of unanticipated receipts after the accounting period.

Finally, we have used a single discount rate and treated it both as constant during the accounting period and, more important, as unaffected by the windfall. In practice, as we have seen, not all assets need yield the same subjective rate, because of imperfections in the capital market. If a windfall adds to or subtracts from a set of assets that have a relatively high or a low subjective rate, the single weighted-average rate r must be adjusted accordingly. Like the other departures from our assumptions, this would require modifications in the wording of the preceding analysis without any substantial change in the conclusions.

These conclusions would remain: (1) transitory income as a rate of flow cannot be defined satisfactorily without specifying an accounting period; (2) a windfall that produces additional receipts within the accounting period in which it occurs will raise transitory income, permanent income, and measured income for that period; (3) the amount of the rise in transitory income depends not only on the magnitude of the additional receipts but also on when they occur and on the length of the accounting period; (4) a windfall that produces additional receipts after the accounting period in which it occurs will lower transitory income and measured income but raise permanent income in that period and subsequent periods up to the one in which the receipt occurs.

3. The Correlation Between Permanent and Transitory Components of Income

Concentration of attention on cash windfalls that may be expected to raise both permanent and transitory components has led to questioning of the assumption that there is a zero correlation between transitory and permanent components of income, an assumption that plays an important role in the permanent-income hypothesis as I have formulated it.[23] The

---

[22] This would be so if there were restrictions on the exchange of assets from one form to another. For example, if the windfall is $1000 found on the street, the individual can convert this sum from cash into a wide variety of other assets, perhaps even increased human capacity. If, however, it is an unexpected increase in earning power, he may not be able to convert it immediately into nonhuman assets.

[23] See the quotation from Eisner in footnote 11. Also:

"If a windfall gain were to cause an increase in permanent income, as well as an increase in transitory income, the two would be correlated, and this Friedman rules out. Eisner's strictures are based on an economic interpretation of permanent income which, whatever its other merits, has little or nothing to do with the statistical assumptions in which the permanent income hypothesis should be expressed, according to Friedman's own exposition" [5, p. 993n].

preceding analysis makes it clear that the questions raised have reflected mainly the incomplete range of windfalls considered. As we have seen, all windfalls raise permanent income. Some raise transitory income, some lower it; when they lower transitory income, they may do so for a number of successive accounting periods. It is possible that windfalls introduce a positive correlation between transitory and permanent components of income; it is possible also that they introduce a negative correlation. I see no way to establish a general presumption one way or the other; the result depends on the distribution of windfalls by kind and on the length of the accounting period. In consequence, I see no reason for revising, on the basis of considerations of this kind, the tentative assumption of zero correlation that is embodied in my formulation of the permanent-income hypothesis. And, of course, similar statements are valid for unanticipated unfavorable changes in circumstances.[24]

It may be, of course, that in a particular problem dealing with specific windfalls affecting a specific group, a presumption can be established that the correlation is in a particular direction and significant in magnitude. For any such problem, the analysis will have to be complicated to allow for the correlation, whose magnitude can probably be inferred from the circumstances that require taking account of it.

More generally, the offsetting effects of windfalls on the correlation between permanent and transitory components of income are further diffused by the existence of transitory components of income of other kinds. As we have seen, for a particular consumer unit and a particular time period, a transitory component may be fully anticipated. When we speak of the correlation between such transitory components and permanent components, we implicitly have in mind either a number of such time periods or a number of consumer units, whereas with windfalls (and their opposite) we can have in mind a single unit and the probability distribution of receipts in a single subsequent time period. We shall not often be misled if we do not specify precisely which of these we have in mind; sometimes, however, as in problems like those mentioned in the preceding paragraph, it is important to consider the situation more explicitly. "Randomness" or "chance," ideas which underly the concept of "zero correlation," are sophisticated concepts. What is "random" to me may be well determined in terms of the information available to someone else; and conversely, what is well determined to me may appear "random" when I am considered as one of a set of entities by an outside observer. The concept of "transitory income" is formally definable for a single consumer unit in terms of its anticipations, as in (6). Its interpretation in empirical work depends on particular circumstances and the particular group of time units or consumer units considered.

---

[24] Is it our optimistic bias that accounts for there being no obvious antonym to "windfall"?

4. The Estimation of Permanent Income

In connection with the analysis of aggregate data, I have used an estimate of permanent income constructed from past data as follows:

$$(20) \qquad \mathrm{E}[y_p(T)] = \beta \int_{-\infty}^{T} e^{(\beta-\alpha)(T'-T)} y_m(T') \, dT',$$

where E denotes "estimate of"; this notation has been slightly altered from that in my book to conform with that used above [3, p. 144]. This estimate has two logically distinguishable elements: (1) an exponentially weighted average of past measured incomes adjusted for trend, the weights being given by $\beta e^{\beta(T'-T)}$, where T is the date for which the estimate is constructed and T' covers the whole range of earlier dates so that the weights decline as one goes farther back; (2) an adjustment for trend at the continuous rate of α per unit of time.

Although I used this estimate in my book only for aggregate data, I shall discuss it here as if it applied to an individual consumer unit, since my present purpose is to see how the value of β can be connected with the concept of horizon discussed above, and that concept is defined strictly for a single consumer unit.

4.1. Weighted Average of Past Measured Incomes. The rationalization that I gave in my book for using a weighted average of past incomes was in terms of the kind of expectations or adjustment model that has become familiar through the work of Cagan, Nerlove, Koyck, and others. In this model, β measures the speed of adjustment of expected magnitudes to actual magnitudes.

This rationalization requires the interpretation of $y_p(T)$ as "the 'expected' or predicted value of current measured income." [3, p. 143]. This is more satisfactory for the aggregate or average permanent income of all consumer units than it would be for an individual consumer unit, since—once allowance is made for secular growth—it is plausible that deviations between expected measured income and expected permanent income, which may well be sizable for individual units, largely or wholly cancel for all units so that one can be taken as an estimate of the other. However, even for all consumer units it is not fully satisfactory. For example, during the great depression, say from 1931 to 1934, it is not implausible that consumer units on the average anticipated that their measured incomes would be lower than their permanent incomes and conversely during booms, so that the figure I have interpreted as equal to expected permanent income cannot also validly be interpreted as expected measured income.

Another difficulty, for our present purpose, with the rationalization that identifies expected measured with expected permanent income is that it gives no rigorous connection between β and the horizon. In my book [3, p. 150], I asserted a connection but did not demonstrate one:

> The value of β turned out to be .4, implying an average lag of $2\frac{1}{2}$ years, or an "effective weighting period" of 5 years. In terms of our hypothesis, this period is presumably related to the horizon implicit in judgment of permanent income by individual consumer units. It seems plausible that this period would be longer for aggregate data than the corresponding horizon for individual units, due to the averaging out of random factors.

The final sentence does not seem unreasonable for an adjustment coefficient used to derive expected measured income but I do not now believe it to be correct for a horizon defined as in the earlier sections of this paper. Suppose all consumer units used the same value of r in discounting future returns. Then that same value of r would be the one to use in converting the aggregate of anticipated returns into aggregate wealth and aggregate permanent income. If the values of r differ, then a rather complex weighted average is relevant, but I see no reason to assert that this weighted average has a systematic bias relative to individual values of r. Similarly, the earlier part of the quotation, with its weasel word "presumably," avoids the key issue: why should the horizon be identified with the "effective weighting period" rather than the average lag? I suspect that the reason I then thought so was because I was implicitly and erroneously thinking of the kind of horizon that I unfortunately used in my initial theoretical analysis, namely, a cutoff period.

An alternative rationalization of the exponential weighting in (20) that is relevant to individual data as well as to aggregate data and that avoids these difficulties is to regard individuals as taking their past experience, adjusted for trend, as the best single estimate of their likely future experience. Set α temporarily equal to zero, to eliminate the problem of a trend. Assume that measured income at time T' in the past is an estimate of anticipated measured income $T - T'$ time units in the future, and set $\beta = r$. Equation (20) then differs from equation (6), which is our basic definition of permanent income, only in being a continuous integral rather than a summation over discrete points in time. And this difference is only expositional, since $y_m(T')$ is in practice a discrete series at annual intervals.[25]

Allowance for trend is required on this interpretation because of differences between current wealth and wealth at the time the past observed measured incomes occurred, as a result either of intended savings or of accidental but known capital gains or losses. Since the unit knows about such differences in wealth, they provide a reason for expecting future

---

[25] Compare (5), (6), and (8). The absence of an explicit term for the depreciation reserve in (20) also reflects its being a continuous integral. An explicit depreciation reserve is needed in (5) to bridge the gaps between the discontinuous receipts.

experience to differ systematically from past experience and hence should be taken into account in estimating permanent income. We can allow for them by treating the past increase in wealth as if it had occurred at a steady percentage rate, which we designate α, and as if it were of the same composition as prior wealth. On these assumptions, the estimate of current permanent income can be regarded as made in two steps. First, each past measured income is adjusted to the value it would have had if wealth then had been equal to its value now. On the assumptions just made, the adjusted value of $y_m(T')$ is $e^{\alpha(T-T')}y_m(T')$. Second, these adjusted values are used as estimates of the future receipts to be expected, the discounted value of which constitutes present wealth.

On this interpretation, β is a direct estimate of r, which, as it happens, yields an estimate of the horizon closer to that yielded by other evidence than did my earlier assertion that $2/\beta$ was an estimate of the horizon. As I have noted, β turned out to be 0.4, which is certainly rather close to the value for r of 0.33 that we have been using.

4.2. Allowance for Trend.

On the interpretation just presented, α is an estimate of the known past rate of increase in wealth. Capital gains and losses may be expected to cancel among consumer units at any point in time as well as over time. Hence α can be approximated by the planned past rate of increase in wealth. If k had been equal to unity throughout, so that consumption equaled permanent income, the value of α in (20) would be zero. If k had been less than unity, the consumer unit would have been saving to raise permanent income, so α should be positive; the converse would have been true if k had been more than unity. If we continue to use a single rate of discount, the rate of change in permanent income is given by

$$(21) \qquad\qquad \alpha = r(1 - k).$$

For $r = \frac{1}{3}$ and $k = 0.9$ (the approximate value of k for the United States as estimated in my book), $\alpha = 0.033$, whereas I used a value of $\alpha = 0.02$ in my analysis of aggregate data. This value of α was derived from the secular trend in estimated per capita real consumption. For several reasons, it is not clear that these two estimates of α are fully comparable.

(1) Savings as defined in computing the numerical value of k include only savings in nonhuman form, whereas for present purposes savings should include all forms of addition to wealth. This has effects working in different directions. It leads to an overestimate of savings (underestimate of k) insofar as saving in nonhuman form is, for the individual consumer unit, simply a conversion of human to nonhuman wealth as the unit ages. It leads to an underestimate of savings insofar as the reverse process is at work: nonhuman capital is being converted into human capital via

expenditures on education or training, or human capital is being created through savings out of current income. If the aggregate α is intended, as I believe it should be, to be an average of the values for individual consumer units, then the effect that dominates will depend on how consumer units judge the expenditures on raising and training children: they may and in large measure doubtless do regard such expenditures as consumption even though for the economy as a whole they constitute replacement or increase in human capital, in which case the first effect will almost surely dominate, and k from empirical data will on this account be an underestimate of the relevant value.

(2) Since $r = \frac{1}{3}$ is intended to include nonpecuniary as well as pecuniary returns from wealth, these returns should also be included as income and consumption, whereas most are excluded in the empirical data from which $k = 0.9$ is computed.[26] Since inclusion of these nonpecuniary returns adds equal absolute amounts to numerator and denominator, it tends to raise the ratio of consumption to income when this ratio is less than unity. Hence their exclusion makes the observed k an underestimate of the relevant value.

(3) The exclusion of nonpecuniary returns may also affect the value of α estimated from the trend in per capita real consumption. If the nonpecuniary returns excluded from the estimates of consumption have grown relative to estimated consumption, as seems highly likely in view of the apparent growth relative to total wealth of consumer durable goods and liquid assets yielding low pecuniary returns, then the trend in per capita consumption underestimates the value of α relevant to (21).

Combining these effects, there seems to be no irreconcilable contradiction between a value of α of 0.033 computed directly from (21) using $r = \frac{1}{3}$ and $k = 0.9$ and the value of α of 0.02 derived from the observed trend in per capita real consumption. For example, adjustment of k to 0.94 because of effects (1) and (2), would alone produce a value of α of 0.02; and adjustment of α to 0.025 because of effect (3), would imply that a value of $k = 0.0925$ would suffice to equate the two estimates.

5. Conclusion

This paper suggests that permanent income of a consumer unit be interpreted as the product of an interest rate r and a stock of wealth W; that the stock of wealth be interpreted as the present value of anticipated future receipts from both human and nonhuman assets discounted back to the present at subjective rates of interest that need not be the same for different categories of receipts but whose average value is r; and that

---

[26] About the only general exception is nonpecuniary returns from owner-occupied housing and from food grown for own use.

the horizon be defined as $1/r$, or "the number of years purchase" corresponding to the interest rate r.

The paper demonstrates that this interpretation permits a straightforward calculation of the effects on consumption to be expected on the permanent-income hypothesis from an unanticipated change in circumstances. It demonstrates further that the occurrence of such unanticipated changes provides no reason to question the zero correlation between permanent and transitory components assumed in the specific version of the permanent-income hypothesis I have proposed.

The paper also offers a new interpretation of the exponentially weighted average of past measured incomes that I have used as an empirical estimate of permanent income from aggregate data. It suggests that the exponent β in the weighting pattern be taken as equal to r, the interest rate used in calculating wealth. This interpretation links the permanent-income hypothesis and this estimation procedure more closely and rigorously than I have done heretofore and for that reason alone is aesthetically preferable. In addition, it links the trend-adjustment parameter α in the weighting pattern with the parameters of the consumption theory, thereby providing another indirect piece of evidence on the value of r, and it makes for a higher degree of consilience in the empirical estimates of the horizon derived from time-series data and budget data.

Throughout the paper, I have tentatively accepted 3 years as an estimate of the average horizon for the United States, which means a subjective rate of discount of 0.33. Nothing in this paper gives any reason to suppose that this estimate is widely in error. If it seems drastically out of line with widely quoted market rates of interest, it should be kept in mind that these rates apply only to a very limited range of assets; that most future receipts whose discounted value constitutes wealth come from assets that cannot be readily bought and sold or for which buying and selling prices differ widely. It should be kept in mind also that the value of r required by the theory includes not only pecuniary but also nonpecuniary returns from the assets. These nonpecuniary returns rationalize the simultaneous ownership by consumer units of assets that have widely varying rates of pecuniary yield.

APPENDIX A

Derivation of Effect of Unanticipated Receipt During Accounting Period on Measured Income

We shall derive equation (15) by evaluating items (a), (b), and (c) of footnote 18.

Item (a) is simply equal to U.

To get items (b) and (c), we need to know the difference between $D(T)$ and $D^*(T)$ at each date in order to integrate. At any date in the accounting period other than T_0,

(i) $$\frac{d[D(T') - D^*(T')]}{dT'} = rUe^{-rfA} + r[D(T') - D^*(T')] .$$

where the first term on the right is the extra drain on the depreciation reserve to finance the increased consumption equal to increased permanent income and the second term is the drain because of lower interest received on the lower depreciation reserve. This is a differential equation whose solution is

(ii) $$D(T') - D^*(T') = Ke^{rT'} - Ue^{-rfA} ,$$

where K can be chosen to satisfy an initial condition. At $T - A/2$, $D^* = D$, so if we use this as an initial condition,

(iii) $$Ke^{r(T-A/2)} = Ue^{-rfA} ,$$

or

(iv) $$K = Ue^{-rfA-r(T-A/2)} ,$$

giving for the time interval $T - A/2$ to T_0,

(v) $$D(T') - D^*(T') = Ue^{-rfA}[e^{r[T'-(T-A/2)]} - 1] .$$

At T_0, since $T_0 - (T - A/2) = fA$, this gives

(vi) $$D(T_0) - D^*(T_0) = U(1 - e^{-rfA}) .$$

This is the value the depreciation reserve approaches before allowance is made for the receipt of U; i.e., its limit as the approach is made from earlier dates. The receipt of U produces a jump of U in D^* at T_0, hence the limit as the approach is made from later dates is

(vii) $$D(T_0) - D^*(T_0) = U(1 - e^{-rfA}) - U = -Ue^{-rfA} ,$$

which is precisely equal in absolute value to the discounted value of the transitory receipt, validating some of the statements made earlier.

If this value is used for the initial value at time T_0, it gives a K equal to zero, which means that, as stated earlier, for the time interval from T_0 to $T + A/2$,

(viii) $$D(T) - D^*(T) = -Ue^{-rfA} ;$$

that is, the depreciation reserve is higher by precisely the amount of the windfall.

Item (b) is equal to the interest on the negative of (viii) for the interval T_0 to $T + A/2$, which is

(ix) $$r(1 - f)AUe^{-rfA}.$$

Item (c) is given by

(x) $$\int_{T-A/2}^{T_0} r[D(T') - D^*(T')] = rUe^{-rfA} \int_{T-A/2}^{T_0} (e^{r[T'-(T-A/2)]} - 1)dT'$$

$$= U(1 - e^{-rfA} - rfAe^{-rfA}).$$

Finally, (a) + (b) − (c) gives, as the increase in measured receipts,

(xi) $$U[1 + r(1 - f)Ae^{-rfA} - 1 + e^{-rfA} + rfAe^{-rfA}] = Ue^{-rfA}(1 + rA).$$

Converted into a rate of flow this gives

(xii) $$y_m^*(T, A) - y_m(T, A) = Ue^{-rfA}\left(\frac{1}{A} + r\right),$$

which is equation (15).

APPENDIX B

Derivation of Effect of Unanticipated Receipt After Accounting Period on Measured Income

Equation (v) needs only slight modification to apply to the whole of the accounting period for this case. It is necessary to replace Ue^{-rfA}, which was the increment in wealth at the outset of the accounting period in the prior case, by Ue^{-rL}, which is the same thing in this case. If we make this substitution, multiply by r, and integrate, we have the loss of interest on the smaller depreciation reserve, or

$$rUe^{-rL} \int_{T-A/2}^{T+A/2} (e^{r[T'-(T-A/2)]} - 1)dT' = Ue^{-rL}(e^{rA} - 1 - Ar).$$

This is the only item for this case affecting measured income. To get an annual rate, we must divide by A. The negative of the result is then the change in measured income as given in equation (19).

REFERENCES

[1] BODKIN, RONALD, Windfall Income and Consumption, and Reply, in IRWIN FRIEND and R. JONES (eds.), *Proceedings of the Conference on Consumption and Saving*, Pennsylvania (1960).

[2] EISNER, ROBERT, The Permanent Income Hypothesis: A Comment, *Amer. Econ. Rev.*, **48** (December 1958), 972-90.

[3] FRIEDMAN, MILTON, *A Theory of the Consumption Function* (Gen. Ser. 63). New York: National Bureau of Economic Research (distr. Princeton Univ. Press), 1957.

[4] FRIEDMAN, MILTON, and SIMON KUZNETS, *Income from Independent Professional Practice* (Gen. Ser. 45). New York: National Bureau of Economic Research (distr. Princeton Univ. Press), 1945.

[5] HOUTHAKKER, HENDRIK S., The Permanent Income Hypothesis: Reply, *Amer. Econ. Rev.*, **48** (December 1958), 991-93.

2

Tests of the Permanent-Income Hypothesis Based on a Reinterview Savings Survey

NISSAN LIVIATAN, *The Eliezer Kaplan School of Economics and Social Sciences, The Hebrew University of Jerusalem, and the Falk Project for Economic Research in Israel*

In his study on the consumption function Friedman [4] devised and performed various tests of the Permanent-Income Hypothesis (PIH), using time series and cross-section data. The most direct tests, however, are those based on a combination of these two types of data, i.e., on a cross section of identical families in different periods of time. The advantage of this sort of data is in the possibility of relating the observed income elasticities of consumption (which, according to the PIH, are biased) to income variability (which, according to the PIH, is the source of this bias). The purposes of this article are (a) to repeat the test used by Friedman on new data—the 1958/9 Israel Reinterview Savings Survey[1]—and (b) to formulate a new scheme of tests for reinterview surveys, and apply them to our data.

The empirical results show that whereas the test formulated by Friedman is successful (i.e., favorable to the PIH), this is not the case for our new tests. Moreover, we shall argue that Friedman's test is a rather roundabout way of attacking the problem whereas the new tests are more direct. On the basis of our tests, one may conclude that although the traditional income elasticities are indeed likely to be downward biased, the size of the bias has been exaggerated by the PIH. This conclusion is based on a particular survey, but our *methods* are of course quite general and can be applied to various data.

The outline of this article is as follows: In Section 1 we review the statistical properties of the PIH that are needed for the subsequent tests. This is followed by various attempts to test the PIH by using external information about the variances of the temporary components. In Section 2 we use *qualitative* information about the importance of errors in observed consumption and income in occupational groups, to explain the differences in

---

I wish to express my thanks to Professors L. R. Klein, S. J. Prais, J. Mincer, D. Jorgenson, and L. Telser for their comments on this article. This paper will be reissued as Falk Project Research Paper No. 12.

[1] See Appendix A for a short description of this Survey.

the observed consumption functions of employees and self-employed. In Section 3 we review Friedman's method of obtaining a *quantitative* estimate of the variance of temporary income from reinterview data and perform similar tests on our data. Thus far the results are favorable to the PIH. In Section 4 we formulate an alternative test that requires fewer assumptions than Friedman's method. This test, which is based on the relation between temporal changes in income and consumption of identical families, contradicts Friedman's model.

Whereas these sections concentrate on testing the PIH through external information about the error variances, the remaining part of the paper concentrates on methods that are supposed to *eliminate* errors in the observed variables and thus make possible an estimate of the true elasticity. In Section 5 we discuss the principle of elimination of errors, with the aid of additional information, by what is known as the "method of instrumental variables." We then apply the method to our data by using, in Sections 6 and 8, lagged or future income and consumption as instrumental variables. It is shown that even when the assumptions underlying this method are not completely satisfied, the tests in Sections 6 and 8 can still provide lower and upper limits for the true income elasticity of consumption. Our empirical results show that the upper limit fails systematically to reach the value of unity, which is assumed by the PIH to be the true value.

1. The Basic Model

The Permanent-Income Hypothesis is, from a statistical point of view, a model of "errors in variables." In a cross section of families, the observed values of consumption (C) and income (Y) of every family are partitioned into systematic ("permanent") components and errors ("temporary components"); thus $C = C' + C''$ and $Y = Y' + Y''$, where a prime and a double prime denote the systematic components and errors, respectively. The statistical properties of the errors in a cross section of families are given by

$$(1) \qquad \operatorname{cov}(Y'', Y') = \operatorname{cov}(C'', Y') = \operatorname{cov}(C'', Y'') = 0 \,.$$

Thus the errors are correlated neither with the systematic components nor among themselves. In his empirical analysis of the model, Friedman often makes the following additional assumptions (which we shall also use in our analysis):

$$(2) \qquad EY'' = EC'' = 0 \,,$$

where E stands for expected value. In other words, we shall assume that the errors cancel out, on the average. (Friedman points out that this is not always the case for a particular time period or group.)

Unlike other linear models of "errors in variables," the permanent-income model assumes strict proportionality between the systematic components in the cross section, i.e.,

$$(3) \qquad\qquad C' = KY'.$$

Assumption (3) clearly implies that the elasticity between the systematic components is unitary. Assumptions (1)–(3) will be called the "basic model."

According to the basic model, the ordinary least-squares regression (in the population) of C on Y yields

$$(4) \qquad B_{cy} = \frac{\text{cov}(C, Y)}{\text{var}(Y)} = KP_y, \quad \text{where } P_y = \frac{\text{var}(Y')}{\text{var}(Y)} < 1,$$

and where the coefficients written in capital letters denote population values.[2] Denoting by $\bar{\eta}$ the (population) elasticity[3] at the point of population means, we have

$$(5) \qquad\qquad \bar{\eta}_{cy} = B_{cy} \frac{EY}{EC} = P_y.$$

The above relations are the most familiar features of Friedman's interpretation of the traditional method of computing income elasticities of consumption. It is, however, important for our subsequent analysis to note (as Friedman does) the complementary relations when we use C as an independent variable, i.e.,

$$(6) \qquad B_{yc} = \frac{\text{cov}(C, Y)}{\text{var}(C)} = \frac{1}{K} P_c, \quad \text{where } P_c = \frac{\text{var}(C')}{\text{var}(C)} < 1$$

and

$$(7) \qquad\qquad \bar{\eta}_{yc} = B_{yc} \frac{EC}{EY} = P_c.$$

Although the least-squares regression coefficients do not yield consistent estimates of K (or $1/K$), the consistent estimation of K is easily performed by computing the average propensity to consume, since it follows from (2) and (3) that

$$(8) \qquad\qquad \frac{EC}{EY} = \frac{EC'}{EY'} = K.$$

---

[2] The corresponding sample estimates will be denoted by lower-case letters: b_{cy}, k, and p_y, respectively.

[3] The sample elasticity will be denoted by η.

The formulation of the model[4] as such does not of course prove anything. Moreover, the fundamental assumption of the model [i.e., assumption (3)] is incapable of being contradicted by empirical evidence, since the errors are not directly observable. In other words, we cannot identify the true parameters from the observed variables[5] C and Y without using assumption (3), but it is precisely that hypothesis we want to test.

To make the model operational requires additional information and assumptions. The basic model plus the additional assumptions will be called an "enlarged model." The difficulty in using an enlarged model is that when it is contradicted by empirical evidence we do not know which part of it is wrong, the basic model or the additional assumptions.

It is often possible to formulate tests that are too weak to give full support to the basic model but are nevertheless sufficient to test whether the traditional estimates of the elasticities are biased in the direction predicted by the PIH. These tests, which we shall call "weak tests," must also rely on additional assumptions. Since, however, the objective of the weak tests is limited, they require weak additional assumptions. Let us now leave the generalities and turn to the actual tests.

Since, according to the PIH, the source of the bias in η_{cy} is the existence of errors in Y, it should be possible to test the PIH if we have some independent information about these errors. Similar use can be made of external information about the errors in C. We shall first consider weak tests which are based on *qualitative* information about the error variances and pass later to strong tests in which the error variances are estimated quantitatively.

2. Qualitative External Information on Error Variances

In this section we shall make use of a sort of outside information about which there is agreement among virtually all economists—that annual incomes of self-employed businessmen are less stable over time than those of employees. It is also well known that the cross-section consumption elasticities of the former are empirically smaller than those of the latter. According to the PIH this constitutes evidence in favor of the Hypothesis, since the smaller stability of self-employed incomes presumably means a lower P_y, which should be reflected in a lower η_{cy}.

Table 1 shows that in the 1958/9 Reinterview Survey, η_{cy} of the self-employed is in fact smaller in each of the two years than the corresponding

---

[4] Friedman formulates an alternative logarithmic model, analogous to the linear model described above. Throughout this article, however, we shall restrict ourselves to the linear model.

[5] We ignore here the possibility of identifying the true parameters by using moments of higher order than the second. This possibility is, of course, ruled out when the variables are normally distributed, which is approximately true for the logarithmic model. See the discussion of this problem in [8].

elasticity of employees.[6] This seems to favor the PIH. However, an alternative explanation of this phenomenon has been offered in [6, p. 202], namely, that the self-employed tend to save a larger fraction of each additional pound since they have better investment outlets than employees. According to the alternative explanation, income variability plays a minor role in the determination of the cross-section elasticity of the consumption curve of the self-employed. Thus the issue remains unresolved.

TABLE 1

INCOME ELASTICITIES OF CONSUMPTION (η_{cy}) BY OCCUPATION AND YEAR

Year[a]	Occupation[b]	Number of Income Units	b_{cy}[c] (1)	C/Y[d] (2)	η_{cy} (1)/(2)
1	E	667	0.827	0.945	0.875
1	SE	216	0.629	0.940	0.669
2	E	667	0.850	0.957	0.889
2	SE	216	0.753	0.950	0.793

[a] Years 1 and 2 are the fiscal years 1957/8 and 1958/9, respectively.

[b] E and SE denote employees and the self-employed, respectively.

[c] Computed by least squares. The squares and cross products are weighted to take into account differential sampling rates. C includes expenditures on durables. Y is net income.

[d] The means are weighted to take into account differential sampling rates. Note that in our data the difference in average propensities between employees and self-employed is very small.

We may note that the economists who have written on this subject have failed to treat the problem systematically from its statistical aspects. Thus they did not see the possibility of utilizing qualitative information on P_c. Since there is no particular reason to suppose that the relative importance of errors in *consumption* is different for the two groups, it seems reasonable to analyze the behavior of these groups by assuming that P_c is in fact equal in both cases.

Now, according to the PIH the *true* elasticities are equal in both groups (i.e., $\eta_{y'c'} = 1$). Therefore the empirical elasticities η_{yc} must also be equal if the relative bias $(1 - P_c)$ is the same. If we find that η_{yc} is in fact similar in both groups, this can be taken as evidence that $\eta_{y'c'} (= 1/\eta_{c'y'})$ is similar as well, and that the differences in the ordinary elasticities η_{cy}

---

[6] Throughout this article we use consumption *including* purchases of durables as the dependent variable. The use of consumption *excluding* durables does not alter the results of our tests. (See Appendix C.)

are in fact due to differences in P_y. It should be noted, however, that this is a weak test, since even if the results are favorable to the PIH, they cannot be used to support the hypothesis $\eta_{c'y'} = 1$.

TABLE 2

η_{cy}, η_{yc}, AND r_{cy}^2 BY OCCUPATION AND YEAR

Year	Occupation	η_{cy} (1)	η_{yc} (2)	r_{cy}^2 (3) = (1) × (2)
1	E	0.875	0.807	0.706
1	SE	0.669	0.715	0.479
2	E	0.889	0.846	0.752
2	SE	0.793	0.885	0.702

The correlation coefficient is denoted by r.

Turning to Table 2, we see that the differences in η_{yc} in the occupational groups [col. (2)] are considerably smaller than the differences in η_{cy} [col. (1)], which implies that the true elasticities ($\eta_{c'y'}$) of the two groups are not as different as it may seem from col. (1). The relatively small differences between the values of η_{yc} imply that it is income variability, and not the alternative hypothesis, that explains the major part of the differences in observed behavior between employees and the self-employed.

An alternative way of looking at this test is as follows: According to the PIH, measured income (Y) is a poorer indicator of "normal" income for the self-employed than for employees. Therefore, in the former group, Y can be expected to explain a smaller proportion[7] of the variance of C [see the values of r_{cy}^2 in col. (3)]. Moreover, according to the PIH, the ratio of the $\bar{r}_{cy}^2$'s (where $\bar{r}$ denotes the correlation coefficient in the population) should be proportional to the ratio of the $\bar{\eta}_{cy}$'s in the two groups. To realize this we note that

$$(9) \qquad \bar{r}_{cy}^2 = B_{cy} B_{yc} = \bar{\eta}_{cy} \bar{\eta}_{yc} = P_y P_c .$$

Therefore, the ratio of the $\bar{r}_{cy}^2$'s in the two groups, assuming P_c to be the same, is equal to the ratio of the corresponding P_y's and the corresponding $\bar{\eta}_{cy}$'s.

It is evident that our test can be carried out for any *single* period cross section, and can therefore be applied easily to many existing data. As an example, we shall apply it to the data given by Fisher [3, App.] in his

---

[7] On the assumption that the relative importance of the random variation in C is the same in both groups.

TABLE 3

COMPARISON OF η_{cy} AND η_{yc} BY OCCUPATIONAL GROUPS IN THE OXFORD 1953 SAVINGS SURVEY

Occupation	η_{cy} (1)	η_{yc} (2)	r_{cy}^2 (3) = (1) × (2)
Manual workers	1.026	0.803	0.824
Managers	0.810	0.883	0.715
Clerical and sales	0.953	0.850	0.810
Self-employed	0.763	0.803	0.613

Source: Fisher [3]. In the Appendix (pp. 265-68) the author gives the regression coefficients of saving (S) on income (to be denoted by b_{sy}) and the square of the correlation coefficients between these variables (r_{sy}^2). Using the identity $C = Y - S$ we computed b_{yc} as follows: $b_{yc} = (1 - b_{sy})/(1 - 2b_{sy} + b_{sy}^2/r_{sy}^2)$. The average propensities $\bar{C}/\bar{Y}$ were computed from p. 264. The figures in col. (2) were then computed by $b_{yc}\,(\bar{C}/\bar{Y})$. The figures in col. (1) were computed from the data in the same pages. Our computations relate only to consumption including durables, and to each occupational group as a whole.

study of the 1953 Oxford Savings Survey. In this study Fisher, following Friedman, explained the differences in η_{cy} between the self-employed and employees by the presumably greater instability of the former's annual incomes (without actually using data on income variability). He did not see, however, the possibility of attacking the above-mentioned alternative explanation. This, nonetheless, can be done easily by computing from his data η_{yc} for the self-employed and employees. A comparison of η_{cy} and η_{yc} in Table 3 shows that the latter elasticities are much more homogeneous than the former. It is particularly interesting to note that while η_{cy} of the self-employed is very small compared with that of manual workers (which are the largest group of employees), the values of η_{yc} are equal in both groups. This lends strong support for Friedman's interpretation of the differences in η_{cy} between employees and the self-employed.

3. Quantitative External Information on Error Variances

As we have already noted, the test based on qualitative outside information is not strong enough to test directly the basic proportionality assumption of the PIH. Friedman, however, devised an ingenious strong test which is based on the estimation of P_y from intertemporal comparison of incomes ([4, chap. 7] and [5, pp. 325-38]).

Although it is intuitively plausible to think that intertemporal stability of incomes is related to P_y, one cannot estimate the latter from income data without making some specific assumptions. The essence of Friedman's additional assumptions is that permanent income, which represents an income stream, is very stable for every individual between two close periods of time. Friedman does not rule out entirely the possibility of intertemporal changes in Y' of identical individuals, but he requires that these changes be of a very well-behaved nature. As a result of this assumption, the major part of intertemporal variability in individual incomes is interpreted as being associated with the temporary components, and this makes possible an estimate of P_y .

An estimate of P_y from income data can be obtained as follows:[8] Suppose that we have income data on a cross section of families in two different years. Now, assume that the relative positions of individuals' *permanent* incomes remain unchanged in the two periods. More specifically, let

$$(10) \qquad Y'_{2q} = MY'_{1q}, \qquad M = \frac{EY'_2}{EY'_1} = \frac{EY_2}{EY_1},$$

where the subscripts 1 and 2 denote the year, and q $(q = 1, \cdots, N)$ denotes the family. This assumption, which Friedman calls the "mean assumption," postulates that Y' of every family changes between the two years in the same ratio as the average incomes in the entire population group.[9] Note that (10) is an *exact* relationship, which postulates a unitary elasticity between the values of Y' in different years.

In addition to (10), assume that the temporary components of income in the two years are not correlated; i.e., let

$$(11) \qquad \operatorname{cov}(Y''_1, Y''_2) = 0 .$$

It now follows that

$$B_{y_2 y_1} = \frac{\operatorname{cov}(Y_2, Y_1)}{\operatorname{var}(Y_1)} = \frac{\operatorname{cov}(MY'_1 + Y''_2, Y'_1 + Y''_1)}{\operatorname{var}(Y_1)} = MP_{y_1},$$

whence we obtain

$$(12) \qquad \bar{\eta}_{y_2 y_1} = B_{y_2 y_1} \frac{1}{M} = P_{y_1} .$$

A similar result holds for P_{y_2}; i.e.,

$$(13) \qquad \bar{\eta}_{y_1 y_2} = P_{y_2} .$$

---

[8] The following exposition differs somewhat from that given by Friedman, whose analysis is based on grouped data. It can be shown, however (see Appendix B), that the two expositions are equivalent.

[9] An alternative assumption, the "variability assumption," used by Friedman, states that the slope of the line relating Y'_2 to Y'_1 is equal to $\sigma_{y_2}/\sigma_{y_1}$, where σ denotes the standard deviation. The variability assumption implies $P_{y_1} = P_{y_2} = \bar{r}_{y_2 y_1}$. Friedman thinks, however, that the "mean assumption" is more appropriate for our present problems [4, p. 185]. The various tests in this article, which were carried out on the basis of the "mean assumption," were computed for the "variability assumption" as well. The differences, however, were not important enough to justify the repetitions in the text.

The basic assumptions (1)–(3), together with assumptions (10) and (11), form an enlarged model that can be tested by the data. A test that suggests itself immediately, in view of (13), is to compare the values of P_y implied by the basic model (i.e., $P_{y_i} = \bar{\eta}_{c_i y_i}$) with those obtained from income data (i.e., $P_{y_i} = \bar{\eta}_{y_j y_i}$, where i and j denote different years).

An alternative way of interpreting the test is as follows: Dropping the proportionality assumption (3), we first interpret the traditional elasticity as

$$(14) \qquad \bar{\eta}_{c_1 y_1} = B_{c_1 y_1} \frac{EY_1}{EC_1} = B_{c_1' y_1'} P_{y_1} \frac{EY_1}{EC_1} = \bar{\eta}_{c_1' y_1'} P_{y_1},$$

which involves the unobserved parameters $\bar{\eta}_{c_i' y_i'}$ and P_{y_1}. We then compute P_{y_1} from income data alone by $\bar{\eta}_{y_2 y_1}$, and obtain $\bar{\eta}_{c_i' y_i'}$ by $\bar{\eta}_{c_1 y_1}/\bar{\eta}_{y_2 y_1}$. If the enlarged PIH is true, we must have

$$(15) \qquad \bar{\eta}_{c_i' y_i'} = \frac{\bar{\eta}_{c_1 y_1}}{\bar{\eta}_{y_2 y_1}} = 1.$$

Thus far we have not said anything about the time interval between the two years (1 and 2). In most cases, the actual data of reinterview surveys are based on two *consecutive* years. In principle, however, this is not necessarily the best sort of data to use. Generally speaking, a short time interval between the two years may result in serial correlation between temporary components; a long interval may lead to a low elasticity between permanent components (i.e., $\eta_{y_i' y_j'}$ may be much less than unity). In his actual tests Friedman uses data based on two consecutive years and on two years with an interval of one year between them [4, pp. 190-95]. Both sorts of data yield favorable results for his model, but the latter type seems to do better. On the basis of these results, Friedman suggests that there

TABLE 4

VALUES OF p_y COMPUTED FROM CONSUMPTION ELASTICITIES AND FROM INCOME DATA ALONE

Year (i)	Occupation	Estimates of P_{y_i}	
		$\eta_{c_i y_i}$ (1)	$\eta_{y_j y_i}$ (2)
1	E	0.875	0.875
1	SE	0.669	0.730
2	E	0.889	0.875
2	SE	0.793	0.790

For the first two rows $j = 2$, and for the last two rows $j = 1$.

is an advantage in using data in which there is an interval of a year between the two years.

Table 4 shows the results of the application of Friedman's test to our data. Clearly, the PIH passes the test with amazing success—the values in cols. (1) and (2) being virtually identical, except for the second row, where there is some difference. In other words, the interpretation of η_{cy} as measuring P_y is confirmed by an independent estimate of P_y from income variability over time. (In view of the above results our data, which are based on *consecutive* years, would naturally be considered appropriate for the enlarged model.)

Thus far there is every reason for PIH supporters to rejoice. However, Friedman used his enlarged model to formulate only one "strong" test. We shall now show that on the basis of the above assumptions it is possible to formulate additional tests. Moreover, some of these new tests are more direct and require fewer additional assumptions. Unforunately, they cast much doubt on Friedman's enlarged model.

4. Marginal Propensities to Consume of Identical Individuals

The test in the previous section compares $\eta_{c_i y_i}$, which is based entirely on interpersonal comparisons in a *given year*, with $\eta_{y_j y_i}$ which is based on *intertemporal changes* of incomes of identical families. We now formulate a test that relates directly the intertemporal changes *both* in income and in consumption. The advantages of this test will become evident as we proceed.

Since we have data on C and Y in two years, we can compute for each individual the ratio between the temporal changes in income and in consumption, i.e.,

$$\frac{C_{2q} - C_{1q}}{Y_{2q} - Y_{1q}} = \frac{\dot{C}_q}{\dot{Y}_q} \qquad (q = 1, \cdots, N),$$

where a dot denotes the time rate of change. Similarly, for a group of individuals we can compute a weighted average of the individual m.p.c.'s by least squares as follows:

$$(16) \qquad\qquad B_{\dot{c}\dot{y}} = \frac{\text{cov}(\dot{C}, \dot{Y})}{\text{var}(\dot{Y})}.$$

Now, what can be said about (16) by the traditional "absolute income hypothesis"? If prices remain constant (or if Y_2 and C_2 are deflated by the price index), there is no reason for $B_{\dot{c}\dot{y}}$ to be different from B_{cy}. Consider now the PIH interpretation of (16). As we have seen, Friedman envisages permanent income as being very stable over time. In other words, the changes in Y are attributed mainly to the temporary components. The latter, however, have (by assumption) no effect on consumption. Therefore, $B_{\dot{c}\dot{y}}$ can be expected to be "very" small, i.e., much smaller than B_{cy}.

Thus a comparison of $b_{\dot{c}\dot{y}}$ and b_{cy} provides a direct attack on the traditional approach. This is one of the advantages of this test compared with Friedman's test, which attacks the traditional approach more indirectly. We shall show later that the present test can also be turned into a critical test of the enlarged model.

TABLE 5

COMPARISON OF "STATIC" AND "DYNAMIC" MARGINAL PROPENSITIES TO CONSUME

Occupation	$b_{\dot{c}\dot{y}}$ (1)	$b_{c_1 y_1}$ (2)	$b_{c_2 y_2}$ (3)
E	0.719 ($\pm$ 0.051)	0.827 ($\pm$0.021)	0.850 ($\pm$ 0.019)
SE	0.520 ($\pm$0.069)	0.629 ($\pm$0.045)	0.753 ($\pm$0.034)

The numbers in parentheses are standard errors of estimates. The change in prices between the two years was very small (3%), so that using deflated values of C_2 and Y_2 did not change the results—instead of the values in col. (1) we obtained 0.713 and 0.511.

In Table 5 we present the comparison between the "dynamic" m.p.c. ($b_{\dot{c}\dot{y}}$) and the ordinary cross-section m.p.c.'s in the two years. It can be seen that $b_{\dot{c}\dot{y}}$ is systematically lower than b_{cy}, which constitutes evidence against the traditional approach. However, although the difference between $b_{\dot{c}\dot{y}}$ and b_{cy} is in the direction predicted by the PIH, it seems to be smaller than expected. We turn now to form a more precise idea of the value of $b_{\dot{c}\dot{y}}$ that is to be expected on the basis of Friedman's enlarged model.

Using the structural equation (and assuming K to be the same in both years),[10] we may write (16) as

$$(17) \qquad B_{\dot{c}\dot{y}} = \frac{\operatorname{cov}(K\dot{Y}' + \dot{C}'', \dot{Y})}{\operatorname{var}(\dot{Y})} = K \frac{\operatorname{var}(\dot{Y}')}{\operatorname{var}(\dot{Y})} + K \frac{\operatorname{cov}(\dot{Y}', \dot{Y}'')}{\operatorname{var}(\dot{Y})}$$

$$+ \frac{\operatorname{cov}(\dot{C}'', \dot{Y}'')}{\operatorname{var}(\dot{Y})} + \frac{\operatorname{cov}(\dot{Y}', \dot{C}'')}{\operatorname{var}(\dot{Y})}.$$

First we note that $\operatorname{cov}(\dot{C}'', \dot{Y}'') = \operatorname{cov}(\dot{C}'', \dot{Y}') = 0$, since $\operatorname{cov}(C_i'', Y_i'') = \operatorname{cov}(C_i'', Y_i') = 0$ by assumption (1), and therefore also $\operatorname{cov}(C_i'', Y_j'') = \operatorname{cov}(C_i'', Y_j') = 0$ for $i \neq j$, since the latter are weaker assumptions than

---

[10] This simplification is justified for our data, since the average propensities are virtually the same in both years (see Table 1).

the former.[11] By similar reasoning it also follows that cov $(\dot{Y}', \dot{Y}'') = 0$; the terms of the type cov (Y_i', Y_i'') vanish by assumption (1), and the terms of the type cov (Y_i', Y_j'') must vanish if the former assumption is to make any sense.[12] Thus, by analogy with (1), we have

$$(1') \qquad \text{cov}\,(\dot{Y}'', \dot{Y}') = \text{cov}\,(\dot{C}'', \dot{Y}') = \text{cov}\,(\dot{C}'', \dot{Y}'') = 0\,.$$

It follows from the above arguments that the only term which remains on the right-hand side of (17) is $K\,[\text{var}\,(\dot{Y}')/\text{var}\,(\dot{Y})]$ or $KP_{\dot{y}}$, where $P_{\dot{y}}$ is the dynamic equivalent of P_y. Note also that $P_{\dot{y}}$ is, on the above assumptions, the square of the correlation coefficient between the changes in permanent income $(\dot{Y}')$ and the changes in measured income $(\dot{Y})$. We may now write (17) as

$$(18) \qquad B_{\dot{c}\dot{y}} = K\,\frac{\text{var}\,(\dot{Y}')}{\text{var}\,(\dot{Y})} = KP_{\dot{y}}\,.$$

We may accordingly compute $P_{\dot{y}}$ by

$$(19) \qquad P_{\dot{y}} = \frac{B_{\dot{c}\dot{y}}}{K} \qquad (K = EC/EY)\,.$$

In Table 6 we present the values of $p_{\dot{y}}$ for the two occupations. The comparison *between* occupations implies that the income changes of the self-employed are of a more temporary nature than those of employees. However, the proportion of income changes that can be regarded as permanent is very high—0.55 and 0.75 for the self-employed and employees, respectively. In fact, $p_{\dot{y}}$ is not strikingly lower than p_y.

TABLE 6

A COMPARISON OF $p_{\dot{y}}$ WITH p_y

Occupation	$p_{\dot{y}} = b_{\dot{c}\dot{y}}\,\dfrac{\overline{Y}_{1+2}}{\overline{C}_{1+2}}$	$p_{y_1} = \eta_{c_1 y_1}$	$p_{y_2} = \eta_{c_2 y_2}$
	(1)	(2)	(3)
E	0.754	0.875	0.889
SE	0.550	0.669	0.793

The values of $p_{\dot{y}}$ were computed according to formula (19) by $b_{\dot{c}\dot{y}}/k$. As an estimate of K we used the average propensity for the two years combined; thus $\overline{Y}_{1+2}$ in the second column is average income in the two years.

---

[11] In fact Friedman uses the assumption cov $(C_i'', Y_j'') = 0$, where $i \neq j$, as a natural implication of cov $(C_i'', Y_i'') = 0$ [4, eq. (7.7), p. 198].

[12] Note also that cov $(Y_i', Y_j'') = \text{cov}\,(Y_i', C_j'') = 0$ by assumption (1) and assumption (10) of the enlarged model.

Having estimated the value of $P_{\dot{y}}$ from the dynamic m.p.c. on the basis of the basic model, we now compute it on the basis of other assumptions of the enlarged model. If the two estimates do not agree, the enlarged PIH cannot be accepted. For the purpose of this test, write (18) in full:

$$(20) \qquad \frac{B_{\dot{c}\dot{y}}}{K} = \frac{\operatorname{var}(\dot{Y}')}{\operatorname{var}(\dot{Y})} = \frac{\operatorname{var}(Y_1') + \operatorname{var}(Y_2') - 2\operatorname{cov}(Y_1', Y_2')}{\operatorname{var}(\dot{Y})}.$$

This can alternatively be written as

$$(21) \qquad \frac{\operatorname{var}(\dot{Y}')}{\operatorname{var}(\dot{Y})} = \frac{\operatorname{var}(Y_1)}{\operatorname{var}(\dot{Y})}\left[P_{y_1}\left(1 - 2\bar{\eta}_{y_2'y_1'}\frac{EY_2}{EY_1}\right) + P_{y_2}\frac{\operatorname{var}(Y_2)}{\operatorname{var}(Y_1)}\right].$$

Using the assumptions of the basic model, we may substitute $\bar{\eta}_{c_iy_i}$ for P_{y_i}. Again using assumption (10) of the enlarged model, we substitute 1 for $\bar{\eta}_{y_2'y_1'}$. Equation (21) can now be rewritten as

$$(22) \qquad \frac{\operatorname{var}(\dot{Y}')}{\operatorname{var}(\dot{Y})} = \frac{\operatorname{var}(Y_1)}{\operatorname{var}(\dot{Y})}\left[\bar{\eta}_{c_1y_1}\left(1 - 2\frac{EY_2}{EY_1}\right) + \bar{\eta}_{c_2y_2}\frac{\operatorname{var}(Y_2)}{\operatorname{var}(Y_1)}\right],$$

where all the components of (22) can be estimated from the sample. Thus (19) and (22) provide two values of $P_{\dot{y}}$; these must be equal if the enlarged PIH is true.

It is important to note that in formulating this test we do not have to resort to assumption (11), which states that $\operatorname{cov}(Y_j'', Y_i'') = 0$. Thus the present test is valid even if there exists a serial correlation between the temporary components of income in the two years (which is not the case with Friedman's test).

A more subtle point is that our test is in effect independent of the proportionality assumption (3) as well, in spite of the fact that in equation (22) we made use of this assumption by substituting $\bar{\eta}_{c_iy_i}$ for P_{y_i}. The proportionality assumption is in fact required only when we want to estimate the *absolute* value of $P_{\dot{y}}$. If, however, we wish merely to test the equality of $P_{\dot{y}}$ as computed from (19) and (22), then our test will hold for any value of K independently of whether $K = EC/EY$ (i.e., $\eta_{c'y'} = 1$) or not.[13] Thus our method provides a test of assumptions (1) and (10) of the enlarged model.

---

[13] This can be seen as follows: Let equation (3) be $C' = \beta_0 + \beta Y'$, where β is any number. Then equation (19) becomes

$$(19') \qquad\qquad \beta P_{\dot{y}} = B_{\dot{c}\dot{y}}.$$

The ordinary consumption elasticity is now interpreted as $\bar{\eta}_{c_iy_i} = \beta(EY_i/EC_i)P_{y_i}$. If we now substitute in (21) the expression for P_{y_i} and use (10), we obtain

$$(22') \quad \beta P_{\dot{y}} = \beta\frac{\operatorname{var}(\dot{Y}')}{\operatorname{var}(\dot{Y})} = \left[\bar{\eta}_{c_1y_1}\frac{EC_1}{EY_1}\left(1 - 2\frac{EY_2}{EY_1}\right) + \bar{\eta}_{c_2y_2}\frac{EC_2}{EY_2}\frac{\operatorname{var}(Y_2)}{\operatorname{var}(Y_1)}\right]\frac{\operatorname{var}(Y_1)}{\operatorname{var}(\dot{Y})}.$$

The right-hand sides of equations (19') and (22'), which are estimated from the data, must

The results of this test are given in Table 7. The values of $P_{\dot{y}}$ estimated from equation (22) are clearly very much lower than $P_{\dot{y}}$ estimated from equation (19). What this means is that Friedman's enlarged model implies a very low correlation between $\dot{Y}'$ and $\dot{Y}$, whereas the basic model implies a rather high correlation between these two rates of change. That the figures in col. (2) are low is not surprising, since this follows logically from the severe restrictions Friedman imposes on intertemporal changes of Y' by means of assumption (10). If, for example, the elasticities $\bar{\eta}_{c_i y_i}$ are the same for both years, and so are EY_i and var (Y_i), then equation (22) reduces to zero. Since in practice the above variables do not change considerably from one year to the next, we may expect $P_{\dot{y}}$, as estimated from equation (22), to be very small.

TABLE 7

A Comparison of $p_{\dot{y}}$ Computed Alternatively on the Basis of Equations (19) and (22)

Occupation	$p_{\dot{y}}$ Computed by Eq. (19) (1)	$p_{\dot{y}}$ Computed by Eq. (22) (2)
E	0.754	0.137
SE	0.550	0.171

For the purpose of these computations k was computed as $\bar{C}_{1+2}/\bar{Y}_{1+2}$.

An alternative way of looking at our test is as follows: The interpretation of $B_{\dot{c}\dot{y}}$ by means of the basic model is given by (18). We then estimate $P_{\dot{y}}$ by means of the *enlarged* model [i.e., using equation (22)] and thus obtain the latter's "prediction" of $B_{\dot{c}\dot{y}}$. In Table 8 we see that $b_{\dot{c}\dot{y}}$ predicted by the enlarged model [col. (3)] is very low compared with the actual $b_{\dot{c}\dot{y}}$ [col. (1)]. The reason for this failure is that the enlarged model implies that intertemporal income changes are mainly of a temporary nature, whereas according to the basic model these changes are mainly of a permanent nature. The traditional prediction of $b_{\dot{c}\dot{y}}$ is simply b_{cy}. This prediction does much better [col. (2)] than the enlarged PIH.

We have noted already that when an enlarged model is contradicted by the data, we still do not know whether the basic model is wrong. Assuming that the *additional* assumptions are wrong, it is always possible to change them so that the "modified" enlarged model will exactly fit the data.

---

be equal regardless of the value β, if assumptions (1) and (10) are true. This is the essence of our test.

Now in our data $k = \bar{C}_{1+2}/\bar{Y}_{1+2}$ is virtually identical with the average propensity in each separate year. Ignoring the differences in average propensities and dividing the right-hand sides of (19') and (22') by EC/EY, we obtain (19) and (22).

Although it is clear that the "modified" model cannot be subjected to any *test* (since we have used up all our degrees of freedom), it can still be used to interpret the data in the light of the basic model.

TABLE 8

PREDICTIONS OF $b_{\dot{c}\dot{y}}$ BASED ON THE TRADITIONAL APPROACH AND ON THE ENLARGED PIH

Occupation	Actual $b_{\dot{c}\dot{y}}$ (1)	Traditional Prediction[a] $b_{\dot{c}\dot{y}} = b_{cv}$ (2)	PIH Prediction[b] $b_{\dot{c}\dot{y}} = k \times$ estimate of eq. (22) (3)
E	0.754	0.839	0.130
SE	0.550	0.691	0.162

[a] In this column we used a simple average of the annual b_{cv}'s.

[b] The value of k was computed as the combined average propensity to consume for the two years.

To be more specific, the failure of the enlarged model to explain the dynamic m.p.c. can be attributed to assumption (10), which permits virtually no changes in permanent income between the two years. If, however, we change this assumption and accept the possibility that Y' may change in a nonsystematic manner between the two years, i.e., that $\bar{r}_{y'_2 y'_1}$ may be smaller than unity, we can always find a value of $\eta_{y'_j y'_i}$ that is consistent with the observed $b_{\dot{c}\dot{y}}$. Thus, in passing from (21) to (22), we do not equate $\bar{\eta}_{y'_2 y'_1}$ to 1 but leave it as an *unknown*. We then equate (22) with $B_{\dot{c}\dot{y}}/K$ [see equation (20)] and solve for $\bar{\eta}_{y'_j y'_i}$. The resulting value of $\eta_{y'_j y'_i}$ must be in exact agreement with $B_{\dot{c}\dot{y}}$, and can be used to *interpret* the concept of permanent income in view of the basic model.

In cols. (1) and (2) of Table 9 we present the values of $\eta_{y'_j y'_i}$ that are consistent (in view of the basic model) with the observed $b_{\dot{c}\dot{y}}$.[14] It can be seen that all these figures are less than unity. This means essentially that there exists nonsystematic ("random") variation in Y' between the two years. Consequently, $r_{y'_j y'_i} < 1$, contrary to assumption (10). This implies that (for our data) Friedman's conception of permanent income, as being a variable capable only of well-behaved changes between consecutive years, is wrong. To put it differently, Friedman's additional assumptions virtually rule out the possibility that changes in current income may lead to a revision of the expectation concerning the entire income stream. Consequently, the changes in income (Y) cannot have any significant effect on changes in C. The observed values of $b_{\dot{c}\dot{y}}$ imply, however, that income changes between consecutive years *do* lead to important changes in expectations. Hence we have a contradiction.

---

[14] See Appendix D for an interpretation of our method of computing $\eta_{y'_2 y'_1}$.

Now, if the enlarged model is wrong, how can we account for the excellent results obtained in the previous section? The discussion of this problem will have to be deferred to a later stage, where we shall be equipped with some additional results.

TABLE 9

ELASTICITIES AND CORRELATIONS BETWEEN PERMANENT COMPONENTS OF INCOME IN TWO CONSECUTIVE YEARS

Occupation	$\eta_{y_2' y_1'}$ (1)	$\eta_{y_2' y_1'}$ (2)	$r_{y_2' y_1}$ $(3) = \sqrt{(1) \times (2)}$	$r_{y_2 y_1}$ (4)
E	0.903	0.889	0.894	0.877
SE	0.867	0.792	0.831	0.762

The values in cols. (1) and (2) were computed on the basis of equations (20), (21), and (22) as follows:

$$\eta_{y_2' y_1'} = \frac{1}{2} \frac{\bar{Y}_1}{\bar{Y}_2} \left[1 - \left(\frac{b_{\dot{c}\dot{y}}}{k} \frac{\Sigma \dot{y}^2}{\Sigma y_1^2} - \eta_{c_2 y_2} \frac{\Sigma y_2^2}{\Sigma y_1^2} \right) \frac{1}{\eta_{c_1 y_1}} \right],$$

where lower-case letters express the variables as deviations from sample means. We compute $\eta_{y_1' y_2'}$ from the same formula by interchanging the indexes 1 and 2. We compute k as $\bar{C}_{1+2}/\bar{Y}_{1+2}$.

5. The Method of Instrumental Variables

We have already pointed out that Friedman's "strong" test (in Section 3) is essentially a method of estimating the true elasticity $\bar{\eta}_{c'y'}$ by using outside information on error variances. An alternative method of using outside information is known as the "method of instrumental variables" [1][15]. With the aid of this method it is possible, under certain conditions, to eliminate the effects of the temporary components and thus obtain consistent estimates of the true elasticity. We now describe the principles of this method, whose advantages will soon become evident.

Let us first drop the proportionality assumption (3) and write the relation between the permanent components as

(23) $C' = \beta_0 + \beta Y'$.

Suppose now that there exists a variable Z (to be called "instrumental variable") which is correlated with Y', but which is *not* correlated with the "errors" Y'' and C''. Consider now the estimate

(24) $b_{cy}^z = \frac{\Sigma cz}{\Sigma yz}$,

---

[15] For an application of this method to Engel Curve analysis, see [7].

where the superscript denotes the particular instrumental variable and the summation is over the families in the sample (the lower-case letters denote variables expressed as deviations from sample means). It is easily seen that b_{cy}^z is a consistent[16] estimate of the true m.p.c.; i.e.,

$$(25) \qquad B_{cy}^z = \frac{\text{cov}\,(C, Z)}{\text{cov}\,(Y, Z)} = \frac{\text{cov}\,(\beta_0 + \beta Y' + C'', Z)}{\text{cov}\,(Y' + Y'', Z)} = \beta$$

(the reader who is not interested in the sampling aspects of this method may skip the following analysis and continue with Section 6).

Suppose now that we have found a proper Z. We then set up the null hypothesis that the least-squares estimate b_{cy} is unbiased (i.e., that the PIH is false). For this purpose write the least-squares estimate in the sample as

$$b_{cy} = \frac{\Sigma(\beta y + c'' - \beta y'')y}{\Sigma y^2} = \beta + \frac{\Sigma wy}{\Sigma y^2},$$

where $w = c'' - \beta y''$. Similarly, write b_{cy}^z as

$$b_{cy}^z = \beta + \frac{\Sigma wz}{\Sigma yz}.$$

Our null hypothesis is then (in terms of population parameters)

$$(26) \qquad H_0: B_{cy}^z = B_{cy} = \beta \quad \text{or} \quad \text{cov}\,(W, Y) = \text{cov}\,(W, Z) = 0.$$

Note that H_0 implies that there is no random variability in income, i.e., that $\text{var}\,(Y'') = 0$, and therefore that $W = C''$ identically. The least-squares bias postulated by the PIH implies, of course, the alternative hypothesis

$$(27) \qquad H_1: (B_{cy}^z - B_{cy}) > 0.$$

To test H_0 it is necessary to compute the standard error of $(b_{cy}^z - b_{cy})$ under the null hypothesis and use it for a one-tailed test (since the sign of the difference is specified by the alternative hypothesis). Suppose, tentatively, that Y and Z are "fixed" in repeated samples, and write

$$(28) \qquad b_{cy}^z - b_{cy} = \Sigma\left(\frac{z}{\Sigma yz} - \frac{y}{\Sigma y^2}\right)w.$$

---

[16] An alternative method of eliminating the errors (and therefore of consistently estimating β) when Z is available is as follows: Divide the range of Z into a given number of classes and compute averages of C and Y for each of these classes. This has the effect of "averaging out" the errors in C and Y so that we are left with approximately the (mean) *systematic* components (provided the number of cases in each subgroup is large). This is in fact the principle adopted by Friedman and by Eisner [2]. However, if Z is an ordinary continuous variable, the estimate (24) has the advantage both of making use of all the information (i.e., by using *individual* data), and of being a more elegant tool for analytical purposes.

Squaring (28) and taking expectations, we obtain under H_0:[17]

$$(29) \qquad \text{var}\,(b_{cy}^z - b_{cy}) = \frac{\text{var}\,(W)}{\Sigma y^2}\left(\frac{1}{r_{yz}^2} - 1\right) = \text{var}\,(b_{cy}) \cdot \left(\frac{1}{r_{yz}^2} - 1\right).$$

It can be shown that the same result is obtained when we treat (as we should) Y and Z as random variables, and compute the *asymptotic* approximation to the variance of (28). Finally, it is important to note that the higher r_{yz}^2 is, the more powerful (statistically) is the test.

It is clear that if we cannot reject H_0, there is no point in continuing the test, and the PIH should be rejected. In this case there is also no point in using b_{cy}^z instead of b_{cy}, since the former is statistically less efficient. Suppose, however, that (28) is significantly positive, as implied by the PIH. We then continue to test whether $\eta_{c'y'}$ is significantly different from unity. This test could be easily performed on the logarithmic variant of Friedman's model. For the linear model, however, this is a complicated matter, since $\eta_{cy}^z = b_{cy}^z(\bar{Y}/\bar{C})$ in a product of two random variables. For simplicity, suppose that EC/EY is known. We then consider whether $b_{cy}^z - (EC/EY)$ is significantly different from zero, the (asymptotic) variance here being[18]

$$(30) \qquad \text{var}\left(b_{cy}^z - \frac{EC}{EY}\right) = \text{var}\,(b_{cy}^z) = \frac{\text{var}\,(W)}{\Sigma y^2}\frac{1}{\bar{r}_{yz}^2}.$$

6. Lagged or Future Income as an Instrumental Variable

Thus far we have dealt with formal considerations. The difficulties arise when we look in practice for a variable with the properties of Z. There is usually no problem of finding various variables that are correlated with Y', but we are often not sure that they are not correlated with the errors in C and in Y.

If, however, Friedman's enlarged model is true, we need not worry about finding a proper instrumental variable, since such a variable is readily provided, for any year i, by lagged or future income Y_j (where $j \neq i$). To see this we note that $\text{cov}\,(C_i'', Y_j) = 0$ and, by assumption (11),[19] $\text{cov}\,(Y_i'', Y_j' + Y_j'') = 0$; hence $\text{cov}\,(W_i, Y_j) = 0$, where $W_i = C_i'' - \beta Y_i''$. Therefore, $b_{c_i y_i}^{y_j}$ is a consistent estimate of the true m.p.c., and $b_{c_i y_i}^{y_j}(\bar{Y}_i/\bar{C}_i)$ is a consistent estimate of the true elasticity $\eta_{c'y'}$, which—according to the PIH—is equal to unity.

It is important to note that in order to use Y_j as an instrumental variable, we do not have to resort to assumption (10) concerning the value of $\bar{\eta}_{y_j'y_i'}$.

---

[17] Note that in (29) we have to assume that W is homoscedastic.

[18] Var (W) is estimated from the sample by $\Sigma\,(c - b_{cy}^z y)^2/(n - 2)$. For the derivation of asymptotic variances of estimates obtained by instrumental variables, see [9].

[19] We assume as usual that cov $(Y_i'', Y_j') = 0$.

In fact, we need no external information at all about the relation between Y_i' and Y_j' (except that they are correlated). Thus, if assumption (11) is true, the addition of assumption (10) to the enlarged model is redundant. In this sense, the use of Y_j as an instrumental variable provides a more direct test of the basic model than the test suggested by Friedman.

One final point should be noted before we turn to the actual tests. As we have pointed out [see equation (29)], the power of the test depends directly on the correlation between Y_i and the instrumental variable. When Y_j is used as the instrumental variable the correlation is very high, so that even a relatively small reinterview survey may provide adequate data for powerful tests.

TABLE 10

INCOME OF A DIFFERENT YEAR (Y_j) AS THE INSTRUMENTAL VARIABLE

Year (i)[a]	Occupation	$b_{c_i \nu_i}$ (1)	$b_{c_i \nu_i}^{\nu_j}$ (2)	$\dfrac{(2) - (1)}{(1)}$ (3)	Standard Error[b] of $(2) - (1)$ (4)	$t = \dfrac{(2) - (1)}{(4)}$ (5)
1	E	0.827	0.858	0.037	0.013	2.39
1	SE	0.629	0.754	0.199	0.051	2.45
2	E	0.850	0.861	0.013	0.012	0.92
2	SE	0.753	0.750	−0.004	0.038	−0.08

[a] For the first two rows $j = 2$, and for the last two rows $j = 1$.
[b] The standard errors in this column were computed on the basis of formula (29) as follows:

$$\text{std. error of } \left(b_{c_i \nu_i}^{\nu_j} - b_{c_i \nu_i} \right) = \text{std. error of } b_{c_i \nu_i} \times \sqrt{ (r_{\nu_j \nu_i}^2)^{-1} - 1 } .$$

In Table 10 we present in col. (2) the estimates of β, using Y_j as an instrumental variable. The comparison of col. (2) with the least-squares estimates in col. (1) is rather disappointing for the PIH; only for the group of self-employed in year 1 do we find a substantial positive difference [see col. (3)]. In two of the other three cases the sign of the difference is as predicted by the PIH, but it is of rather small magnitude. In col. (5) we divide these differences by their standard errors and find that two of the differences are "highly" significant according to the usual criteria (note that we are dealing with a one-tailed test, so that $t \geqslant +2.33$ is significant at the 1 per cent level).

Even if we accept the idea that the $b_{c_i \nu_i}^{\nu_j}$ provide better estimates of the true m.p.c. than $b_{c_i \nu_i}$, we can see from Table 11 that (even in the most favorable cases) the former are much smaller than the average propensities.

Alternatively, we may consider the elasticities in col. (3), which are still much closer to the ordinary least-squares elasticities than to unity. Thus, the results of this test are clearly unfavorable to the PIH.

TABLE 11

CONSUMPTION ELASTICITIES $\eta_{c_i v_i}^{v_j}$ COMPUTED WITH Y_j AS THE INSTRUMENTAL VARIABLE

Year (i)	Occupation	$b_{c_i v_i}^{v_j}$ (1)	$\bar{C}_i/\bar{Y}_i$ (2)	$\eta_{c_i v_i}^{v_j} = (1)/(2)$ (3)
1	E	0.858 ($\pm$.021)	0.945	0.907
1	SE	0.754 ($\pm$.045)	0.940	0.802
2	E	0.861 ($\pm$.019)	0.957	0.900
2	SE	0.750 ($\pm$.034)	0.950	0.789

The numbers in parentheses are standard errors of estimates, computed on the basis of equation (30).

7. Evaluation of the Tests in Sections 3 Through 6

In view of the fact that the results of the tests in Sections 4 and 6 contradict Friedman's enlarged model, one is faced with the usual problem of whether it is the *basic* model that is false, or the *additional* assumptions, or both. Unfortunately, there is not enough information to provide a definite answer to this question. There is also the puzzling problem of explaining the success of the PIH in Section 3 in view of its failures in Sections 4 and 6.

Some insight into these problems can be obtained by assuming tentatively that the basic model is true and working out, on the basis of this assumption, the implications of the tests in terms of the nature of permanent and temporary components of income. It should be stressed at the outset that this experiment cannot be used as a formal test of any kind; it can only help in forming a better subjective judgment on the plausibility of the PIH.

Let us try first to reconcile the results of the test in Section 3 with those of Section 4. Assuming the basic model to be true, what is the reason for the success of "Friedman's test" in Section 3 and the failure of the test in Section 4? In order to answer this question, let us write the expression for $\bar{\eta}_{y_j y_i}$, assuming only that cov $(Y_j', Y_i'') = 0$ for $i, j = 1, 2$ (according to the basic model). Using the latter assumption and the definition of $\bar{\eta}_{y_j y_i}$, we obtain [see equation (3b) in Appendix B]

$$(31) \qquad \bar{\eta}_{y_j y_i} = \bar{\eta}_{y_j' y_i'} P_{y_i} + B_{y_j'' y_i''} (EY_i/EY_j)(1 - P_{y_i}).$$

Using the proportionality assumption, we substitute $\bar{\eta}_{c_i y_i}$ for P_{y_i}, and rewrite (31) as

$$(32) \qquad \bar{\eta}_{y_j y_i} = \bar{\eta}_{y'_j y'_i} \bar{\eta}_{c_i y_i} + B_{y''_j y''_i} \, (EY_i/EY_j) \, (1 - \bar{\eta}_{c_i y_i}) \, .$$

Now if assumptions (10) and (11) are true, (32) reduces to $\bar{\eta}_{y_j y_i} = \bar{\eta}_{c_i y_i}$, which corresponds to "Friedman's test" in Section 3. However, on the basis of Section 4, assumption (10), which states that $\eta_{y'_j y'_i} = 1$, must be rejected. If, empirically, $\eta_{y_j y_i}$ is nevertheless close to $\eta_{c_i y_i}$ (as shown in Section 3) this must imply $B_{y''_j y''_i} > 0$. In other words, if the basic model is to be consistent with *both* tests, there must exist between temporary components of income a positive serial correlation just sufficient to compensate for the fact that $\eta_{y'_j y'_i}$ is less than unity.

Now if $B_{y''_j y''_i} > 0$, then the use of Y_j as an instrumental variable is inappropriate. This "explains" the failure of the PIH in Section 6. To see this, consider the meaning of $B^{y_j}_{c_i y_i}$ when Y''_j is positively correlated with Y''_i. Under these conditions we have

$$(33) \qquad B^{y_j}_{c_i y_i} = \frac{\mathrm{cov}\,(C_i, Y_j)}{\mathrm{cov}\,(Y_i, Y_j)} = \beta \, \frac{\mathrm{cov}\,(Y'_i, Y'_j)}{\mathrm{cov}\,(Y'_i, Y'_j) + \mathrm{cov}(Y''_i, Y''_j)}$$

$$= \beta \, \frac{1}{1 + (B_{y''_j y''_i}/B_{y'_j y'_i}) \, (1 - P_{y_i})/P_{y_i}} \, .$$

This implies that $B^{y_j}_{c_i y_i} < \beta$. It follows that a sufficiently high serial correlation may account for the discrepancy of $\eta^{y_j}_{c_i y_i}$ from unity.

Independently of assumption (3), we may expect (33) to be higher than the downward-biased $b_{c_i y_i}$. To see this, write (33) as

$$(34) \qquad B^{y_j}_{c_i y_i} = \beta P_{y_i} \, \frac{1}{P_{y_i} + (B_{y''_j y''_i}/B_{y'_j y'_i}) \, (1 - P_{y_i})} \, .$$

Note, however, that $\beta P_{y_i} = B_{c_i y_i}$, and therefore

$$(35) \qquad \frac{B_{c_i y_i}}{B^{y_j}_{c_i y_i}} = P_{y_i} + \frac{B_{y''_j y''_i}}{B_{y'_j y'_i}} \, (1 - P_{y_i}) \, .$$

This implies that in spite of its bias, $B^{y_j}_{c_i y_i}$ must be larger than the least-squares coefficient $B_{c_i y_i}$, inasmuch as the regression coefficient of the temporary components is smaller than that of the permanent components of income. This explains the tendency of $b^{y_j}_{c_i y_i}$ to be larger empirically than $b_{c_i y_i}$, quite independently of the proportionality assumption. Thus $b^{y_j}_{c_i y_i}$ is the effective lower limit for β.

If this assumption is true, we may substitute $\bar{\eta}_{c_i y_i}$ for P_{y_i} in (35) and solve for $B_{y''_j y''_i}/B_{y'_j y'_i}$. Moreover, since we can estimate $B_{y'_j y'_i}$ by the procedures indicated in Section 3,[20] we can also obtain a separate estimate of $B_{y_i' y_j'}$. (These can be computed on the basis of either (35) or (32), the two methods being equivalent.)

TABLE 12

VALUES OF $b_{v_j'' v_i''}$ AND OF $b_{v_j' v_i'}$ IMPLIED BY THE PIH

Year (i)	Occupation	$b_{v_j'' v_i''}$ [a] (1)	$b_{v_j' v_i'}$ [b] (2)	(1)/(2) [c] (3)
1	E	0.758	1.064	0.712
1	SE	0.485	0.974	0.498
2	E	0.668	0.756	0.883
2	SE	0.719	0.706	1.019

a The values of $b_{v_j'' v_i''}$ were computed by (3) × (2).
b The values of $b_{v_j' v_i'}$ were computed by $\frac{1}{2} (\Sigma c_j y_i + \Sigma c_i y_j)/\Sigma c_i y_i$.
c This ratio was computed on the basis of formula (35), with $\bar{\eta}_{c_i y_i}$ substituted for P_{y_i} .

The estimates of $B_{y_i' y_j'}$ as implied by the basic model, are given in col. (1) of Table 12. It can be seen that the PIH implies an extremely high stability of temporary components (in Friedman's terminology this means an extremely long income "horizon"). Indeed, as shown in col. (3), the temporary components are not strikingly less stable than the permanent components.

The high ratios in col. (3) seem to contradict the intuitive notion of the nature of temporary and permanent components of income. If, however, we think (as we should) that the ratios in col. (3) should be lower, we imply that $P_{y_i} > \bar{\eta}_{c_i y_i}$, since these calculated ratios can be reduced only if we substitute for P_{y_i} in (35) values larger than $\bar{\eta}_{c_i y_i}$.[21] This, however, implies that the relative "least-squares bias" $(1 - P_{y_i})$ is smaller than is suggested by the PIH, or in other words that $\eta_{c'y'} < 1$. The success of "Friedman's test" in Section 3 must accordingly be attributed to compensating errors in the enlarged model.

8. Past and Future Consumption (C_j) as an Instrumental Variable

The experiment of using Y_j as an instrumental variable leads us naturally to consider the use of lagged or future consumption (C_j) in the same manner. The condition required for this purpose is that there be no serial correlation

---

[20] That is, using the assumptions of the basic model, it follows that $B_{v_j' v_i'} = \text{cov } (Y_j, C_i)/\text{cov } (Y_i, C_i)$. See Appendix D.

[21] It can be shown that this must be true if empirically we have $b_{c_i y_i}^{v_j} > b_{c_i y_i}$.

between the random elements in C in the two years. Since there is no way of verifying whether C_i'' is in fact not correlated with C_j'' (i.e., without making use of all the assumptions of the basic model), it is important to consider the possible *sign* of this correlation *if it does exist*.

General considerations lead one to expect a *positive* serial correlation between temporary components in income or in consumption. After all, the dividing line between two consecutive years is arbitrary, and therefore the same factors which caused a discrepancy between actual Y or C and their permanent components in the first year are likely to continue to operate (though to a smaller extent) in the second year. This is in fact the way Friedman analyzes the problem. Although his main concern is with explaining the nature of the serial correlation between temporary components of *income*, his analysis applies of course to temporary components in consumption as well. In fact, when the latter problem arises, Friedman goes as far as to assume not only that the serial correlation between the C''''s is of the same *sign* as between the Y''''s but also that these two correlations are *equal*.[22]

For the purpose of the subsequent analysis we shall accordingly assume that the correlation between C_j'' and C_i'' is non-negative. Suppose first that the correlation is zero, and form the instrumental variables estimate

$$(36) \qquad b_{c_i y_i}^{c_j} = \frac{\sum c_i c_j}{\sum y_i c_j} = \beta + \frac{\sum w_i c_j}{\sum y_i c_j},$$

where $w_i = c_i'' - \beta y_i''$. Using the assumption cov $(C_j'', C_i'') = 0$ and the other usual assumptions concerning the properties of temporary components, we have cov $(W_i, C_j) = 0$, and hence $B_{c_i y_i}^{c_j} = \beta$.

Suppose, alternatively, that cov (C_j'', C_i'') is positive. Then, using the usual assumptions of the model, we have cov $(W_i, C_j) = $ cov $(C_j'', C_i'') > 0$, and consequently $b_{c_i y_i}^{c_j}$ is an *upward*-biased estimate of the true m.p.c. (i.e., β). This implies that in using C_j as an instrumental variable we obtain an *upper* limit for β. For this reason, using C_j as instrumental variable does not provide a direct attack on the traditional approach, but it is very useful in testing whether the true elasticity is in fact as high as unity.

In the actual computations we used as an instrumental variable not only C_j, but also C_j excluding expenditures on durables (to be denoted C_j^x). There is some advantage in experimenting with the latter variable, since it is probably more stable than C.

The empirical results of using C_j and C_j^x as instrumental variables are given in cols. (2) and (3) of Table 13. A comparison with the values of $b_{c_i y_i}$ in col. (1) shows that the estimated value of m.p.c. is always higher in

---

[22] He points out of course that this is a very rough approximation. See [4, pp. 196-99, esp. eqs. (7.10) and (7.12)].

cols. (2) and (3), as should be expected on the basis of the PIH. Moreover, all the differences are statistically significant and quite substantial in size. It seems, therefore, that if the serial correlation between C_j'' and C_i'' is zero, or small, then the least-squares bias is by no means negligible.

TABLE 13

CONSUMPTION OF A DIFFERENT YEAR AS INSTRUMENTAL VARIABLE

Year[a] (i)	Occu-pation	$b_{c_i v_i}$ (1)	$b_{c_i v_i}^{c_j}$ [b] (2)	$b_{c_i v_i}^{c_j^x}$ [c] (3)	$\dfrac{(2) - (1)}{(1)}$ (4)	$\dfrac{(3) - (1)}{(1)}$ (5)	(2) − (1)[d] Standard Error (6)	(3) − (1)[d] Standard Error (7)
1	E	0.827	0.885	0.893	0.070	0.080	2.64	2.14
1	SE	0.629	0.880	0.889	0.399	0.413	2.89	3.02
2	E	0.850	0.888	0.902	0.045	0.061	1.81	2.48
2	SE	0.753	0.875	0.826	0.162	0.097	1.85	1.22

[a] For the first two rows $j = 2$ and for the last two rows $j = 1$.
[b] The instrumental variable is consumption including durables.
[c] The instrumental variable is consumption *excluding* durables.
[d] The difference between $b_{c_i v_i}^{c_j}$ (or $b_{c_i v_i}^{c_j^x}$) and $b_{c_i v_i}$ divided by the standard error of the difference. The latter was computed according to formula (29), i.e., on the null hypothesis that $b_{c_i v_i}$ is consistent.

An outstanding feature of the results in col. (2) is that not only does the use of C_j as an instrumental variable raise the m.p.c.'s, but it also virtually equates the m.p.c.'s of the self-employed with those of employees. Since, in our data, the average propensities in these two groups are very similar, our results suggest that the income elasticities of consumption are the same in both groups, as postulated by the PIH. These results diminish the likelihood that our estimates are biased. This is so because it is hard to believe that the biases in the $b_{c_i v_i}^{c_j}$'s of the self-employed and employees are such as to compensate for the large differences in the traditional estimates. This is too much of a coincidence, especially when there is a theory which states beforehand that the true elasticities are equal.

Although the values of m.p.c., estimated by instrumental variables, are considerably higher than $b_{c_i v_i}$, they are still systematically lower than the average propensities, as can be seen in Table 14. Alternatively, the elasticities in cols. (4) and (5) are systematically smaller than unity. Moreover, if in fact there exists a serial correlation between the temporary components of consumption, then the elasticities in cols. (4) and (5) should

TABLE 14

CONSUMPTION ELASTICITIES COMPUTED WITH C_j AND C_j^x AS INSTRUMENTAL VARIABLES

Year (i)	Occupation	$b_{c_i v_i}^{c_j}$ (1)	$b_{c_i v_i}^{c_j^x}$ (2)	$\dfrac{\bar{C}_i}{\bar{Y}_i}$ (3)	$\eta_{c_i v_i}^{c_j}$ = (1) ÷ (3) (4)	$\eta_{c_i v_i}^{c_j^x}$ = (2) ÷ (3) (5)
1	E	0.885 ($\pm$.027)	0.893 ($\pm$.026)	0.945	0.936	0.945
1	SE	0.880 ($\pm$.071)	0.889 ($\pm$.071)	0.940	0.936	0.946
2	E	0.888 ($\pm$.025)	0.902 ($\pm$.025)	0.957	0.928	0.943
2	SE	0.875 ($\pm$.053)	0.826 ($\pm$.051)	0.950	0.921	0.870

be lowered. This clearly implies that Friedman's fundamental hypothesis, which claims that the elasticity between permanent components of C and Y is unity, cannot be accepted. This, however, should not belittle the basic fact that the elasticities in cols. (4) and (5) are closer to unity than to the traditional elasticities.

9. Conclusions

Our empirical results show that the model formulated by Friedman to test the PIH from reinterview surveys is contradicted by the data. Although this cannot be seen when we copy Friedman's test in Section 3, the contradiction comes out clearly when we use new and more direct tests in Sections 4 and 6.

Although these results are based only on the Israel 1958/9 Reinterview Savings Survey, it is not unlikely that they will be confirmed by other savings surveys, since there is usually a considerable similarity among the various surveys in these matters. Therefore, our results lead to serious doubts about the interpretation of the success of the test (of the type described in Section 3) carried out by Friedman on reinterview data. To disperse these doubts Friedman has to show that the data he used in his tests are consistent with the tests we formulated in Sections 4 and 6. The latter can of course be applied not only for consecutive years but also for two years with any time interval between them.

An important conclusion from our theoretical analysis is that only *one* additional requirement (i.e., in addition to the basic model) is needed to estimate the true consumption elasticity: that there be no serial correlation between temporary components over time. Friedman's additional assumption concerning the form of the relationship between *permanent* components (i.e., the "mean assumption" or the "variability assumption") is redundant as far as the testing of the PIH is concerned. Since we need not be concerned about the *form* of the relationship between permanent components, it is clear that, in principle, the best tests of the PIH are those in which the time interval between the two years is long enough to eliminate the possible serial correlation between temporary components.[23] From this point of view the data used by Friedman in some of his tests, where there is an interval of one year between the two years, are more appropriate than our data for the application of the method of instrumental variables [with income of a different year (Y_j) as instrumental variable].

These remarks apply equally to the use of consumption of a different year (C_j) as an instrumental variable. The best check on our results of using that method is to lengthen the interval between the two years and thus eliminate the possible serial correlation between the temporary components of consumption.

Finally, what can we learn from the results of the tests presented in this article about the value of the true income elasticity of consumption ? We may first point out that the results indicate a downward bias in the traditional elasticities. This is particularly true of elasticities relating to the self-employed, as can be seen by the results of computing regressions of income on consumption, or of using consumption as an instrumental variable.

The results obtained by using Y_j as an instrumental variable indicate that the elasticities relating to employees are also downward-biased. Although that bias turned out to be rather small, it is not unlikely that this is due to the existence of positive serial correlation between temporary components of income. (This hypothesis can be checked by using data with an appropriate time interval between the two years.) Thus the elasticities obtained by using Y_j as an instrumental variable can be regarded as lower limits for the true elasticities. These limits are 0.90 and 0.80 for employees and the self-employed, respectively.[24] An upper limit is obtained by using C_j as an instrumental variable. Thus in the most favorable case the true elasticity is, for both employees and the self-employed, around 0.94. This is still less than what is required by the strict proportionality assumption. On the basis of the discussion in the preceding section, we suggest that the true elasticity is likely to be represented better by the upper limit.

---

[23] The only disadvantage of this procedure is the increase in sampling errors, since the correlation between the permanent components is reduced. However, the correlation between Y_i' and Y_j is still likely to be stronger than that between Y_i' and any other instrumental variable.

[24] The corresponding least-squares elasticities are 0.88 and 0.73 (using averages for the two years).

APPENDIX A

The Data

Our data are based on two savings surveys carried out in Israel as a joint effort of several institutions.[25] The first survey relates to the fiscal year 1957/8 and included some 3000 Jewish urban families ("income units"). The 1958/9 survey is based on about 1000 of these families who were reinterviewed in the subsequent year. In the analysis in this article we purposely did not include the retired and unoccupied, a group that comprises about 10 per cent of the families.

The survey methods and definitions[26] are very similar to those of the Oxford Saving Surveys and of the Survey of Consumer Finances in the United States. In particular, saving was estimated directly on the basis of the various transactions on capital account. Only retained earnings of the self-employed were estimated by the residual approach, i.e., profits minus withdrawals.

The data on income (Y) used in this article represent *net* income, i.e., after direct taxes (including national insurance). The latter taxes were *imputed* on the basis of tax schedules. The average net income per family is virtually the same for employees and the self-employed (about IL 3100 and IL 3400 in the first and second year, respectively). Income does not include imputed income of owner-occupied flats.

Consumption (C) has been calculated as the difference between income and saving. Throughout this article we used as the dependent variable consumption (C) *including* expenditures on durables. In fact, we repeated all the computation given in the text for nondurable consumption as well. The differences in the results were, however, too small to justify a duplication of all the tables in the text. On this point see Appendix C.

Finally, we should point out that all our computations are weighted to take into account differential sampling rates.

APPENDIX B

Implications of the "Mean Assumption"

Friedman's presentation of his method of estimating P_y from income data is in terms of group means. We shall now show that his presentation implies (a) that the relation between Y_2' and Y_1' of *individual* families is

---

[25] Bank of Israel, Central Bureau of Statistics, Department of Economics of the Hebrew University, Falk Project for Economic Research in Israel, and Israel Institute of Applied Social Research.

[26] The survey methods and definitions, as well as the main findings, are described in *Bank of Israel Bulletin No. 10* and. *Bank of Israel, Annual Report 1959*, pp. 319-27. These were reissued as *Research Papers 8 and 9*, Falk Project for Economic Research in Israel.

exact, as given in equation (10) in the text, and (b) that his presentation implies $\text{cov}(Y_2'', Y_1'') = 0$; i.e., there is no temporal serial correlation between transitory components. Assumption (b) refers, of course, to the case to which the test described in Section 3 is applicable.

Friedman presents his "mean assumption" as follows [5, pp. 329-30]:

> Suppose we classify the families in year 1 by T (measured) income classes $(t = 1, \cdots, T)$, and
>
> Let $\bar{Y}_{1t}$, $\bar{Y}'_{1.1t}$ be the average income and permanent income, respectively, in year 1 of a year 1 income class t.
>
> Let $\bar{Y}_{2.1t}$, $\bar{Y}'_{2.1t}$ be the average income and permanent income, respectively, in year 2 of a year 1 income class t.
>
> Let $\bar{Y}_1$, $\bar{Y}_2$ be the over-all average income in years 1 and 2, respectively (these are also the over-all averages of permanent income).

The "mean assumption" is then stated as

(1b)
$$\bar{Y}'_{2.1t} - \bar{Y}_2 = \frac{\bar{Y}_2}{\bar{Y}_1}(\bar{Y}'_{1.1t} - \bar{Y}_1)$$

or

(2b)
$$\bar{Y}'_{2.1t} = m\bar{Y}'_{1.1t} \qquad [m = (\bar{Y}_2/\bar{Y}_1)].$$

Thus the "mean assumption" states that all the (conditional) group means of *permanent* income change between the two years in precisely the same ratio as the *over-all* means. Since the range of the income classes is arbitrary, (2b) must presumably hold for *any* possible classification. This in turn implies that the relation between the values of Y_2' and Y_1' of *individual* families is *exact*.

Alternatively, suppose that we classify the families by classes of Y_2. Then, according to the "mean assumption," the (conditional) group means of permanent income must lie on a straight line with slope $1/m$. Since the slopes m and $1/m$ relate also to Y' of *individual* families, this implies that the correlation is unity. A similar argument applies to the "variability assumption" (see footnote 9). Friedman also assumes $\bar{Y}'_{2.1t} = \bar{Y}_{2.1t}$; i.e., $\bar{Y}''_{2.1t} = 0$. This means that the temporary components in year 2 are not correlated with those in year 1. Alternatively, we shall now show that if Friedman's assertion that $\bar{\eta}_{y_2y_1} = P_{y_1}$ is true, then the mean assumption implies $\text{cov}(Y_1'', Y_2') = 0$. Writing $\bar{\eta}_{y_2y_1}$ in full yields

(3b)
$$\bar{\eta}_{y_2y_1} = \frac{\text{cov}(Y_2' + Y_2'', Y_1' + Y_1'')}{\text{var}(Y_1)} \frac{EY_1}{EY_2}$$

$$= \bar{\eta}_{y_2'y_1'} P_{y_1} + \frac{\text{cov}(Y_2'', Y_1'')}{\text{var}(Y_1'')} \frac{EY_1}{EY_2}(1 - P_{y_1})$$

$$+ \frac{\text{cov}(Y_1', Y_2'') + \text{cov}(Y_2', Y_1'')}{\text{var}(Y_1)} \frac{EY_1}{EY_2}.$$

Note that cov $(Y_1', Y_2'') = 0$ since $Y_1' = (1/m)Y_2'$ and

$$\text{cov}\,[(1/m)Y_2', Y_2''] = (1/m)\,\text{cov}\,(Y_2', Y_2'') = 0\,.$$

Similarly, cov $(Y_2', Y_1'') = 0$, so that the last term on the right-hand side vanishes. Note also that according to the mean assumption, $\bar{\eta}_{y_2' y_1'} = 1$, so that (3b) reduces to

(4b) $$\bar{\eta}_{y_2 y_1} = P_{y_1} + \frac{\text{cov}\,(Y_2'', Y_1'')}{\text{var}\,(Y_1'')}\,\frac{EY_1}{EY_2}\,(1 - P_{y_1})\,.$$

Now if $\bar{\eta}_{y_2 y_1} = P_{y_1} < 1$, we must have cov $(Y_2'', Y_1'') = 0$.
Similar results follow for the "variability assumption."

APPENDIX C
Nondurable Consumption as the Dependent Variable

Ideally, consumption should include the value of *services* derived from the stock of durable goods, but should not include current purchases of durables. Cross-section data, however, do not permit us to use this refined concept. Consequently, research workers use either consumption *in*cluding or consumption *ex*cluding purchases of durables. (The former procedure, which has been followed in the text, is the more common one.) Sometimes *both* alternative definitions are used for computing the consumption elasticities in the hope that the "true" elasticity is in between.

In our analysis we have in fact repeated all the computations presented in the text for nondurable consumption (C^x) as well. However, the results of the tests were not substantially different. This conclusion is illustrated in Tables C-1 and C-2.

TABLE C-1

COMPARISON OF "STATIC" AND "DYNAMIC" m.p.c.'s FOR NONDURABLE CONSUMPTION (C^x)

Occupation	$b_{c^x y}$ (1)	$b_{c_1^x y_1}$ (2)	$b_{c_2^x y_2}$ (3)
E	0.659 ($\pm$.043)	0.754 ($\pm$.018)	0.767 ($\pm$.016)
SE	0.486 ($\pm$.065)	0.595 ($\pm$.039)	0.717 ($\pm$.032)

In Table C-1, which is equivalent to Table 5 in the text (except that here we use C^x instead of C), we still find that the m.p.c. of identical individuals is very close to the ordinary cross-section m.p.c.

TABLE C-2

INCOME ELASTICITY OF NONDURABLE CONSUMPTION COMPUTED BY
THREE ALTERNATIVE METHODS

Year (i)	Occupation	$\eta_{c_i^x y_i}$	$\eta_{c_i^x y_i}^{y_j}$	$\eta_{c_i^x y_i}^{c_j^x}$	$\dfrac{(2) - (1)}{(1)}$	$\dfrac{(3) - (1)}{(1)}$
		(1)	(2)	(3)	(4)	(5)
1	E	0.849	0.870	0.917	0.025	0.080
1	SE	0.673	0.802	0.896	0.192	0.331
2	E	0.852	0.870	0.917	0.021	0.076
2	SE	0.777	0.785	0.876	0.010	0.127

In col. (1) we have the ordinary least-squares elasticity, while in cols. (2) and (3) we use Y_j and C_j^x ($j \neq i$) as instrumental variables.

Table C-2 shows that although the use of Y_j as an instrumental variable [col. (2)] raises in all cases the consumption elasticity [as compared with col. (1)], the "improvement" is of a rather small magnitude [see col. (4)]. Again, as in the results presented in the text, the use of C_j^x as an instrumental variable [col. (3)] raises the elasticities considerably, but they still fall short, systematically, from unity.

APPENDIX D

A Simple Interpretation of Our Method of Computing $\eta_{y_2' y_1'}$

Our formula for computing $\eta_{y_2' y_1'}$ is given by (see note to Table 9)

(1d)
$$\frac{1}{2} \frac{\bar{Y}_1}{\bar{Y}_2} \left[1 - \left(\frac{b_{\dot{c}\dot{y}}}{k} \frac{\Sigma \dot{y}^2}{\Sigma \dot{y}_1^2} - \eta_{c_2 y_2} \frac{\Sigma y_2^2}{\Sigma y_1^2} \right) \frac{1}{\eta_{c_1 y_1}} \right].$$

Ignoring the difference between $\bar{C}_1/\bar{Y}_1$ and $\bar{C}_2/\bar{Y}_2$ (which is in fact negligible), the above formula reduces to

(2d)
$$\frac{\frac{1}{2}(\Sigma c_2 y_1 + \Sigma c_1 y_2)}{\Sigma c_1 y_1} \cdot \frac{\bar{Y}_1}{\bar{Y}_2} .$$

Using the assumption of zero correlation between permanent and temporary components and between temporary components of y and c, and taking probability limits, we have

$$\text{plim} \frac{1}{N} (\Sigma c_2 y_1) = \text{plim} \frac{1}{N} (\Sigma c_1 y_2) = K \operatorname{cov} (Y_2', Y_1')$$

and

$$\text{plim} \frac{1}{N} (\Sigma c_1 y_1) = K \text{ var } (Y_1').$$

Hence, in the population, equation (2d) yields

(3d)
$$\frac{\text{cov} (Y_2', Y_1')}{\text{var} (Y_1')} \frac{EY_1'}{EY_2'} = \eta_{y_2' y_1'}.$$

Note that (3d) is *independent* of the value of K; i.e., our method is valid independently of the proportionality assumption (3).

REFERENCES

[1] DURBIN, J., Errors in Variables, *Rev. Int. Stat. Inst.*, **22** (1954), 23.

[2] EISNER, R., The Permanent Income Hypothesis: Comment, *Amer. Econ. Rev.*, **48** (1958), 972.

[3] FISHER, M. R., Exploration in Savings Behavior, *Bull. Oxford Univ. Inst. Stat.*, **19** (1956), 99.

[4] FRIEDMAN, M., *A Theory of the Consumption Function* (Gen. Ser. 63). New York: National Bureau of Economic Research (distr. Princeton Univ. Press), 1957.

[5] FRIEDMAN, M., and S. KUZNETS, *Income from Independent Professional Practice* (Gen. Ser. 45). New York: National Bureau of Economic Research (distr. Princeton Univ. Press), 1945.

[6] KLEIN, L. R., Pattern of Savings: The Surveys of 1953 and 1954, *Bull. Oxford Univ. Inst. Stat.*, **17** (1955), 173.

[7] LIVIATAN, N., Errors in Variables and Engel Curve Analysis, *Econometrica*, **29** (1961), 336.

[8] MADANSKY, A., The Fitting of Straight Lines when Both Variables are Subject to Error, *J. Amer. Stat. Assoc.*, **54** (1959), 173.

[9] SARGAN, J. D., The Estimation of Economic Relationships Using Instrumental Variables, *Econometrica*, **26** (1958), 393.

NOTE ON NISSAN LIVIATAN'S PAPER

MILTON FRIEDMAN, *University of Chicago*

This is an extremely ingenious, original, and penetrating paper, and I am full of admiration for it. At the same time I am not persuaded by Liviatan's substantive results. The purpose of this note is to point out briefly an alternative explanation for some of them.

Liviatan's Section 3

The first result that bothered me was one that Liviatan interprets as favorable to the permanent-income hypothesis, namely, the close agreement between the elasticities of consumption with respect to income computed (1) directly from contemporaneous data on consumption and income and (2) indirectly from the correlation between incomes in successive years (Table 4). Liviatan interprets this agreement both as supporting the permanent-income hypothesis and as implying that the horizon can be taken as equal to two years for these data, i.e., that transitory components of income in successive years can be treated as uncorrelated.

My uneasiness arose from what seems to me a wide range of evidence that the horizon is almost surely longer than two years. In *A Theory of the Consumption Function*, I concluded that three years was a plausible estimate. Other data I have looked at since have suggested that this is, if anything, an underestimate. The interpretation of the horizon discussed in my contribution to this volume (as the reciprocal of an interest rate) leads to the same conclusion.

The length assigned to the horizon is important not only for Section 3, but also for the estimates using income and consumption of one year as instrumental variables for a neighboring year. This technique will in fact eliminate bias only if the transitory components (of income or consumption, as the case may be) are uncorrelated in successive years.

But if the horizon for Liviatan's data is in fact longer than two years, how is it that the elasticity estimates in his Table 4 agree so closely?

One plausible explanation is based on an important difference between Liviatan's data and the budget data that I have analyzed in detail. Liviatan's data are from a savings survey and consist of independent estimates for individual consumer units of income and savings. His estimate of consumption is derived by subtracting savings from income. The bulk of the data I analyzed were from expenditure surveys, and consist of independent estimates of income and consumption. In most, there are also independent estimates of savings. However, as far as I recall, I made no use of the independent estimates of savings.

With savings survey data, observed consumption and income clearly have a common component aside from the effect of permanent income. Let there be a straightforward measurement error in income. Consumption, computed as income minus an independently estimated figure for savings, will contain the same measurement error. But as I have pointed out in my book, it is impossible in most applications to distinguish measurement error from a transitory component proper. As long as income and consumption are estimated independently, this fact does not give any reason for questioning the assumed zero correlation between transitory components of income and consumption; on the contrary, it gives an additional reason why the correlation embodied in the empirical data might be expected to be close to zero; even if there were nonzero correlation between transitory components proper, it would be diluted by the zero correlation between the measurement errors. However, when consumption is estimated as it is in

Liviatan's data, the common measurement error means that even if the correlation between transitory components proper were zero, the correlation embodied in the empirical data would be positive.

As a formal matter, the common measurement error can be introduced into Liviatan's analysis by setting his terms C'' and Y'' equal to $C''' + M$ and $Y''' + M$, respectively, where Y''' is the transitory component proper of income, M is the measurement error of income, and C''' is the transitory component proper of consumption plus the measurement error of savings. Once this is done, it is clear that Liviatan's equations (1) no longer hold, and hence that the PIH in the form of the basic model as he defines it does not hold for these data.

The effect of the common measurement error is to impart an upward bias to the estimates in column (1) of Liviatan's Table 4. These become, instead of estimates of P_y alone, estimates of $P_y + 1/m(P_e)$, where P_e is the fraction of the variance of measured income accounted for by the measurement error M. Adjustment of these estimates for this bias would therefore lower all of them and make them all lower than the estimates in column (2) based on incomes in successive years. But this is precisely what the relation should be if the horizon is longer than two years. Some rough calculations suggest that a value of P_e of 0.06 would lower the estimates in column (1) by enough so that they would bear roughly the same relation to those in column (2) as I found for the corresponding numbers computed from U.S. expenditure survey data. No significance should be attached to this particular estimate of 0.06 except as an indication of the order of magnitude of the effect required to eliminate the apparent discrepancy between these results and my earlier results.

It should be emphasized that the bias in question is not conjectural. The character of the data enforce it, hence the PIH as I formulated it, if applied rigorously to these data, does not imply the particular estimates Liviatan has used for savings surveys (and that I and others have also). The only question at issue is the magnitude of the bias. And it is clear from the calculations just cited that a bias sufficient to alter significantly the results can arise from measurement errors that are by no means implausibly large.

Liviatan's Section 4

The common measurement error in consumption and income affects also the formulas used by Liviatan in his Section 4. It turns out that if his equation (22) is revised to take account of the common measurement error, it yields an estimate of P_y that is necessarily higher than that given by the equation in its original form. Again, rough calculations suggest that a value of P_e of the order of 0.06 would be high enough to eliminate most of the discrepancies between columns (1) and (2) of Liviatan's

Table 7. Hence this section does not contain any evidence contradicting the PIH when it is correctly applied to Liviatan's data. The apprearance to the contrary arises solely from an invalid application of the PIH, which is to say, from the use of formulas that are a correct implication of the PIH for expenditure survey data as if they were also a correct implication for savings survey data, when in point of fact they are not.

Liviatan's Sections 6 and 7

Given that the horizon is longer than two years, income of one year is no longer an appropriate instrumental variable for a neighboring year. As Liviatan notes, the effect of a positive correlation between transitory components is to give a downward bias to the computed elasticities as estimates of the elasticities between the permanent components. In addition, the translation of some of the numerical results into estimates of elasticities is affected by the common error of measurement. Liviatan has made some calculations using a P_e of 0.06 and a correlation between transitory components in successive years of 0.25 (suggested by some of my U. S. results). The effect is to give estimated elasticities between permanent components notably higher than in Liviatan's Table 11 but also still appreciably less than unity.

The crudeness of the estimates of P_e and the correlation between transitory components lead me to regard these calculations as suggestive but hardly very strong evidence that the elasticity between the permanent components is less than unity.

Liviatan's Section 8

This is the one section that seems to me to offer evidence based solely on Liviatan's data that is relevant to judging whether the elasticity between the permanent components is less than unity. If the correlation between transitory components of consumption is positive, whether because this is true of the transitory components proper or because the measurement errors in saving are positively correlated or because the measurement errors in income are, then, as Liviatan demonstrates, the use of consumption in one year as an instrumental variable introduces an upward bias into the elasticity of consumption with respect to income as an estimate of the elasticity between the permanent components. Yet Liviatan's estimates are consistently less than unity.

As a theoretical matter, such a result is to be expected only if transitory components of consumption in successive years are negatively correlated. It is not impossible for the correlation to be negative, especially since the data measure consumption expenditures, not the value of services consumed. For example, unusually large expenditures this year could portend unusually low expenditures next year. Such an inverse connection seems particularly plausible for durable goods, as is confirmed by the fact that Liviatan obtains higher estimates for three out of four cases when he uses consumption excluding durables than when he uses consumption including durables. However, the increase is very small and even the higher estimates are less than 0.95. On the whole, a negative correlation between the transitory components of consumption does not strike me as a plausible explanation of Liviatan's results.

I conclude that if these results should be confirmed for other bodies of data, they would constitute relevant and significant evidence that the elasticity of permanent components is less than unity.

Final Comment

None of the questions raised in this comment detracts from the significance of Liviatan's theoretical contribution. It is most desirable that his analysis be applied to data not marred by common errors of measurement in income and consumption. It would further be highly desirable to have such data spanning at least a three-year period so that income and consumption for one year could be used as an instrumental variable for a year at least two years later or earlier.

A REPLY

NISSAN LIVIATAN

It seems that there are two difficulties connected with the data used in this study (as well as in many other studies). The first difficulty arises from the possible correlation between temporary components of different years. This problem has already been dealt with in various parts of the text, and its implications will be summarized below.

The second difficulty, which is the central point in Professor Friedman's note, is of a purely statistical character and has to do with ordinary measurement errors in savings-survey data. Clearly, no one can deny that there are statistical deficiencies in measuring annual income. Neither can anyone dispute the logic of Friedman's argument that in savings surveys these errors are transmitted automatically to the consumption figures. It is also obvious that Friedman presents a reasonable alternative explanation to some (but not all) of the results in my article, which is particularly relevant to the test in Section 4.

On this, then, there is no disagreement. Nevertheless, we should not overlook the basic fact that Friedman has not presented any independent evidence on the *importance* of these measurement errors. Thus, while the element of common errors undoubtedly exists, it may still be an unimportant factor in the interpretation of the results. It is true that even a "small" value of P_e (i.e., var (M)/var (Y) in Friedman's notation) of say 0.06, can explain the large values of $b_{\dot{c}y}$ in Section 4. It is possible however that $P_e = 0.06$ is not small for the problem in question. Thus, compared with var (Y'')/var (Y) (where Y'' is the temporary component proper), the assumed value of P_e is very large indeed.

Friedman's numerical calculations bring out very clearly the sensitivity of the test in Section 4 to common errors. This finding suggests, however, a more general inference, namely, that the test in Section 4 is very sensitive to a correlation between *any* type of error in C and Y. Suppose, for example, that there is a correlation between temporary components *proper* of (contemporaneous) income and consumption. Then a relatively small correlation of, say, $r^2_{c_i''y_i''} = 0.06$ can explain the large values of $b_{\dot{c}y}$ in Section 4, and has the same implication on our results as Friedman's explanation. Note, however, that the existence of $r^2_{c''y''} > 0$ contradicts the basic model of the PIH, while Friedman's explanation does not. This example is not meant to suggest that $r^2_{c''y''} > 0$ is a more plausible explanation than Friedman's. It only shows that there are various simple theories which can explain the large values of $b_{\dot{c}y}$ (including the explanation given in text) and that in order to establish his case Friedman needs to present more direct statistical evidence.

Assuming that the two above-mentioned problems are really important, what are their implications on further research on the lines suggested by the present article? Consider first the test in Section 4, which deals with m.p.c.'s of identical individuals. As I pointed out in the text, this test has the great merit of being independent of the first difficulty, i.e., of any possible correlation between temporary components in different years. However, as Friedman demonstrates, this test is very sensitive to common measurement errors. Therefore, it is highly desirable that this test should be performed on *expenditure* data, since the latter are free from the common error problem. Clearly, the comparison of the results of this test, performed on expenditure survey and savings survey data, provides indirect test of Friedman's alternative explanation.

As for the test in Section 6, which is based on using income of a neighboring year as an instrumental variable, we have to distinguish between the parts played by the two difficulties. The common error problem disturbs the *comparison* between $\eta_{c_i y_i}$ and $\eta^{y_j}_{c_i y_i}$, since the former is upward-biased as a result of the common error. The latter elasticity, however, is unlikely to be affected by common measurement errors, since it is based entirely on covariances of variables measured in *different* years. Hence the only possible difficulty with $\eta^{y_j}_{c_i y_i}$ is due to the first problem only. Therefore, as pointed out by Friedman and by myself, it is most desirable to use data spanning three years (or even more). It is only under these conditions that we should expect, according to the PIH, to find that $\eta_{c_i y_i}^{y_j}$ strictly equals unity. This test can be performed on savings survey data since it is independent of common errors. This holds *a fortiori* for expenditure survey data. It is a pity that this test, in its stringent form, can be applied only to a limited body of existing data, but these data may be sufficient to settle the issue.

For the more usual type of reinterview data, namely, that based on two *consecutive* years, the test in Section 6 can be applied profitably to *expenditure* survey data. In this case the comparison between $\eta_{c_i y_i}$ and $\eta_{c_i y_i}^{y_j}$ is unaffected by measuremnt errors, and therefore we should expect, according to the PIH, to find a considerable difference between the above elasticities. Whereas it is not possible to make a precise statement on the magnitude of the difference $(\eta_{c_i y_i}^{y_j} - \eta_{c_i y_i})$, which is to be expected on the basis of the PIH, it is reasonable to require that $\eta_{c_i y_i}^{y_j}$ should be at least halfway between $\eta_{c_i y_i}$ and unity. (Clearly, even a smaller value of $\eta_{c_i y_i}^{y_j}$ is sufficient for rejecting the traditional approach.)

Thus far we have dealt with using *income* of a neighbouring year as an instrumental variable. When we turn to the test in Section 8, which is based on using *consumption* (preferably not including durables) of a neighboring year as an instrumental variable, none of the above-mentioned difficulties arises. As pointed out in Section 8 and in Friedman's note, any reasonable assumption leads us to the conclusion that $\eta_{c_i y_i}^{c_j}$ is larger than or equal to the true elasticity, independently of the two difficulties. This test can therefore be applied to any reinterview savings survey based on two consecutive years.

Finally, I wish to point out a method of testing directly Friedman's theory of the importance of common errors in savings survey data, provided we have *independent* measurements on income, saving, and consumption of families in the cross section. Suppose that each of these measurements contains a random measurement error that is independent of the other errors. Then the fraction of the variance of measured income accounted for by the measurement error (P_e in Friedman's notation) can be estimated as follows. Compute each family's consumption as the difference between the independent estimates of income and savings. Denote this residual estimate by C_r and the *independent* estimate of C by C_n. Compute the regression coefficients of C_r and C_n on income Y. P_e is then simply the difference between these two coefficients; i.e., $P_e = B_{c_r y} - B_{c_n y}$. Note also that $B_{c_r y}$ is the m.p.c. computed according to the savings survey procedure, while $B_{c_n y}$ is the m.p.c. computed according to the expenditure survey procedure.

The difficulty with this method of computing P_e stems from the fact that there are only a few surveys in which all three independent measurements were taken simultaneously (as, for example, in the surveys mentioned in Friedman's note). It is also questionable whether the magnitude of P_e in these surveys is comparable with P_e in the more recent savings surveys, in which the technique of measurement is greatly improved.

It is, however, interesting to note that in principle our method can be applied not only to the case of simultaneous measurements of all three variables, but also to the case in which the m.p.c.'s are computed from *different* savings and expenditure surveys. In practice, however, this method will be rather unreliable (quite apart from the relatively large sampling errors), since it requires that the savings and expenditures surveys be drawn from the same population, a requirement that is rarely satisfied. Just as a matter of curiosity, I looked up Table 1 in Friedman's book (1957), where there is a list of $b_{c_r y}$'s and $b_{c_n y}$'s, and I found no systematic difference between them. Although this fact is suggestive, I do not consider it as important evidence because of the reservation noted earlier.

I hope that this exchange of ideas has pointed out not only the shortcomings of the existing data, but also the direction toward improving future research on the theory of the consumption function.

3

Market Prices, Opportunity Costs, and Income Effects

JACOB MINCER, *Columbia University and the National Bureau of Economic Research*

The purpose of this paper is to point out a class of specification biases that affect the estimation of parameters of economic relations; such biases are a result of neglecting certain easily overlooked or misunderstood price variables. The error is most likely to occur in cross-section estimation, since one of the generally appreciated advantages in using cross sections is that no attention need be paid to price variables. Except for the obvious cases of geographic diversity and price discrimination, it is reasonable to assume that market prices do not vary systematically in cross sections.[1] However, for a number of products and services, market prices alone do not provide sufficient information on the theoretically relevant opportunity costs. Moreover, such costs are specific to individuals and are likely to be linked to their incomes. Price variables, in this general sense, are not fixed in cross sections, and cannot be left out of the analysis without creating misinterpretations of income effects.

The notion of opportunity costs is not usually considered in the framework of consumption or demand analysis. But just as productive processes involve some elements of consumption (utility) to participating human factors, many consumption activities involve some specific costs to consumers over and above the money price paid to the seller of the consumption goods. The specific costs involve contributions by the consumer of complementary economic resources such as labor, time, and other goods. For the proper specification of a demand function, prices must somehow be imputed to these items. And, of course, the budget constraint must be correspondingly redefined.[2] It is the opportunity cost of time which is most likely to be overlooked in the specification of relevant prices in demand

I am indebted to Gary S. Becker for very illuminating discussions of issues raised in this paper. Helpful comments were also received from Victor Zarnowitz, Carl S. Shoup, Donald Dewey, and Dave O'Neill.

[1] The existence of price dispersion in a local area is often a matter of quality differences. Price dispersion for *identical* goods reflecting imperfect information is discussed on pp. 79-81.

[2] Income at a zero rate of leisure is the relevant constraint in the demand for leisure.

functions. Since the opportunity cost of time is linked, at the margin, to the wage rate, this price element is positively related to income.

The properly defined price with which the consumer is faced is not p, the market selling price, but $P = p + c$, where c is the opportunity cost of time. The relative size of components p and c differs by commodities and by individuals. In the usual case, c is considered to be negligible, though the assumption may be questioned. At the other extreme, as in the case of leisure, $p = 0$, and $P = c$.

Generally, the demand function for a particular commodity should be written

$$(1) \qquad Y_i = \alpha + \beta X_i + \gamma_1(p_1 + c_{1i}) + \gamma_2(p_2 + c_{2i}) + \cdots + u_i,$$

where Y_i is consumption of that commodity by consumer i, X_i is income of consumer i, p_1 is the market price of the good and c_{1i} its opportunity cost to consumer i, p_2 is the market price of a related good and c_{2i} its opportunity cost to consumer i. It is clear that even if the p's are fixed in cross sections, the c's are not, and if the c's are a function of the wage rate W, the omission of the c's will bias the coefficient β, the estimate of β. Since c_1 is related negatively to Y and positively to X, its omission will bias β downward. The omission of c_2, if good 2 is a complement for good 1, will bias β in the same direction. This omission will result in an upward bias if good 2 is a substitute.

The same problem exists in time-series estimation, with aggregate (average) c's replacing the individual c in the linear case, and with the distribution of c (hence of wage rates) entering the price variables in the nonlinear case. But the more important the opportunity cost c in the total price P, the greater the multicollinearity with income. This is recognized, in the extreme case, in the usual treatment of the demand for leisure, where the income (wage) coefficient is interpreted as the sum $(\beta + \gamma_1)$, defining leisure in time units equal to the length of the period over which the wage is received. Even in that case it is not clear that the neglect of related goods is unimportant. In the general time-series case, the omission of c biases both income and price coefficients.

The relevance of these considerations is illustrated in sections 1 through 5 by examples of economic relations in which the important price variables appear mainly or partly in the form of opportunity costs. Aspects of transportation, labor supply, domestic servants, family size, and market information are discussed from this point of view.

1. Transportation Costs

A basic dimension of quality changes in transportation is increased speed. This is considered an improvement precisely because time is not a free good. Such quality changes can be translated into price changes, provided an opportunity cost (c) of time is imputed: Increasing speed by a factor of m leads to a less-than-proportionate decline in price of a given trip from $P_1 = p + c$ to $P_2 = p + (1/m)\,c$.

Some interesting implications for passenger transportation can be derived under the simplifying assumptions that the trip serves purely the purpose of moving a person from location A to location B, and affords no other utility or disutility. Under these conditions, and on the assumption of constant marginal opportunity costs, c can be expressed as a multiple of the wage, $c = aW$.

If ticket prices do not change relative to the price level, increases in real wages make the real or total price of the trip ($P = p + aW$) more costly to the passenger. If real wages increase by a factor of k and speed of transportation by a factor of m, and if $k > m$, increases in total prices are underestimated when measured by p only and overestimated when $k < m$. Estimates of price elasticities based on time series are too large in absolute value in the former case, too small in the latter.

Cross-sectional surveys of demand for air travel indicate very high income elasticities. These are likely to be overestimates, because the assumption that relative prices are fixed misses a price effect which works in favor of air travel as the individual's earning power increases.[3] Consider the price of air travel relative to travel by rail: for a given trip, the ticket price ratio p_a/p_r is, of course, fixed in the cross section. But the relevant price ratio is not p_a/p_r, but $R = (p_a + c)/(p_r + mc)$, where c is the opportunity cost of time in air travel, and m is the time of rail travel expressed as a multiple of air travel time. It is easily seen[4] that $\partial R/\partial c < 0$, provided that $p_r < mp_a$, a condition that is empirically satisfied. This means that with given ticket prices, the relevant cost of air travel declines relative to the cost of rail travel as c, the opportunity cost (and hence the wage rate of the passenger), increases. Thus the neglect of opportunity costs biases the income parameter upward. Incidentally, larger distances are usually associated with larger m, so relative prices also move in favor of air travel as the distance of the trip increases: $\partial R/\partial m < 0$. And because $\partial^2 R/\partial c\,\partial m < 0$, it follows that the income bias becomes stronger as the distance increases.[5] By the same token, of course, the true income effect on railway travel is

---

[3] We assume that the wage does not continue to be paid during travel. If it is a business trip, the opportunity cost becomes a business expense to the firm. The same considerations and results hold.

[4] $\dfrac{\partial R}{\partial c} = \dfrac{(p_r + mc) - (p_a + c) \cdot m}{(p_r + mc)^2} = \dfrac{p_r - m \cdot p_a}{(p_r + mc)^2} < 0$, when $p_r < mp_a$.

[5] $\dfrac{\partial R}{\partial m} = \dfrac{-c(p_a + c)}{(p_r + mc)^2} < 0$ and

$\dfrac{\partial^2 R}{\partial m\,\partial c} = \dfrac{(p_r + mc)^2\,(-p_a - 2c) - 2c(p_a + c)\,(p_r + mc)\,m}{(p_r + mc)^4} < 0.$

underestimated when prices are neglected in cross sections. The interesting implication for time series is that, even if relative market (ticket) prices of air and rail travel remained fixed and technological changes did not affect relative speeds of transportation media, an increase in society's wage level would produce a shift from rail to air travel, provided the absolute money prices of tickets did not rise as fast as money wages.

2. The Supply of Labor

Ever since Robbins's illuminating discussion of labor–leisure choices [6] this aspect of labor supply has been analyzed in terms of demand for leisure time considered as a consumption good. In the demand for leisure function, the income variable is properly redefined to mean "potential" income at a zero rate of leisure, and the price variable is generally understood to be the opportunity cost of leisure time, that is, the foregone wage rate. Prices of related goods that might play a part in the analysis are usually neglected in this context.

Even though the demand function for leisure is multidimensional in principle, the supply of labor function derived from it has been studied in a two-dimensional fashion, as a simple relation between wage rates and hours of work. This Procrustean approach results from: (a) the restriction of the demand function to two variables, income (X_1) and price of leisure (X_2), and (b) viewing X_1 as a fixed multiple of X_2. The latter assumption means that sources of income other than labor income of the individual are neglected, or kept in fixed proportion to it. The empirically estimated coefficient of the single variable, the wage rate or income defined as a multiple of it, represents the sum of the "pure" (partial) income and price parameters. The "backward-bending" supply curve of labor is an empirical statement about the negative sign of that sum: the negative effect of income on hours of work exceeding the positive effect of price–opportunity cost of the foregone wage rate.

The approach to the supply of labor by way of the theory of consumer demand is perfectly general, but the empirically motivated collapse of the multidimensional demand function into a single-variable supply curve of labor is of limited merit. If variables other than income and price are neglected, this approach serves at best as a first approximation in estimating the structure underlying secular trends in the length of the workweek. This assumes that such changes reflect mainly the behavior of adult males, the bulk of the labor force. But it is a blunt and misleading approach when applied to cross sections, or to population subgroups other than adult males. A cross-sectional regression of hours of work on wages or income yields neither a pure price effect, nor an income effect, nor a sum of the two. Prices (opportunity costs of leisure) are not fixed either in cross sections or in relation to total family income as distinguished from labor income of the individual whose decisions are studied. Separate coefficients of the several relevant variables must be estimated to avoid gross misinterpretations.

Thus inverse cross-sectional relations between wages of adult males and labor-force participation rates of females, whether by areas or by income brackets of husbands, cannot be interpreted as empirical representations of the "backward-bending" supply curve of labor. Such interpretations create spurious puzzles and paradoxes. Perhaps the most striking example is the continuing secular increase in labor-force rates of females, particularly of married women, depite the growth of real income.

The confusion arises because a derivative construct, the backward-bending supply curve—which may be valid when labor–leisure choices are truly dichotomous—has been misapplied. This does not detract from the generality of the approach suggested by Robbins. The primary analytical tool is the theory of choice. It must be the starting point of any supply-of-labor analysis.

The study of labor force participation of married women indeed provides a good illustration.[6] It shows how an improper understanding of the nature of the price variable—inherent in the inapplicable backward-bending supply curve—leads to a variety of estimation biases.

Starting from the choice problem, it is immediately obvious that labor choices are not simply between an increment of leisure and an increment of money income currently obtainable in the market. The third alternative is a non-market productive activity that is not leisure. In the case of married women it is mainly production of goods and services in the home. Thus both the demand for leisure and demand for services in the home must be considered.

Secondly, the relevant income concept in demand both for leisure and for home goods is total family income. A change in family income, whatever its origin, results in a changed consumption of most goods, including leisure. Where opportunity costs are unimportant, the distribution of consumption among family members depends on tastes. However, the distribution of leisure, market work, and home work among family members is determined not only by tastes, but by relative prices that are specific to individual members of the family. Opportunity costs (that is, earning powers in the market and marginal productivities in alternative pursuits) differ among individual family members.

The opportunity cost of the time spent outside the labor market is the market wage rate of the individual, but the income variable is family income. In cross section both sets of relative prices—of income (wage goods) vs. leisure, and of wage goods vs. home goods—are reflected in the market wage

---

[6] The discussion and findings in this section are based on the author's "Labor Force Participation of Married Women" [5].

rate of the woman, on the assumption that her productivity at home is uncorrelated with her productivity in the market. The price and income variables defined as the market wage of the woman and family income do not bear fixed proportions to one another. Nor can the two be assumed to be uncorrelated. Thus a complete specification is necessary. Furthermore, the interpretation of the price (wage-rate) parameter is different from that in the usual supply-of-hours analysis, which is at best applicable to adult males: In the latter case the price (wage-rate) parameter reflects substitution mainly between leisure time and wage goods. In the case of married women, the main substitution is between services of the homemaker and wage goods. Only if the two substitution effects here compared were equal in size, would a backward-bending shape be imparted to the supply curve of female market labor, when compressed to a two-dimensional form. But there is no reason to expect this. The evidence on substitution between home services and wage goods is much more pervasive than on substitution between leisure time and wage goods. Household appliances, domestic servants, and TV dinners are obvious exhibits. And, indeed, the empirically estimated price parameter [γ in equation (2)] is much larger than the implicit price parameter in the adult male labor supply function (see footnote 6).

The simplest specification of a labor-market supply function for married women is

$$(2) \qquad\qquad m = \beta_p y_p + \gamma w + u .$$

where m is the quantity of labor supplied to the market, y_p is a long-run level of family income, computed at a zero rate of leisure and of home production, w is the wife's full-time market wage rate, and u reflects other factors or "tastes." All variables are written as deviations from their means. Writing $y_p = x_p + w$ (where x_p stands for the long-run level of family income, not including earnings of the wife),

$$(3) \qquad\qquad m = \beta_p(x_p + w) + \gamma w + u = \beta_p x_p + \alpha w + u .$$

Since $\alpha = \beta_p + \gamma$, the supply function can be estimated by means of (3), given the availability of data on incomes of husbands, a rough empirical representation of x.

The theoretical expectation is that $\beta_p < 0$ and $\gamma > 0$. These expectations were fulfilled in the empirical analyses. More interestingly, the α coefficient was positive, indicating that the price effect—the attractive power of the wage rate in drawing women into the labor market—outweighs the inhibiting effect of income. The α coefficient was positive also in a logarithmic regression of the same variable. This implies that if in a set of observations the female wage rate changed at the same rate as total family income, the two-dimensional relation between wage rates and participation in the labor market would not be backward-bending, but forward-sloping. But this is precisely what happened over time: participation rose as wages rose.

If the income and price variables varied in the same direction and at the same rate in cross section, one would similarly expect a positively sloping two-dimensional supply relation whether wage rates or income were used as the independent variable. This is not the case, because (a) the covaration between wives' earning power and husbands' current income is relatively weak in the usual family surveys and (b) "transitory components" in current income accentuate the negative relation. (It was found that the negative impact of transitory income on labor supply is stronger than that of long-run income.) The size of the covariation between the wives' and husbands' earning power and the importance of transitory components in income vary in different bodies of data, giving rise to a variety of apparently different relations between labor force rates and the classifying variables. These relations are puzzling only when the specification biases are misconstrued as genuine structural parameters.

Specifically, let husbands' current income x consist of two components: x_p (long-run or normal income) and x_t (transitory income or the difference between current and normal income). The supply function of female labor (3) is expanded, for purposes of cross-sectional analysis, to

$$(4) \qquad m = \beta_p x_p + \beta_t x_t + \alpha w + u .$$

Multiplying by x and summing both sides of (4) over all observations, then dividing by Σx^2 and assuming that x_t is independent of x_p and of u, we get

$$(5) \qquad b_{mx} = \beta_p \cdot P + \beta_t (1 - P) + \alpha b_{wx} ,$$

where P is the ratio of the variance of permanent income to that of current income, b_{mx} is the least-squares regression of m on X, and b_{wx} the least-squares regression of w on x, in large samples. Elasticities replace slopes and relative variances when (4) is specified in logarithms.

In terms of elasticities, the point estimate for β_p was roughly -0.5, -1.6 for β_t, $+1.5$ for α, and $+0.4$ for b_{wx} (see footnote 6). With P of a magnitude 0.8 to 0.9, this leads to a negative b_{mx}, as usually observed in family surveys. The negative sign of b_{mx} cannot be construed as evidence for the backward-bending supply curve, or as an estimate of $(\beta_p + \alpha)$. This sum is clearly positive. And indeed, in long-run time series, (5) becomes $b_{mx} = \beta_p + \alpha$, since $P = 1$ and $b_{wx} = 1$ (female wage rates grew at least as fast as wages of males). When income is related to labor-force rates by averages of areas, as it was by Douglas [3] and Long [4], P approximates 1, eliminating the second term in (5). Depending on the size of b_{wx} for the selected set of areas, b_{mx} may be positive or negative. It was negative prior to 1950, and positive in 1950, simply because of a small change in b_{wx}.

By the same procedure as in (5), and using an additional assumption that x_t is independent of w, the slope of the gross regression of m on w in family surveys becomes $b_{mw} = \beta_p b_{xw} + \alpha$. Since $b_{xw} < 1$, this is clearly positive. Both b_{mx} and b_{mw} are resultants of several specification biases. That b_{mx} normally shows a negative sign in cross sections is no more than an accident. The interpretation of such observed negative relations between income, by family unit or area, and labor force rate of married women as *the* supply curve of female labor is due to a misunderstanding of the opportunity cost variable resulting from an improper attribution of generality to the "backward-bending" supply curve.

3. The Demand for Domestic Servants

A related example in which the neglect of opportunity costs leads to estimation biases is the cross-sectional study of demand for domestic service. A regression of quantity of domestic service on family income does not yield a proper estimate of the income effect. This is true even if the wage rate of the servant (standardized for quality) is held constant. The reason is simple: The wage rate of the servant is not the only price variable in the demand function. The market wage rate of the (female) employer is also important.

Consider family members (particularly the housewife) and domestic servants as substitutable factors of production in the home. Changes in relative prices of these factors will affect their relative employments in the home. The wage rate of the domestic servant must be viewed in relation to the price of employing the wife at home, which is the opportunity cost of foregone earnings in the market. The higher the market wage rate of the wife, other things equal, the greater the employment of domestic servants. A cross-sectional demand function must contain both price variables, in addition to family income. Of the price variables, the wage rate of the servant can be considered fixed in local markets, abstracting from quality differentials. The opportunity cost variable, however, varies even within local markets. Its omission biases the income coefficient upward to an extent that depends on the covariation of the female wage rate with family income and on the size of the parameter of the omitted variable.

Empirical observations relating consumption of domestic service to income of the household indicate relatively high income elasticities. Employment of servants per family increased by 2 per cent when family income rose 1 per cent, according to the 1935–6 Consumer Purchases Study [2]. The magnitude was similar when based on averages by states in 1939, even when standardized for the wage rate of domestic servants [1, pp. 32, 44].

Data contained in the 1950 BLS Survey of Consumer Expenditures suggest an even higher gross income elasticity, about $+3$. Evidence that the elasticity is overestimated is provided by several sets of data: Indirect evidence is contained in the findings that among families with the same income, those in which the wife works hire more servants. This was shown in the 1935–6 Consumer Purchases Study [2, pp. 57-58]. The decisions to work outside the home and to employ a domestic both positively depend on the wage rate of the employer, hence they are positively related to each other in the data.

More direct evidence was obtained in area regressions relating the employment of domestic servants per family (X_0) to husband's income (X_1), the full-time annual female wage (X_2), and the full-time annual income of domestic servants (X_3). The two regressions shown below are for state urban areas and standard metropolitan areas, respectively, in the North in 1950.

(i)
$$X_0 = 0.11X_1 + 0.25X_2 - 0.33X_3 \qquad R^2 = 0.31 ,$$
$$\quad\; (.05) \qquad (.14) \qquad (.24)$$

(ii)
$$X_0 = 0.09X_1 + 0.28X_2 - 0.21X_3 \qquad R^2 = 0.18 .$$

Numbers in parentheses are standard errors of regression coefficients.

Defining long-run family income as $X_f = X_1 + X_2$ and expressing the regressions in terms of X_f ,

(i')
$$X_0 = 0.11X_f + 0.14X_2 - 0.33X_3 ,$$

(ii')
$$X_0 = 0.09X_f + 0.15X_2 - 0.21X_3 .$$

Clearly, when family income is held constant, an increase in the female wage rate results in an increased utilization of domestic service. Omission of the opportunity cost variable biases the income variable by more than 50 per cent.

The upward bias depends partly on the relation between family income and wives' earnings. The higher apparent income elasticity of demand for domestic servants in 1950 than in 1935–36 budget data is probably attributable to the greater influence of working wives' earnings on family incomes in the more recent period.

4. Income and Family Size

The Malthusian emphasis on the effect of income on family size stimulated empirical studies of the relation between income and fertility. Such studies usually contradict Malthus' prediction of a positive effect of income on family size, at least in the economically developed parts of the world. Family size declined historically in countries where per capita incomes increased, and at a given time more children are found in families with low economic status than in wealthy families. United States census data for 1910, 1940, and 1950 show a negative relation between fertility and father's occupation, mother's education, or monthly rental. Inverse relations with current family income have been observed in a variety of data, particularly in the Current Population Survey of the U.S. Census, and in the Indianapolis Study [9].

One interpretation of the cross-sectional findings of differential fertility is that it largely reflects differential prevalence of family planning among population groups differing in socio-economic status. The higher status groups presumably have more knowledge of birth control techniques. Alternatively, the negative relation between fertility and income is interpreted as reflecting the variation of tastes with income in a way that, in the language of demand theory, makes the number of children an "inferior good." According to recent empirical studies, however, it would seem that the relation between income and fertility tends to be positive, when variables that are assumed to represent the level of contraceptive knowledge are held constant.[7] This result is consistent with demand theory, in which the typical income effect is positive. Now, if the economic aspects of decisions about family size can be conceptually organized along the lines of demand analysis, then another major variable whose effect should be taken into account before the pure income effect can be estimated is the price variable, or the cost of children [1, pp. 210-15].

Data on costs of children ideally require an index of prices of the various categories of expenditures. The major reason for omission of the cost factor in empirical population studies is the enormous difficulty in compiling such data. The cost variable receives no attention in cross-section data, except in the obvious rural–urban comparisons, presumably because prices are fixed in cross sections. There is one relevant cost element, however, that varies in cross sections—the opportunity cost of child care. This is the only cost element with respect to which families differ in cross sections. Again, this cost can be measured by the foregone wage obtainable by the mother in the labor market.

The simplest specification of a demand function is

$$(6) \qquad X_0 = \beta_1 X_1 + \beta_2 X_2 + \beta_3 X_3 + u \,,$$

where X_0 is the fertility variable, X_1 is the husband's income, X_2 is the wife's full-time earnings, and X_3 is a variable representing level of contraceptive knowledge.

This can be rewritten as

$$(7) \qquad X_0 = \beta_1 X_f + \alpha X_2 + \beta_3 X_3 + u \,,$$

where $X_f = X_1 + X_2$, or potential family income, and $\alpha = \beta_2 - \beta_1$.

---

[7] Gary S. Becker, "An Economic Analysis of Fertility" [1]. See also the literature quoted therein.

Economic theory predicts that $\beta_1 > 0$ and $\alpha < 0$. It does not predict the sign of β_2, which is a price effect not compensated for by an equivalent change in income. An increase in X_2 of \$1000 is a \$1000 increase in opportunity cost, which tends to curtail planned family size, but it is also a \$1000 increase in family income, which tends to increase the demand for children. The sign of β_2 depends, therefore, on whether the positive income effect or the negative substitution effect dominates.

A few preliminary results of an empirical investigation designed to explore these relations will be reported here.

A sample of about 400 families was selected from the 1950 BLS Survey of Consumer Expenditures. The criteria for selection specified that they be urban white husband–wife families whose heads were fully employed during the year and that the wife be between 35 and 45 years of age and employed in the labor market some time during the year. Numbers of children (X_0) were related to husband's full-time income $(X_1$, in thousands of dollars) to wife's full-time earnings $(X_2$, in thousands of dollars), and to years of husband's schooling (X_3):

(8)
$$X_0 = 0.10X_1 - 0.09X_2 - 0.02X_3 .$$
$$(.04) \qquad (.05) \qquad (.02)$$

Numbers in parenthesis are standard errors of regression coefficients. In terms of family income,

(9)
$$X_0 = 0.10X_f - 0.19X_2 - 0.02X_3 .$$

The expectation of a positive income coefficient and of a negative price (opportunity cost) coefficient is fulfilled. And indeed, the cost parameter is stronger than the income parameter. The negative relation with the differential knowledge proxy-variable X_3 is also discernible, but not statistically significant.

Similar analyses were carried out with area averages as observations. The three regression equations presented below refer to: (a) 25 large cities in the North in 1950, (b) urban and rural nonfarm areas in 32 Northern States in 1950, and (c) 29 large cities in the North in 1940. The analyses are restricted to the North because of the differentials in structural parameters between white and Negro populations, a topic not considered here. In all regressions except the third, X_0 is the number of children per 1000 married women, age 35–44. In the third regression, X_0 is the completed family size reported by ever-married women, age 45–49; X_1 is median full-time income of males, X_2 is median full-time income of females, X_3 is the percentage of population over 25 years of age with completed high school education, and X_4 is the labor-force rate of wives of the given age groups, husband present.

(a)
$$X_0 = 0.12X_1 - 0.17X_2 + 0.06X_3 - 0.02X_4 \qquad R^2 = 0.49 .$$

Neither X_3 nor X_4 was statistically significant. When they were dropped,

$$X_0 = 0.10X_1 - 0.14X_2 \qquad R^2 = 0.44 ,$$

(b) $\qquad X_0 = 0.05X_1 - 0.11X_2 + 0.06X_3 - 0.04X_4 \qquad R^2 = 0.41 .$

Again X_3 and X_4 were not statistically significant:

(c) $\qquad\qquad X_0 = 0.07X_1 - 0.13X_2 - 0.02X_4 \qquad R^2 = 0.35 .$

Converting X_1 into family income X_f, as defined before, and restricting the equations to two variables,

(a') $\qquad\qquad\qquad X_0 = 0.12X_f - 0.29X_2 ,$

(b') $\qquad\qquad\qquad X_0 = 0.05X_f - 0.16X_2 ,$

(c') $\qquad\qquad\qquad X_0 = 0.07X_f - 0.20X_2 .$

Several implications of these results are worth noting: Given that the regression of X_2 on X_1 and on X_f is positive, it is clear that the omission of X_2 in the gross comparison of fertility rates with income level will reduce the income coefficient. The reduction, or downward bias, will be greater when the comparison is with current family income than when it is with husband's income:[8] This trend occurs because current family income is more strongly related to the female wage rate than is husband's income. And indeed, the usual demographic findings confirm these inferences. Thus current population surveys indicate little or no differences in fertility of urban women by income of husband, and a negative relation with current family income, as well as with monthly rent. It is this reversed direction of effect that has been traditionally interpreted as the true income effect.

Another finding that has been emphasized recently is that fertility is negatively related to labor-force participation of women. The argument runs both ways: The greater responsibility of child care prevents women with more children from entering or re-entering the labor force. Conversely, women who are in the labor force deliberately restrict the size of their families. The economic analyses of fertility and of labor-force participation here presented suggest that the choices of labor and family size are not causally related to one another. Rather, these choices are simultaneously determined by the same basic economic variables. The higher the female wage rate and the lower the husbands' earning power, the higher the labor-force rate and the smaller the fertility rate. The relation between

---

[8] In the BLS sample the gross regression coefficient of family size on husbands' income was $+ 0.05$, on family income -0.03. These were families with husbands fully employed. In the general population surveys, current incomes are much more heavily weighted with "transitory" components, resulting in an augmented downward bias in the income coefficients.

fertility rate and labor-force participation is not autonomous; it does not provide new insight once the two structural relations are specified. And indeed, as the empirical findings indicate, a labor-force variable (X_4) introduced in addition to the income and price variables is redundant; it adds little or nothing to the explanation.

5. Information, Prices, and Income

This section is devoted to some additional illustrations of potential biases in the estimation of income effects arising from the neglect of opportunity costs. We shall now drop the assumption of perfect markets (markets where identical goods are sold at exactly the same price by different sellers). The existence of some price dispersion would not create any estimation problems if buying prices were not correlated with buyers' incomes. The economic theory of information, however, implies that a systematic relation exists.

Price dispersion in product markets, and dispersion in rates of return as well as in borrowing and lending rates in capital markets are market imperfections due to imperfect information and to restrictions of various sorts. Advantages in the form of lower prices for a given product and higher rates of return on investment are available to consumers and investors with greater knowledge of prices and rates. This knowledge is either accumulated through past experience or currently obtainable at a cost. If we think of the acquisition of information about prices or rates in terms of actual physical "shopping" or "search,"[9] the following equilibrium process can be envisaged: The larger the buyer's expenditures on the commodity, the larger the marginal revenue, or savings from an additional unit of search (measured in time units). The marginal cost is the opportunity cost of the time spent on an additional unit of search. At the margin, this may be equaled to the wage rate. As Stigler has shown [8] the marginal revenue curve that relates the gains from search to the amount of search is downward-sloping. Hence an equilibrium amount of search can be determined, as in Fig. 1.

Figure 1 illustrates the behavior of two consumers. The wage rate of consumer 2 is twice as high as the wage rate of consumer 1: With zero investment in information and no differences in the stock of information already embedded in the individuals, assume that the richer one normally buys twice as many units of the (identical) commodity in question as does the poorer one. The reduction in price per unit from an additional unit of search is the same (statistically speaking, i.e., on the average) for both consumers, but the total gain (in dollar terms) is twice as large for the richer individual. Thus, for each point on the horizontal axis, $MR_2 = 2MR_1$.

---

[9] The analysis and terminology follow Stigler [8].

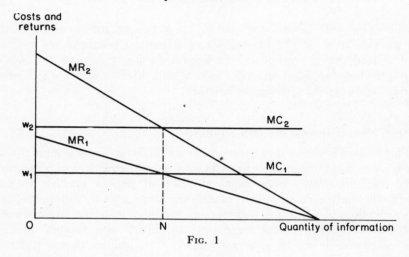

Fig. 1

In this case the equilibrium amount of search ON is the same for both consumers. Hence they will pay, on the average, the same prices for identical goods.

Suppose now that individual 2 consumes more than twice the amount consumed by individual 1. Then MR_2 shifts upward, and the equilibrium investment will be larger for individual 2 than for individual 1. The converse is true if the richer individual normally consumes less than twice as much as the other.

The three cases just discussed correspond to classes of commodities with income elasticities equal to, greater than, and less than unity. The conclusion is that the same prices are paid by rich and poor for items with unitary elasticity, lower prices are paid by the rich for "luxury" goods, and by the poor for "necessities." The result is an obvious bias in cross-section estimates of income effects: In the case of luxury goods, the omitted price variable moves in favor of purchases as incomes go up, so that the income coefficients are overestimated. In the case of necessities, the income coefficients are underestimated.

Pushing the analysis a step further, the assumption that the marginal cost of acquiring information rises *pari passu* with the buyer's wage rate must be relaxed. Clearly, there is an opportunity for arbitrage and specialized middlemen, and the information industry comes into being. The consumer will buy information services, rather than conduct the search himself, so long as the price per unit of additional information is less than the opportunity cost of acquiring it and less than the marginal revenue resulting from it.

Assuming the polar case of a perfect market in the supply of information, consumers of varying incomes are now confronted with identical prices for units of a given information service. In the diagram above, the relevant marginal cost curve is now the price, common to all buyers. For example, let this price line be identical with MC_1. If $P = MC_1$ and $MC_1 < W_1$, both individuals will buy information, but the higher the income, the greater will be the investment in (expenditure on) information. If $W_1 < P < W_2$, the rich consumers will buy information, the poor ones will sacrifice leisure. In both cases the money expenditures on information and the amount of information acquired will increase with consumer income. Buying prices of all goods and services except information will be lower for richer consumers, both for luxuries and for necessities, so long as the income elasticity is positive. Cross-sectional income elasticities of all superior goods are biased upward, and as before, the higher the "true" income elasticity, the stronger the bias.

To put it another way, the difference in money income of the two consumers in our diagram underestimates the difference in real income (in the sense of purchasing power). Hence "true" income elasticities are overestimated.

It is interesting to note that the analysis predicts a positive income effect on purchases of information. It also predicts a positive relation between income elasticities of demand for various goods and services, and for information media specializing in them.[10] These phenomena, once more, are essentially relative price effects masquerading as income effects, when they are viewed as consumption expenditures.

6. Concluding Remarks

The substantively diverse economic relations discussed here have the common feature of involving price variables that are not coextensive with market prices but include a non-market opportunity-cost component.

The emphasis in this paper has been on the estimation problems created by the usual omission of the invisible price component in empirical analyses. Generally, the omission of opportunity costs results in over- or underestimation of parameters of economic variables. In time-series analyses both income and price coefficients are biased. The bias in the income parameter is particularly likely and important in cross sections in which price variables are altogether neglected. In some cases the reduction or increase in parameter due to the specification bias is sufficient to impart an opposite sign to the parameter, a situation leading to both quantitatively and qualitatively faulty interpretations. Thus lack of recognition of the

---

[10] This is analogous to, and indeed reflects, the law of derived demand for a factor in production theory. A striking empirical illustration is the high income elasticity of demand ($+3.0$ to $+8.0$, depending on the income range) for *Consumer Reports*, a publication of the Consumers Union of the U.S., a product-testing and -rating organization. Thus information theory predicts the selectivity toward high income (and related education) levels of Consumers Union subscribers.

proper price variables is in part responsible for the traditional interpretations of relations between wages and labor-force participation, and between income and family size.

In a more general sense the point to be emphasized is that the final price to the consumer is not the selling price, say at retail as distinguished from wholesale or from manufacturer's price. There is also a "value added" by the consumer at the final stage of consumption. This "value added," the component c, creates differences in effective prices of the "same commodity" among different consumers. It also creates differences between prices as quoted by sellers and as viewed by buyers, yet the latter determine the demand curves facing the industry and the firm. The interesting problem of resulting *market* adjustments is outside the scope of this paper.

References

[1] BECKER, GARY S., An Economic Analysis of Fertility, in *Demographic and Economic Change in Developed Countries* (Special Conference Series 11). New York: National Bureau of Economic Research (distr. Princeton Univ. Press), 1960.

[2] Department of Agriculture, *1935-6 Consumer Purchases Study* (*Miscellaneous Bulletins*, No. 432). Washington, D.C., Supt. of Documents.

[3] DOUGLAS, PAUL H., *The Theory of Wages*. New York: Macmillan, 1934.

[4] LONG, CLARENCE D., *The Labor Force Under Changing Income and Employment* (Gen. Ser. 65). New York: National Bureau of Economic Research (distr. Princeton Univ. Press), 1958.

[5] MINCER, JACOB, Labor Force Participation of Married Women, in *Aspects of Labor Economics* (Spec. Conf. Ser. 14). New York: National Bureau of Economic Research (distr. Princeton Univ. Press), 1963.

[6] ROBBINS, LIONEL, On the Elasticity of Demand for Income in Terms of Effort, *Economica*, 10 (June 1930), 123-29.

[7] STIGLER, GEORGE J., *Domestic Servants in the United States, 1900-1940* (Occasional Paper 24). New York: National Bureau of Economic Research, 1946.

[8] STIGLER, GEORGE J., The Economics of Information, *J. Polit. Econ.*, 69 (June 1961), 213-25.

[9] WHELPTON, P. K., and C. V. KISER, eds., *Social and Psychological Factors Affecting Fertility*. Milbank Memorial Fund, 1951.

4

Demand Curves and Consumer's Surplus

DON PATINKIN, *The Eliezer Kaplan School of Economics and Social Sciences, The Hebrew University of Jerusalem, and the Falk Project for Economic Research in Israel*

The assumptions underlying the construction of a demand curve—and their implications for the problem of measuring consumer's surplus—have been much discussed in recent years. Similarly, there has been a renewed interest in the nature of Marshall's demand curve. The present paper adds little in a technical way to these discussions; nevertheless, it is hoped that the graphical device of Section 1 will clarify the nature of the interrelationships among the various demand curves that have been employed in the literature. Similarly, it is hoped that the approach to consumer's surplus in Section 2 will place it in a somewhat broader context than heretofore, as well as bring out its common-sense meaning. Particular attention will also be devoted to an analysis of consumer's surplus within a general-equilibrium framework. These two sections will then serve as the basis for an interpretation of the Marshallian demand curve, offering a simple solution to the prolonged debate that has taken place on this question in recent years.

1. Three Types of Demand Curves

1.1. Consider an individual who comes to market with an initial endowment of the (composite) good Y and exchanges part of it for the

This paper was completed while I held a Ford Foundation Visiting Research Professorship at the University of California, Berkeley. I have benefited greatly, on questions of exposition as well as substance, from the searching and patient criticism of E. J. Mishan. There are, however, still some points on which we remain in disagreement. I am also indebted to William J. Baumol, Nissan Liviatan, and Jerome Rothenberg for their helpful comments.

The subject of this paper is one that was close to the heart of Yehuda Grunfeld. In keeping with his Chicago training, he was continuously concerned with the assumptions that underlie the demand curve, and I remember many absorbing hours spent with him discussing this subject. One of Grunfeld's planned projects was a critical examination of the literature on empirical demand functions, the purpose being to bring out the implicit definitions of "real income" used in these studies, and to show that the failure to understand the economic significance of these definitions had frequently led to an incorrect interpretation (in terms of substitution and income effects) of the estimated parameters.

This paper was written after Grunfeld's death. But I did discuss with him the material of Section 1, and particularly the interrelationships of Fig. 2. As always, his comments were quick, to the point, and provocative.

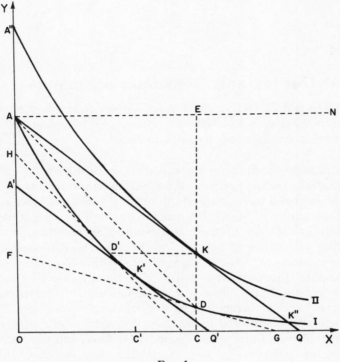

FIG. 1

(composite) good X. Let A in Fig. 1 represent the individual's initial position. Assume now that we confront the individual with a price of X represented by the slope of the budget line AQ and ask him to tell us the respective amounts he will buy of X under the following three alternative conditions:

(a) The individual is to buy the maximum amount of X that he can buy without making himself worse off than he was in his initial position A. This will bring him to point K'' on the original indifference curve, I. For reasons that will become apparent below, let us denote the demand curve generated by varying the price in this sort of experiment an "all-or-none demand curve." It is represented by MP in Fig. 2. The assumed convexity and negative slope of the indifference curve imply that the slope of this demand curve must always be negative.[1]

(b) The individual is to buy the amount of X that will maximize his

---

[1] If the indifference curve through A should intersect the X-axis, then this curve is not defined for prices corresponding to budget lines which intersect this axis rightward of this point of intersection.

I am indebted to Eytan Sheshinsky for this observation.

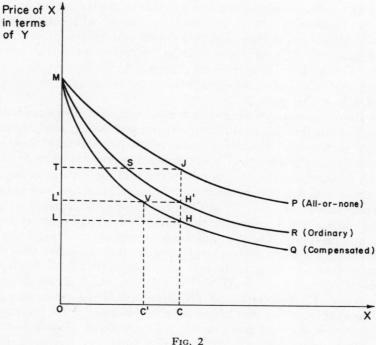

FIG. 2

utility. This will bring him to point K on the higher indifference curve II. Clearly, K cannot lie rightward of K'' on AQ, for under no circumstances will anyone freely choose to carry out a market transaction that will make him worse off. Indeed, we can see from the graph that K must actually lie leftward of K''. This is the obverse side of the fact that the individual in experiment (a) is forced to go beyond his optimum. The demand curve generated in this way will be called an "ordinary demand curve" and is represented in Fig. 2 by MR. As just explained, it must lie leftward of the all-or-none curve.

(c) As in (b), the individual chooses the utility-maximizing amount of X; but in contrast to (b), compensating variations are made in his initial endowment of Y ("income") to keep him on indifference curve I. In the case at hand, this means that we deduct AA' units of Y from his initial endowment so that the individual chooses the optimum point K' on the budget line, $A'Q'$ (parallel to AQ in Fig. 1). If X is a normal good (i.e., income elasticity greater than zero), K' must lie leftward of K. Hence the "compensated demand curve," MQ, in Fig. 2 must lie leftward of MR. The convexity of the indifference curve once again implies that MQ must be negatively sloped—whether X is normal or inferior. This is simply an expression of the familiar fact that under the convexity assumption the Hicksian substitution effect—which is what our experiment actually isolates—is always negative. (Note that in the present case we cannot generate MQ by compensating variations in prices instead of income. For as long as income is unchanged, the budget line must go through the initial point A, and hence can be tangent to indifference curve I only at that point.)

The above experiments derive the demand curves in Walrasian fashion by confronting the individual with a given price and asking him to specify the quantity demanded. A more precise relationship among these curves can be derived by conducting the experiments in the alternative Marshallian way: by asking the individual to tell us the maximum he is willing to pay for X under different circumstances, on the assumption that he is consuming a given quantity of it (say, OC). Thus the all-or-none demand curve (and this, of course, is the reason for the name) is derived by determining the maximum per-unit price the individual is willing to pay for OC of X rather than go entirely without it. In Fig. 1, the maximum *total* amount the individual is willing to forego for this quantity is ED. Hence the maximum *per-unit* price is $ED/OC = ED/AE$, which is the slope of the radius vector AD with respect to AN. From this viewpoint we also see that the convexity and negative slope of the indifference curve imply that the all-or-none demand curve is not only negatively sloped, but also of greater-than-unity elasticity. Note too that since the decision here is *not* a marginal one, the individual is at a point on his indifference curve where the marginal rate of substitution is *not* equal to the price.

In contrast, the ordinary demand curve is derived by asking the individual to tell us the maximum price he is willing to pay for X at the margin— when he is consuming OC units of it, and when he obtains all units at the price he designates. This is Marshall's "marginal demand price."[2] The fact that in this case the individual is making a marginal decision means that he must be at a point on an indifference curve whose marginal rate of substitution equals the price he designates; and the fact that all units are

---

[2] "Suppose, for instance, that tea of a certain quality is to be had at 2s. per lb. . . . he buys perhaps 10 lbs. in the year; that is to say, the difference between the satisfaction which he gets from buying 9 lbs. and 10 lbs. is enough for him to be willing to pay 2s. for it: while the fact that he does not buy an eleventh pound, shows that he does not think that it would be worth an extra 2s. to him. That is, 2s. a pound measures the utility to him of the tea which lies at the margin or terminus or end of his purchases; it measures the marginal utility to him. If the price which he is just willing to pay for any pound be called his *demand price*, then 2s. is his *marginal demand price*" [17, 8th ed., pp. 94-95; italics in original].

I believe the conceptual experiment described here is also the one Marshall had in mind in Note II of his "Mathematical Appendix" [17, 8th ed., pp. 838-39]. Correspondingly, the phrase "price which he is just willing to pay for an amount x" that appears there should be understood as "total amount" that he is just willing to spend—when he can buy all units at the "marginal demand price" of the amount x.

purchased at the same price means that he must be on a straight budget line originating in point A in Fig. 1. Hence the "marginal demand price" must equal the slope of that budget line originating in A and tangent to an indifference curve at the given quantity of X. On the assumption that the demand curve is single-valued, any other budget line originating in A will intersect an indifference curve at this quantity; hence its slope will represent a price different from the one the individual "is just willing to pay." In Fig. 1 the marginal demand price for OC of X is thus equal to the slope of AQ with respect to AN, which is necessarily less than that of AD.

Finally, the compensated demand curve is derived in the same way as the ordinary one—with the difference that compensating changes are made in income to keep the individual on indifference curve I. For OC of X, this compensating reduction in income is AF. The corresponding maximum price is given by the slope of FG with respect to AN—represented by OL in Fig. 2. Alternatively, we can conceive the compensated demand curve as representing the maximum price the individual will pay for an additional unit of X—on the assumption that we have exacted from him the respective maximum prices that he is willing to pay for each preceding unit. For this too is measured by the marginal rate of substitution of indifference curve I at the quantity of X in question.

From this last description it is clear that the compensated demand curve is related to the all-or-none as the marginal is to the average [12, pp. 84-88]. This can be seen most simply by turning Fig. 1 upside down and comparing the slopes of FG and AD with respect to AN. Hence we can make use of the familiar relationship between average and marginal to state that the fact that MP in Fig. 2 is always declining (see above) implies that MQ must lie below it.

At first there seems to be something paradoxical about the fact that the all-or-none and compensated experiments—both of which keep the individual on the same indifference curve I—should nevertheless yield different demand curves. But as has just been seen, this simply reflects the difference between the curves that are, respectively, average and marginal to the same indifference curve. A less technical way of resolving the paradox is to note that in the case of curve MQ the individual surrenders Y both in payment for X and in payment of compensation; in the case of the curve MP, however, he surrenders Y only in payment for X. Since for any given quantity of X the total amount of Y surrendered must be the same in both cases (in order to remain on the same indifference curve), this implies that the per-unit market price in the all-or-none case must be higher.

Indeed, this line of reasoning brings us to the familiar fact that we can measure in Fig. 2 the size of the compensating variation AF in Fig. 1. For the total amount of Y surrendered in the all-or-none case is represented in Fig. 2 by the area $OCJT$. In the compensated case, however, only area $OCHL$ is surrendered via the market place. This means that an amount of

Y equal to area $LHJT$ ($= OCJT - OCHL$) must have been surrendered via the compensating mechanism. Alternatively, by the marginal-average relationship existing between curves MQ and MP, area $OCJT =$ area $OCHM$; hence the compensating variation is represented by the area of the triangle-like figure LHM ($= OCHM - OCHL$).

Consider now the special and much discussed case in which the good X has zero-income elasticity throughout. This implies that parallel shifts in the budget line in Fig. 1 will generate points of tangency corresponding to the same quantity of X. In other words, the indifference curves must be parallel for every value of X. This in turn implies that, for example, points K' and D must coincide. Hence the ordinary demand curve MR in Fig. 2 must coincide with the compensated curve MQ. The fact that in this way the same demand curve describes the individual's behavior both when his utility is constant and when it is changing (as he moves along the curve) should not disturb us, for the essence of the zero-income-elasticity assumption is precisely that changes in the level of utility ("real income") do not affect the demand for X.

1.2. Before leaving this discussion, three further—and unrelated—points might be noted. First, only the second of the six experiments described above can be conducted solely on the basis of observation of the individual's behavior.[3] Hence only this experiment, with its resulting demand curve, is properly part of "positive economics." All the others—and particularly all of the Marshallian ones—are not, for they can be conducted only if the individual provides us with true information about the positions or slopes of his (to us) unobservable indifference curves. An individual intent on bluffing (designating prices really below his maximum) could not be detected.

Second, the negative slope of the all-or-none curve has some simple implications for the case of the perfectly discriminating monopolist. Consider in particular the familiar problem of a monopolist whose costs are too high to permit him to operate if all units must be sold at the same price. This implies that the total costs of producing the first unit are greater than the demand price for that unit. Hence the negative slope of the all-or-none curve implies that even perfect discrimination will not enable the monopolist to operate unless he enjoys decreasing average costs over a certain region. This is clearly a necessary and not sufficient condition, for in order to reach a profit situation, the monopolist's average costs must fall more sharply than the all-or-none price over the relevant region.

---

[3] There is, however, a variant of the third experiment that also comes within this category; in this variant, the compensation is of the Slutzky type (that is, enabling the individual to buy his initial basket). As Mosak has shown, for infinitesimal changes the Hicks and Slutzky substitution effects are equal. But this equality obviously does not hold for finite changes [21, pp. 69-74].

Third, if we conceive the foregoing demand curves as being aggregated over all individuals, then the compensated demand curve would represent a "constant real income" curve in the sense of describing movements along a given (community) indifference curve. It would *not* represent a constant "real income" curve in the sense of describing the demand that would prevail under the assumption of constant productive capacity and techniques.[4] Hence even an exogenous change that shifts the economy to another point on the same production-possibility curve will generally involve a shift in the compensated "constant-real-income" demand curve no less than in the ordinary one.

On the grounds of invariance under such a change, then, there is little to choose between the compensated and ordinary demand curves as analytical tools. But even if this were not so, I can see little point to a *methodenstreit* on this question.[5] We need exactly the same amount of information to carry out an analysis with one type of curve as with another. And if account is taken of all the interrelationships, the results obtained by using the alternative demand curves must be the same. In technical terms, the way in which we choose to take two-dimensional cross sections of a demand function dependent on relative prices and "real income" can obviously not affect the outcome of the general-equilibrium analysis of a problem.[6] Thus it would seem to me that the only valid—if not very edifying—methodological prescription that can be given here is that we should adopt a general-equilibrium approach to our problems that will take account of these interrelationships. There would, nevertheless, be a point to insisting on the advantages of using the compensated demand curve if it were to be shown that the failure to use this curve has tended to lead to a neglect of these interrelationships and to consequent error. This is a meaningful hypothesis that can be tested empirically by adducing relevant evidence from the literature, but no such valid evidence has as yet been adduced.[7]

---

[4] The way in which such a "constant-productive-capacity" demand curve can be derived is neatly shown by Bailey [2].

[5] The recrudescence of this *methodenstreit* is, of course, due to Friedman [7]. Friedman's methodological criticism of the ordinary demand curve has been restated in an even more extreme way by Buchanan [5]. See footnote 7.

For a detailed discussion of the issues involved, see Yeager [27].

[6] It is worth noting that Friedman himself shows just this in the example he considers [7, pp. 59-62].

[7] It is noteworthy that Friedman concedes that the type of error he is interested in averting by use of the compensated demand curve had already been corrected by other economists, who did not make use of such a construct [8, pp. 101-2, fn. 3]. See also his reply to Bailey [2].

Ironically enough, Buchanan's treatment of the hypothesis just mentioned actually reduces it to a tautology. For he attempts to prove that failure to use the compensated demand curve has led to error by dividing his examples from the literature into two categories: those in which this failure has been accompanied by error, and those in which this failure has not so been accompanied, but in which (it is asserted) error is absent despite the failure to use the

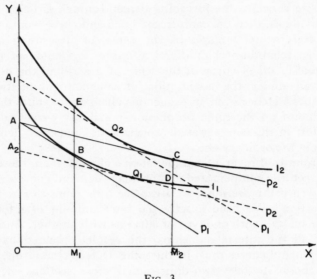

FIG. 3

2. The Common Sense of Consumer's Surplus[8]

2.1. A given individual with a given "money" income achieves different levels of welfare under different trade situations; this is the essence of consumer's surplus. It follows that the magnitude of this surplus is a function of the situations being compared. If utility were a cardinal quantity, we would be able to measure this surplus in terms of "utils." But if utility is only ordinal, we must resort to other—and necessarily arbitrary—measures.

The ordinary way in which we measure a difference in welfare is by means of a quantity index. In its "true" form this measures the magnitude of a shift from one level of utility to another by the ratio of the respective minimum money costs of acquiring these levels under competitive conditions [23, pp. 160-61; 16, pp. 507-8]. Clearly, this ratio depends on the prices used to compute these costs. Consider then the individual in Fig. 3 whose income is OA and who is initially permitted to trade in a competitive market at price p_1, so that he is at B on indifference curve I_1. Let the individual now be permitted to trade at the lower price p_2, so that he moves to point C on the higher indifference curve I_2. If we measure this

---

compensated-demand curve, and not because of it! [5, pp. 262-69]. Thus Buchanan's procedure makes it impossible ever to refute the hypothesis he wishes to test.

It might also be noted that Buchanan's emphasis on the desirability of points on demand curves being potentially observable [5, p. 264] is much more fruitfully discussed as part of the general problem of identification, so familiar from the econometric literature.

[8] For a critical survey of the "new" development of this subject by Hicks, Henderson, Little, and others, see [20, pp. 238-45]; fig. 3 is reproduced from p. 240 of this article.

On the arbitrariness of the measure of consumer's surplus, see [23, pp. 195-202].

increase in welfare by a quantity index using the original prices (i.e., evaluating the respective indifference curves at the price p_1), we obtain OA_1/OA. On the other hand, if we use the final prices, we obtain OA/OA_2. In principle, however, there is no reason to restrict ourselves to these two alternatives, and we can measure the shift from I_1 to I_2 in terms of a true quantity index using any set of prices that we choose.

In actual practice, of course, the indifference map is unknown, and so resort is had instead to the Laspeyre and Paasche approximations. Unfortunately, however, these approximations fail us in just that case which plays such a crucial role in the theory of consumer's surplus: the one depicted in Fig. 1, in which the two situations being compared are those of no-trade (point A) and competitive trade at a given price (point K), respectively. For the impossibility of trading at A is represented by an infinite price for X, which renders the Laspeyre quantity index meaningless, while the fact that A and K are by assumption on the same budget line implies that the Paasche index must always be unity. This indicates, as it must, an increase in welfare, but it obviously fails to reflect the elementary fact that the lower the price at which trade is opened up, the greater this increase.

Whether or not for this reason, the traditional discussion of consumer's surplus has never been in terms of the relative movement measured by index numbers but in absolute, money terms. This obviously does not diminish—and might even be said to increase—the arbitrariness already noted in connection with measures of changes in utility. Thus, corresponding to the true quantity index OA_1/OA in Fig. 3, there is the measure of consumer's surplus AA_1. This is Hicks' "equivalent variation." Again, corresponding to the index OA/OA_2, there is the measure AA_2. This is Hicks' "compensating variation." In a similar way we could define a "variation" to correspond to any one of the infinite number of true quantity indexes that can be constructed to measure the shift from indifference curve I_1 to I_2.

However, as Henderson emphasized in his classic article [10], for any specific question only one of these measures of consumer's surplus will usually be relevant. Thus, if in Fig. 3 we want to know the maximum amount of money ("tax") our individual with income OA and price p_1 will pay for the privilege of being able to buy at the lower price p_2, then it is only the compensating variation AA_2 that is relevant. On the other hand, if in Fig. 1 we want to know the minimum amount of money we must pay our individual with income OA and price ratio AQ for withdrawing entirely the privilege of buying X (that is, raising its price to infinity), then it is only the equivalent variation AA'' that is relevant. Note that though the compensating variation cannot exceed the individual's income, there is no such limit on the equivalent variation, for though the individual's income necessarily sets an upper limit on what he can *pay*, it obviously cannot limit what he can *receive* [12, pp. 105-6].

Thus far we have restricted the two trade situations being compared to competitive ones (from the viewpoint of the buyer) that differ only in their given prices. There is, however, no reason why we should not broaden our scope to make comparisons involving other types of situations. As we shall now see, once this is done, there will no longer be a one-to-one correspondence between measures of consumer's surplus and true quantity indexes. This is what should be expected, for as already indicated—and as the straight budget lines used in their computation show—these indexes themselves are based on the assumption of perfect competition. Indeed, we might reverse the direction of our argument and contend that index-number theory should be generalized so as to provide measures relevant for noncompetitive situations too.

In any event, let us now assume, for example, that our individual with income OA in Fig. 1 is initially subject to a perfectly discriminating monopolist who has exacted from him the maximum price he is willing to pay for each successive unit, and has brought him to point D on indifference curve I. (Alternatively, we can assume that the individual has been brought to this point by an all-or-none monopolist who has forced him to take OC units of X.) Then the line segment AH measures the maximum amount of money our individual would pay to convert this situation into a competitive one with a price equal to the *average* one now being paid to the discriminating monopolist. On the other hand, our individual would be willing to pay AF to obtain a competitive price equal to the *marginal* one now being paid. Since the marginal is less than the average, AF must clearly exceed AH. Note too that the individual buying competitively at the erstwhile marginal price FG will—after paying AF—continue to consume OC units of X. Obviously, AF and AH also represent the compensating variation for a movement from the no-trade situation represented by point A to competitive trade at the prices represented, respectively, by the slopes of AD and FG. This simply reflects the fact that, from the viewpoint of welfare, no-trade and trade under a perfectly discriminating monopolist are equivalent.

Let us now consider the opposite case, in which our individual is initially buying OC units of X in a competitive market and is at K. The minimum amount that we must pay him to convert this into a situation in which he must buy this same quantity from a perfectly discriminating monopolist (or on an all-or-none basis) is KD. This would seem to be closest to Marshall's own notion of consumer's surplus as "the excess of the price [i.e., total expenditure] which he would be willing to pay rather than go without the thing, over that which he actually does pay."[9] Note that this

---

[9] See [17, 8th ed., p. 124]. The first to identify KD with Marshall's surplus was, of course, Hicks [11, pp. 38-41].

See, however, Appendix Note A for evidence that Marshall also thought in terms of the surplus as measured by the equivalent variation, AA''.

surplus, too, cannot exceed income; for even though, as interpreted here, it is an amount *received* by the individual, its magnitude is determined by a hypothetical experiment in which he would be *paying* it.

All of these are relevant measures of consumer's surplus under the circumstances defined. Indeed, in principle it would seem possible to define a set of circumstances that would enable us to interpret as consumer's surplus any of the infinite ways there are of measuring the "distance" between two indifference curves. The common element of all these surpluses would be that they measure the welfare difference between two trade situations in terms of the amount of money an individual would pay—or insist on receiving—in order to move from one to another. The differing element would be a reflection of the fact that this amount of money obviously varies in accordance with the situations being compared. In brief, the "distance" between two indifference curves depends on the nature of the path followed.[10]

2.2. It is recognized, of course, that the foregoing surpluses can be presented alternatively in terms of the demand curves of Fig. 2. For simplicity, we shall—in the case of compensating and equilibrating variations—restrict our attention to the total surplus, i.e., to that measuring the welfare difference between no-trade and competitive trade at a given price. In the case of the Marshallian surplus, however, no such restriction is actually needed; for according to the foregoing interpretation, this necessarily refers to the surplus on the total amount of X purchased by the individual.

Let us start with the compensating variation AA' in Fig. 1. Let the

---

Actually, the interpretation of Marshall's surplus just presented differs from the usual one in ways that cannot be fully discussed here. Suffice it to say that the usual interpretation does not clearly represent the Marshallian surplus as the outcome of a comparison of perfect monopoly and competition. Instead, it essentially compares two competitive price situations (from the consumer's viewpoint), in one of which the consumer is prevented from attaining his optimum position [20, pp. 240-41]. In this way it defines the Marshallian surplus as CD in Fig. 3, and describes BE as its counterpart. Correspondingly, it does not present the surpluses AH and AF in a Marshallian context.

We might also note that in his original article Henderson does initially describe the Marshallian surplus as "the maximum increase in returns which the seller could obtain through negotiating all-or-none bargains with each consumer" [10, pp. 119-20]. But he unfortunately concludes his article with the diagram reproduced here as Fig. 3—and with the statement that the Marshallian surplus is measured by CD and EB. It is this last version that became accepted in the literature.

[10] This multiplicity of measures is emphasized here because of Mishan's contention that "in all plausible circumstances" only the compensating and equilibrating variations are "tenable" [20, p. 241; 18, pp. 27, 30-32].

Mishan's contention is correct if we restrict our attention to perfectly competitive equilibrium situations; but (as is evident from the foregoing discussion) it ceases to be correct as soon as we broaden the scope of our analysis to other types of situations.

price represented by the slope of AQ (or $A'Q'$) in Fig. 1 equal OL' in Fig. 2. Then it is clear from Section 1.1 (pp. 87-88) that AA' can be represented by the triangular area $L'VM$ defined by the price OL' and the compensated demand curve MQ. For, to repeat the argument, the maximum the individual would be willing to pay for the quantity OC' in the all-or-none experiment is given by the area $OC'VM$ under this curve. The amount he actually does pay in the compensated experiment (i.e., "after tax") is $OC'VL'$. Hence, since he remains on the same indifference curve, he must have been taxed a compensating payment of $OC'VM - OC'VL' = L'VM$ units of Y.

In a similar way it can be shown that the equivalent variation AA'' equals the triangular area defined by the price OL' and a compensated demand curve constructed so as to keep the individual at the utility level represented by indifference curve II in Fig. 1. Clearly, if X is a normal good, this demand curve must be rightward of MQ in Fig. 2. (See [18] and the references to Hicks cited therein.)

In general, however, no such simple representation exists for the Marshallian surplus, KD, in Fig. 1, for this equals the difference between the areas defined by *two* different demand curves: the first, to tell us the maximum he would pay for the given quantity of X under all-or-none conditions; the second, what he actually does pay under competitive ones. In particular, the surplus equals (Fig. 2) area $OCJT$ defined by curve MP *less* the necessary smaller area $OCH'L'$ defined by curve MR. Alternatively, it equals $OCHM - OCH'L'$. Thus it can be represented either by $L'H'JT$ or by $L'VM - VH'H$.[11] From this it is clear that both the triangular area under MQ (namely, $LHM = OCHM - OCHL$) and the triangular area under MR (namely, $L'H'M = OCH'M - OCH'L'$) are overestimates of Marshall's measure, the former because its subtrahend $OCHL$ is too small, the latter because its minuend $OCH'M$ is too large. Only in the special case where the demand for X is of zero income elasticity—so that MR and MQ coincide—will the triangular area under the ordinary demand curve provide a correct measure of Marshall's consumer's surplus. For only under this assumption will the total area under this demand curve tell us the maximum the individual is willing to pay. As Hicks has shown [11, pp. 38-40], this is indeed the assumption Marshall made.

Finally, let us consider the other Marshallian surpluses defined above: AF and AH. Since these can be interpreted alternatively as compensating

---

[11] Thus, in the case of a normal good, the Marshallian surplus is less than the compensating one. This could also be deduced directly from Fig. 1 by noting that if both X and Y are normal goods, AA' must be greater than KD.

Note, however, that this inequality is reversed in the case of an inferior good. From this it is clear that there is no basis for the contention—frequently found in the literature—that the foregoing inequality necessarily results from the inherent nature of the Marshallian and compensating surpluses.

variations (see p. 92) their relationship to the compensated demand curve is obvious. Note that in the zero-income-elasticity case, $AA' = AA'' = KD = AF$, so that all these measures of consumer's surplus are represented by the same triangular area.

2.3. Other aspects of these interrelationships have been sufficiently discussed elsewhere,[12] so that we can go on to some more general points.

First, consider the criticism levied against Marshall that since in the light of his budget restraint an individual cannot plan to spend more than he actually does on all his commodities simultaneously, consumer's surplus in the aggregate must be identically zero.[13] It is clear from the preceding discussion that this contention is based on a misunderstanding of the nature of consumer's surplus. True, Marshall's definition of this surplus (as the difference between the maximum the individual is willing to pay for a commodity and what he actually pays) does lend itself to such misunderstanding. But it is clear from other passages of the *Principles* that Marshall did conceive of consumer's surplus as measuring the welfare difference between two trade situations, and hence as remaining meaningful even when the totality of the consumer's purchases is considered.[14]

Second, let us see how the magnitude of consumer's surplus is affected by changes in price or quantity. Continuing to restrict our attention to total consumer's surplus, we note that the necessarily negative slope of the compensated demand curve (or, equivalently, the convexity of the indifference curves) implies that the lower the price at which competitive trade is initiated, the greater both the compensating and equivalent variations. This is self-evident, for the lower the price at which the individual can convert his initial endowment of Y into X, the greater the advantages of trade as compared with no-trade.

From this we can also see that (as long as the ordinary demand curve is negatively sloped) the greater the volume of the competitive trade that is opened up, the greater the compensating and equivalent variations. On the other hand, if X is an inferior good, this relationship obviously need not hold. For if the inferiority is sufficiently marked, a greater quantity will be associated with a higher demand price.

In contrast, the Marshallian surpluses AH and AF will be increasing functions of quantity even in the case of a highly inferior good. For—as the negatively sloped all-or-none curve and compensated curve of Fig. 1 show— the greater the quantity of X purchased in the initial monopolistic situation, the lower its average and marginal price, respectively, hence the greater the advantage of converting these prices into uniform competitive ones.

---

[12] See the references cited in footnote 8. See also [4; 10; 12, chaps. 10 and 18].

[13] See [25, p. 575] and the reference to Allyn Young cited therein. See also [3, pp. 432-33] and the description there of the debate between Marshall and J. S. Nicholson.

[14] See Appendix Note A.

On the other hand, the Marshallian surplus KD will not always increase with quantity consumed, even in the case of a normal good. This is the simple counterpart of the fact that KD also measures the potential profit of a perfectly discriminating monopolist, and monopoly profits are generally not a monotonically increasing function of quantity sold. That is, there is generally some finite quantity at which these profits are at a maximum.

In technical terms, the Marshallian surplus equals $OCJT - OCH'L'$ in Fig. 2. Now, the all-or-none curve in this diagram is necessarily of greater-than-unitary elasticity (p. 86); hence, as the quantity of X increases, the area of the rectangle corresponding to $OCJT$ must also increase. If, now, the ordinary demand curve is of less-than-unitary elasticity, then the area of the rectangle corresponding to $OCH'L'$ will at the same time decrease, so that the surplus will increase. If, however, the ordinary demand curve is elastic, this rectangle will increase. Hence, over ranges in which the elasticity is sufficiently pronounced, the Marshallian surplus will decrease with increases in X.

This indeterminacy can also be seen in terms of Fig. 1, where the Marshallian surplus is measured as $ED - EK$. As the quantity of X increases, ED must also increase; but the direction of the change in EK depends on the elasticity of demand. In graphical terms, the vertical distance between indifference curve I and the relevant initial indifference curve can either increase or decrease with X. Note that this remains true even if X is always a normal good, for normality expresses itself as a narrowing vertical distance between any two *given* indifference curves as X increases. In the Marshallian case, however, the intial indifference curve to be compared with curve I will change as X itself changes.[15]

The third point that emerges from the preceding analysis is the fundamental one that consumer's surplus is a function also of the individual's initial position. (For simplicity, the following discussion is restricted to the compensating and equivalent variations; the extension to the Marshallian surplus is immediate.) Thus, for example, if the individual were initially at K in Fig. 1, both the compensating and equivalent variations would be zero at the price AQ. This absence of surplus would also manifest itself in demand-curve diagrams, for these would show a zero demand at the price AQ; hence all of the relevant triangular and rectangular areas would also be zero. Note that we are here making use of "demand" in the sense of amount purchased, and not in Wicksteed's sense of including also "reservation demand." This is as it should be, for what is measured by the compensating and equivalent variations is the increased welfare

---

[15] Even though this is also true of the equivalent variation, no such indeterminacy characterizes that case. The reason for this difference is that no matter what the value of X in the initial situation, the equivalent variation is measured on the Y-axis—i.e., for the same (zero) value of X. Hence a higher level of utility must correspond to a higher level of Y. This is obviously not the case for the Marshallian measure just discussed.

generated by the possibility of carrying out transactions in a competitive market.

Clearly, if the individual does start from the initial position K (or any other point representing a greater-than-zero quantity of X) he will—for sufficiently high prices—be a supplier of X instead of a demander. Once again, we can construct a triplet of curves corresponding *mutatis mutandis* to the all-or-none, compensated, and ordinary experiments described in the preceding section [4]. The relationship between these curves is depicted in Fig. 4, where the negative quantities of X represent amounts supplied and OQ represents the individual's initial endowment of X. Thus the curves in this figure are of the excess-demand variety. The all-or-none curve in the negative region represents the *minimum* per unit price at which the individual will supply X rather than make no sale at all; alternatively, it represents the maximum amount of X he can supply at a given price without worsening his initial position. Just as on the demand side of Fig. 4, the compensated curve on the supply side is marginal to the all-or-none curve and (in the case of a normal good) lies below the ordinary one. This latter relationship reflects the fact that whether the individual uses the market to buy or sell X, he achieves thereby a higher level of real income (i.e., higher

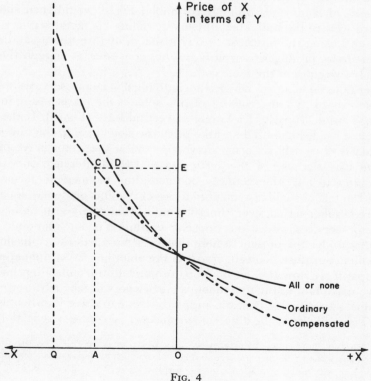

FIG. 4

indifference curve) and hence consumes a larger amount of X. Hence only at the point-of-no-trade P can the compensated and ordinary curves coincide.

As before, the various areas subtended by the supply curves can be used to provide different measures of consumer's surplus [4]. Thus area $BFEC = PCE$ is the compensating variation: the maximum amount the individual is willing to pay in his initial position for the privilege of selling X at the uniform price OE. On the other hand, the Marshallian seller's surplus has no simple representation, and the area subtended by the ordinary curve no welfare connotation, except for the case in which a zero-income elasticity for X causes the ordinary and compensated curves to coincide throughout. Note, however, that in this case the corresponding curves for Y cannot coincide, for the income effect then expresses itself exclusively in an increased demand for this commodity.

Since the initial position plays such a crucial role in the analysis of consumer's surplus, it is worth dwelling a little longer on its nature. In a modern economy individuals generally come to the market with initial quantities of factor endowments, and not commodities. Hence it is more realistic to consider Y in Fig. 1 as representing the individual's own-use of these endownments: leisure, in the case of labor; enjoyment of nature, in the case of land; and so on. Accordingly, Fig. 1 would then show the increased welfare the individual obtains by selling his factor services in the market and using the proceeds to buy goods. Thus we might say that the diagram shows producer's surplus, and not consumer's—though these are obviously two sides of the same coin.[16]

In the special case in which the individual's factor services have no own-use—that is, no alternative to being sold on the market—the indifference map would consist of a family of vertical lines (Fig. 5). If the initial quantity of the factor is OA and the price the slope of AB, the individual's optimum is obviously at corner B, where none of the factor is retained for his own. use. Because of the verticality of the indifference curves, it is meaningless to talk of exacting a compensating payment in terms of Y. But we can talk of such a payment in terms of X. This obviously equals OB. In more familiar terms, everything the individual receives in exchange for his factor services under our present assumptions is "economic rent." Note that under the present assumptions OB measures the equivalent and Marshallian surpluses as well. For it is the amount of X we must pay the individual if we now (i.e., at point B) prohibit him from selling his labor, or if we make him sell it to a monopsonist (who will take advantage of the individual's completely inelastic supply of labor to drive its price down to zero). This equality of the different surpluses is, of course, a reflection of the

---

[16] A fact duly emphasized by Marshall: " . . . when we have reckoned the producer's surplus at the value of the general purchasing power which he derives from his labour. . . , we have reckoned implicitly his consumer's surplus too. . ." [17, 8th ed., p. 831]. On this and the following paragraph, see Mishan [19].

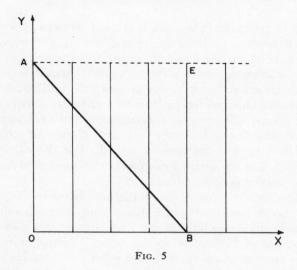

FIG. 5

absence of an income effect on the demand for Y, for this demand is zero no matter what the level of X.

Returning to the case of ordinary indifference curves, we now note that the foregoing discussion exaggerates the extent of the surplus generated by permitting the individual to sell his labor on a competitive market. For if we let Y in Fig. 6 once again represent the individual's leisure, and let AF represent his own production curve (that is, the amounts of X he himself can produce by foregoing leisure and working instead), then a Crusoe with no access to a market would not stay at point A, but would

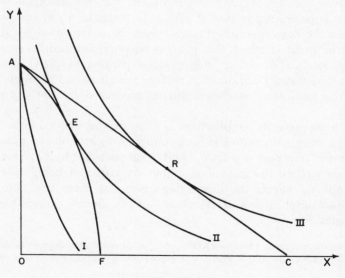

FIG. 6

move instead to point E. Thus the increased welfare generated by the opening up of market facilities is represented by the movement from indifference curve II to III, and not by the movement from I to III. In other words, the advantages of trading on a market should be compared not with a no-trade situation, but with one in which the individual "trades with nature" by means of his isolated productive activity. In a modern economy, however, the greater efficiency of specialization and exchange is so overwhelming that the distance between A and E can be assumed to be negligible relative to that between A and R. For the same reason the individual in Fig. 6 is represented as moving to corner A of his production curve after the market is opened up.

We note finally the complete parallelism between Fig. 6 and the familiar diagram demonstrating the gains from international trade [14]. Indeed, the only difference is that the "after-trade" position in Fig. 6 is assumed to be one of "complete specialization." In this way we see once again that the essence of consumer's and seller's surplus (as measured by the compensating variation) are the gains from trade enjoyed by both parties to any free-market transaction.

2.4. Until now the analysis has been restricted to the case of an individual who buys only one commodity. Let us now briefly indicate some of the problems involved in extending it to the case of several commodities. For simplicity, we shall restrict our attention to the compensating variation.

In order to fix our ideas, let us consider the three-dimensional construct represented by Fig. 7. Once again, Y is the (composite) commodity with which the individual is initially endowed. Let OA represent this initial endowment, and let X_1 and X_2 represent the commodities which the individual is permitted to buy at prices (in terms of Y) p_1 and p_2, respectively. Let the corresponding budget plane be represented by ABC, and let P be the point at which this plane is tangent to an indifference surface. Similarly, let $A'B'C'$ be a budget plane parallel to ABC and tangent (at Q) to that (lower) indifference surface which passes through A. Then AA' is the total consumer's surplus as measured by the compensating variation.

What must now be emphasized is that in the general case of interdependent marginal utilities it is meaningless to attempt to partition this surplus into "that part due to X_1" and "that part due to X_2," for the total increase in welfare the individual enjoys by virtue of being able to trade in X_1 and X_2 reflects the interactions between these two commodities. The welfare implications of X_1 alone—or X_2 alone—cannot logically be disentangled.[17]

---

[17] The argument here is analogous to the one that demonstrates the meaninglessness of a cost-of-living index when both prices and money are changing. For details, see [16, pp. 530-36].

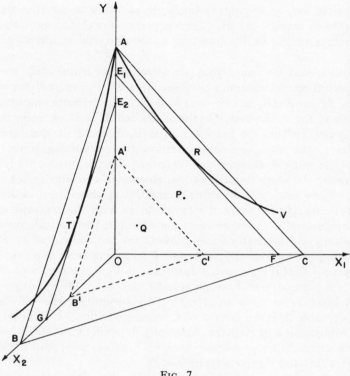

FIG. 7

But what must also be emphasized is that it is difficult to conceive of policy questions for which such a disentanglement would be of interest. For what concerns us in practice is the total surplus generated by any particular action. The abstract accounting imputation of this total to particular commodities is of no operational significance.

Thus for example, we might want to determine the compensating tax that could be levied if the individual at A were permitted to buy only (say) X_1, while the market for X_2 remained closed to him. The relevant compensating variation in this case can readily be measured in Fig. 7 as the distance AE_1. It is determined by the intersection with the Y-axis of that budget line in the OX_1Y plane which is parallel to AC and tangent to the indifference curve ARV (in the same plane) going through A. (The quantity AE_1 can also be represented by the relevant triangular area under the compensated demand curve corresponding to the indifference curve ARV; in other words, the demand curve drawn for the individual at A on the assumption that X_2 does not exist or is priced infinitely high.) Clearly, we would obtain a different compensating variation if instead of assuming the market for X_2 closed, we were to assume that the individual is buying a certain fixed quantity of it; or, more appropriately, if we were to assume that he is initially able to acquire X_2 at a certain price. But this is as it should be, for the nature of the policy question confronting us would then also be different.

In a similar way we can define the consumer's surplus AE_2, measuring the compensating variation for opening up only the market for X_2. The quantities AE_1 and AE_2 can be used to define the "relative importance" of X_1 and X_2 to the individual. On the other hand, it is obvious that they will not generally sum up to AA'. That is, because of the interactions noted above, the compensating variation for permitting trade in both X_1 and X_2 is not the sum of the variations for permitting trade in each one separately. In more familiar terms, consumer's surplus is not additive. For policy questions, however, this nonadditivity should not bother us.

Figure 7 can also be adapted to provide us with the relevant measures of consumer's surplus for other cases [for example, the equivalent variations for abolishing one or both of the markets for the individual at P, or the compensating (or equivalent) variations for moving from the price system p_1^0, p_2^0 to p_1', p_2']. But if consumer's surplus is to be a practical tool of policy-making, it is necessary that we be able to measure these variations not by means of indifference-map analysis, but by computing the relevant areas under observable demand curves—or, more generally, by carrying out the relevant integrations of demand functions dependent on the whole array of relative prices. The problems involved here are very complicated and still await a full and rigorous treatment.[18]

On the other hand, it is important to note that the total compensating variation in any multi-commodity case (that is, the surplus generated by introducing trade in all the commodities) can conceptually be readily computed from demand curves by making use of Hicks' well-known theorem that a group of commodities whose prices move proportionately can be treated as a single composite one. (See [11, pp. 33-34, 312-13]; for a graphical exposition, see [26, pp. 108-10].) Let us accordingly define the composite commodity $X = p_1 X_1 + p_2 X_2$ (where p_1 and p_2 are the prices in terms of Y), and let MQ in Fig. 2 represent its compensated demand curve.

---

[18] For an indication of some of the problems involved, see [15, pp. 173-82] and the references to Henderson and Hicks given therein.

Little actually devotes most of his attention to analyzing the welfare implications of introducing a new good into the economy. The nature of this problem can be defined formally as follows: Assume that an economy with n goods is at a certain point on its n-dimensional production surface. Introducing a new good adds a dimension to this surface. The question is then whether it is possible to move on the resulting $(n + 1)$-dimensional production surface to an $(n + 1)$-dimensional (community) indifference surface that is "higher" than the original one.

Little's discussion of the various consumer's and producer's surpluses is essentially an attempt to answer the foregoing question. At the same time Little points out certain methodological objections (similar to those which arise whenever a "change in tastes" occurs) that might make this whole question meaningless [15, p. 173, fn.].

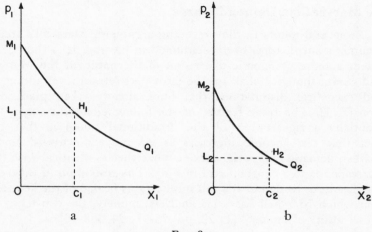

Fig. 8

Similarly, let M_1Q_1 in Fig. 8(a) represent the compensated demand curve for X_1 *drawn on the assumption that changes in p_1 are accompanied by proportionate changes in p_2*. A corresponding statement holds *mutatis mutandis* for M_2Q_2 in Fig. 8(b). Finally, let OL_1 and OL_2 be the respective prices of X_1 and X_2 corresponding to the price OL of their composite X. Since by definition the individual's expenditure on this composite good equals the sum of his expenditures on X_1 and X_2, the rectangle $OCHL$ in Fig. 2 is the sum of $OC_1H_1L_1$ and $OC_2H_2L_2$ in Fig. 8. By similar reasoning, $OCHM = OC_1H_1M_1 + OC_2H_2M_2$. Hence total consumer's surplus LHM can be measured as the sum of the triangles L_1H_1M and $L_2H_2M_2$.[19]

Needless to say, these last two triangles have no welfare connotation in themselves. We can, if we wish, *define* triangle $L_1H_1M_1$ as that part of the total surplus "due to" X_1, but this would be quite arbitrary. It should in particular be emphasized that this triangle is *not* a measure of the compensating variation AE_1 defined above.

We note finally that the foregoing procedure (whose simplicity stems from the fact that it effectively reduces a multi-commodity case to a two-commodity one) indicates how total consumer's surplus can be measured in a perfectly competitive economy in which all income is from labor. The initially endowed good (Y) of this economy is, of course, potential labor service (see Fig. 6). Total surplus would then be the sum of the relevant triangles under the individual demand curves for the various commodities, where each of these curves is drawn as a function of price in terms of the wage unit, on the assumption that the prices of all other commodities change in the same proportion.

---

[19] For a different approach to the multi-commodity case, see [12, chap. XVIII].

3. The Marshallian Demand Curve

3.1. At several points in the preceding argument, Marshall's treatment of consumer's surplus has been mentioned in passing. It is thus desirable to present a more systematic discussion of the nature of the Marshallian demand curve, though I shall for the most part refrain from adding to the detailed exegetical disputations that have already taken place on this question [7, 1]. The basic feature of the following interpretation (which is essentially a rigorization of the "traditional" one) is that despite the fact that real income increases as we move downward along the Marshallian demand curve, the curve is nevertheless identical with the one that corresponds to a constant real income. The resolution of this seeming paradox lies in drawing out the full implications of one of the key assumptions on which Marshall bases his analysis: namely, the constancy of the "marginal utility of money" [1; 22, pp. 75-91; 24, 388-90].

This term, of course, has nothing to do with the marginal utility of cash balances, but denotes instead what might better be called the marginal utility of expenditure. I also accept the view (though it is not essential for the following) that Marshall considers this constancy to be an approximation resulting from the assumption that the good whose demand is being analyzed (say, X) forms only a small part of the individual's total expenditure.[20, 21] Marshall's two further assumptions are that the marginal utilities of the various goods are independent and diminishing.[22]

The individual's utility-maximizing position is then described by the marginal conditions

$$(1) \qquad \frac{u_X(X)}{p} = u_Y(Y) = m \,,$$

together with the budget restraint

$$(2) \qquad pX + Y = I \,,$$

where X is the good whose demand is being analyzed, Y represents all other goods, p is the price of X in terms of Y, $u_X(\ )$ and $u_Y(\ )$ are the marginal utilities of X and Y, respectively, m is the marginal utility of money, and I is the individual's given income in units of Y.[23] Clearly, m is

---

[20] This is the view of Samuelson [22, p. 80, fn.] and Stigler [24, p. 370]. On the other hand, it is an essential element of Friedman's interpretation that Marshall did not make this assumption [7, p. 81]. For further discussion see Appendix Note B.

[21] For a rigorous analysis of the implications of this approximate constancy, see [9].

[22] See [17, 8th ed., pp. 93, 845]. By "independent marginal utilities" is meant that the marginal utility of any good is dependent only on the quantity consumed of that good.

[23] Note that the foregoing assumptions actually imply the impossibility of any good's being an inferior one. For by budget restraint (2), an increase in I necessarily increases the

measured in "utils" per unit of "money" and so is dependent on the cardinal utility function chosen for the analysis. It is not invariant under a positive monotonic transformation of this function [22, pp. 76-78].

The meaning of Marshall's approximation can now be seen. If X is an unimportant good, a change in its price will cause a small variation in the individual's expenditures on it relative to his total income. Hence the total quantity of Y purchased will not be much affected, and hence $u_Y(Y)$—and therefore m—will remain approximately the same. It should be emphasized that in actuality the law of diminishing utility is assumed to hold for both X and Y; it is only the relatively small variation in the consumption of the latter that enables us to ignore it in this case.

If, for simplicity, we now assume m to remain exactly constant at m_0, we can immediately "translate [the] law of diminishing utility into terms of price" [17, 8th ed., p. 94]. We then have, from (1),

$$(3) \qquad p = \frac{u_X(X)}{m_0},$$

or, alternatively,

$$(4) \qquad X = f(p),$$

where (to use inverse-function notation) $f(p) \equiv u_X^{-1}(m_0, p)$. Correspondingly, the demand function for Y can be deduced from (2) as

$$(5) \qquad Y = I - pf(p).$$

Now, since by assumption the marginal utility curve $u_X(X)$ is negatively sloped, its inverse—and hence the demand curve for X—must also be negatively sloped. This is the crux of Marshall's famous argument.

This argument can be reinterpreted in modern Hicksian terms by noting from (4) that Marshall's assumptions imply a demand function for X that is independent of income.[24] Hence, for example, a decrease in price will cause the amount of X demanded to increase only because of the substitution

---

demand for at least one good. This then decreases the marginal utility of that good. Hence in order to restore equality in (1), the amounts demanded of all goods must increase. (This is actually a special instance of the Paretian assumptions discussed by Hicks in [11, p. 28, fn. 2]). From Marshall's discussion of the Giffen paradox, however, it would seem that he was not aware of this implication [17, 8th ed., p. 133].

[24] Provided that the total expenditure on X is less than the individual's income. In other words, an additional (if tacit) restriction under which the individual is behaving is that Y in equation (5) cannot be negative. In graphical terms, the demand curve for X cannot lie rightward of the rectangular hyperbola representing a total expenditure on X equal to the individual's income.

Clearly, this limitation need not concern us within the framework of Marshall's assumption that X is an unimportant good.

effect. It must be emphasized that such a price decrease *will* generate an income effect, but as equations (4) and (5) show, this will express itself entirely in an increased demand for Y.

This zero-income elasticity of demand for X can also be deduced directly from equation (1). This is so because, if we assume an increase in I to take place, p constant, then if the marginal utility of X is declining while that of Y is constant, utility maximization will clearly lead the individual to spend all of his increased income on Y [6, pp. 153-56]. By assumption, this leaves m unaffected. Thus Marshall's assumptions imply constancy of m with respect to both p and I.

There are several additional points that should be emphasized. First, the zero-income elasticity of demand for X depends no less on the two additional assumptions of declining marginal utility of X and independence of marginal utilities than on the constancy of the marginal utility of Y. Thus if we assumed, for example, that $u_X( )$ were also constant, then an increase in income would be used in indeterminate proportions to increase the demand for both X and Y. Alternatively, if we assumed that $u_X( )$ depended on Y as well as on X, then we would no longer be able to infer from equation (3)—modified accordingly—that the demand for X depended only on p, to the exclusion of I.[25]

Second, it would be a serious misinterpretation of Marshall to attribute to him the belief that the marginal utility of money (and hence the demand for a commodity) actually remains constant under a change in income, no matter how large. On the contrary, he devoted Section 3 of Book III, Chapter III to an analysis of how an increase in income causes a decrease in m and hence an increase in the demand for X. In modern terminology, Section 2 of Marshall's argument analyzes the substitution effect, while Section 3 analyzes the income effect. The proper relation between these two sections is, however, somewhat obscured by what is presumably an unnoticed typographical error in all editions of the *Principles* subsequent to the third.[26]

Third, there is no relationship whatsoever between constancy of the marginal utility of money and constancy of real income in the sense of staying on the same indifference curve. In general, a compensated change in price that will leave the individual on the same indifference curve will not leave m unchanged, although in the Marshallian case it will.[27] Conversely, under Marshallian assumptions a decrease in the price of X moves the individual to a higher indifference curve, on which he is consuming more of

---

[25] From this it is clear that Hicks' well-known demonstration that constancy of $u_Y( )$ implies zero-income elasticity of demand for X is actually invalid for it overlooks these two additional assumptions [11, p. 26]. For further details see Appendix Note C.

[26] See Appendix Note D.

[27] See Appendix Note E.

both X and Y, and yet his marginal utility of income is constant. This is no more surprising than the fact that, say, constant marginal costs do not imply constant total costs. Yet I feel that the failure to recognize this lack of relationship has been a stumbling block in the path toward an understanding of Marshallian demand theory.

Finally, nothing essential in the forgoing interpretation would be changed if instead of assuming that Marshall intended to keep *m approximately* constant, we were to assume that he intended to keep it *absolutely* constant by means of compensating variations in the prices of other goods.[28] The main point is that the constancy achieved by these compensating variations is that of the marginal utility of money, and not (as Friedman would have it)[29] of the level of utility. In modern terms, the compensating variations are intended to eliminate the income effect not in its entirety, but only from the market for X.

We can now summarize our interpretation in the following words: The Marshallian demand curve is identical with the compensated demand curve of Section 1 above, not because it is conceptually generated by an experiment in which compensating variations eliminate the income effect

---

[28] Note that under these assumptions we must divide all other goods into two classes, those whose prices are kept constant and thus serve as the unit of measure (denoted, say, by W) and those whose prices are varied compensatingly (say, Z). The optimum conditions then become

(a)
$$\frac{u_X(X)}{p_X} = u_W(W) = \frac{u_Z(Z)}{p_Z},$$

(b)
$$p_X X + W + p_Z Z = I,$$

where p_X and p_Z are the prices of X and Z, respectively, in terms of W. All goods are now assumed to be subject to diminishing marginal utility, hence the assumption that $u_W(W)$ is constant implies that W is also constant. Thus (a) and (b) are effectively three equations in the four variables Z, X, p_Z, and p_X. The first three of these variables can then be solved out as functions of the fourth. Clearly, the resulting demand function for X depends only on p_X and is independent of income.

[29] Friedman relies primarily for his interpretation on Note II of Marshall's Mathematical Appendix [7, p. 84]. But it seems to me that the conceptual experiment referred to in this Note is not the compensated one described by Friedman, but rather the one described in footnote 2 above. The interpretation of this footnote also resolves the other difficulties of textual interpretation which Friedman raises earlier [7, pp. 82-83]. Furthermore, it enables the straightforward acceptance of Marshall's Appendix as a description of the same conceptual experiment described in his text, and not (as Friedman contends) of a different one. Similarly, our approach avoids the very strained interpretation of Marshall's discussion of consumer's surplus into which Friedman (by virtue of his constant-real-income approach) is forced [7, pp. 51-52, 68-72]. See the next paragraph of the text.

Note too how the correct version of Marshall's argument cited in Appendix Note D makes it even clearer than in later editions of the *Principles* that whatever compensating variations Marshall is making in order to keep "other things . . . equal," their purpose is to achieve constancy of the marginal utility of money.

created by the price change and thus leave the individual at the same level of utility, but because the income effect is assumed to expend itself entirely in other markets, leaving only a substitution effect in the market for X. For this reason the Marshallian demand curve tells us at one and the same time the maximum amount the individual would be willing to spend for X under perfectly discriminating monopoly conditions that keep his level of utility constant, and the amount he actually does spend under conditions in which a falling price raises this level. Hence it can be used as Marshall does use it to provide an accurate measure of consumer's surplus.

APPENDIX NOTES

(Superior figures in parentheses following key letter refer to respective text footnote.)

A[9] The passages from the *Principles* [17, 8th ed.] (with italics added) are as follows. Note that they create the impression that Marshall was thinking more along the lines of the equivalent surplus AA'' than of the surplus KD (Fig. 1).

> In other words, he derives this 45s. worth of surplus enjoyment from his conjuncture, from the adaptation of the environment to his wants in the particular matter of tea. *If that adaptation ceased, and tea could not be had at any price,* he would have incurred a loss of satisfaction at least equal to that which he could have got by spending 45s. more on extra supplies of things that were worth to him only just what he paid for them (p. 127).

> ... there might be use, when comparing life in Central Africa with life in England, in saying that, though the things which money will buy in Central Africa may on the average be as cheap there as here, *yet there are so many things which cannot be bought there at all,* that a person with a thousand a year there is not so well off as a person with three or four hundred a year here. If a man pays 1d. toll on a bridge, which saves him an additional drive that would cost a shilling, we do not say that the penny is worth a shilling, but that the penny together with the advantage offered him by the bridge (the part it plays in his conjuncture) is worth a shilling for that day. *Were the bridge swept away on a day on which he needed it,* he would be in at least as bad a position as if he had been deprived of eleven pence (p. 127, footnote).

> It is a common saying in ordinary life that the real worth of things to a man is not gauged by the price he pays for them: that, though he spends for instance much more on tea than on salt, yet salt is of greater real worth to him; *and that this would be clearly seen if he were entirely deprived of it.* This line of argument is but thrown into precise technical form when it is said that we cannot trust the marginal utility of a commodity to indicate its total utility (p. 129).

It yields to him, as consumer, a surplus consisting of the excess of the total utility to him of the commodity over the real value to him of what he paid for it. For his marginal purchases, those which he is only just induced to buy, the two are equal: but those parts of his purchases for which he would gladly have paid a higher price rather than go without them, yield him a surplus of satisfaction: a true net benefit which he, as consumer, derives from the facilities offered to him by his surroundings or conjuncture. *He would lose this surplus, if his surroundings were so altered as to prevent him from obtaining any supplies of that commodity,* and to compel him to divert the means which he spends on that to other commodities (one of which might be increased leisure) of which at present he does not care to have further supplies at their respective prices (p. 830).

B[20] The contention that Marshall restricts his discussion of the demand curve to an unimportant commodity is supported by Stigler [24, p. 390] by reference to the following passage from the first edition of the *Principles*:

When a person buys anything for his own consumption, he generally spends on it a small part of his total resources; while when he buys it for the purpose of trade, he looks to re-selling it, and therefore his total resources are not diminished. In either case, the marginal utility of money to him is not appreciably changed (p. 393; the corresponding passage in the eighth edition appears on p. 335, with the last sentence changed to: "In either case, there is no appreciable change in his willingness to part with money.")

Though mentioning this passage, Friedman apparently feels that it is offset by the fact that "nowhere in Book III, Ch. III does Marshall explicitly restrict his discussion to unimportant commodities" [7, p. 81, fn. 45]. Friedman also finds much significance in the fact that the first time Marshall does make such an explicit restriction is in connection with his discussion of consumer's surplus [17, p. 842], where according to Friedman's interpretation too it is necessary [7, p. 72]. The significance of this contrast is, however, much attenuated, if not eliminated, by Guillebaud's recent explanation that the critical passage on p. 842 was inserted by Marshall "partly in response to a letter from John Neville Keynes who was reading the proofs of Marshall's 1st edition of the *Principles* and asked him to consider the possible effects on consumer's surplus of a transfer of expenditure to other commodities" [17, 9th ed., Vol. 2, p. 832]. Thus, if the vital restriction to unimportant commodities was originally left only implicit in Marshall's discussion of consumer's surplus, there is certainly nothing unreasonable in assuming that it was (and is) also implicit in his discussion of the demand curve.

Another point that should be emphasized is that Marshall's discussion of the demand curve in Book III, Chapter III (and in the attached Mathematical Notes) is supported by repeated references to Jevons—who, in order to treat the "utility of money as a constant" explicitly restricted his analogous discussion to the case of goods that are not "the main elements of expenditure" [13, 2d ed., pp. 159-60. This was the edition used by Marshall. The corresponding passages in the fourth edition occur on pp. 147-48].

C[(25)]   Hicks' argument is as follows:

> What is meant by the marginal utility of money being constant? Making our translation, it would appear to mean that changes in the consumer's supply of money (that is, with respect to the problem in hand, his income) will not affect the marginal rate of substitution between money and any particular commodity X. (For the marginal rate of substitution equals the ratio of the marginal utilities of X and money.) Therefore, if this income increases, and the price of X remains constant, the price of X will still equal the marginal rate of substitution, without any change in the amount of X bought. The demand for X is therefore independent of income [11, p. 26].

Now, unless there is independence of the marginal utilities, an increase in money may affect the marginal utility of X, and hence the marginal rate of substitution of money for X, even though the marginal utility of money is constant. On the other hand, if the marginal utility of X were also constant under a change in money, the marginal rate of substitution could remain constant even if the demand for X were to increase.

These same results can be obtained analytically by making use of the fact that

$$\frac{\partial X}{\partial I} = \frac{\begin{vmatrix} 0 & 1 & u_Y \\ u_X & 0 & u_{XY} \\ u_Y & 0 & u_{YY} \end{vmatrix}}{\begin{vmatrix} 0 & u_X & u_Y \\ u_X & u_{XX} & u_{XY} \\ u_Y & u_{XY} & u_{YY} \end{vmatrix}}$$

(see [11, pp. 307-8]). Hicks assumes only that $u_{YY} = 0$; but this clearly does not assure the vanishing of the numerator. It will, however, vanish if $u_{XY} = u_{YY} = 0$.

On the other hand, if $u_{XX} = u_{YY} = u_{XY} = 0$, both numerator and denominator are zero, so that the income effect with respect to X is indeterminate.

D[(26)]   The relevant text of Marshall's third edition (p. 170) is as follows:

> An increase in the amount of a thing that a person has will, other things being equal (i.e. the purchasing power of money, and the amount of money at his command being equal) diminish his marginal demand price for it.

§3. This last sentence reminds us that we have as yet taken no account of changes in the marginal utility of money, or general purchasing power. At one and the same time, a person's material resources being unchanged, the marginal utility of money to him is a fixed quantity, so that the prices he is just willing to pay for two commodities are to one another in the same ratio as the utility of those two commodities.

Of course, a greater utility will be required to induce him to buy a thing if he is poor than if he is rich. . . .

In all subsequent editions, Section 3 is erroneously designated as starting a paragraph later than in the third edition. Furthermore, an additional paragraph has been inserted before the one beginning "This last sentence..." As a result, the antecedent of "last" is misrepresented in all of these editions.

E[27] In the two-commodity case it can be shown [21, pp. 70-71, fn. 3] that for a compensated change which keeps the individual on the same indifference curve,

$$\frac{\partial m}{\partial p} = \frac{\begin{vmatrix} 0 & u_X & u_Y \\ m & u_{XX} & u_{XY} \\ 0 & u_{XY} & u_{YY} \end{vmatrix}}{\begin{vmatrix} 0 & u_X & u_Y \\ u_X & u_{XX} & u_{XY} \\ u_Y & u_{XY} & u_{YY} \end{vmatrix}} = \frac{-m \begin{vmatrix} u_X & u_Y \\ u_{XY} & u_{YY} \end{vmatrix}}{U},$$

which is generally not zero.

Under the Marshallian assumption that $u_{XY} = u_{YY} = 0$, this will, however, vanish. The reason this invariance characterizes both the compensated and uncompensated Marshallian cases is intuitively obvious. For these two cases differ only in the amount of Y demanded, the demand for X being the same in both. But since the marginal utility of Y is assumed constant, m must also be constant.

REFERENCES

[1] ALFORD, R. F. G., Marshall's Demand Curve, *Economica*, **23** (1956), 23-48.
[2] BAILEY, M. J., The Marshallian Demand Curve, *J. Polit. Econ.*, **62** (1954), 255-61.
[3] BISHOP, ROBERT, Consumers' Surplus and Cardinal Utility, *Quart. J. Econ.*, **57** (1942-43), 421-49.
[4] BOULDING, KENNETH, The Concept of Economic Surplus, *Amer. Econ. Rev.*, **35** (1945), 851-69. [As reprinted in WILLIAM FELLNER and BERNARD F. HALEY (eds.), *Readings in the Theory of Income Distribution*. Philadelphia: Irwin, 1946, pp. 638-59.]
[5] BUCHANAN, JAMES, *Ceteris Paribus;* Some Notes on Methodology, *South. Econ. J.*, **24** (1958), 259-70.

[6] FRIEDMAN, MILTON, Professor Pigou's Method for Measuring Elasticities of Demand from Budgetary Data, *Quart. J. Econ.*, **50** (1935·36), 151-63.

[7] FRIEDMAN, MILTON, The Marshallian Demand Curve, *J. Polit. Econ.*, **57** (1949). [As reprinted in MILTON FRIEDMAN, *Essays in Positive Economics*. Chicago: Univ. Chicago Press, 1953, pp. 47-99.]

[8] FRIEDMAN, MILTON, The "Welfare" Effects of an Income Tax and an Excise Tax, *J. Polit. Econ.*, **60** (1952). [As reprinted in MILTON FRIEDMAN, *Essays in Positive Economics*. Chicago: Univ. Chicago Press, 1953, pp. 100-13.]

[9] GEORGESCU-ROEGEN, N., Marginal Utility of Money and Elasticities of Demand, *Quart. J. Econ.*, **50** (1935·36), 533-39.

[10] HENDERSON, A., Consumer's Surplus and the Compensating Variation, *Rev. Econ. Studies*, **8** (1941), 117-21.

[11] HICKS, J. R., *Value and Capital: An Inquiry into some Fundamental Principles of Economic Theory*, 2d ed. London: Oxford Univ. Press, 1946.

[12] HICKS, J. R., *A Revision of Demand Theory*. London: Oxford Univ. Press, 1956.

[13] JEVONS, W. S., *Theory of Political Economy*. London: Macmillan, 1879 (2d ed.), 1911 (4th ed.).

[14] LEONTIEF, W., The Use of Indifference Curves in the Analysis of Foreign Trade, *Quart. J. Econ.*, **47** (1933). [As reprinted in H. S. ELLIS and L. A. METZLER (eds.), *Readings in the Theory of International Trade*. Philadelphia: Irwin, 1949, pp. 229-38.]

[15] LITTLE, I. M. D., A Critique of Welfare Economics, 2d ed. London: Oxford Univ. Press, 1957.

[16] LIVIATAN, N., and D. PATINKIN, On the Economic Theory of Price Indexes, *Econ. Devel. and Cult. Change*, **9** (1961), 502-36.

[17] MARSHALL, ALFRED, *Principles of Economics*. London: Macmillan, 8th ed., 1920; St Martin's, 9th ed. (variorum), edited by C. W. GUILLEBAUD, 1961.

[18] MISHAN, E. J., Realism and Relevance in Consumer's Surplus, *Rev. Econ. Studies*, **15** (1947·48), 27-33.

[19] MISHAN, E. J., Rent as a Measure of Welfare Change, *Amer. Econ. Rev.*, **49** (1959), 386-95.

[20] MISHAN, E. J., A Survey of Welfare Economics, 1939-59, *Econ. J.*, **70** (1960), 197-265.

[21] MOSAK, JACOB, On the Interpretation of the Fundamental Equation of Value Theory, in O. LANGE *et al.* (eds.), *Studies in Mathematical Economics and Econometrics*. Chicago: Univ. Chicago Press, 1942.

[22] SAMUELSON, P. A., Constancy of the Marginal Utility of Income, in O. Lange *et al.* (eds.), *Studies in Mathematical Economics and Econometrics*. Chicago: Univ. Chicago Press, 1942.

[23] SAMUELSON, P. A., *Foundations of Economic Analysis*. Cambridge, Mass.: Harvard Univ. Press, 1947.

[24] STIGLER, G. J., The Development of Utility Theory: II, *J. Polit. Econ.*, **58** (1950), 373-96.

[25] VINER, JACOB, *Studies in the Theory of International Trade*. New York: Harper, 1937.

[26] WOLD, H., *Demand Analysis*. New York: Wiley, 1953.

[27] YEAGER, LELAND B., *Methodenstreit* Over Demand Curves, *J. Polit. Econ.*, **68** (1960), 53-64.

II. Theory and Measurement of Production

5

Capital Stock in Investment Functions:
Some Problems of Concept and Measurement

ZVI GRILICHES, *University of Chicago*

This paper originated as a report on an econometric study of total farm investment in machinery and motor vehicles. For this study I needed a measure of the stock of machinery on farms, and the available "official" measures seemed to be the obvious choice. But the more I worked with the model and these data the more dissatisfied I became with the official measures and with my own understanding of the problem. Although it was not too difficult to point out the flaws in the available measures, it was not at all clear to me what the right measure should be. Thus my interest shifted from the substantive question of the determinants of farm machinery investment to the methodological question of the role of capital stock in investment functions and the quest for the right concept of capital.

In pursuing the literature on this subject, mostly in the accounting and national accounting field and not too familiar to an econometrician, I found that almost everything worth saying has already been said by somebody some place, but not, I think, loud enough or often enough.[1] In this paper I will not be able to solve all or even many of the conundrums in this field. At best, it will be a guide to some unsolved problems of concept and measurement.

1. The Role of Capital in Investment Functions

The first question to be asked is "why is it necessary to have a capital variable in the investment function in the first place?" Is it not possible to explain investment without getting involved in the semi-metaphysical issues of defining capital? The answer is clearly no. What we need is a behavior equation, an equation that summarizes the most important determinants of investment and allows us to interpret and, hopefully, to predict this

This paper is part of a larger study of technical changes in agriculture that is being supported by a grant from the National Science Foundation. A study of the demand for tractors, touching on some of these same problems, was reported in [8]. A draft of this paper was read on December 29, 1959, at the Econometric Society meeting in Washington, D.C.

[1] Even though I do not agree with his main conclusions, the best discussion of many of these problems is to be found in Denison's paper [3]. See also Kuznets [15, 16].

variable. But at best, the investment function is a derived function. There is no such thing as demand for investment. Farmers or entrepreneurs do not desire a particular annual flow of purchased capital equipment *per se*. The fundamental desire or demand is for particular levels of capital, for a particular stock of capital equipment. To the extent that the desired stock does not equal the actual, there will be investment, but this investment is derived from the demand for a stock of capital—it is not an independent function.

Let me beg most of the crucial measurement and definition problems in this section and consider a very simple model in which the desired level of capital K^* is a function of a *set* of variables that I shall call X (say, the expected level of output, the rate of interest, wages, etc.).

Thus

(1) $$K^* = f(X) .$$

Now, if at the end of the period actual capital always equals desired capital, i.e., all of the adjustment is completed within the unit period of analysis, *net* investment depends only on the change in $f(X)$. Thus, only if we believe that all adjustments are completed within a year (or whatever is the unit of analysis) can we disregard capital (or the past history of net investment that is summarized in the capital concept) in explaining current net investment. In this particular case net investment is a function of the changes in X and will be zero unless X changes. Thus, net investment functions that do not contain a capital variable should have all their independent variables in first-difference form or have some other provision that would reduce net investment to zero eventually if there are no continuing changes in the independent variables. Of course, if the dependent variable is gross investment, there may be no escape from the capital stock variable, since gross investment is the sum of net investment and replacement, and replacement is definitely some function of the existing level of stock and its age distribution.

The assumption that all the desired change in the stock of capital is completed within one year is clearly unrealistic. Investment takes time. There are lags in budgeting, ordering, delivering, and installing new equipment. Often one investment (e.g., a new plant) will result in a stream of investment expenditures that are spread over quite a number of years. Moreover, in a world of rapidly changing economic conditions one may discount rather heavily changes that would indicate a very different level of desired capital stock. There is little point in completing the adjustment quickly if changing economic conditions are likely to outdate this decision quickly. The best policy may be to adjust only a little at a time, arriving at the goal eventually and only if the conditions that made this level desirable persist for a long enough period. (For an extensive survey of the literature on this type of model, see Nerlove [17].)

Such considerations lead to a very simple adjustment equation,

$$(2) \qquad \Delta K = g(K^* - K),$$

where K is the actual stock of capital and ΔK is net investment. Thus net investment is a function g of the difference between the desired and the actual stock of capital. For practical purposes and to simplify the exposition, I shall assume that net investment is actually a fixed fraction of this difference, though it is easy to think of reasons why this may not be so.[2] We have thus

$$(3) \qquad K_{t+1} - K_t = \gamma(K^*_{t+1} - K_t),$$

where γ is the adjustment coefficient and the stock of capital is measured at the beginning of the period.

Putting equations (1) and (3) together gives us

$$(4) \qquad K_{t+1} - K_t = \gamma f(X_t) - \gamma K_t.$$

We are interested, however, in gross rather than net investment. It is gross investment that is the output of the capital goods industries and the variable that we would like to predict. Also, gross investment is the datum of the economy and its explanation is a fairer test of one's model than explaining net investment, which may be largely a construct of one's (questionable) depreciation procedure. But gross investment equals net investment plus replacement:

$$(5) \qquad I_t = K_{t+1} - K_t + R_t,$$

where I_t is gross investment and R_t is replacement. If in addition we assume that replacement demand is proportional to the existing stock of capital, an assumption that I shall question later on, we have

$$(6) \qquad R_t = \delta K_t,$$

where δ is the implicit depreciation coefficient.[3] Putting (3), (4), and (5)

---

[2] Adjustments may not be symmetric: it may take longer to disinvest than to invest, the adjustment path may be nonlinear, and so on. The rate of adjustment may depend on other variables, e.g., "liquidity." It seems quite clear that the usual liquidity variables have no place in the desired-capital function. What they affect is not the desired level of capital, but only the rate at which these desires can be satisfied. Thus, such variables, if included at all in investment functions, should be entered in a form in which their influence will die out eventually.

[3] Note that this is equivalent to assuming a declining balance depreciation scheme (the capital stock "disappears" at a constant percentage rate), and it immediately implies one particular way of measuring K—as a weighted average of all past investments, with weights declining geometrically.

together, we have

(7)
$$I_t = \gamma f(X_t) - \gamma K_t + \delta K_t$$
$$= \gamma f(X_t) + (\delta - \gamma)K_t.$$

This form has been used widely in various investment studies [1, 11, 14]. The role of capital stock is here twofold: it has a negative influence on investment, measured by γ, owing to the damping effect of the existing stock of capital on the adjustment process, and a positive influence, measured by δ, owing to the larger replacement demand generated by a larger stock of capital. The net effect of the capital stock on investment is indeterminate; it depends on whether δ is smaller or larger than γ.

2. Which Concept of Capital?[4]

Besides the usual index number problems of adding cars and manure spreaders together and taking care of changing quality and price levels, which will not be discussed here, the main difficulty with capital measures arises from the most important property of capital—its durability. Most of my remarks will deal with the problem of how to compare and count new machines and 10-year-old machines.

There is a variety of possible capital measures (e.g., gross stock, adjusted gross stock, net stock, market value, depreciation or capital consumption, flow of services), and I shall discuss each of these measures briefly. The thing to remember throughout this discussion, however, is the difference between the *quantity* of capital in some physical units and its *value*. For many purposes we will be interested mainly in the first concept, whereas most of the available measures are approximations of the second concept. The reason for this distinction should be made clear: Almost all of our theorizing about investment and the desired stock of capital rests implicitly on some technological considerations and is derived from some kind of general production function. As long as we stick to the production function framework, it is clear that *quantity* rather than *value* is the relevant dimension, since the production function is defined as a relationship between the quantity of output and the quantity of various inputs. (See, e.g., Smith [18], and also Chap. 5 in the very interesting recent book by Hood and Scott [13].) That is, if we are interested in the demand for tractors, changes in the desired level of output will imply a desire to change the *number* of machines on farms. Whether these machines are new or old is a secondary problem.

---

[4] I am greatly indebted to Trygve Haavelmo in whose seminar on investment theory (Winter 1958, at the University of Chicago) I participated, for some of the ideas in this section. See also his monograph on investment theory [12]. He, of course, is not responsible for my interpretation and mistakes.

Of course, if we are interested in problems of technical change, and the new machines are also "better" machines, then the distinction between old and new machines becomes important again and we might want to rephrase our model in terms of capital vintages. On this see the paper by Solow [19].

Perhaps the simplest and least ambiguous measure is the gross stock concept. A machine is carried at its original value until it is retired. This is equivalent to a one-hoss-shay assumption—the machine is as good as new until the day of its "death." There are two major variants of this measure when one comes to deal with a large number of machines. The first retires (writes off) all machines at the end of their expected (average) life span, say 20 years. This is equivalent to measuring capital stock by a moving sum of past investment expenditures, the length of the summation being determined by the average life span of the particular machine. The second variant takes into account the variance around the expected life span and retires items on the basis of survival curves, machine mortality tables, or some other information on the distribution of retirements with age. The second variant seems to be clearly preferable to the first, since the first results in the writing off of all the capital by the time its average life span is exhausted, while in fact half of the original capital stock (gross) is still "alive."

Neither of these measures, however, takes care of the case of the same machines having different degrees of durability. The best procedure would be to count machines. In this fashion, the same machines have the same weight in the total, irrespective of the differences in their durability. In practice, however, we are faced with the problem of adding together machines of different size and type, and we wind up using some measure of total investment expenditures in constant dollars. Doing this, we are likely to give a machine that lasts 10 years (approximately) twice the weight of a new machine of the same capacity and annual productivity that will last only 5 years. The thing to do in this case is to deflate gross investment for changes in the expected life span, giving the more durable machine the same weight as the standard machine but carrying it for a longer period. It may be very difficult in practice to apply this type of deflation, but it is useful to keep it in mind as one possibly ideal measure, which I shall call *adjusted gross stock*.

The net stock concept is motivated by the observed fact that the value of a capital good declines with age (and/or use). This decline is due to several factors, the main ones being the decline in the life expectancy of the asset (it has fewer work years left), the decline in the physical productivity of the asset (it has poorer work years left), and the decline in the relative market return for the productivity of this asset due to the availability of better machines and other relative price changes (its remaining work years are worth less). One may label these three major forces as exhaustion, deterioration, and obsolescence. Net stock concepts will differ, depending on which (if any) of these factors govern the rate at which the gross stock is "written down." Some depreciation patterns have very little economic justification (except accounting convenience), but most of them at least purport to approximate the decline in the economic value of the remaining services (i.e., market value). Of the various possible depreciation schemes (net stock measures), two measures seem to be of the most interest: (a) a net stock concept based on a purely physical deterioration depreciation scheme,[5] and (b) the market value of the existing stock of capital. The latter figure can be approximated by the use of depreciation rates derived from studies of used machinery prices. The first concept is of interest because it is likely to be proportional to the available *current* flow of productive services. The second concept is of interest because it represents the market valuation of the current *and* all future flows of services that will be available from a given capital stock. Since many decisions about the future are made today, the market's valuation of the available *future* services of capital should not be ignored.

Two concepts of depreciation are of special interest to us: (1) "deterioration" (the loss in physical productivity or in the capacity of the existing capital to supply *current* services)[6] and (2) devaluation (the decline in the economic value [price] of the current and all future services derivable from the given capital stock).[7] The usefulness of either of these concepts is limited mainly to computing the appropriate net stock of capital. Neither of them is a good measure of the flow of current productive capital services. Ideally, the available flow of services would be measured by machine-hours or machine-years. In a world of many different machines we would weight the different machine-hours by their respective rents.[8] Such a measure would approximate most closely the flow of productive services from a given stock of capital and would be on par with man-hours as a measure of labor input.

Although we have explored briefly an array of possible "reasonable" measures of capital, the choice of a particular capital measure to be used in

---

[5] Deterioration would be subtracted from the adjusted gross stock. Ideally, this net stock would equal the number of existing machines times one minus the percentage decline in their average physical productivity.

[6] I am well aware of the fact that it is extremely difficult in practice to distinguish between physical and economic aspects of a factor of production and that only economically relevant physical aspects are of interest to us. Nevertheless, it seems to me both important and useful to keep these distinctions in mind, even if there is very little that we can do about them in practice.

[7] In Fabricant's language [4], the latter would include both capital consumption and capital adjustment.

[8] In a perfectly competitive world, the annual rent of a machine would equal the marginal product of its services. The rent itself would be determined by the interest costs on the investment, the deterioration in the future productivity of the machine due to current use, and the expected change in the price of the machine (obsolescence). To the extent that the world deviates from the competitive model, this weighting scheme may not be fully appropriate.

the investment function is still not very clear. Each of these measures is of some interest and will be found useful in answering particular questions. It is important, however, to decide first what question we want our measure to answer. For this purpose it is useful to distinguish between the two different roles of capital in the investment function: (a) the depressing effect of the existing stock of capital on the *rate of adjustment* to the new equilibrium, and (b) capital stock as a measure of replacement demand.

If we stick to our prejudice in favor of physical measures of the *quantity* of capital (i.e., if we derive the demand for capital from some underlying production function in which the relevant dimension is the *number* of machines), it seems quite clear that it is the existing *quantity* of machines which will affect the rate at which entrepreneurs adjust to changes in underlying conditions. It is clear that the pressure to close a given gap will be less if there are many machines, even if they are somewhat dilapidated, than if there are only a few and they are new. The desired stock of capital that is derived from production function considerations is a demand for the services of a number of machines, and the rate of adjustment of stock is a function of the difference between the desired number of machines and the existing number. These considerations lead to the following ranking of the relevant capital measures for this purpose: (1) the currently available flow of services, (2) net stock based on deterioration depreciation only, (3) adjusted gross stock (adjusted for the changing expected life span of machines), and (4) gross stock (survival curve retirement). The first measure is probably proportional to the second, and hence we may concentrate on the second and fourth measures, since we do not have the data to do an adequate job on the third. The net stock based on deterioration and the gross stock differ only in their assumption about deterioration. How the productivity of machines actually declines with age is a major empirical question to which we have very few answers. The range of possibilities extends from gross stock with the assumption of no deterioration at all to net stock based on declining balance depreciation at a relatively high rate.

The fact is that we know almost nothing about the deterioration with age in the performance of a machine. For many purposes, in particular for productivity comparisons, the one-hoss-shay assumption seems to be reasonable, or at least less extreme than some of the more commonly used assumptions (e.g., declining balance). When we turn to scattered data on hours worked by age of machine, gasoline consumption, etc., some deterioration with age is quite evident, but it is rather slow and concave to the origin. Figure 1 presents some evidence on the influence of age on the performance of tractors in the U. S. [20, pp. 70, 71]. [See the curves labeled (2) and (3)]. Data on the market value depreciation of tractors show, however, a strongly convex pattern [see (4) in the same figure].[9] Since market depreciation is

---

[9] For an interesting discussion of a particular depreciation model, see [2].

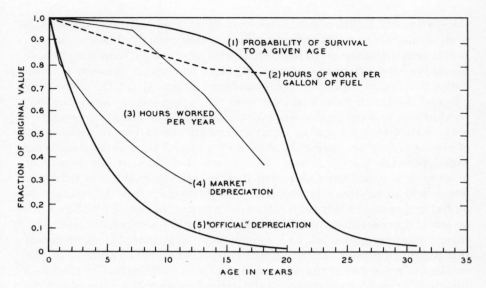

FIG. 1. THE AGING OF TRACTORS

(1) From A. P. Brodell and A. R. Kendall, *Life of Farm Tractors*, USDA, BAE, F. M. 80. Washington, D.C., Supt. of Documents, June 1950. The estimates are based on purchase data and the estimated 1948 stock of tractors on farms by age.

(2) The reciprocal of an index of fuel consumption per hour of work for wheel tractors 25 horsepower and over (this index equals 1.00 for less-than-5-year-old tractors). From A. P. Brodell and A. R. Kendall, *Fuel and Motor Oil Consumption and Annual Use of Farm Tractors*, USDA, BAE, F. M. 72. Washington, D. C., Supt of Documents, 1950. Data based on a 1940 survey.

(3) Average hours worked in 1940 by wheel tractors of different ages, with hours worked by less-than-5-year-old tractors equaling 1.00. From Brodell and Kendall, USDA, F. M. 72, *op. cit.*

(4) Average resale price of different-age tractors of same make and model in 1958 (new price = 1.00). Based on a sample of 23 models from the *Official Tractor and Farm Equipment Guide*. St. Louis, Mo.: National Retail Farm Equipment Association, 1958.

(5) "Official" depreciation based on 18.5 per cent declining balance depreciation, the rate and method used by the USDA in its estimates of farm machinery depreciation, net income, and the value of the stock of tractors on farms. See USDA, *Agriculture Handbook No. 118*, Vol. 3, p. 17.

composed of the change in interest costs, deterioration, and obsolescence, and since the change in interest costs by itself would produce a concave pattern of depreciation, either deterioration must be strongly convex (in spite of our scattered evidence) or, more likely, the impact of obsolescence is all-pervasive. If there is a high enough rate of obsolescence, it will produce a convex pattern in market values, even though the other two components of depreciation are concave. The fact is that we do not know what assumption is correct, and until we gather better information we should try several measures incorporating different assumptions about deterioration.

If we follow the same logic, the choice of the appropriate replacement measure is also quite clear. Replacement is the replacement of a number or units of machines; it is the replacement of productive capacity. Hence, if we assume no deterioration, replacement is just equal to retirements. If we do allow for some deterioration, it is equal to retirements plus deterioration. Thus it is equal to the depreciation in the *gross* stock, or to the depreciation in the net stock based on deterioration depreciation. Note that only if we assume a constant percentage rate of deterioration (i.e., declining balance) is replacement proportional to capital. Only then can we use the same variable to represent both roles of capital in the investment function. All other depreciation schemes require two different measures for these purposes.

We may, however, be proving too much. In a world in which the basic demand is for a *number* of machines and in which competition prevails, the prices of machines will be adjusted in such a fashion that the alternatives of using a new or an old machine are equally attractive. But there is nothing, then, in this model that would determine the age distribution of machinery, and hence the *value* as opposed to the quantity of capital.

The main determinants of the age distribution of capital are probably on the supply side. The price at which new machines can be substituted for old ones is the most important of these. But we are also abstracting from some of the most important aspects of the capital-equipment markets, from the fact that at given prices entrepreneurs differ in their preferences about different-age machines, that they differ in the value they put on reliability and in their evaluation of the risks of obsolescence. These differences of opinion and the possible different uses of the same machine make for a market in used machinery and result in the well-known downgrading in use of machinery with age.[10]

Moreover, we have up to now left out from consideration the impact of technological change or "obsolescence" on the demand for new equipment. But a theory of investment without obsolescence is like *Hamlet* without the

---

[10] It is really outside the scope of this paper to pursue these interesting problems further. For an outline of what a theory of used-machinery markets should contain, see Fox [6]. Also, see Farrell [5].

Prince. The main reason for the continuing high levels of gross investment is probably not so much the wearing out of old machinery as the availability of better new machinery [20]. Ideally, we should have taken account of it in our definition of X, including it as one of the variables determining the desired level of capital (in constant quality units). One way of doing this would have been through a continuously declining price of new machinery per constant quality unit. In practice, however, there is very little that we can do about it, and the whole effect of obsolescence is likely to be ignored in empirical work.[11]

One way of taking some of this into account is to assume that replacement is not only replacement of retired or worn-down machines but includes also the replacement of obsolete machines, even though the obsolete machines have not been retired but only downgraded in use. The amount of obsolescence (and deterioration) can be approximated quite well by the decline in the market value of the existing capital. More generally, we may postulate that there is a set of variables which determines the desired *value* of the stock of capital (e.g., the cost of durability, speculative considerations, and transaction costs), even though our simple production-function-based theory of the demand for capital determines only the desired *quantity* of capital. If these variables remain unchanged, it would appear reasonable to assume that replacement is desired not only for the quantity of capital but also for the value of capital. If this is true, market depreciation may be the best measure of replacement, defined broadly to include not only deterioration and retirement but also the reduction in the expected life span and the loss in earning power due to obsolescence.

We still have no very strong *a priori* reason for choosing any one capital measure over the others. One can, however, summarize three distinct approaches to the problem. At one extreme is the position that assumes that market values reflect all the relevant calculations and that the *value* of capital and the changes in it are the only relevant aspects of capital. At the other extreme is the "technological" position, claiming that only the number of machines matters, that the *quantity* of capital is the relevant and the only relevant dimension. In this section an attempt was made to outline an intermediate position, recognizing the different questions answered by different measures of capital, and suggesting that perhaps two different measures of capital are both relevant to the explanation of gross investment. The intermediate position would come close to the quantity extreme if we were able to include the impact of the availability of better machines on the demand for new machinery explicitly among our independent variables (the X's).

---

[11] Since this was first written, I have become somewhat more optimistic about the possibility of adjusting machinery price indexes for quality change. For an example of such an attempt, see [10].

Although we have expressed a preference for the intermediate approach, the evidence for it is not overpowering and some experimentation with alternative measures is in order. Moreover, even if we did decide *a priori* on a particular *concept* of capital, we should still experiment with alternative *measures* of capital, since empirical knowledge on the right depreciation or deterioration formula is almost nonexistent. The next section, therefore, will be devoted to a report on the experimental use of different measures of capital in explaining the fluctuations of farm gross investment in machinery and motor vehicles.

3. The Farm-Investment Function and Different Measures of the Stock of Machinery on Farms

The more substantive aspects of the farm-investment study will not be presented here. It will suffice to note that the major candidates for X (the set of independent variables) were the price of machinery, the prices of farm products, farm wages, prices of machinery supplies (complements) the price of land, the rate of interest, farmers' net worth, farm income, stocks of substitutes (horses and mules), and trend. After a substantial amount of experimentation the list was narrowed down to only two useful variables: the ratio of farm machinery prices to the index of prices received by farmers (machines–product price ratio) and the stock of horses and mules on farms. None of the other *a priori* important variables seemed to add significantly to the explanation of gross investment. The farm-wage variable and the price of machinery supplies had the right sign (positive for wages and negative for the price of machinery supplies) and were, in some cases, on the verge of being significant. The coefficient of the interest-rate variable was negative and highly significant in the absence of the horses-and-mules variable, but it became insignificantly different from zero when the horses-and-mules variable was introduced. These two variables turned out to be almost perfect substitutes for each other. The main substantive result of this study was the high significance of the real price of farm machinery in explaining the fluctuations in farm-machinery investment, most of it being accounted for, however, by the fluctuations in the denominator (farm products prices) of this variable rather than by its numerator (farm machinery prices). The coefficient of the latter variable was not significantly different from zero when the two parts of the real price were introduced separately in the regression. The estimated short run elasticity of investment with respect to changes in the real price of machinery was between -1.6 and -2.4 at 1957 levels of investment. This estimate was remarkably stable with respect to the introduction or deletion of various other independent variables. Another result of some interest was the almost complete insignificance of the farm-income or net-real-wealth-of-farmers variables. These variables had been introduced as proxy variables for liquidity.

Apparently, however, either liquidity considerations were not very important during this period or, more likely, these widely used proxy measures
of liquidity are very poor measures of it.

Since this paper is focused on the choice of the appropriate capital
measure, I shall report here the results of using different capital measures to
account for the fluctuations in gross farm-machinery investment only in
conjunction with the two finally selected independent variables. A large
portion of the same experiments was also performed in conjunction with
many other independent variables, with essentially similar results.

Our dependent variable is gross farm investment in machinery and
motor vehicles in 1935–39 prices.[12] All of the capital stock variables are
some function of these same gross investment series, and will be described
briefly below. The real price of farm machinery is the ratio of a Paasche
Farm Machinery Price Index to the USDA Prices Received by Farmers
Index as of March 15 of *the same year*.[13] The Farm Machinery Price
Index is the "implicit farm gross investment deflator" arrived at by dividing
the gross investment figures on farm machinery and motor vehicles in
current dollars by the estimated gross expenditures in 1935–39 dollars.
The stock of horses and mules on farms is the product of the number of
horses and mules on farms times their average price in 1935–39.[14] All
the stock and flow variables enter linearly into the regressions; all the
others (in the reported regressions only the "real price") are defined
as logarithms of the original values.[15] The period of analysis is 1920–41
and 1947–57.

Before we consider the different capital measures in detail, it is worthwhile to establish first that different measures of capital differ enough
to matter. Although it is quite true that in a stationary world most measures
of capital would come to the same thing, it is very misleading to apply this
reasoning to the real world. Given changing rates of growth and substantial
cyclical fluctuations, different measures of capital will differ both in the

---

[12] Actually, it is equal to farmers' expenditures on farm machinery, tractors, trucks, and
40 per cent of the expenditures on automobiles, since only 40 per cent of the total automobile
expenditures are considered by the USDA as a *productive* investment, the rest being classified
as consumption expenditures. In retrospect, I feel that it might have been better either to
include all automobile purchases or to exclude all. At the time this study was begun, however,
I wanted to cover all productive investment excluding construction, and it seemed easiest
to follow the USDA definition. I am indebted to the Farm Income Branch, AMS, USDA,
for making available to me these unpublished estimates of gross investment in 1935–39
prices.

[13] Wherever I use the word "machinery" alone it is a shorthand for all farm machinery,
tractors, trucks, and 40 per cent of automobiles.

[14] Weighting horses and mules separately according to age groups did not lead to appreciably
different results.

[15] This form was chosen to allow for the linear identities between stocks and flows and
for some nonlinearity in the behavior relation. The result is a semi-logarithmic desired-
demand function with a linear adjustment equation and identities.

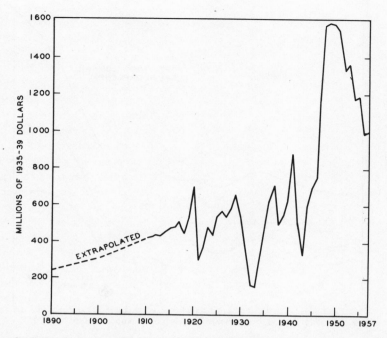

FIG. 2. GROSS FARM CAPITAL EXPENDITURES ON MACHINERY AND MOTOR VEHICLES
(FOR PRODUCTION PURPOSES), IN 1935-39 PRICES

Gross farm-machinery investment — gross farm investment in farm machinery, tractors, trucks and 40 per cent of the gross investment in automobiles, all in 1935-39 prices. Based on unpublished data (from USDA, AMS, Farm Income Branch) underlying the official depreciation rates. The figures in current prices are published in USDA, The Farm Income Situation. All the subsequent stock estimates are based on these series. Since the USDA figures go back only to 1910, when more years were needed for the particular stock measure, the data were extrapolated backward on the basis of decade investment averages from M. W. Towne and W. D. Rasmussen, "Farm Gross Product and Gross Investment in the 19th Century" [21].

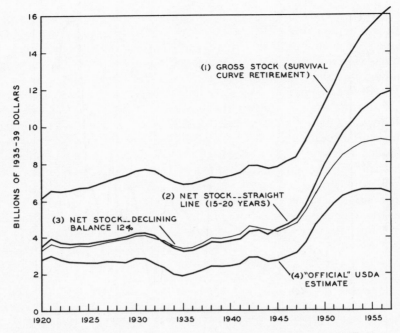

FIG. 3. DIFFERENT MEASURES OF THE STOCK OF MACHINERY ON FARMS

(1) Gross stock (survival-curve retirement)—based on survival information for tractors and grain binders (tractor survival tables from A. P. Brodell and A. R. Kendall, *Life of Farm Tractors*, USDA, BAE, F.M. 80, Washington, D.C., Supt. of Documents, June 1950, and A.P. Brodell and R. A. Pike, *Farm Tractors: Type, Size, Age, and Life*, USDA, BAE, F. M. 30, Washington, D.C., Supt. of Documents, February 1942. Survival table for grain binders from E. L. Butz and O. G. Lloyd, *The Cost of Using Farm Machinery in Indiana*, Purdue University Agricultural Experiment Station, Bulletin No. 437, May 1939). It is assumed that an investment depreciates to 10 per cent of its original value in 25 years and is scrapped after that. The pattern of depreciation is as follows: 0.990, 0.985, 0.975, 0.97, 0.96, 0.95, 0.93, 0.91, 0.88, 0.85, 0.81, 0.77, 0.71, 0.65, 0.59, 0.52, 0.45, 0.38, 0.31, 0.26, 0.21, 0.17, 0.13, 0.10.

(2) Net stock—straight-line depreciation: 15 years length of life before 1940, 20 years since 1940. Comparable to Goldsmith estimates [7].

(3) Net stock—declining-balance depreciation at 12 per cent per year. Consistent with market depreciation figures [9].

(4) Net stock—based on unpublished USDA data underlying the official depreciation estimates, using the declining balance method at a rate of (in recent years) 18.5 per cent for tractors, 22.0 per cent for automobiles, 21 per cent for trucks, and 14 per cent for other farm machinery. Average rate used is about 17 per cent (using 1950 stock values as weights). The estimates from 1940 to date are published in *The Balance Sheet of Agriculture*.

slope of their trends and in cyclical timing. Figure 2 presents the gross investment figures underlying all the various capital measures. Figure 3 presents a selected number of these capital measures and illustrates the resulting differences in level and movement. The differences in movement are minor, but the differences in trend are striking, particularly in the post-World-War-II period. On the whole, however, the series look enough alike to throw some doubt on the profitability of our search for "the" capital measure based on a goodness-of-fit criterion.[16]

Four capital measures were chosen for extensive analysis, and two more were added to cover more completely the range of possible assumptions. The first measure, K_1, is the unpublished "official" USDA estimate of the net stock of machinery on farms underlying the published official estimates of depreciation and net farm income. It is based on a declining balance depreciation scheme for the different items at a rather high rate (approximately 17 per cent per year). The second measure, K_2, is also a net-stock measure based on declining balance depreciation but at a lower rate (12 per cent). This rate is closer to the rates of depreciation observed in the market for used machinery. The third concept of net stock, K_3, is based on straight-line depreciation (15 years of life until 1940, 20 thereafter). This type of capital measure is probably the one used most widely by economists and statisticians, and the resulting estimates are comparable and very close to Goldsmith's estimates for similar categories. The last of the first four measures, K_4, is a measure of the gross stock where depreciation is only retirement depreciation, and its form is based on survival curve data. Since for K_3 and K_4 depreciation or replacement is not proportional to the measured stock, two measures of depreciation, D_3 and D_4, were also added to the analysis. Finally, two additional net stock variables were added—K_{30} and K_{05}, each based on declining balance depreciation, but one at the very high rate of 30 per cent per year and the other at the relatively low rate of 5 per cent per year. We can think of K_4 as approximating the *quantity*-of-capital concept, the *number* of machines on farms, whereas K_1 and K_2 are approximations of the *value* of capital on farms. The other measures are intermediate to these two extremes, expressing different assumptions about the pattern and the rate of depreciation.

The results of using these different capital measures to explain gross farm-machinery investment in 1920–41 and 1940–57, in conjunction with the real price of farm machinery and the stock of horses on farms, are presented in Table 1. Several interesting results emerge from these calculations: None of the measures of capital is statistical significant by itself. All the coefficients are small and most of them are smaller than their standard errors.

---

[16] From the point of view of productivity analysis, these same differences would loom much larger, implying substantially different rates of growth in "total factor productivity" in the post-World-War-II period. (See [9].)

TABLE 1

COEFFICIENTS OF DIFFERENT CONCEPTS OF THE STOCK OF MACHINERY ON FARMS
IN GROSS FARM-MACHINERY INVESTMENT REGRESSIONS

| | Coefficients | | | | | | | | |
	K_1	K_2	K_3	D_3	K_4	D_4	K_{30}	K_{05}	R
1	0.007 (.027)								0.954
2		−0.005 (.025)							0.954
3			−0.013 (.016)						0.955
4					−0.021 (.016)				0.956
5							−0.060 (.040)		0.957
6								−0.020 (.022)	0.955
7			0.118 (.053)	−2.78 (1.08)					0.964
8					0.012 (.013)	−4.46 (.085)			0.978
9	0.326 (.047)				−0.205 (.028)				0.984
10		0.381 (.063)			−0.259 (.041)				0.981
11					−0.110 (.017)		+0.281 (.042)		0.984

The dependent variable is gross farm investment in machinery (farm machinery, tractors, trucks, and 40 per cent of automobiles) in billions of dollars at 1935–39 prices. Each of the regressions contains two additional independent variables. The logarithm of the real price of farm machinery (index of farm-machinery prices divided by the index of prices received by farmers), and the stock of horses and mules on farms in billions of dollars at 1935–39 prices. The coefficients of these two variables are always significantly different from zero at conventional significance levels in all the regressions and vary between −1.7 and −2.4 for the coefficient of real price and between −0.5 and −1.0 for the coefficient of the stock of horses and mules on farms.

The numbers in parentheses are the estimated standard errors of the coefficients, and R is the coefficient of multiple correlation.

K_1 = USDA estimate of the stock of machinery on farms based on declining-balance depreciation scheme for the individual items at an average 17 per cent rate.

K_2 = net stock of machinery on farms based on 12 per cent declining-balance depreciation per year.

K_3 = net stock based on straight-line depreciation (15 years life before 1940, 20 thereafter).

$D_{3t} = K_{3t} - K_{3t+1} + I_t$.

K_4 is the gross stock of machinery on farms based on survival-curve depreciation. The assumed pattern of depreciation is as follows: 0.990, 0.985, 0.975, 0.97, 0.96, 0.95, 0.93, 0.91, 0.88, 0.81, 0.77, 0.71, 0.65, 0.59, 0.52, 0.45, 0.38, 0.31, 0.26, 0.21, 0.17, 0.13, 0.10, 0.00.

$D_{4t} = K_{4t} - K_{4t+1} + I_t$.

K_{30} = net stock based on 30 per cent declining-balance depreciation.

K_{05} = net stock based on 5 per cent declining-balance depreciation.

When depreciation measures are included for those concepts which are not proportional to depreciation, K_3 and K_4, the coefficient of depreciation is significant but has the wrong sign *a priori*. Its coefficient is negative, rather than positive as we would expect if depreciation were a good measure of replacement demand. The most interesting result is represented in lines 9 and 10, where K_1 and K_4 are included together. Separately, the contribution of neither concept was statistically significant, but when they are included together, the coefficients are highly significant at conventional significance levels but *opposite in sign*. The coefficient of the approximation to market value (K_1, K_2, or K_3) is positive, whereas the coefficient of the approximation to gross stock (K_4 and D_3) is negative. The results are similar when we use K_2 or K_{30} instead of K_1. Also, the results of 4.0 using K_3 and D_3 can be interpreted similarly. Straight-line-based depreciation is proportional to gross stock (based on a fixed-life assumption), whereas net stock is closer to market value than to anything else. Thus, the results support our hypothesis that to explain gross investment adequately we may need *two* capital concepts: (1) a quantity or number-of-machines concept for the adjustment mechanism, and (2) a value concept for replacement demand. As we have seen, a single capital concept by itself does not work, and when two concepts are included together not only do they contribute significantly to the explanation of gross investment, but also the concepts that approximate market value most closely always have a positive sign, whereas the approximations to the quantity of capital emerge with a negative sign.[17]

Before we take these results too seriously, we should discuss some alternative hypotheses that might explain them. A very simple statistical explanation of these results has been suggested to me by Milton Friedman. Consider the possibility that there is serial correlation in gross investment, which our model does not capture via the few independent variables that it uses. For various reasons, when investment is high in one year it is also more likely to be high in the next year and vice versa. But when investment has been relatively high in the recent past, the *value* concept of capital will be higher relative to the *quantity* concept and will contribute positively to the prediction of next year's investment. When investment has been below the average for some time, the *quantity* concept will be higher relative to the *value* concept and will contribute negatively to the prediction of next year's investment. That is, for various reasons we should have

---

[17] Similar results were obtained in the tractor-demand study. The two concepts of capital used there were the USDA estimated net value of tractors on farms (based on 18.5 per cent declining-balance depreciation) and the actual *number* of tractors on farms. In this case each of the variables was also significant separately. Together, however, they contributed distinctly more to the explanation of gross investment with the coefficient of net stock having a positive sign, whereas the coefficient of the *number* of tractors on farms had a negative sign. For details of this study see [8].

included lagged gross investment in our model. Since we have not done this, the use of these two capital measures approximates the use of lagged investment, and this also explains the different signs that we get for the two measures.

This result can be derived rigorously from a model in which the desired stock of capital depends not only on X but on expected X^*, and the expectations are formed by the function

$$X_t^* - X_{t-1}^* = \beta(X_t - X_{t-1}^*) ;$$

i.e., expectations are revised by some fraction of the difference between the realized X and the previously expected X^*. This assumption, together with the adjustment equation and the stock-flow identities, leads to the following model:

$$S_{t+1}^* = aX_t^* ,$$

$$S_{t+1} - S_t = \gamma(S_{t+1}^* - S_t) ,$$

$$X_t^* - X_{t-1}^* = \beta(X_t - X_{t-1}^*) ,$$

$$I_t = S_{t+1} - S_t + \delta S_t .$$

All these equations, substituted into each other and lagged twice, result in the following estimating equation:

$$I_t = \gamma\beta aX_t + \frac{(\delta - \gamma)\,(\beta - \delta)}{(1 - \delta)}\,S_t + \frac{(1 - \beta)\,(1 - \gamma)}{(1 - \delta)}\,I_{t-1} .$$

Thus, the introduction of an expected X equation on top of the adjustment equation transforms the resulting estimating equation from a first-order difference equation to a second-order difference equation (in S) and introduces I_{t-1} explicitly into it.

We can test this explanation of our results by including lagged investment explicitly in our model. Table 2 presents the results of substituting lagged gross investment for the various capital measures and the results of including it together with two measures of capital. It is clear from this table that there is something to the charge that we may have ignored the serial correlation in investment, but it does not invalidate our previous conclusions. Although lagged investment contributes significantly to the explanation of current investment both by itself and in conjunction with other capital measures, it does not supersede the contribution of either of the capital measures nor does it change their sign. It works in addition to, rather than instead of, the two capital measures. Both K_1 and K_4 retain their statistical significance and their opposite signs in the presence of I_{t-1}.

Another possible explanation of these results is that, using two extreme-assumption capital measures together, we allow, in effect, for an inter-

TABLE 2

FARM-MACHINERY INVESTMENT REGRESSIONS: DIFFERENT MEASURES OF STOCK VERSUS LAGGED INVESTMENT

	Coefficients			
	K_1	K_4	I_{t-1}	R
1	0.326 (.047)	−0.205 (.028)		0.984
2			0.416 (.082)	0.976
3	−0.068 (.020)		0.571 (.084)	0.984
4		−0.0414 (.0099)	0.496 (.068)	0.985
5	0.162 (.080)	−0.125 (.042)	0.291 (.120)	0.987

Note: The same comments apply as in Table 1. The new variable, I_{t-1}, is farm gross investment in machinery in the previous year. It is the dependent variable lagged one year.

mediate measure of capital based on a more complicated depreciation scheme. Let us then explore briefly the depreciation pattern implied by our results. Take, for example, line 10 in Table 1, where the coefficients of K_2 and K_4 are $+0.381$ and -0.259, respectively. We know that

$$K_{2t+1} = \sum_{i=0}^{\infty} I_{t-i}(0.88)^i \quad \text{and} \quad K_{4t+1} = \sum_{i=0}^{25} I_{t-i}W_i,$$

where the W's are the weights given in the notes to Figure 2. Thus

$$0.381K_{2t+1} - 0.259K_{4t+1} = + 0.125I_t \quad + 0.080I_{t-1} + 0.040I_{t-2}$$
$$+ 0.008I_{t-3} - 0.020I_{t-4} - 0.044I_{t-5}$$
$$- 0.062I_{t-6} - 0.080I_{t-7} - 0.091I_{t-8}$$
$$- 0.098I_{t-9} - 0.103I_{t-10} - 0.104I_{t-11}$$
$$- 0.100I_{t-12} - 0.096I_{t-13} - 0.088I_{t-14}$$
$$- 0.078I_{t-15} - 0.067I_{t-16} - \cdots\cdots\cdots.$$

We can see that the net weights have different signs in different years, and no one depreciation scheme could produce these results. Figure 4 presents a graphic picture of the estimated influence of past gross investment on current gross investment. It is evident that the impact of past gross

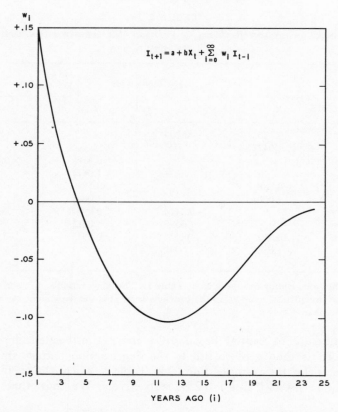

$$I_{t+1} = a + bX_t + \sum_{i=0}^{\infty} w_i I_{t-i}$$

FIG. 4. The Estimated Impact of Investment i Years ago on Current Investment (from Line 10, Table 1).

investment on current gross investment is positive for the first four years, becomes negative in the fifth year, and reaches a peak of negative influence at 12 years, after which the influence of past investment declines slowly to about zero at age 25. The positive impact of the previous few years is due either to serial correlation in the left-out variables or to the fact that replacement demand is strongly correlated in adjacent years. After the first few years this influence wears off, and the contribution of past investment becomes strongly negative, reflecting the depressing effect of the existing stock of capital on new investment. The fact that the impact of past investment is, on balance, strongly negative should not surprise us. Given our simple model, we would expect the stock of capital to have a negative net effect on gross investment, since the depreciation coefficient should not exceed 0.2, whereas the adjustment coefficients are likely to be higher than that, on the order of 0.3 to 0.5. Be that as it may, it is clear that the resulting pattern of the effects of lagged investment cannot be rationalized on the basis of some intermediate depreciation scheme. It seems preferable, and much easier, to interpret this as the result of the working of two distinct measures of capital, each having a different influence on gross investment.

4. Summary

In the previous sections I have argued that it is not obvious what kind of measure of capital we want to use in an investment function, but that most of the argument favors the use of two different measures of capital simultaneously, one approximating the idea of capital as a quantity (or number) of machines and the other measure approximating the idea of capital as the current value of the existing stock of machines. I have also argued that I would expect these two different measures to affect gross investment in opposite directions.

TABLE 3

SIMPLE CORRELATION COEFFICIENTS BETWEEN FARM MACHINERY INVESTMENT, LAGGED INVESTMENT, AND DIFFERENT MEASURES OF THE STOCK OF MACHINERY ON FARMS, 1920-41, 1947-57[a]

	I_t	K_1	K_2	K_3	D_3	K_4	D_4	K_{30}	K_{05}
K_1	0.741								
K_2	0.734	0.989							
K_3	0.693	0.986	0.994						
D_3	0.587	0.945	0.968	0.980					
K_4	0.672	0.969	0.991	0.996	0.988				
D_4	0.606	0.783	0.865	0.856	0.886	0.897			
K_{30}	0.809	0.985	0.978	0.957	0.906	0.940	0.779		
K_{05}	0.742	0.948	0.984	0.975	0.959	0.985	0.936	0.944	
I_{t-1}	0.917	0.857	0.841	0.798	0.717	0.773	0.642	0.921	0.814

[a] For the definition of variables see Table 1.

In spite of the very high multi-colinearity among the different measures of capital (the simple intercorrelation coefficients are presented in Table 3), our empirical results tend to support this position. The results are not very clear-cut and are subject to different interpretations, but they still suggest that two measures of capital are better than one. To gain more insight into these problems we shall have to improve our empirical knowledge about what happens to machines as they age. We have very little information about the expected life of different machines, about the rate of deterioration in their physical productivity with age, or about the factors that determine the relative prices of different age machines in the used-machinery markets. Without this knowledge, we don't know how to measure any kind of capital. With this knowledge, we will still need different measures of capital to answer different questions.

REFERENCES

[1] CHENERY, HOLLIS, Overcapacity and the Acceleration Principle, *Econometrica*, **20** (January 1952), 1-28.

[2] CRAMER, J. S., The Depreciation and Mortality of Motor Cars, *J. Roy. Stat. Soc.*, Ser. A, **121**, Part I (1958).

[3] DENISON, EDWARD F., Theoretical Aspects of Quality Change, Capital Consumption, and Net Capital Formation, in *Problems of Capital Formation: Concepts, Measurement, and Controlling Factors* (Conference on Research in Income and Wealth 19). New York: National Bureau of Economic Research (distr. Princeton Univ. Press), 1957, pp. 215-60.

[4] FABRICANT, SOLOMON, *Capital Consumption and Adjustment*. New York: National Bureau of Economic Research, 1938.

[5] FARRELL, M. J., The Demand for Motor Cars in the U.S., *J. Roy. Stat. Soc.*, **117** (1954), 171-93.

[6] FOX, ARTHUR H., A Theory of Second-Hand Markets, *Economica*, **24** (May 1957), 99-115.

[7] GOLDSMITH, RAYMOND W., *Study of Saving in the United States*, Vols. I–III. Princeton, N.J.: Princeton Univ. Press, 1955–56.

[8] GRILICHES, ZVI, The Demand for a Durable Input: U.S. Farm Tractors, 1921-1957, in A. C. HARBERGER (ed.), *The Demand for Durable Goods*. Chicago: Univ. Chicago Press, 1960.

[9] GRILICHES, ZVI, Measuring Inputs in Agriculture: A Critical Survey, *J. Farm Econ.*, XLII (December 1960), 1411-27.

[10] GRILICHES, ZVI, Hedonic Price Indexes for Automobiles: An Econometric Analysis of Quality Change, in *The Price Statistics of the Federal Government* (Gen. Ser. 73). New York: National Bureau of Economic Research (distr. Princeton Univ. Press), 1961, pp. 173-96.

[11] GRUNFELD, YEHUDA, The Determinants of Corporate Investment, in A. C. HARBERGER (ed.), *The Demand for Durable Goods*. Chicago: Univ. Chicago Press, 1960.

[12] HAAVELMO, TRYGVE, *A Study in the Theory of Investment*. Chicago: Univ. Chicago Press, 1960.

[13] HOOD, WM. C., and ANTONY SCOTT, *Output, Labour and Capital in the Canadian Economy*, Royal Commission on Canada's Economic Prospects, February 1957 (Queen's Printer: Hull).

[14] KUH, EDWIN, The Validity of Cross-Sectionally Estimated Behavior Equations in Time Series Applications, *Econometrica*, **27** (April 1959), 197-214.

[15] KUZNETS, SIMON, Comment, *Studies in Income and Wealth*, Vol. XIV (Conference on Research in Income and Wealth 14). New York: National Bureau of Economic Research (distr. Princeton Univ. Press), 1951.

[16] KUZNETS, SIMON, Comment, in *Problems of Capital Formation: Concepts, Measurement, and Controlling Factors* (Conference on Research in Income and Wealth 19). New York: National Bureau of Economic Research (distr. Princeton Univ. Press), 1957.

[17] NERLOVE, MARC, *Distributed Lags and Demand Analysis of Agricultural and Other Commodities*, USDA Agriculture Handbook No. 141, Washington, D.C., Supt. of Documents, June, 1958.

[18] SMITH, VERNON L., The Theory of Investment and Production, *Quart. J. Econ.*, LXXIII (February 1959), 67-87.

[19] SOLOW, R. M., Investment and Technical Progress, in KENNETH J. ARROW, SAMUEL KARLIN, and PATRICK SUPPES (eds.), *Mathematical Methods in the Social Sciences, 1959*. Stanford: Stanford Univ. Press, 1960, pp. 93-104.

[20] TERBORGH, GEORGE, *Dynamic Equipment Policy*. New York: McGraw-Hill, 1949.

[21] TOWNE, M. W., and W. D. RASMUSSEN, "Farm Gross Product and Gross Investment in the 19th Century," in *Trends in the American Economy in the 19th Century* (Conference on Research in Income and Wealth 24). New York: National Bureau of Economic Research (distr. Princeton Univ. Press), 1960.

6

Estimation of Production and Behavioral Functions from a Combination of Cross-Section and Time-Series Data

YAIR MUNDLAK, *Faculty of Agriculture, The Hebrew University of Jerusalem, and the Falk Project for Economic Research in Israel*

This paper surveys some of the problems encountered in the estimation of production and behavioral functions, with major emphasis on the Cobb-Douglas form. The reason for concentrating on a particular function is convenience in exposition. The approach and the results obtained can be extended to models in which other functions are used.

The correspondence between the behavioral equations and the production function is briefly considered in Section 1, which deals with the specification of the model [9]. The problems of estimation are introduced in Section 2, which deals with limitations of single-equation estimation. The possibility of using the reduced form is then considered in Section 3. This method makes full use of the one-to-one correspondence that exists between the production function and the behavioral equations, which are the equations of the reduced form. The limitations of this approach can be overcome by applying more direct methods of estimation. In Section 4 the Marschak and Andrews case is analyzed, and it is shown how, with the use of a combination of time-series and cross-section data, the system can be identified and solved. This result is considered from various statistical points of view. It is then generalized to the case in which some inputs are and some are not independent of the error terms in the production function. The relation to least squares is explored by comparing the asymptotic standard errors in a case favorable to least squares. It is found that in this case there is no loss of efficiency in using the suggested procedure. This method of estimation is then further generalized to allow for price variations over firms and over time.

In Section 9 still another approach is considered. It calls for the use

---

This paper will be reissued as Falk Project Research Paper No. 13. It was written during my tenure as Visiting Associate Professor at the University of California at Berkeley. An earlier version of it was read at the winter meeting of the Econometric Society, New York, December 1961. I am indebted to Zvi Griliches, George Kuznets, Nissan Liviatan, Albert Madansky, and Marc Nerlove for helpful comments. I have also benefited from stimulating discussion with Irving Hoch.

of lagged inputs as instrumental variables for eliminating the dependence of current inputs on current disturbances, and the covariance analysis for elimination of firm and time effects.

Finally, in Section 10, the method of estimation from factor shares is considered, and it is argued that although the method is subject to serious limitations when used by itself, it could be used efficiently together with covariance analysis. We thus suggest three direct methods and one indirect (reduced-form) method for obtaining consistent estimates of the production function. Most of the results could be achieved only through the use of repeated observations per firm; such data are therefore required for actual applications. This will become clear from the text, although in some places it will not be explicitly emphasized.

The discussion is in terms of a homogeneous product. Problems involved in aggregation over products will be dealt with elsewhere.

1. Specification

In this paper we shall only deal with industries in which the individual firm has no control over prices.[1] Rather than going into a detailed discussion of the problem of specification, we shall simply indicate that the following specification accounts for the fact that the size of the firm is determined, that firms differ in size and in the combinations in which the various inputs are employed, and that the size of the firm may change over time. We shall deal explicitly with a Cobb-Douglas production function, but we believe that part of the discussion has a more general implication.

Let the production function be

$$(1.1) \qquad X_{0it} = \alpha_0 K_{0t} \prod_{h=1}^{H} X_{hit}^{\alpha_h} M_{0i}^{\alpha_{H+1}} U_{0it} ,$$

where X_0 = output, X_h = input of factor h, M_{0i} = level of technical efficiency or, simply, management of firm i, and U_0 is a random disturbance that accounts for variations in output obtained from a given bundle of resources in repeated experimentation on firm i in year t. The coefficient α_h is the production elasticity with respect to factor h, and K_{0t} is a coefficient representing productivity in year t.

The first-order conditions for profit maximization are

$$(1.2) \qquad \alpha_h \frac{X_{0it}}{X_{hit}} = P_{hit} M_{hi} K_{ht} U_{hit} ,$$

---

[1] The analysis could be extended to cover cases where this condition is relaxed. Marschak and Andrews followed a more general formulation from this point of view in [7].

where P_h is the ratio of the price of factor h and that of the product, M_{hi} reflects the behavioral pattern of firm i in adjusting to the appropriate price ratio, and K_{ht} reflects the degree of adjustment, common to all firms, to the same price at year t. The main source for differences in behavior among firms or over time is the uncertainty that exists with respect to future prices or with respect to the production process. Except for one example in Section 2, we shall not elaborate on this point, since we are only interested here in the consequences of the specification.

The full implications of the specification are reflected in the reduced-form equations, where the endogenous variables are expressed as functions of prices and the various disturbances. For the case $H = 2$, we can express the reduced form as:

(1.3) $$X_r = B_{r0}\, B_{rt}\, P_1^{\beta r1}\, P_2^{\beta r2}\, \mu_{ri}\, V_r\,,$$

where

$$r = 0, 1, 2; \quad h = 1, 2, \qquad\qquad B_{00} = (\alpha_0 \alpha_1^{\alpha_1} \alpha_2^{\alpha_2})^D,$$

$$\beta_{rh} = -\alpha_h D - \delta_{rh}\,, \qquad\qquad B_{h0} = B_0 \alpha_h\,,$$

$$\delta_{rh} = \begin{cases} = 1,\ r = h \\ = 0,\ r \neq h, \end{cases} \qquad\qquad B_{rt} = K_{0t}^D\, K_{1t}^{\beta r1}\, K_{2t}^{\beta r2}\,,$$

$$\beta_{03} = \alpha_3 D\,, \qquad\qquad \mu_{ri} = M_0^{\beta 03}\, M_1^{\beta r1}\, M_2^{\beta r2}\,,$$

$$D = \frac{1}{1 - \alpha_1 - \alpha_2}\,, \qquad\qquad V_r = U_0^D\, U_1^{\beta r1}\, U_2^{\beta r2}\,.$$

Thus, when the production function is known, we can derive the supply elasticity of the product and the demand elasticities for the factors of production. Further, it is possible to evaluate explicitly the impact of technology and the certainty conditions on the level of output, as well as the impact of management and behavioral patterns of the firms. It is for that reason that it is useful to concentrate on the production and behavioral function at the same time. Whatever is said about one is reflected in the other.

Equation (1.3) represents the long-run equilibrium solution of X_r. From the point of view of estimation, this solution is too restrictive, since it is generally inappropriate to assume that firms are located at that point. In the short run their decisions are constrained by certain fixed factors, such as plant capacity. In such cases the model should be modified, as we shall see in Section 3.

Since most of the discussion will be conducted in terms of the logarithmic transformation, we shall rewrite the equations in this form, using lower-case letters to denote logarithms. Equations (1.1) and (1.2) can be rewritten as

$$
\begin{bmatrix} 1 & -\alpha_1 & -\alpha_2 \\ 1 & -1 & 0 \\ 1 & 0 & -1 \end{bmatrix}
\begin{bmatrix} x_{0it} \\ x_{1it} \\ x_{2it} \end{bmatrix}
-
\begin{bmatrix} 0 \\ p_{1it} \\ p_{2it} \end{bmatrix}
+
\begin{bmatrix} -\alpha_0'' \\ \alpha_1'' \\ \alpha_2'' \end{bmatrix}
$$

$$
=
\begin{bmatrix} k_{0t} \\ k_{1t} \\ k_{2t} \end{bmatrix}
+
\begin{bmatrix} m_{0i} \\ m_{1i} \\ m_{2i} \end{bmatrix}
+
\begin{bmatrix} u_{0it} \\ u_{1it} \\ u_{2it} \end{bmatrix},
$$

where also $\alpha_r'' = \log \alpha_r$ and $m_{0i} = \log M_{0i}^{\alpha_2}$, or simply

$$(1.4) \qquad Ax - p + A_0 = \epsilon$$

for $\epsilon_{it} = k_t + m_i + u_{it}$. We shall deal mainly with the variables defined as deviations from their respective means, in which case we will have

$$(1.5) \qquad Ax - p = \epsilon,$$

and the reduced form is given by

$$(1.6) \qquad x = A^{-1}p + A^{-1}\epsilon.$$

The following notations will be used for the partitioned matrixes:

$$
A = \begin{bmatrix} 1 & -\alpha' \\ \hline L & -I \end{bmatrix}
$$

with dimensions

$$
\begin{bmatrix} 1 \times 1 & 1 \times H \\ \hline H \times 1 & H \times H \end{bmatrix};
$$

$$
x = \begin{bmatrix} x_0 \\ \hline x_h \end{bmatrix}, \qquad
p = \begin{bmatrix} 0 \\ \hline p_h \end{bmatrix}, \qquad
k_t = \begin{bmatrix} k_0 \\ \hline k_h \end{bmatrix}, \qquad
m_i = \begin{bmatrix} m_0 \\ \hline m_h \end{bmatrix}, \qquad
u = \begin{bmatrix} u_0 \\ \hline u_h \end{bmatrix}.
$$

All of dimensions $\left(\begin{smallmatrix} 1 \times n \\ H \times n \end{smallmatrix}\right)$ for $n = IT$. Also,

$$(1.7) \qquad A^{-1} = D \begin{bmatrix} 1 & -\alpha' \\ \hline L & B \end{bmatrix} \quad \text{for } B = -(L\alpha' + ID^{-1}) \text{ and } D = (1 - L\alpha)^{-1}.$$

The components of ϵ are the disturbances associated with the year, with the firm, and with repeating the production process for the same firm at the

same year, respectively. The common feature of these three error terms is
that none of them is observed. However, given the year, k_t is fixed; and
given the firm, m_i is fixed; but given the year and the firm, u_{it} is a random
vector that may take different values in repeated experiments. Marschak and
Andrews were concerned mainly with the firm variable, since they dealt
with a cross-section problem only, but they indicated that there may be a
similar term for a year effect.

In our discussion we will be concerned with the distribution of the
random components conditional on k_t (in other words, for fixed k_t). That is,
we are not interested in the population, if such exists, from which k_t was
drawn. We shall thus have only two sources for randomness in any given
year, the firm vector m_i and u. We shall conceive of m as having been drawn
from an infinitely large population of entrepreneurs, and of u as having
been drawn from an infinitely large population of repeated experiments on
a given firm in a given year. We make the following assumptions:

$$E(\epsilon_{it}|_{it}) = k_t + m_i , \qquad E(\epsilon_{it}|_t) = k_t ,$$

(1.8)

$$\sum_{\epsilon} = E(\epsilon\epsilon') = k_t k_t' + \sum_m + \sum_u ,$$

where Σ_x denotes the variance matrix of vector x.

Whenever plim is used, it will be done for given t's and evaluated over
the population of u or of m as the particular case requires.

2. Direct Estimation of the Production Function

Direct least-squares estimates of the production function have their
optimum properties only if the explanatory variables, x_h, are independent
of the disturbance of that equation, $m_{0i} + k_{0t} + u_{0it}$. From (1.6) it can be
seen that this condition is not met, since the inputs depend, among other
things, on the same error components as output. The better managers are
likely to employ more inputs and, by definition, will obtain larger output
for a given bundle of resources. Similar interpretation can be given for the
year effect and for u. The latter will be examined in more detail below.

The first two sources can be eliminated by the use of covariance analysis
[3, 8]. Such a procedure utilizes the fact that for a given firm and year,
$m_{0i} + k_{0t}$ are fixed and therefore cannot account for within-firm-year
deviations in inputs or in output. We can rewrite the production function
and also the appropriate averages to get

(2.1) $$x_{0it} - \alpha_1 x_{1it} - \alpha_2 x_{2it} = \epsilon_{0it} ,$$

(2.2) $$\epsilon_{0it} = k_{0t} + m_{0i} + u_{0it} .$$

With no loss in generality we can assume that in the sample

$$\sum_t k_{0t} = \sum_i m_{0i} = 0$$

the averages

$$\epsilon_{0.t} = k_{0t} + \qquad + u_{0.t},$$
$$\epsilon_{0i.} = \qquad m_{0i} + u_{0i.},$$
$$\epsilon_{0..} = \qquad\qquad u_{0..}.$$

are considered, where

$$\epsilon_{0.t} = \frac{1}{I}\sum_i \epsilon_{0it}, \qquad \epsilon_{0i.} = \frac{1}{T}\sum_t \epsilon_{0it}, \qquad \epsilon_{0..} = \frac{1}{IT}\sum_i \sum_t \epsilon_{0it},$$

and consequently,

(2.3) $$\epsilon_{0it} - \epsilon_{0.t} - \epsilon_{0i.} + \epsilon_{0..} = u_{0it} - u_{0.t} - u_{0i.} + u_{0..}$$

or we introduce the notation $\epsilon_0^{IT} = u_0^{IT}$. But, by using (2.1) for ϵ_{0it}, we get

(2.4) $$x_0^{IT} - \alpha_1 x_1^{IT} - \alpha_2 x_2^{IT} = u_0^{IT}$$

for

$$x_r^{IT} = x_{rit} - x_{r.t} - x_{ri.} + x_{r..}.$$

The α's can now be estimated by using least squares:

(2.5) $$\hat{\hat{\alpha}} = \left(x_h^{IT} x_h^{IT'} \right)^{-1} x_h^{IT} x_0^{IT'}.$$

The estimates $\hat{\hat{\alpha}}$ will be referred to as covariance analysis estimates.[2] The estimates do not, in general, possess the optimum properties, since x_h^{IT} may still depend on u_0^{IT}. If such dependence did exist originally, it did not disappear by the transformation into year-firm deviations. This can best be seen by making the same transformation on the reduced form in (1.6):

(2.6) $$x^{IT} = A^{-1} p^{IT} + A^{-1} u^{IT}.$$

An assumption under which this source will be eliminated was pointed out by Hoch [2]. It is based on the observation that the nature of the production process is such that inputs precede output in time and, therefore, that at the date when inputs are determined the actual output that will be realized is

---

[2] Admittedly, this is general, but in most of the discussion there will be no room for ambiguity. Wherever it is necessary, we shall use more specific wording, e.g., "estimates obtained after allowing for year and firm effects."

not known with full certainty, the reason being the dependence of output on the disturbance U_0. Thus the firm can base its decision on expected output or choose another criterion, such as minimizing the expected loss resulting from deviation between anticipated output and actual output or any other decision criterion. The result is that in setting the first-order condition he will consider some parameters of the density function of U_0 rather than U_0 itself. That is, the first-order conditions will be obtained by differentiating

$$\bar{X}_0 = \alpha_0 K_{0t} X_1^{\alpha_1} X_2^{\alpha_2} M_0^{\alpha_3} \eta ,$$

where η could be $E(u)$ or any other function of the parameters of $f(u)$. As a consequence, the first-order condition will be

(2.7) $$\frac{\delta \bar{X}_0}{\delta X_h} = \alpha_h \frac{\bar{X}_0}{X_h} = P_h M_{hi} K_{ht} U_h$$

instead of that presented in (1.2). Consequently, when the reduced form is written out, U_0 will not appear in the demand equations for the factors.

Another consequence of this assumption offers some insight into the interpretation of the behavior variable M_{hi}. Note that $\bar{X}_0 = (X_0/U_0)\eta$, and if this is substituted in (2.7) and η is moved to the right, we obtain a term M_h/η, which could be defined as the new M_h. That is, among other things, M_h represents the lack of full knowledge of the outcome of the production process. The value of η may vary over firms as producers may differ in their anticipations and actions in the world of uncertainty.

Finally, to complete the conditions that secure independence, we have to make one more assumption, that of independence between U_0 and the set U_h. However, U_{hit} need not be independent of $U_{h'it}$. This may seem to be a plausible assumption in view of the fact that the main sources of dependence, those of firm and year effects, were considered explicitly. It is, therefore, under the following two assumptions that covariance analysis yields unbiased estimates.

(1) Consideration of "expected output" (in the sense indicated above) rather than actual output in the firm's decision in response to prices.

(2) Stochastic independence between the disturbance (U_0) in the production function and the disturbances (U_h) in the first-order conditions.

The validity of the first assumption can be questioned, even in cases in which the time factor plays an important role in production, e.g., in agriculture. In many cases it may be possible to divide the production process into two stages, say, planting and harvesting. Let the logarithmic form of the production function that describes the planting stage be

(2.8) $$x_{01} = \alpha_{11} x_1 + u_1 ,$$

where x_{01} is the output before harvest, x_1 is the input at the planting season, and u_1 is the disturbance of the first stage. At this stage, x_1 is determined according to expected output, since there is no way to tell in advance what u_1 is going to be. The second stage consists of the harvest operation. The logarithmic form of the production function that describes the harvest operation is

$$(2.9) \qquad x_{02} = \alpha_{21}x_{01} + \alpha_{22}x_2 + u_2 \,.$$

There are two inputs in this process, the stand in the field, x_{01}, and the "labor" employed in picking, x_2.

Here again x_2 is determined according to expected value of x_{02} and is independent of u_2. Thus we have a recursive situation, which allows us to estimate each equation separately by least squares. However, this can seldom be accomplished, since there are no data on the various stages of the production process. Instead, we estimate

$$(2.10) \qquad x_{02} = \beta_1 x_1 + \beta_2 x_2 + (\alpha_{21}u_1 + u_2) \,.$$

It is clear that x_2 is not independent of u_1, since the determined quantity of x_2 depends on x_{01}, which in turn depends on u_1. That means that we are back in a situation where at least some inputs are not independent of the disturbance in the production function. It is possible that the resulting bias may be small, but that, of course, depends on the particular case under investigation. Consequently, it turns out that another solution to the problem has to be sought.

There is another implication of this formulation. If x_1 and x_2 are inputs of the same factor, say labor, then instead of $\beta_1 x_1 + \beta_2 x_2$ in (2.10) there will be one term only, βx, where x stands for total labor. Unless $\beta_1 = \beta_2$, or unless x_2 is constant or proportional to x_1, which contradicts our assumption that it depends on u_1, that will lead to a specification error. For

$$(2.11) \qquad (\beta_1 x_1 + \beta_2 x_2) = \beta_1(x_1 + x_2) + (\beta_2 - \beta_1)x_2 \,.$$

Thus, if we include in the equation only the term βx, the term $(\beta_2 - \beta_1) x_2$ is omitted from the formulation and a bias is incurred. The direction of the bias depends on the sign of $(\beta_2 - \beta_1)$ and on the correlation of x_2 with the other variables in the regression.

3. Estimation of the Reduced Form

The formulation in the foregoing discussion secures exact identification, since in each first-order condition there are two endogenous variables and one exogenous variable, P_h. It is therefore possible to estimate the reduced form and then to solve for the coefficients of the production function.[3] The estimation of the reduced form can only be carried out if there are sufficient variations in prices, which is not always the case, especially if the study is conducted only for one year. It then may well be that price variations among firms are not sufficiently large to yield reliable estimates. In fact, it is this case which was discussed in the paper by Marschak and Andrews, where the simultaneous relationships between output and inputs were first formulated. This problem will be discussed subsequently, but as will be seen, there are other methods of estimating the production functions.

The estimation of the reduced form deserves some comments on formulation and on the method of estimation. Usually, the period of observation in a cross-section study is a year. During the year some inputs, such as the size of the plants, are fixed. That means that the reduced-form equation will be expressed in terms of the available quantities of the fixed factors rather than in terms of their prices. Thus we can assume, for illustration, that x_2 is fixed at the level x_2^* . Consequently, the first-order condition with respect to x_2 has no meaning and (1.5) should then be rewritten as

$$\begin{bmatrix} 1 - \alpha_1 \\ 1 - 1 \end{bmatrix} \begin{bmatrix} x_0 \\ x_1 \end{bmatrix} - \begin{bmatrix} \alpha_2 & 0 \\ 0 & 1 \end{bmatrix} \begin{bmatrix} x_2^* \\ p_1 \end{bmatrix} = \begin{bmatrix} k_{0t} \\ k_{1t} \end{bmatrix} + \begin{bmatrix} m_{0i} \\ m_{1i} \end{bmatrix} + \begin{bmatrix} u_{0it} \\ u_{1it} \end{bmatrix},$$

which we shall denote as

(3.1) $Ax - Cz = \epsilon$.

From the point of view of our discussion, this is a more general formulation than (1 5). In the extreme case where all the inputs vary during the year, then (3.1) is the same as (1.5). On the other hand, if all the inputs are fixed, then (3.1) simply collapses to the production function. Thus, in general, the number of rows in (3.1) is equal to the number of endogenous variables, and the matrixes in (3.1) are defined accordingly.

The reduced form of (3.1) is

(3.2) $x = \pi z + v$,

where $\pi = A^{-1}C$ and $v = A^{-1}\epsilon$.

There is no reason to assume that z is independent of v. It is possible that there is dependence between firm effects and prices, or what is more likely, between firm effects and the fixed factors in z. Better managers may operate larger firms. Thus, to avoid biased estimates, the reduced form

---

[3] Such an approach was attempted by the author in [10]. This is also essentially the approach followed by Nerlove in Returns to Scale in Electricity Supply, in this volume, pp. 167–98.

should be estimated by using covariance analysis. That is, instead of (3.2), estimate

$$(3.3) \qquad\qquad x^{IT} = \pi z^{IT} + v^{IT}.$$

The stucture of A makes it possible to solve for the production elasticities from knowing the coefficients of any one of the reduced-form equations, as can be verified by observing the definition in (1.3). This may create the problem of obtaining unique results if more than one equation is estimated. It may therefore be desirable to estimate the various equations under a constraint that will secure a unique solution.

It seems that the reduced-form estimates are relatively inefficient. It is certainly true in the extreme case where no variations in prices exist. In that case the reduced form cannot be estimated at all, but there may be considerable variation in output as a result of variations in the various error components. Hence methods that utilize these variations, such as the methods discussed below, are likely to be more efficient. It should be noted that what is required is to have within-firm-year price variations if the covariance analysis is to be used. Thus differences of a more permanent nature, such as those reflecting location differences, will be washed out.

Finally, the reduced-form estimates depend to a larger extent on the specifications of the model and therefore are more susceptible to errors in specifications. To illustrate, prices are not actually known to the firms and therefore the results are likely to be affected by the particular measure that is selected to represent the expected price.

4. The Marschak and Andrews Case

4.1. Identification and Solution. Marschak and Andrews [1; see also 2, 11, 13] investigated the case in which (1) all inputs are endogenous (that is, $z = p$); (2) there are no price variations among firms; and (3) there is only one observation per firm.

We shall discuss this case with one modification: the use of repeated observations per firm. We shall thus show that when repeated observations are available on each firm the production function is estimable. In fact, the solution could be obtained in several ways, as will be indicated below.

Under the assumptions specified above, (3.1) is the same as (1.5) and they both collapse to

$$(4.1) \qquad\qquad Ax = \epsilon.$$

It is thus implied that variations among firms reflect only the firm effects and random disturbances, and that variations over time reflect only the time effects and random disturbances. In the Marschak-Andrews formulation ϵ consisted only of the firm effects, whereas in our case it also contains the year effects and random disturbance.

In discussing the identification, it will be preferable first to refer to (1.4), in which the variables do not appear as deviations from the mean. Since there are no price variations, we can rewrite (1.4) as

$$(4.2) \qquad A x_{it} + (A_0 - p) = \epsilon_{it} .$$

Although the first-order conditions in (4.2) are identified, the production function is not, in the sense that one could get a linear combination of the three equations that will be similar in form to the production function. In fact, let, the coefficients of such a linear combination be δ_0, δ_1, δ_2. The error term in the new equation thus formed will be $\bar{\epsilon}_0 = \delta_0 \epsilon_0 + \delta_1 \epsilon_1 + \delta_2 \epsilon_2$. It is apparent that $\bar{\epsilon}_0$ is not independent of ϵ_1 and ϵ_2.

If, however, ϵ_0 were independent of ϵ_1 and ϵ_2, that is, $\mathrm{cov}\,(\epsilon_0 \epsilon_1) = \mathrm{cov}\,(\epsilon_0 \epsilon_2) = 0$, then the new error term $\bar{\epsilon}_0$ will differ in distribution from ϵ_0, and identification of the production function is established [5, 13]. However, it was not in this case that Marschak and Andrews were interested, since they assumed that such dependence in fact does exist and, therefore, sought other restrictions to be imposed in order to limit the possible values of the parameters. The reasoning for rejecting the assumption of independence is clear; there is no *a priori* justification for assuming that m_{0i} is independent of m_{hi} or that the product $k_{0t} k_{ht} = 0$ for all h and t. In terms of (1.8), we do not restrict the first row of $k_t' k_t$ or of Σ_m to be zero.

A possible way to eliminate the dependence is to use within-firm-year variations, as discussed in Section 2. Instead of (4.2) we then have

$$(4.3) \qquad A x^{IT} = u^{IT} ,$$

and it can be shown that

$$(4.4) \qquad \sum_{u^I T} = \frac{(I - 1)\,(T - 1)}{IT} \sum_{u} .$$

Thus to assume $E(u_0^{IT} u_h^{IT}) = 0$ implies $E(u_0 u_h) = 0$. This assumption seems to be quite plausible in view of the fact that the main sources for such dependence, the time and the firm effects, were eliminated. It is not necessary to assume independence between u_h and $u_{h'}$, nor is it necessary to assume the contrary. As we shall see, such independence does not lead to overidentification.

In order to simplify the notation, we shall use $y = x^{IT}$ and $f = u^{IT}$ and write out (4.3) explicitly in terms of the new notation:

$$(4.5) \qquad y_0 - \alpha_1 y_1 - \alpha_2 y_2 = f_0 ,$$

$$(4.6) \qquad \begin{aligned} y_0 - \;\; y_1 \qquad\;\; &= f_1 , \\ y_0 \qquad\quad - \; y_2 &= f_2 . \end{aligned}$$

We then have $Ay = f$, where y and f are both of dimension $3xn$, where $n = IT$ is the number of observations, $ff' = ASA'$.

Taking expectations, we have

$$(4.7) \qquad \sum_f = AE(S) A',$$

where, by definition,

$$\sum_f = \frac{(I-1)(T-1)}{IT} \sum_u.$$

In subsequent discussion we shall omit the subscript f from Σ_f or its components, the typical one to be denoted as $\sigma_{rr'}$. Now $S = (yy'/n)$ is a matrix of the sample moments of y. We shall omit the y from the index of the elements of S, the typical element of which is $s_{rr'}$. We shall denote either expectations or asymptotic limits of the variables by bar. In order to see the nature of the solution, we partition (4.7) to get

$$(4.8) \qquad \begin{bmatrix} \sigma_{00} & \sigma_{0h}' \\ \sigma_{0h} & \sigma_{hh'} \end{bmatrix} = \begin{bmatrix} 1 & -\alpha' \\ L & -I \end{bmatrix} \begin{bmatrix} \bar{S}_{00} & \bar{S}_{0h}' \\ \bar{S}_{0h} & \bar{S}_{hh'} \end{bmatrix} \begin{bmatrix} 1 & L' \\ -\alpha & -I \end{bmatrix},$$

where $L = \begin{pmatrix} 1 \\ 1 \end{pmatrix}$. Multiplying out,

$$(4.9) \qquad \sigma_{00} = \bar{S}_{00} - 2\alpha' \bar{S}_{0h} + \alpha' \bar{S}_{hh'} \alpha,$$

$$(4.10) \qquad \sigma_{hh'} = \bar{S}_{00} LL' - \bar{S}_{0h} L' - L\bar{S}_{0h}' + \bar{S}_{hh'},$$

$$(4.11) \qquad \sigma_{0h}' = \bar{S}_{00} L' - \alpha' \bar{S}_{0h} L' - \bar{S}_{0h}' + \alpha' \bar{S}_{hh'}.$$

The six unknown population parameters in Σ are expressed in terms of the sample moments and the two unknown elasticities in α, altogether six equations and eight unknowns.

It should be noted that the three parameters in $\sigma_{hh'}$ are estimable from (4.10), for which no restrictions need be made. That means that we are left with three equations, (4.9)–(4.11), and five unknowns. Imposing $\sigma_{0h} = 0$ leads to the same number of unknown parameters as equations, and the system can be solved. The solution for the α will follow from (4.11):

$$(4.12) \qquad \alpha' = (\bar{S}_{0h}' - \bar{S}_{00} L') (\bar{S}_{hh'} - \bar{S}_{0h} L')^{-1}.$$

The solution for σ_{00} is obtained by substituting (4.12) for α in (4.9).

It then follows that the estimates of α and σ_{00} which are obtained by using the sample values of S instead of $\bar{S}$ are consistent, whereas the estimates of $\sigma_{hh'}$ are also unbiased.

4.2. Identity with Instrumental Variable Estimates. It is interesting to note that the statistics derived from (4.12) could be obtained from estimating (4.5) by the method of instrumental variables, where the instrumental variables are f_1 and f_2 as defined in (4.6).[4] Such a procedure will lead to two equations of the form

$$(4.13) \qquad \sum_{it} y_0 f_h - \alpha_1 \sum_{it} y_1 f_h - \alpha_2 \sum_{it} y_2 f_h = \sum_{it} f_0 f_h .$$

By the independence assumption, $E[\Sigma f_0 f_h] = 0$, and the system is soluble, the solution being given by (4.12). To show this, write (4.13), including the independence assumption, in matrix notation:

$$(4.14) \qquad \bar{S}_{f0} = \bar{S}_{fh} \alpha ,$$

where

$$S_{f0} = \frac{1}{n} f_h y_0' \quad \text{and} \quad S_{fh} = \frac{1}{n} f_h y_h' ,$$

but from (4.6), $f_h = L y_0 - y_h$; hence

$$S_{f0} = L S_{00} - S_{h0} \quad \text{and} \quad S_{fh} = L S_{0h}' - S_{hh'} .$$

By substituting these expressions in (4.14), we can verify that the statistics in the two cases are identically the same.

4.3. Identity with Theil's Suggestion. The solution in (4.14) could also be obtained by following the approach suggested by Theil as quoted by Hoch [2, fn. 11, p. 572]. The suggestion is based on the assumption of independence between f_0 and f_h, and calls for least-squares estimates of the equation

$$(4.15) \qquad y_0 = - D(\alpha_1 f_1 + \alpha_2 f_2 - f_0) .$$

Equation (4.15) is obtained by substituting $y_h = y_0 - f_h$ in (4.5). The least-squares estimates of (4.15) are obtained from

$$(4.16) \qquad S_{f0} = - D S_{ff} \tilde{\alpha},$$

but

$$(4.17) \qquad S_{ff} = \frac{1}{n} f_h f_h' = \frac{1}{n} f_h (y_0' L' - y_h') = S_{f0} L' - S_{fh} .$$

Substituting (4.17) in (4.16), rearranging terms, and noting that $D^{-1}(I + L'\alpha DI) = I$, we get the statistics derived from (4.14). We have

---

[4] For exposition of the method, see [1, 12].

thus shown that the statistics obtained from least-squares estimates of (4.15) are the same as those obtained from using f_h as instrumental variables. It is therefore concluded that the statistics obtained for the Marschak-Andrews case, for the instrumental variable case, and for the Theil suggestion are identically the same.

4.4. Least-Squares Bias and Hoch's Solution. The asymptotic bias of the direct least-squares estimates of (4.5) can be evaluated from (4.12). With rearrangement of the terms we get

$$(4.18) \qquad \tilde{\alpha}' = \alpha' [I - \bar{S}_{0h}L'\bar{S}_{hh}^{-1}] + \bar{S}_{00}L'\bar{S}_{hh}^{-1},$$

where $\tilde{\alpha}'$ is the least-squares estimate of α', and $\bar{\tilde{\alpha}}'$ is its asymptotic limit. Thus the necessary condition for α to be asymptotically unbiased is

$$[\bar{S}_{00} - \alpha'\bar{S}_{0h}]L'\bar{S}_{hh}^{-1} = 0 .$$

This is fulfilled by .

$$(4.19) \qquad \bar{S}_{00} = \alpha'\bar{S}_{0h} ,$$

which in the present framework implies that $\sigma_{00} = 0$. This can be verified by solving for $\bar{S}$ in (4.8), from which we get

$$(4.20) \qquad \begin{aligned} \bar{S}_{00} &= D^2(\sigma_{00} + \alpha'\sigma_{hh}\alpha) , \\ \bar{S}_{0h} &= D^2(\sigma_{00}L - B\sigma_{hh}\alpha) , \end{aligned}$$

where $B = -(L\alpha' + ID^{-1})$.

Noting that $\alpha'B = -\alpha'$, and substituting (4.20) in (4.19), we verify the proposition. The implication of this statement is that when the production function remains fixed, then variations in the adjustment equations will trace out the production function, or in other words, if there are no variations in f_0 , there can be no dependence between f_0 and y_h .

The least-squares bias and estimates of the variances were evaluated by Hoch for a more restrictive case in which $\sigma_{12} = 0$, that is, zero covariance between the errors of the equations of the first-order conditions [2]. It can be shown that the results obtained above reduce to the results obtained by Hoch, if this restriction is imposed. Whether such a restriction is acceptable or not could be determined from the sample, since its imposition introduces a linear dependence between some sample moments. This can be seen from (4.10):

$$(4.21) \qquad \sigma_{12} = 0 = \bar{s}_{00} - \bar{s}_{01} - \bar{s}_{02} + \bar{s}_{12} .$$

As a consequence, the identification of the remaining parameters is not disturbed; our results hold and, in fact, can be simplified. For instance, a consistent estimate for α_h is obtained from

$$(4.22) \qquad \bar{\bar{\alpha}}_h = \frac{s_{0h} - s_{00}}{D\sigma_{hh}} \,.$$

If we know α_1 and α_2, D can be derived, and from (4.10) we get

$$\bar{\bar{\sigma}}_{hh} = s_{00} - 2s_{01} + s_{11} \,,$$

which is substituted in (4.22). This solution is very simple to compute, since no matrix inversion is required.

In concluding this section, we note that the Marschak-Andrews case is estimable if repeated observations on the same firms are available. The model can then be formulated in terms of within-firm-year variations. The estimates will be consistent. Their sampling variance is evaluated in Section 6.

5. A Generalization: Exogenous Inputs

The results of Sections 2 and 4 can now be combined and considered as the extremes of a general case in which some inputs are and some are not independent of the disturbances in the production function f_0.[5] In introducing the case, it is helpful to think of the estimates in Section 2 as if they were obtained by using the inputs as instrumental variables. Likewise, a possible interpretation of the estimates presented in Section 4 is to consider them as if they were obtained by using the disturbances of the first-order conditions as instrumental variables.

The suggested procedure for the general case is to estimate the elasticities with the aid of instrumental variables. These variables will be either inputs or disturbances in the first-order conditions, depending on whether the inputs are or are not independent of f_0. To illustrate, in the estimation of (4.5) let us assume that y_2 is independent of f_0, whereas y_1 is not. The relevant system will then be reduced to

$$(5.1) \qquad \begin{aligned} y_0 - \alpha_1 y_1 - \alpha_2 y_2 &= f_0 \qquad [E(f_0 f_1) = 0]\,. \\ y_0 - y_1 &= f_1 \end{aligned}$$

Using $-f_1$ and y_2 as instrumental variables, we get, for a sufficiently large sample,

$$(5.2) \qquad \sum f_0 f_1 = \sum y_2 f_0 = 0 \,.$$

---

[5] See the discussion in Section 2. It is in this sense that the term exogenous in the title should be interpreted. That is, the inputs are still dependent on the firm and year components, which are here eliminated.

Substituting for f_0, and f_1, the system to be solved is

(5.3)
$$s_{10} - s_{00} = \tilde{\alpha}_1(s_{11} - s_{01}) + \tilde{\alpha}_2(s_{12} - s_{02}),$$
$$s_{20} = \tilde{\alpha}_1 s_{12} + \tilde{\alpha}_2 s_{22}.$$

To generalize, suppose there are H inputs, the first H_1 are not independent of f_0, and the last $H - H_1$ are independent of f_0. The estimates of the H elasticities are obtained from

(5.4)
$$\left[S_{hh} - \binom{H_1}{0} S'_{0h} \right] \tilde{\alpha} = S_{0h} - \binom{H_1}{0} S_{00},$$

where $\binom{H_1}{0}$ is a column vector whose first H_1 rows consist of ones and the last $H - H_1$ rows consist of zeros. When $H = 0$, (5.4) reduces to least-squares estimates. When $H_1 = H$, (5.4) is the same as (4.12).

The estimates of the variances and covariances in question can be derived, following the pattern used in Section 4.1.

In using (5.4), one must classify the inputs according to whether they are dependent or independent of f_0. As indicated in Section 2, the classification depends on the stage of the production process at which the input is used. The decision may be somewhat arbitrary, as is sometimes the case in classifying variables as exogenous or endogenous. Hoch suggested that the relative size of the variances may help in the classification, but this method is not exhaustive [2]. To see what is involved, we shall express the asymptotic limit of sample moments in the desirable form. Instead of solving for the moments from (4.8), let us rewrite (4.15), thus expressing y_0 as a function of the errors

(5.5)
$$y_0 = D \left(f_0 - \sum_h \alpha_h f_h \right).$$

From (4.6) we get

(5.6)
$$\bar{s}_{11} = \bar{s}_{00} + \sigma_{11} - 2\sigma_{y_0 f_1}.$$

Using (5.5), we get

(5.7)
$$\sigma_{y_0 f_1} = -D(\alpha_1 \sigma_{11} + \alpha_2 \sigma_{12}).$$

Hence

$$\bar{s}_{11} = \bar{s}_{00} + \sigma_{11} + 2D\alpha_1 \sigma_{11} + 2D\alpha_2 \sigma_{12}.$$

If $\sigma_{12} = 0$, then $\bar{s}_{11} > \bar{s}_{00}$. Thus, for the input to be endogenous, the probability limit of its variance should be larger than that of the output. If, however, $\sigma_{12} < 0$, this is no longer so. Further, the classification is not reversible in that not all inputs with variances larger than that of the output are endogenous. Finally, the variance of the input whose value is determined according to expected output, and therefore is independent of f_0, may be larger or smaller than s_{00}. Consequently, if we divide the production process according to stages, it is possible that an input will not be independent of f_0, but will have a smaller variance than s_{00}. For all that, it seems that the classification requires some judgment.

In concluding this section, it should be pointed out again that the only justification for imposing the assumption of independence between f_0 and f_h is the allowance made for the firm and year effects, which are believed to be the main sources for the dependence, the implication being that the variables are defined according to (2.3) and the sample moments in S are

$$(5.8) \qquad s_{kj} = \frac{1}{n} \left\{ \sum_t \sum_i x_{kit} x_{jit} - T \sum_i x_{ki.} x_{ji.} - I \sum_t x_{k \cdot t} x_{j \cdot t} + IT x_{k..} x_{j..} \right\}.$$

If for some reason there are no variations over time in the amount of some inputs used by the firms, the elasticities of these inputs could not be estimated by (5.4), since the relevant sample moments, as they appear in (5.8), will be zero. It seems that one possible way to handle such a situation would be to estimate first all the elasticities that could be estimated. The remaining elasticities could be estimated either by using the factor share approach, as discussed below, or by substituting the estimates obtained from (5.4) for the true values of the corresponding parameters and then estimating the remaining elasticities by regular regression rather than by covariance analysis.

6. Standard Errors and Further Comparison with Least Squares

As was pointed out by Durbin [1], elimination of the bias by use of instrumental variables is achieved with some loss in efficiency. It is therefore interesting to explore the implication of this result in the context of our model. We shall do it for the case in which all the instrumental variables are the disturbances in the first-order conditions (f_h). This is the most extreme deviation from least squares and therefore the most convenient for such a comparison. The implications for the general case, which is the mixed case, follow without difficulty.

Following the results obtained by Sargan [12], we can write the variance matrix of the estimated coefficients as

$$(6.1) \qquad \sum_{\tilde{\alpha}} = \frac{\sigma_{00}}{n} \bar{S}_{fh}^{-1} \sigma_{hh'} \bar{S}_{hf}^{-1},$$

where, as before, $n = IT$, $S_{hf} = (y_n f_n')1/n$ is the matrix of sampling moments between y_h and f_h, and S_{fh} is its transpose. In order to obtain the asymptotic limit of S_{hf}, we derive, from (4.5) and (4.6),

$$(6.2) \qquad y_h = D(Lf_0 + Bf_h),$$

where B is defined as in (1.7). Using (6.2) and setting $E(f_0 f_h') = 0$, we get

$$(6.3) \qquad \bar{S}_{hf} = \frac{1}{n} (\overline{y_h f_h'}) = DB\sigma_{hh'}.$$

Substituting (6.3) in (6.1), we get

$$(6.4) \qquad \sum_{\tilde{\alpha}} = \frac{\sigma_{00}}{n} D^{-2} \{B\sigma_{hh'} \cdot B'\}^{-1}.$$

This expression can be compared with the variance of the least-squares estimates in the case where least-squares estimates are usable:

$$(6.5) \qquad \sum_{\hat{\alpha}} = \frac{\sigma_{00}}{n} S_{hh}^{-1}.$$

As we recall, least squares can be used if y_h is independent of f_0, which implies that expected rather than actual output is used in the first-order condition. In this case, instead of (6.2) we get[6]

$$(6.6) \qquad y_h = DBf_h,$$

and (6.4) could then be written as

$$(6.7) \qquad \sum_{\tilde{\alpha}} = \frac{\sigma_{00}}{n} S_{hh}^{-1},$$

which is identical with (6.5).

This means that in circumstances where least squares are usable there is no loss of efficiency in using f_h rather than y_h as the instrumental variable. Further investigation indicates that in this case the two statistics are identical. This can be verified by using (6.6) in (4.14), which yields

$$(6.8) \qquad \begin{aligned} S_{f0} &= CS_{h0} \\ S_{fh} &= CS_{hh} \end{aligned} \quad \text{for } C = D^{-1}B^{-1};$$

hence in this case the statistics implied by (4.14) will become

$$(6.9) \qquad S_{h0} = S_{hh} \tilde{\alpha}$$

which is the least-squares statistic.

This result is not the general rule for instrumental variable estimates, which have lower efficiency in the case favorable to least squares. The result in this case reflects the underlying structure.

---

[6] In this case, what was noted above as f_h can now be written as $f_h + f_0 L = f_h^*$. Upon substitution in (6.2), factoring out, and noting that $BL = -L$, the statement is verified.

The approach followed by some authors implies the use of instrumental variables if it can be asserted empirically that least-squares estimates are subject to a bias [1, 6]. This is done with the understanding that such a choice is not necessarily the best choice for small samples, in which case the variances of the instrumental variables estimates may be relatively large. The choice between the two methods depends on the size of the bias and the standard error of the least-squares estimates as compared with the standard error of the consistent estimates. The asymptotic limit of the standard error of the least-squares estimates has not been developed for the case in which such estimates are biased. Therefore, instead of deriving a definite criterion for determining which procedure to follow when samples are small, we shall attempt to see when we can expect the variance of the instrumental-variables estimates to be relatively small.

We shall start with the simple case in which there is only one input. From (6.4) we get

$$(6.10) \qquad \sigma_{\tilde{\alpha}}^2 = \frac{\sigma_{00}}{n\sigma_{11}} (1 - \alpha)^2 .$$

The variance is then directly related to σ_{00} and indirectly related to σ_{11}. This result is familiar, and it implies that for given σ_{00}, α, and n the variance could be reduced by taking a sample with a large spread in f_1, that is, large deviations in the average productivities.

Expression (6.10) can be written in a form that is more familiar in the discussion of instrumental variables by noting that $\sigma_{y_1}^2 = D^2(\sigma_{11} + \sigma_{00})$ and the correlation coefficient in the population between f_1 and y_1 is $\rho_{y_1 f_1}^2 = \sigma_{11}/\sigma_{00} + \sigma_{11}$. We then have, for (6.10),

$$(6.11) \qquad \sigma_{\tilde{\alpha}}^2 = \frac{\sigma_{00}}{n\sigma_{y_1}^2 \rho_{y_1 h}^2} .$$

This appears to be the same as the variance of the least-squares estimate divided by the square of the correlation coefficient, but it is not so when the condition of least squares is violated. However, if the condition is met, the statement holds, but we also have $\rho_{y_1 f_1}^2 = 1$, which would imply the same expression, as is expected from the discussion above.

Extending the analysis to two inputs, it can be shown that (6.4) leads to[7]

$$(6.12) \qquad \sigma_{\alpha_1}^2 = \frac{\sigma_{00}}{n(1 - \rho_{12}^2)} \left\{ \frac{(\alpha_1 - 1)^2}{\sigma_{11}} + \frac{\alpha_1^2}{\sigma_{22}} - \frac{2(\alpha_1 - 1)(\alpha_1)\rho_{12}}{\sigma_1\sigma_2} \right\} .$$

Thus the variance is again inversely related to σ_{hh} and directly related to the square of the correlation coefficient (ρ_{12}^2) between f_1 and f_2. Hence a

---

[7] $\sigma_h = \sqrt{\sigma_{hh}}$.

desirable situation is to have f_1 and f_2 with large variances and uncorrelated.

It is interesting now to observe how the least-squares bias is related to the same parameters. To do so we can show that asymptotically the bias that was developed in Section 4.4 can be written as

$$\text{(6.13)} \qquad \tilde{\alpha} - \alpha = \bar{S}_{hh}^{-1}\, \bar{S}_{hf_0}.$$

Using (6.2) for evaluating (6.13), we obtain

$$\text{(6.14)} \qquad \tilde{\alpha} - \alpha = D^{-1}\sigma_{00}[B\sigma_{hh}B' + \sigma_{00}LL']^{-1}L.$$

Thus, conditions that decrease the variance of the instrumental variable estimates also lead to a decline in the bias of the least-squares estimates. In the simple case of one input, (6.14) takes the form

$$\text{(6.15)} \qquad \tilde{\alpha} - \alpha = (1-\alpha)\,\frac{\sigma_{00}}{\sigma_{00}+\sigma_{11}} = (1-\alpha)\,(1-\rho_{y_1 f_1}^2).$$

Thus, the bias is directly related to σ_{00} and inversely related to σ_{11}. But when conditions of least squares are met the bias is zero, since in this case $\rho_{y_1 f_1}^2 = 1$.

7. A Generalization: Nonvanishing Prices

The original discussion by Marschak and Andrews, as well as subsequent discussions of the same model, assumed no price variations among firms; consequently, the vector p in (1.4) is identically equal to zero. What emerges from the foregoing discussion is that a less restrictive assumption is appropriate, namely,

$$p_{hit} - p_{h.t} - p_{hi.} + p_{h..} = 0 \quad \text{for all } h, i, \text{ and } t.$$

Since a solution to the model is obtained by working with within-firm-year variations, interfirm differences in prices which remain constant over time, or follow a particular time pattern, are washed out in the analysis.[8] It is therefore possible that this model adequately covers some situations. However, the difficulty is that when price variations do exist the solution should be modified, and a different statistic has to be used. This statistic, as we shall see below, takes into account the variations in prices and represents, in fact, a more general case, which collapses to that of Section 4 where p^{IT} is zero. It is therefore appropriate to consider now the more general case.

---

[8] By the phrase "following a particular pattern over time," we mean differences that are equal to the year effect. That is $p_{hit} - p_{hi.} = p_{h.t} - p_{h..}$. The difference in prices between firms i and i'' is $p_{hit} - p_{hi't} = p_{hi.} - p_{hi'.}$ regardless of t.

We shall start with (1.4), which, after allowance for firm and year effect, can be written as

$$(7.1) \qquad\qquad Ay - w = f,$$

where $p^{IT} = w$, and (4.7) is now generalized to

$$(7.2) \qquad\qquad n \sum_f = A\overline{yy'}A' - A\overline{yw'} - \overline{wy'}A' + \overline{ww'}.$$

Using the partitioning

$$y = \left[\frac{y_0}{y_h} \right], \qquad w = \left[\frac{0}{w_h} \right],$$

we get

$$(7.3) \qquad\qquad A\overline{yw'} = \left[\begin{array}{c|c} 0 & \overline{y_0 w_h'} - \alpha'\overline{y_h w_h'} \\ \hline 0 & L\overline{y_0 w_h'} - \overline{y_h w_h'} \end{array} \right],$$

$$\overline{wy'}A' = (A\overline{yw'})',$$

and

$$(7.4) \qquad\qquad \overline{ww'} = \left[\begin{array}{c|c} 0 & 0 \\ \hline 0 & \overline{w_h w_h'} \end{array} \right];$$

and $A\overline{yy'}A'$ is the right side of (4.8) or as written explicitly in (4.9)–(4.11). We can now substitute (7.3), (7.4), and (4.9)–(4.11) to get explicit expressions for the components of Σ_f [σ_{00} is the same as in (4.9)]:

$$(7.5) \qquad \sigma_{0h}' = \sigma_{0h}'[\text{as in } (4.11)] - (\overline{y_0 w_h'} - \alpha'\overline{y_h w_h'}) \frac{1}{n}$$

$$= \frac{1}{n} \left\{ (\overline{y_0 y_0'}L' - \overline{y_0 y_h'} - \overline{y_0 w_h'}) - \alpha'(\overline{y_h y_0'}L' - \overline{y_h y_h'} - \overline{y_h w_h'}) \right\}$$

and by using $\sigma_{0h}' = 0$, we obtain

$$(7.6) \qquad \alpha' = (\overline{y_0 y_0'}L' - \overline{y_0 y_h'} - \overline{y_0 w_h'})(\overline{y_h y_0'}L' - \overline{y_h y_h'} - \overline{y_h w_h'})^{-1},$$

which replaces (4.12). Again, we can show that (7.6) is a solution for a system generated by using f_h as instrumental variables. Simply rewrite (7.5) as

$$(7.7) \qquad \sigma_{0h}' = \text{plim} (y_0 - \alpha' y_h)(y_0'L' - y_h' - w_h') = 0$$

or plim $(y_0 - \alpha' y_h)f_h' = 0$, by definition of f_h'. Thus the only difference is in the definition of f_h. The expression for $\sigma_{hh'}$ can be obtained in a similar way, but it may be more useful to approach it somewhat differently. Note that (7.1) can also be written as

$$(7.8) \qquad\qquad A(y + w) - (A + I)w = f,$$

where $(y + w)$ represents the log of the original variables measured in value terms (output being numéraire). But

$$(7.9) \qquad (A + I)w = \begin{bmatrix} 2 & -\alpha' \\ L & 0 \end{bmatrix} \begin{bmatrix} 0 \\ w_h \end{bmatrix} = \begin{bmatrix} -\alpha' w_h \\ 0 \end{bmatrix},$$

and Σ_f can be evaluated by using (7.8) rather than (7.2). By so doing, it can be shown that $\sigma_{hh'}$ can be represented by (4.10) except that the variables are now $(y + w)$ rather than y or, in other words, are measured in value terms. The result is

$$(7.10) \quad n\sigma_{hh'} = y_0 y_0' LL' - (y_h + w_h)y_0' L' - L y_0 (y_h' + w_h') + (y_h + w_h)(y_h + w_h)'.$$

In concluding this section we observe that the solution obtained in Section 4 is actually a special case of the more general one, which takes into account price variations. When no such variations exist, the solution in Section 4 is applicable. However, the contrary should be emphasized: when price variations do exist, the statistics developed in this section should be used instead. The reason for emphasizing this lies in the fact that often it will be impossible to follow this approach, owing to a lack of information on prices. For instance, it may be difficult to obtain data on prices of capital inputs. We shall therefore consider a different approach in Section 9.

8. Final Generalization: Nonvanishing Prices and Exogenous Inputs

We shall now conclude the generalization by accommodating the case in which some inputs are independent of the disturbance f_0. The problem was dealt with in Section 5 for the case in which there were no variations in prices.

Changing the formulation in (3.1), we can write

$$(8.1) \qquad \begin{bmatrix} 1 & -\alpha_1 & -\alpha_2 \\ L & -I & 0 \\ 0 & 0 & 0 \end{bmatrix} \begin{bmatrix} y_0 \\ y_1 \\ y_2 \end{bmatrix} - \begin{bmatrix} 0 \\ w_1 \\ 0 \end{bmatrix} = \begin{bmatrix} f_0 \\ f_1 \\ 0 \end{bmatrix},$$

where y_1 is the vector of H_1 inputs that are not independent of f_0, and y_2 is the vector of H_2 inputs that are independent of f_0. The other matrices are defined accordingly.

We use the approach of Section 5; the instrumental variables are now f_1 and y_2. We can then write

$$(8.2) \qquad \text{plim} f_0 \begin{bmatrix} f_1' \\ y_2' \end{bmatrix} = \text{plim} (y_0 - \alpha' y_h) \begin{bmatrix} L y_0 - y_1 - w_1 \\ y_2 \end{bmatrix}' = 0,$$

where $\alpha' = (\alpha'_1 \; \alpha'_2)$ and $y_h = \left[\begin{smallmatrix} y_1 \\ y_2 \end{smallmatrix} \right]$ and α' is obtained by solving

$$(8.3) \qquad \alpha' = \left[\begin{array}{c} \overline{y_0 y_0'} L' - \overline{y_0 y_1'} - \overline{y_0 w_1'} \\ \hline \overline{y_0 y_2'} \end{array} \right] \left[\begin{array}{c} \overline{y_h y_0'} L' - \overline{y_h y_1'} - \overline{y_h w_1'} \\ \hline \overline{y_h y_2'} \end{array} \right]^{-1}.$$

This is the most general solution. When $y_2 = 0$, then $y_h = y_1$ and (8.3) reduces to (7.6). If $w_1 = 0$ (that is, there are no price variations for the endogenous inputs), then (8.3) reduces to (5.4). We have already indicated that (7.6) and (5.4) are generalizations of (4.12), which by itself is a generalization of least-squares estimates.

The estimates for σ_{00} and $\sigma_{hh'}$ can be obtained as before:

$n\sigma_{00} = \overline{f_0 f_0'}$ is the same as (4.9).

$n\sigma_{h_1 h_1'} = \overline{f_1 f_1'}$ is the same as (7.10), with y_1 and w_1 now replacing y_h and w_h

in (7.10).

9. An Alternative Approach and the Decomposition of the Bias

From the discussion of Section 2, it appears that there are two sources for the bias of the regression coefficients. The first is the omission of the time and firm variables. The second is the dependence of some inputs on the "true" disturbance of the production function. The biases caused by those sources are referred to as the time and management bias and the simultaneous equations bias, respectively.[9] In this section we shall show how consistent estimates can be obtained not only for the production elasticities, but also for the components of the bias. Essentially, the procedure amounts to the elimination of the management and time bias by covariance analysis, and the elimination of the simultaneous equations bias by using lagged values as instrumental variables.[10] The justification for this procedure is the very reason for which we did not accept the assumption of independence between x_h and u_0. In terms of the discussion in Section 2, the inputs at the harvest stage are affected by the disturbances of the earlier stages and hence the dependence is established. However, it is clear that inputs of last year are independent of the disturbance of the present year. We shall thus consider three sets of coefficients, those obtained from (a) regression analysis, (b) covariance analysis, and (c) instrumental variables.

---

[9] In this section we are avoiding the term "least-squares bias" since we shall want to compare the bias of a regular regression with that obtained from covariance analysis, both of which are least-squares procedures.

[10] For the use of lagged values as instrumental variables in consumption study, see Nissan Liviatan, Tests of the Permanent-Income Hypothesis Based on a Reinterview Savings Survey, in this volume, pp. 29-59.

These will then be utilized for obtaining consistent estimates of the production elasticities and of the components of the bias.

In this section it will be more convenient to use the original notation for covariance analysis (that is, x^{IT} instead of y, and z^{IT} instead of w). The three sets of estimates are

(9.1)   regression $\hat{\alpha} = (x_h x_h')^{-1} (x_h x_0')$,

(9.2)   covariance analysis $\hat{\hat{\alpha}} = (x_h^{IT} x_h^{IT'})^{-1} (x_h^{IT} x_0^{IT'})$,

(9.3)   instrumental variables $\tilde{\alpha} = (x_{h-1} x_h')^{-1} (x_{h-1} x_0')$,

where x_{h-1} equals the matrix of inputs of year $t-1$.

Rewriting (2.1) and (2.4) as

$$x_0 = \alpha' x_h + \epsilon_0 \,,$$

$$x_0^{IT} = \alpha' x_h^{IT} + u_0^{IT} \,,$$

and substituting in (9.1)–(9.3), we get

(9.4) $\hat{\alpha} = \alpha + (x_h x_h')^{-1} (x_h \epsilon_0')$,

(9.5) $\hat{\hat{\alpha}} = \alpha + (x_h^{IT} x_h^{IT'})^{-1} (x_h^{IT} u_0^{IT'})$,

(9.6) $\tilde{\alpha} = \alpha + (x_{h-1} x_h')^{-1} (x_{h-1} \epsilon_0')$.

The bias in (9.4) can now be decomposed by considering the various components of ϵ_0. The vector $(x_h x_h')^{-1}(x_h k_0')$ represents the bias due to omission of the year effect from the regression. Similarly, the vector $(x_h x_h')^{-1}(x_h m_0')$ represents the bias due to the omission of the management term.[11]

A similar interpretation, but in terms of the instrumental variables, can be given to the bias in (9.6). The vector $(x_h x_h')$ $(x_h u_0')$ represents the simultaneous equations bias that reflects the dependence of the inputs on u_0'. A similar interpretation is given to the bias in (9.5). In order to get a better insight into the determinants of the bias and the procedure for solving for α and for the bias components, we proceed as follows:

From (1.6) and (1.7) we derive for x_h

(9.7) $x_h = G(p + \epsilon)$

for $G = D\,(L \vdots B)$.

---

[11] In terms of the discussion of specification error, the two vectors represent coefficients of auxiliary regressions, that of technology (k_0) on the inputs and that of management on inputs. For empirical evaluation of the latter coefficients, see [8].

Substituting (9.7) in (9.4)–(9.6), write out ϵ, evaluate plim (denoted by a bar), and assume $E(u_t u_{t-1}) = 0$. We get

$$\hat{\alpha} = \alpha + \bar{c}_{11} + \bar{c}_{12} ,$$

(9.8)
$$\hat{\hat{\alpha}} = \alpha + 0 + \bar{c}_{22} ,$$

$$\tilde{\alpha} = \alpha + \bar{c}_{31} + 0 ,$$

where

$$\bar{c}_{11} = (\overline{x_h x_h'})^{-1} G \left[\overline{p(k_0' + m_0')} + kk_0' + \sum_{m_0} \right] ,$$

$$\bar{c}_{31} = (\overline{x_{h-1} x_h'})^{-1} G \left[\overline{p_{-1}(k_0' + m_0')} + k_{-1} k_0' + \sum_{m_0} \right] ,$$

$$\bar{c}_{12} = (\overline{x_h x_h'})^{-1} G \left[\sum_{u_0} \right] ,$$

$$\bar{c}_{22} = (\overline{x_h^{IT} x_h^{IT'}})^{-1} G \left[\sum_{u_0} \right] \frac{(T-1)(I-1)}{IT} .$$

The terms $\bar{c}_{11}$ and $\bar{c}_{31}$ indicate the plim of the bias terms due to management and year effects. The terms involving price disappear when prices are not correlated with management and technology. This, of course, includes the case of no price variations. No generalization can be made along this line, except that even if correlation does exist we can perhaps assume that $(p - p_{-1})(k_0' + m_0') = 0$, that is, that the first differences in time are uncorrelated with technology and management.

The term $k_t k_{0t}'$ is the first column of $k_t k_t'$. Again, it is assumed that $(k_t - k_{t-1}) k_0' = 0$.

Under these two assumptions, we can then write

$$\bar{c}_{31} = \lambda_1 \bar{c}_{11} \quad \text{for } \lambda_1 = (\overline{x_{h-1} x_h'})^{-1} (\overline{x_h x_h'}) .$$

Using (4.4), we can write

$$\bar{c}_{22} = \lambda_2 \bar{c}_{12} \quad \text{for } \lambda_2 = (\overline{x_h^{IT} x_h^{IT'}})^{-1} (\overline{x_h x_h'}) \frac{(T-1)(I-1)}{TI} ,$$

and instead of (9.8) we can now write

$$\hat{\alpha} = \alpha + \bar{c}_{11} + \bar{c}_{12} ,$$

(9.9)
$$\hat{\hat{\alpha}} = \alpha + 0 + \lambda_2 \bar{c}_{12} ,$$

$$\tilde{\alpha} = \alpha + \lambda_1 \bar{c}_{11} + 0 ,$$

which yields the solution[12]

(9.10) $$\bar{c}_{11} = \lambda_1^{-1}(\bar{\tilde{\alpha}} - \alpha)\,, \qquad \bar{c}_{12} = \lambda_2^{-1}(\bar{\tilde{\tilde{\alpha}}} - \alpha)\,,$$

(9.11) $$\alpha = (I - \lambda_1^{-1} - \lambda_2^{-1})^{-1}\,(\bar{\tilde{\alpha}} - \lambda_1^{-1}\bar{\tilde{\alpha}} - \lambda_2^{-1}\bar{\tilde{\tilde{\alpha}}})\,.$$

The use of sample values instead of plim yields a consistent estimator for α and for the various bias components. The bias components depend on p and therefore should not necessarily remain constant over time.

Strictly speaking, this approach may be the most appropriate one to use. We need assume nothing about price variations, or about classification of inputs as endogenous or exogenous, or about independence of $u_0 u_h$.

This approach may also be more efficient than the one discussed in the previous sections. In both cases we depend on covariance analysis for the elimination of the management and time bias. However, in the elimination of the simultaneous equations bias we are now using a better instrumental variable; instead of dealing with deviations from the firm-year averages we get full advantage of the spread that exists between firms and possibly over time. In fact, the larger the firm-time effects are, the better are the results we can expect to obtain from this method. This is especially true if there is a good spread in m_{hi} and k_{ht}, which will reduce the intercorrelation between the instrumental variables and thus will increase their efficiency.

10. Estimation from Factor Shares

Going back to equation (4.2), it was then stated that the equations of the first-order conditions are always identified. This property was used by Klein in proposing the estimation of the elasticities from their factor shares [4]. The estimate is

(10.1) $$\breve{\alpha}_h'' = \frac{I}{IT} \sum_i \sum_t \log \frac{X_h}{X_0}\, P_h\,,$$

but from (1.4) we have

$$\log\left(\frac{X_h}{X_0}\, P_h\right) = \alpha_h'' - (k_{ht} + m_{hi} + u_{hit})\,,$$

and hence

(10.2) $$E\,(\breve{\alpha}_h'') = \alpha_h'' - \Delta_h - \frac{I}{IT} \sum \sum E\,(u_{hit})\,,$$

---

[12] Equation (9.11) can then be reduced to

$$\alpha = \left[x_h x_h' - x_{h-1} x_h' - dx_h^{IT} x_h^{IT'}\right]^{-1} \left[x_h x_0' - x_{h-1} x_0' - dx_h^{IT} x_0^{IT'}\right]\,,$$

where $d = (I - 1)(T - 1)/IT'$.

where

$$\varDelta_h = \frac{E}{IT} \sum_i \sum_t (m_{hi} + k_{ht}) \, .$$

Here $\overset{\vee}{\alpha}_h''$ is an unbiased estimator of α_h'' if $E(u_h) = 0$ and $\varDelta_h = 0$. The introduction of the parameter $\varDelta_h$ secures the first equality, but it is not clear that $\varDelta_h$ will always be zero. The parameter $\varDelta_h$ measures the average discrepancy in the population from the first-order conditions. A value different from zero implies that some additional considerations are taken into account by the firms in making their decision. These considerations are not traced out or formulated explicitly in our analysis, but their net effect is allowed for by introducing the variables M_{hi} and K_{ht}, whose logarithms are not required to distribute with zero means around α''. Whether the bias $\varDelta_h$ is large or not is a matter of fact that could only be found out empirically. In fact, many of the empirical estimations of production function are undertaken with the aim of finding whether firms do equate the value of the marginal productivities to the corresponding wages, hence following the method of the factor shares would be to assume an answer to the question asked. Aside from this, it should be pointed out that at best we only have an unbiased estimator for $\log \alpha_h$, whereas the estimator of α_h itself is consistent.

On the positive side, the virtues of this method are (1) It does not require repeated observations on the same firms—cross-section data are sufficient. (2) It yields estimates that are free from the simultaneous equations bias and that are very simple to compute. Thus, it seems that if the problem of simultaneity is serious, this method solves it—at some cost, but it may not be too high. This cost could be reduced by using a combination of the factor share and covariance analysis. Such an approach would utilize the fact that the inputs which cause the violation of the assumptions of least-squares estimates are those whose estimated elasticities are likely to have low, and perhaps zero, bias when estimated by their factor shares. On the other hand, the inputs whose estimates by factor shares are likely to have large bias meet the assumption of the least-squares estimates. To justify this statement we emphasize that the main source for the variable m_{hi} and k_{ht} is uncertainty, either with respect to the outcome of the production process or with respect to market prices. At the later stages of the production process both sources of uncertainty are reduced and therefore the m_h's of inputs that are used mainly at this stage are likely to have a narrow spread around a value of zero. In the extreme case, when all is known, there would be no reason—except mistakes that balance off— to deviate from the first-order condition. Thus the elasticities of inputs that are acquired or used at the later stages of the production process could be estimated from their factor shares. As we further recall, the limitations of using least-squares estimates of a single equation rose from the dependence of inputs used at the later stages of the production process on the disturbances realized at the earlier stages.[13] If estimates for the elasticities of these inputs are now available, the problem may be resolved. To illustrate, we shall consider the estimation of (2.10) where x_2 is not independent of the error term. Let $\check{\beta}_2$ be the factor share estimate of β_2. We can then rewrite (2.10) as

$$(10.3) \qquad \bar{x}_{02} = x_{02} - \check{\beta}_2 x_2 = \beta_1 x_1 + (\beta_2 - \check{\beta}_2)x_2 + u \ ,$$

and the least-squares estimate for β_1,

$$\hat{\beta}_1 = \frac{\sum \bar{x}_{02} x_1}{\sum x_1^2} \ ,$$

is consistent as long as $\check{\beta}_2$ is consistent.

REFERENCES

[1] DURBIN, J., Errors in the Variables, *Rev. Inst. Internat. Statistique*, **22**, 1 (March 1954), 23-33.

[2] HOCH, IRVING, Simultaneous Equation Bias in the Context of the Cobb-Douglas Production Function, *Econometrica*, **26**, 4 (October 1958), 566-78.

[3] HOCH, IRVING, Estimation of Production Function Parameters Combining Time Series and Cross Section Data, *Econometrica* (forthcoming).

[4] KLEIN, LAWRENCE R., *A Textbook of Econometrics*. Evanston, Ill.: Row, Peterson, 1953.

[5] KOOPMANS, TJALLING C., Identification Problems in WILLIAM C. HOOD and T. C. KOOPMANS (eds.), *Economic Model Construction, Studies in Econometric Methods* (Cowles Commission for Research in Economics, Monograph 14). New York: Wiley, 1953.

[6] LIVIATAN, NISSAN, Errors in Variables and Engel Curve Analysis, *Econometrica*, **29**, 3 (1961), 336-63.

[7] MARSCHAK, J., and WILLIAM H. ANDREWS, JR., Random Simultaneous Equations and the Theory of Production, *Econometrica*, **12**, 3 & 4 (July & October, 1944), 143-206.

[8] MUNDLAK, YAIR, Empirical Production Function Free of Management Bias, *J. Farm Econ.*, **43**, 1 (February 1961), 44-56.

[9] MUNDLAK, YAIR, "A Specification of Production Function and Economic Behavior and Its Implication." University of California, Berkeley, Giannini Foundation Mimeographed Report (forthcoming).

[10] MUNDLAK, YAIR, "Economic Analysis of Established Family Farms in Israel." Falk Project for Economic Research in Israel (forthcoming).

---

[13] See Section 2.

[11] NERLOVE, MARC, "Notes on the Identification and Estimation of Cobb-Douglas Production Functions." Duplicated (revised May 18, 1959).

[12] SARGAN, J. D., The Estimation of Economic Relationships Using Instrumental Variables, *Econometrica*, **26**, 3 (July 1958), 393-416.

[13] WALTERS, A. A., "Some Notes on Simultaneous Equations and the Cobb-Douglas Production Function." Series A, Report No. 17, Faculty of Commerce and Social Science, University of Birmingham, Birmingham, England, June 1960.

7

Returns to Scale in Electricity Supply

MARC NERLOVE, *Stanford University*

The study of returns to scale in public-utility enterprises has a long, if not always honorable, history. The question of whether there are increasing or decreasing returns to scale and over what range of output has, as we know, an important bearing on the institutional arrangements necessary to secure an optimal allocation of resources. If, as many writers in the field appear to believe, there are increasing returns to scale over the relevant range of outputs produced by utility undertakings, then these companies must either receive subsidies or resort to price discrimination in order to cover costs at socially optimal outputs.

In addition, as Chenery [2] has pointed out, the extent of returns to scale is a determinant of investment policies in growing industries. If there are increasing returns to scale and a growing demand, firms may find it profitable to add more capacity than they expect to use in the immediate future.

In studying the problem of returns to scale, the first question one must ask is "To what use are the results to be put?" It is inevitable that the purpose of an analysis should affect its form. In particular, the reason for obtaining an estimate of returns to scale will affect the *level* of the analysis: industry, firm, or plant. For many questions of pricing policy, for example, the plant is the relevant entity. On the other hand, when questions of taxation are at issue, the industry may be the appropriate unit of analysis. But if we are concerned primarily with the general question of public regulation and with investment decisions and the like, it would seem that the economically relevant entity is the firm. Firms, not plants are regulated, and it is at the level of the firm that investment decisions are made.

The U.S. electric power industry is a regulated public utility. Privately

I am indebted for a great deal of helpful advice to I. Adelman, K. J. Arrow, A. R. Ferguson, W. R. Hughes, S. H. Nerlove, P. A. Samuelson, and H. Uzawa. Had I been able to take all the advice I received, perhaps I could lay a part of the blame for the deficiencies of this paper on these people. The situation, however, is otherwise.

Support, in part, for the research on which this paper is based has been received from the Department of Economics, University of Minnesota, and under a grant from the Rockefeller Foundation at Stanford University. Stenographic assistance was received from the Office of Naval Research under Contract Nonr-225(50).

I wish also to acknowledge the help of M. S. Arora, G. Fishman, J. Johnston, H. Kanemitsu, and N. K. Rao, who performed the computations on which this paper is based.

owned firms, with which I am exclusively concerned in this study, account for nearly 80 per cent of all power produced. The technological and institutional characteristics of the electric power industry that are important for the model I shall develop are as follows:

1. Power cannot be economically stored in large quantities and, with few exceptions, must be supplied on demand.
2. Revenues from the sale of power by private companies depend primarily on rates set by utility commissions and other regulatory bodies.
3. Much of the fuel used in power production is purchased under long-term contracts at set prices. The level of prices is determined in competition with other uses.
4. The industry is heavily unionized, and wage rates are also set by contracts that extend over a period of time. Over long periods, wages appear to be determined competitively.
5. The capital market in which utilities seek funds for expansion is highly competitive and the rates at which individual utilities can borrow funds are little affected by individual actions over a wide range. Construction costs vary geographically and also appear to be unaffected by an individual utility's actions.

From these characteristics we may draw two conclusions, which lead to the model presented below. First, it is plausible to regard the output of a firm and the prices it pays for factors of production as exogenous, despite the fact that the industry does not operate in perfectly competitive markets. Second, the problem of the individual firm in the industry would appear to be that of minimizing the total costs of production of a given output, subject to the production function and the prices it must pay for factors of production. I shall adopt this last conclusion in what follows, although it is subject to some qualifications.

There are two basic objections to the cost-minimization hypothesis. First, rates in the industry are governed by a "cost plus" principle designed to secure investors "a fair return on fair value" (whatever that may mean). Although the application of this principle is a complicated matter in practice, it is clear that if a utility minimizes costs too much, i.e., decreases its costs to such an extent that, under the current rate structure, it obtains a substantial increment in earnings, the regulatory body may initiate an investigation and wipe out the increment through a decrease in rates. My impression, however, is that most utilities operate at a considerable distance from this "danger point."

A second objection to the cost-minimization hypothesis is that it is implicitly static; i.e., it does not reflect the fact that utilities are less concerned with cost minimization at a *point in time* than they are with minimization *over time*. In a dynamic formulation capital costs may be particularly affected. However, two contrary tendencies seem to exist: On the one hand, a steady rate of technological improvement has been experienced and may be expected to continue in this industry; thus, it is advantageous to postpone investment commitments. On the other hand, if there are increasing returns to scale, the steady growth in demand might be expected, *à la* Chenery [2], to lead to capital expenditures in excess of current needs. This tendency to over-capitalization may be aided and abetted by rate commissions, which are often inclined to support it after the fact through an increase in rates.

A related objection has been raised by William Hughes. He pointed out, in effect, that the existence of several power pools among companies treated separately in my analysis means that the outputs of such companies may not be truly exogenous as I have assumed.

Previous empirical investigations that have a bearing on returns to scale in electricity supply are those of Johnston [10, pp. 44-73], Komiya [11], Lomax [12], and Nordin [16]. All of these are concerned with returns to scale at the level of the plant, not the firm, and present evidence which suggests that there are increasing or constant returns to scale in the production of electricity. It is shown in Appendix A, however, that because of transmission losses and the expenses of maintaining and operating an extensive transmission network, a firm may operate a number of plants at outputs in the range of increasing returns to scale and yet be in the region of decreasing returns when considered as a unit. Although firms as a whole have been treated in this investigation, the problem of transmission and its effects on returns to scale has not been incorporated in the analysis, which relates only to the *production* of electricity. The results of this analysis are in agreement with those of previous investigators and suggest that the bulk of privately owned U.S. utilities operate in the region of increasing returns to scale, as is generally believed. Nevertheless, the results also suggest that the *extent* of returns to scale at the firm level is overestimated by analyses that deal with individual plants.

As indicated in Table 1, the production of electric power is carried out in three main ways:

1. By internal combustion engines. This method accounts for a negligible fraction of the power produced.

2. By hydroelectric installations. This method accounts for about one-third of all U.S. power production.

3. By steam-driven installations. This method accounts for the remaining two-thirds of U.S. power production.

Few firms rely solely on hydroelectric production because of the unreliability of supply. Furthermore, suitable sites for hydroelectric installations are rather limited and, except for those sites requiring an immense capital investment, almost fully exploited. Because of the great qualitative difference between steam and hydraulic production of electricity, this analysis is limited to steam generation. Since the variable costs of hydro-electric production are extremely low and it appears that firms fully exploit these possibilities, neglect of hydraulic generation should little affect the results on returns to scale.

The costs of steam-electric generation consist of (a) energy costs, and (b) capacity costs. The former consist mainly of the costs of fuel, of which coal is the principal one (see Table 2). Energy costs tend to vary with total output, and depend little on the distribution of demand through time. Capacity costs include interest, depreciation, maintenance, and most labor costs; these costs tend to vary, not with total output, but with the maximum anticipated demand for power (i.e., the peak load). Unfortunately, available data do not permit an adequate treatment of the peak-load dimension of output, hence it has been neglected in this study.

Even if the temporal distribution of demand does not differ systemat-ically from one size firm to another, however, the results may be affected. A large firm with many plants and operating over a wide area has a greater

TABLE 1

PER CENT OF TOTAL KILOWATT-HOURS PRODUCED
BY TYPE OF PLANT, 1930–1950, U.S.

Year	Steam Generating Plants	Hydroelectric Installations	Internal Combustion Engines
1930	65.1	34.2	0.7
1940	65.6	33.4	1.0
1950	69.8	29.1	1.1

TABLE 2

PER CENT OF TOTAL STEAM-ELECTRIC GENERATION (KWH)
BY TYPE OF FUEL, 1930–1950, U.S.

Year	Coal	Oil	Gas
1930	84.8	4.7	10.5
1940	81.9	6.6	11.5
1950	66.4	14.5	19.1

Source: R. E. Caywood, *Electric Utility Rate Economics*. New York: McGraw-Hill, 1956.

diversity of customers; hence, a large firm is more likely to have a peak load that is a small percentage of output than a small firm. It follows that capacity costs per unit of output tend to be less for larger firms. But this is a real economy of scale, and one reason for looking at firms rather than plants is precisely to take account of such phenomena. Of course, explicit introduction of peak-load characteristics would be better than the implicit account that is taken here.

1. The Model Used

As indicated, the characteristics of the electric power industry suggest that a plausible model of behavior is cost minimization, and that output and factor prices may be treated as exogenous. This suggests that traditional estimation of a production function from cross-section data on inputs and output is incorrect; fortunately, it also suggests a correct procedure. Let

c = total production costs,

y = output (measured in kwh),

x_1 = labor input,

x_2 = capital input,

x_3 = fuel input,

p_1 = wage rate,

p_2 = "price" of capital,

p_3 = price of fuel,

u = a residual expressing neutral variations in efficiency among firms.

Suppose that firms have production functions of a generalized Cobb-Douglas type:

$$(1) \qquad y = a_0 x_1^{a_1} x_2^{a_2} x_3^{a_3} u .$$

Minimization of costs,

$$(2) \qquad c = p_1 x_1 + p_2 x_2 + p_3 x_3 ,$$

implies the familiar marginal productivity conditions:

$$(3) \qquad \frac{p_1 x_1}{a_1} = \frac{p_2 x_2}{a_2} = \frac{p_3 x_3}{a_3} .$$

If the efficiency of firms varies neutrally,[1] as indicated by the error term in (1), and the prices paid for factors vary from firm to firm, then the levels of input are not determined independently but are determined jointly by the firm's efficiency, level of output, and the factor prices it must pay. In short, a fitted relationship between inputs and output is a *confluent* relation that does not describe the production function at all but only the net effects of differences among firms. (For a more general discussion, see [13, 15].)

In such cases, however, it may be possible to fit the *reduced form* of a system of structural relations such as (1) and (3) and to derive estimates of the structural parameters from estimates of the reduced-form parameters. Not only does it turn out to be possible in this case, but an important reduced form turns out to be the cost function:

(4) $$c = k y^{1/r} p_1^{a_1/r} p_2^{a_2/r} p_3^{a_3/r} v \, ,$$

where

$$k = r(a_0 a_1^{a_1} a_2^{a_2} a_3^{a_3})^{-1/r} \, ,$$

$$v = u^{-1/r} \, ,$$

and

$$r = a_1 + a_2 + a_3 \, .$$

The parameter r measures the degree of returns to scale. The fundamental duality between cost and production functions, demonstrated by Shephard [17], assures us that the relation between the cost function, obtained empirically, and the underlying production function is unique.[2] Under the cost minimization assumption, they are simply two different, but equivalent ways of looking at the same thing.

Note that the cost function must include factor prices if the correspondence is to be unique. The problem of changing (over time) or differing (in a cross section) factor prices is an old one in statistical cost analysis; see [10, pp. 170-76]. Most generally, it seems to have been handled by deflating cost figures by an index of factor prices, a procedure that Johnston [10] shows typically leads to bias in the estimation of the cost

---

[1] A model incorporating non-neutral variations in efficiency of the form

$$y = (a_0 u_0) x_1^{a_1 u_1} x_2^{a_2 u_2} x_1^{a_3 u_3}$$

was discussed in my paper "On Measurement of Relative Economic Efficiency," abstract, *Econometrica*, 28 (July 1960), 695. It is interesting to note that despite the complex way in which the random elements u_0, u_1, and u_2 enter, there are circumstances under which it is possible to estimate the parameters in such a production function.

[2] I owe this point to Hirofumi Uzawa. It is true, of course, only if all firms have the same production function, except perhaps for differences in the constant term, so that aggregation difficulties may be neglected.

curve unless correct weights, which depend on (unknown) parameters of the production function, are used. It seems strange that no one has taken the obvious step of *including factor prices directly in the cost function*. If price data are available for the construction of an index and prices do not move proportionately, in which case no bias would result from deflation, why not use the extra information afforded?

What form of production function is appropriate for electric power? The generalized Cobb-Douglas function presented above is attractive for two reasons: First, it leads to a cost function that is linear in the logarithms of the variables

$$(5) \qquad C = K + \frac{1}{r} Y + \frac{a_1}{r} P_1 + \frac{a_2}{r} P_2 + \frac{a_3}{r} P_3 + \mathrm{V} \,,$$

where capital letters denote logarithms of the corresponding lower-case letters. The linearity of (5) makes it especially easy to estimate. Second, a single estimate of returns to scale is possible (it is the reciprocal of the coefficient of the logarithm of output), and returns to scale do not depend on output or factor prices. (The last-mentioned advantage turns out to be a defect as we shall see when we come to examine a few statistical results.) But does such a function accurately characterize the conditions of production in the electric power industry?

A casual examination of trade publications suggests that once a plant is built, fixed proportions are more nearly the rule. Support for this view is given by Komiya [11], who found that data on inputs and output for individual plants were better approximated by a fixed-proportions model that allowed differences in the proportions due to scale. A simplified version of Komiya's model is[3]

$$x_1 = a_1 y^{b_1} \,,$$
$$(6) \qquad x_2 = a_2 y^{b_2} \,,$$
$$x_3 = a_3 y^{b_3} \,.$$

At the firm level, however, there are many possibilities for substitution that may go unnoticed at the plant level; for example, labor and fuel may be substituted for capital by using older, less efficient plants more intensively or by using a large number of small plants rather than a few large ones.

---

[3] Since y is exogenous, it would be appropriate to estimate the coefficients in (6) by least squares. An objection to this, however, is the fact that, if individual plants are considered, the output allocated to *each* is not exogenous; see Westfield [19, pp. 15-81). Furthermore, Komiya does not use output but name-plate rated capacity and input levels adjusted to full capacity operation. It is even more doubtful whether the former can be considered as exogenous in a cross section. My objection here is closely related to the one raised by Hughes (see p. 169); however, while the endogenicity of output at the plant level is clear, its endogenicity at the firm level for a member of a power pool is conjectural.

Given persistent differences in the factor prices paid by different firms, cross-section data should reflect such possibilities of substitution. Certainly, as a provisional hypothesis, a generalized Cobb-Douglas function may be appropriate.

It would, of course, be preferable to *test* whether significant substitution among factors occurs at the firm level. The use of the generalized Cobb-Douglas unfortunately does not permit us to do so except in a very general way, since its form implies that the elasticity of substitution between any pair of factors is one. A more general form, which has both the Cobb-Douglas and fixed coefficients as limiting cases, has recently been suggested by Arrow, Minhas, Chenery, and Solow [1]. Constant returns to scale are assumed, but the form can be easily generalized; in a more general form it is

$$(7) \qquad y = [a_1 x_1^b + a_2 x_2^b + a_3 x_3^b]^{1/f}.$$

In this case returns to scale are given by the ratio b/f and the elasticity of substitution between any pair of factors can be shown to be $1/(1 - b)$. In the special case in which $b = f$ it can be shown that the limiting form of (7) as the elasticity of substitution goes to zero is

$$(8) \quad y = \min \left\{ \frac{x_1}{(a_1 + a_2 + a_3)^{1/b} - 1}, \frac{x_2}{(a_1 + a_2 + a_3)^{1/b} - 1}, \frac{x_3}{(a_1 + a_2 + a_3)^{1/b} - 1} \right\},$$

or fixed coefficients, and the limiting form as the elasticity of substitution goes to one is

$$(9) \qquad y = (a_1 + a_2 + a_3)^{1/b} x_1^{a_1/(a_1+a_2+a_3)} x_2^{a_2/(a_1+a_2+a_3)} x_3^{a_3/(a_1+a_2+a_3)},$$

or Cobb-Douglas. Although I have not formally demonstrated the fact, it is possible that the limiting form of the more general case (7) is something like the Komiya model as the elasticity of substitution tends to zero, and like the generalized Cobb-Douglas as it tends to one.

Unfortunately, in its generalized form (7) is quite difficult to estimate from the data available. Furthermore, although clearly superior to the generalized Cobb-Douglas form, (7) still implies that the elasticity of substitution between any pair of factors (e.g., labor capital and fuel capital) is the same, which hardly seems reasonable. Other generalizations are possible, but none that I have found thus far offers much hope of being amenable to a reasonable estimation procedure.

If the generalized Cobb-Douglas form is adopted, however, relatively simple estimation procedures can be devised for evaluating the parameters of the production function. The reduced form of (1) and (3) that incorporates all but one of the restrictions on the parameters in the derived demand equations (which are the more usual reduced form) is nothing but the cost function.

The only restriction not incorporated in (4) or (5) is that the coefficients of the prices must add up to one. It is a simple matter to incorporate this restriction, however, by dividing costs and two of the prices by the remaining price (it doesn't matter either economically or statistically which price we choose). When fuel price is used as the divisor, the result is

$$(10) \qquad C - P_3 = K + \frac{1}{r} Y + \frac{a_1}{r} (P_1 - P_3) + \frac{a_2}{r} (P_2 - P_3) + V,$$

which will be called Model A.

Model A assumes that we have relevant data on the "price" of capital and that this price varies significantly from firm to firm. If neither is the case, we are in trouble. Most of the results presented here are based on Model A, but the data used for this price of capital are clearly inadequate. (See Appendix B.) If one supposes, however, that the price of capital is the same for all firms, which is not implausible, one can do without data on capital price and use the restriction on the coefficients of output and prices to estimate the elasticity of output with respect to capital input. The assumption that capital price is the same for all firms implies

$$(11) \qquad\qquad C = K' + \frac{1}{r} Y + \frac{a_1}{r} P_1 + \frac{a_3}{r} P_3 + V,$$

where $K' = K + (a_2/r)P_2$, since the exponents of the input levels in (1) are assumed to be the same for all firms. Equation (11) is called Model B.

2. Some Statistical Results and Their Interpretation

Estimation of Model A from a cross section of firms requires that we obtain data on production costs, total physical output, and the prices of labor, capital, and fuel for each firm; for Model B we do not need the price of capital, since it is assumed to be the same for all firms. Details of the construction of these data for a sample of 145 privately owned utilities in 1955 are given in Appendix B and are not discussed here at any length. Suffice it to say that these data are far from adequate for the purpose, and I now believe that a better job could have been done with other sources.

The results from the least-squares regression suggested by equation (10) are given in line I of Table 3; the interpretation of these results in terms of the parameters of the production function is given in line I of Table 4. The R^2 is 0.93, which is somewhat unusual for such a large number of observations; increasing returns to scale are indicated, and the elasticities of output with respect to labor and fuel have the right sign and are of plausible magnitude; however, the elasticity of output with respect to capital price has the wrong sign (fortunately, it is statistically insignificant).

TABLE 3

RESULTS FROM REGRESSIONS BASED ON MODEL A FOR 145 FIRMS IN 1955

Regression No.	Coefficient				R^2
	Y	$P_1 - P_3$	$P_2 - P_3$	x	
I	0.721 (±.175)	0.562 (±.198)	−0.003 (±.192)	—	0.931
II	0.696 (±.173)	0.512 (±.199)	0.033 (±.185)	−0.046 (±.022)	0.932
IIIA	0.398 (±.079)	0.641 (±.691)	−0.093 (±.669)	—	0.512
IIIB	0.668 (±.116)	0.105 (±.275)	0.364 (±.277)	—	0.635
IIIC	0.931 (±.198)	0.408 (±.199)	0.249 (±.189)	—	0.571
IIID	0.915 (±.108)	0.472 (±.174)	0.133 (±.157)	—	0.871
IIIE	1.045 (±.065)	0.604 (±.197)	−0.295 (±.175)	—	0.920
IVA	0.394 (±.055)			—	
IVB	0.651 (±.189)			—	
IVC	0.877 (±.376)	0.435 (±.207)	0.100 (±.196)	—	0.950
IVD	0.908 (±.354)			—	
IVE	1.062 (±.169)			—	

Figures in parentheses are the standard errors of the coefficients.

The dependent variable in all analyses was $C - P_3$.

The variables are defined as follows:

C = log costs Y = log output P_1 = log wage rate P_2 = log capital "price"

$$P_3 = \text{log fuel price} \qquad x = \left| \frac{\text{output 1955} - \text{output 1954}}{\text{output 1954}} \right|.$$

TABLE 4

RETURNS TO SCALE AND ELASTICITIES OF OUTPUT WITH RESPECT TO VARIOUS INPUTS DERIVED
FROM RESULTS PRESENTED IN TABLE 3 FOR 145 FIRMS IN 1955

Regression No.	Returns to Scale	Elasticity of Output with Respect to		
		Labor	Capital	Fuel
I	1.39	0.78	−0.00	0.61
II	1.44	0.74	0.01	0.69
IIIA	2.52	1.61	−0.02	0.93
IIIB	1.50	0.16	0.53	0.81
IIIC	1.08	0.44	0.27	0.37
IIID	1.09	0.52	0.15	0.42
IIIE	0.96	0.58	−0.29	0.67
IVA	2.52	1.10	0.25	1.17
IVB	1.53	0.65	0.15	0.73
IVC	1.14	0.50	0.11	0.53
IVD	1.10	0.48	0.11	0.51
IVE	0.94	0.41	0.09	0.44

The difficulties with capital may be due in part to the difficulty I encountered in measuring both capital costs and the price of capital. The former
were measured as depreciation charges plus the proportion of interest on
long-term debt attributable to the production plant; the figure for capital
price was compounded of the yield on the firm's long-term debt and an
index of construction costs. Depreciation figures reflect past prices and
purchases of capital equipment, whereas the price of capital as I constructed
it does not; it is perhaps not so surprising then that the price has little
effect on costs. Model B is designed to evade this difficulty. Results based
on Model B are presented in line V of Table 5 and the implications of this
regression for the parameters in the production function are given in line V
of Table 6. It is apparent that the estimates of returns to scale and the
elasticities of output with respect to labor and fuel are changed very little;

TABLE 5

RESULTS FROM REGRESSIONS BASED ON MODEL B FOR 145 FIRMS IN 1955.
DEPENDENT VARIABLE WAS $C = $ LOG COSTS

Regression No.	Coefficient			R^2
	Y	P_1	P_3	
V	0.723 ($\pm$.019)	0.483 ($\pm$.303)	0.496 ($\pm$.106)	0.914
VIA	0.361 ($\pm$.086)	0.212 ($\pm$1.259)	0.655 ($\pm$.350)	0.438
VIB	0.661 ($\pm$.106)	−0.401 ($\pm$.333)	0.490 ($\pm$.134)	0.672
VIC	0.985 ($\pm$.180)	−0.014 ($\pm$.261)	0.330 ($\pm$.138)	0.647
VID	0.927 ($\pm$.106)	0.327 ($\pm$.228)	0.426 ($\pm$.064)	0.884
VIE	1.035 ($\pm$.067)	0.704 ($\pm$.272)	0.643 ($\pm$.132)	0.934

Figures in parentheses are the standard errors of the coefficients.

TABLE 6

RETURNS TO SCALE AND ELASTICITIES OF OUTPUT WITH RESPECT TO VARIOUS INPUTS DERIVED
FROM RESULTS PRESENTED IN TABLE 5 FOR 145 FIRMS IN 1955.

Regression No.	Returns to Scale	Elasticity of Output with Respect to		
		Labor	Capital	Fuel
V	1.38	0.67	0.03	0.69
VIA	2.77	0.59	1.39	0.74
VIB	1.51	−0.62	0.69	0.33
VIC	1.02	−0.01	0.27	0.46
VID	1.08	0.35	−0.34	0.62
VIE	0.97	0.68	0.03	0.68

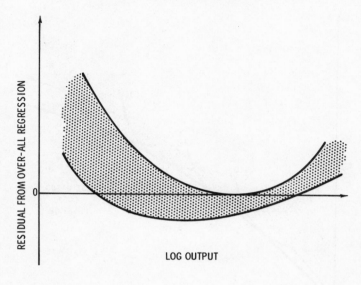

FIG. 1

the elasticity with respect to capital is of the right sign but still unreasonably low for an industry that is so capital-intensive.[4]

A second difficulty with these regressions is not apparent from an examination of the coefficients and their standard errors. As part of these analyses, the residuals from the regressions were plotted against the logarithm of output. The result is schematically pictured in Fig. 1. It is clear that neither regression relationship is truly linear in logarithms. To test this visual impression the observations were arranged in order of ascending output, and Durbin-Watson statistics were computed; the values of the statistics indicated highly significant positive serial correlation, which confirmed the visual evidence.

Aside from difficulties with the basic data, there appear to be at least two plausible and interesting hypotheses accounting for the result.

---

[4]K. Arrow has pointed out that considerations of plausibility implicitly involve an alternative method of estimating the coefficients in the production function: From the marginal productivity conditions (3), we find that for any pair of inputs i and j,

$$\frac{p_i x_i}{p_j x_j} = \frac{a_i}{a_j}.$$

Hence, by constructing some average of the ratios of expenditures on factors, we obtain estimates of the ratios of exponents in the production function. Had the data been arranged in such a manner as to facilitate computation of expenditures on individual factors, a comparison of the ratios a_i/a_j obtained in this way with those derived from the cost function would have been a useful supplement to the analysis. Arrow also pointed out that one could also verify the results by the fit of the production function derived from them. Unfortunately, it is not feasible to obtain good physical measures of the inputs, and such measures are required for this test.

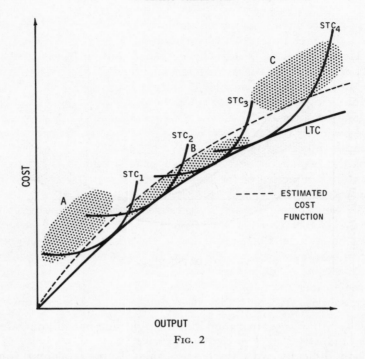

Fig. 2

1. The first explanation of the result derives from dynamic considerations closely related to those underlying Friedman's Permanent-Income Hypothesis [7]. The important thing to note is that actual costs are underestimated by the regressions at both high and low outputs. Consider the situation pictured in Fig. 2. Firms operate not on the long-run cost curve, but at points on the various short-run curves. If firms are evenly distributed about their optimal outputs (i.e., outputs at which long-run marginal cost equals short-run marginal cost), the effect will be to increase the estimate of the extent of increasing returns to scale if they are increasing, or diminish further the estimate of returns to scale if they are decreasing.[5] But elsewhere Friedman holds that a uniform distribution is not likely to occur; in fact he says, "The firms with the largest output are unlikely to be producing at an unusually low level: on the average they are likely to be producing at an unusually high level; and conversely for those that have the lowest output" [14, p. 237].

The situation described by Friedman is pictured in Fig. 2 by the shaded areas A, B, and C, which refer, respectively, to observations on firms with unusually low, usual, and unusually high outputs. The Friedman explana-

---

[5] This argument rests partly on the form of the function that constrains it to pass through the origin.

tion does produce a residual pattern similar to that observed. Regression II, Table 3, is designed to test this explanation for Model A. A corresponding test for Model B was not made. Since "usual" output cannot be directly observed, the hypothesis was modified slightly by identifying departure from the usual with large changes in output from the previous year, the assumption being that firms with stable output were likely to be near the optimal long-run output.[6] Thus, the absolute percentage changes in output should be positively related to total costs. Unfortunately, they are negatively related and significantly so.

Part of the explanation for this unexpected result is suggested by a more careful examination of the data. Almost all firms with large changes had positive changes and had been experiencing rapid growth for some time. It is well known, though unfortunately not taken into account in these analyses, that there is a steady rate of technological progress in generating equipment. Since expanding firms purchase new equipment in the process, the average age of a plant in those firms experiencing large changes in output is lower than that of firms with more stable outputs. Hence, the former tend to have lower costs because of the inadequacy of the capital-cost data to reflect obsolescence.[7] Thus, while one would not want to reject the Friedman hypothesis on the basis of this evidence, it clearly does not explain the residual pattern.

2. Fortunately, the observed result can be explained by a much simpler hypothesis, namely, that the degree of returns to scale is not independent of output, but varies inversely with it. Figure 3 illustrates this explanation: The solid line gives the traditional form of the total cost function, which shows increasing returns at low outputs and decreasing returns at high outputs. If we try to fit a function for which returns to scale are independent of the level of output, e.g., one linear in logarithms, a curve such as the dashed one will be obtained. The shaded areas A and B show the output ranges, high and low, for which total costs are underestimated.

---

[6] Capacity figures might have been used. However, those available appear to be somewhat unrealistic. These are based on generator name-plate ratings, which refer to the maximum output that can be produced without overheating. According to the Federal Power Commission, however, units of the same size, general design, and actual capability may show as much as a 20 per cent difference in rating [5, p. xi]. Furthermore, in a multiple-plant firm, total generator capacity is not the only factor to be considered. Such defects in the capacity figures also led to grouping firms by output rather than by capacity in the analyses of covariance presented below.

[7] Treatment of capital costs is the source of one of the most serious shortcomings of the present study, as indeed capital measurement is in most studies of production. Solow's recent contribution to the study of the aggregate production function [18] offers considerable promise of an appropriate measure of capital used in the production of electric power. I hope, in future work, to make use of a model of production that involves fixed coefficients *ex post* at the plant level, but that permits substitution of inputs and that changes over time *ex ante*.

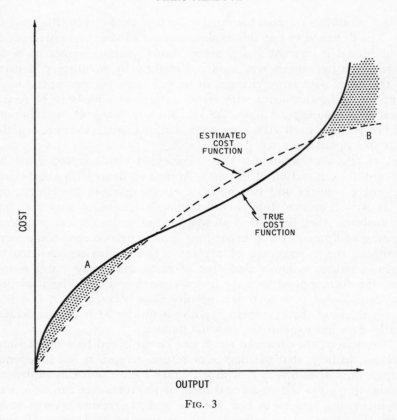

FIG. 3

If the true cost function is not linear in logarithms, we can either fit an over-all function that reflects this fact or attempt to approximate the actual function by a series of segments of functions linear in logarithms. Because of fitting difficulties and the problem of determining the form in which factor prices enter the cost function, I initially chose the latter course. Firms, arrayed in order of ascending output, were divided into 5 groups containing 29 observations each. A list of the firms used in the analysis appears in Appendix C. The results of fitting five separate regressions of the form indicated by Model A are given in lines IIIA through IIIE of Table 3 and the corresponding implications for the parameters in the production function in lines IIIA through IIIE of Table 4. Similar results for regressions of the form indicated by Model B are presented in lines VIA through VIE of Tables 5 and 6.

The results of these regressions with respect to returns to scale are appealing: Except for statistically insignificant reversal between groups C and D, returns to scale diminish steadily, falling from a high of better than 2.5 to a low of slightly less than 1, which indicates increasing returns at a diminishing rate for all except the largest firms in the sample. However, in the case of regressions III, the elasticity of output with respect to capital price behaves very erratically from group to group and has the wrong sign in groups A and E; in regressions VI the elasticity of output behaves erratically, both with respect to labor and with respect to capital, having the wrong sign in groups B and C for the former and in group D for the latter.

Analyses of covariance for regressions III and VI, compared with the over-all regressions I and V, respectively, gave F-ratios of 1.569 and 1.791 in that order. With 141 and 125 degrees of freedom, these ratios are significant at better than the 99 per cent level. Thus, breaking the sample into five groups significantly reduces the residual variance. However, because of the erratic behavior of the coefficients of independent variables other than output, it appears that we may have gone too far. Regressions III and VI are based on the assumption that *all* coefficients differ from group to group. Economically, this may be interpreted as the hypothesis of *non-neutral variations in returns to scale*; i.e., scale affects not only returns to scale but also marginal rates of substitution.

A halfway house between the hypothesis of no variation in returns to scale with output level and the hypothesis of non-neutral variations in scale is the hypothesis of *neutral variations in returns to scale*. A general test of this hypothesis is equivalent to testing the hypothesis that the coefficients for the various prices in the individual group regressions are the same for all groups while allowing the constant terms and the coefficients of output to differ.[8] The hypothesis of neutral variations in returns to scale is tested in this way only in the context of Model A. The regression results are presented in lines IVA through IVE of Table 3 and their implications for the production function in Table 4. An analysis of covariance comparing regressions III and IV gives an F-ratio of 1.576. With 133 and 125 degrees of freedom, a ratio this high is significant at better than the 99 per cent level; hence, we cannot confidently reject the hypothesis of non-neutral variations in returns to scale on statistical grounds alone with this test. Examining the results derived from regressions IV, however, we find that the degree of returns to scale steadily declines with output until, for the group consisting of firms with the largest outputs, we find some evidence of diminishing returns to scale.[9] Furthermore, the elasticities of output with

---

[8] For a generalized Cobb-Douglas the marginal rate of substitution between x_i and x_j is

$$\frac{\partial y/\partial x_i}{\partial y/\partial x_j} = \frac{a_i/a_j}{x_i/x_j}.$$

Hence, if the ratio of a_i to returns to scale, r, is restricted to be the same for each output group, the marginal rates of substitution will be invariant with respect to output level at each given factor ratio.

[9] Note, however, that the estimated value is insignificantly different from one, so that we cannot reject the hypothesis of constant returns to scale for this group of firms.

respect to the various input levels are all of the correct sign and of reasonable magnitude, although I still feel that the elasticity with respect to capital is implausibly low.[10] Thus, on economic grounds, one might tentatively accept the hypothesis of neutral variations in returns to scale.

If one accepts the hypothesis of neutral variations in returns to scale, a somewhat more refined analysis is possible, since we may then treat the degree of returns to scale as a continuous function of output. That is, instead of grouping the firms as we did previously, we estimate a cost function of the form

$$(12) \qquad C = K + \frac{1}{r(Y)} Y + \frac{a_1}{r} P_1 + \frac{a_2}{r} P_2 + \frac{a_3}{r} P_3,$$

where $r(Y)$, the degree of returns to scale, is a function of the output level. Since neutral variations in returns to scale are assumed, the coefficients of the prices are unaffected. A preliminary graphical analysis indicated that returns to scale as a continuous function of output might be approximated by a function of the form

$$(13) \qquad r(y) = \frac{1}{\alpha + \beta \log y}.$$

Thus, instead of regressions of the form suggested by (10) or (11), we fit

$$(14) \quad C - P_3 = K + \alpha Y + \beta Y^2 + \frac{a_1}{r} [P_1 - P_3] + \frac{a_2}{r} [P_2 - P_3] + V$$

(Model C)
and

$$(15) \qquad C = K' + \alpha Y + \beta Y^2 + \frac{a_1}{r} P_1 + \frac{a_3}{r} P_3 + V$$

(Model D).

The results obtained for regressions based on Model C and Model D are reported in Table 7 for regressions VII and VIII, respectively. The implications of these results for the production function are given in Table 8. Note that returns to scale and the other parameters have been computed at five output levels only, so that the results in Table 8 may be readily compared with those in Tables 4 and 6.

Perhaps the most striking result of the assumption of continuously and neutrally variable returns to scale of the form suggested in (13) is the substantial increase in our estimate of the degree of returns to scale for firms in the three largest size groups. Whereas before, we found nearly

---

[10] See p. 179.

TABLE 7

RESULTS FROM REGRESSIONS BASED ON MODELS C AND D FOR 145 FIRMS IN 1955; CONTINUOUS NEUTRAL VARIATIONS IN RETURNS TO SCALE

Model C: Dependent Variable Was $C - P_3$

Regression No.	Coefficient				R^2
VII	Y	Y^2	$P_1 - P_3$	$P_2 - P_3$	
	0.151	0.117	0.498	0.062	0.958
	($\pm$.062)	($\pm$.012)	($\pm$.161)	($\pm$.151)	

Model D: Dependent Variable Was C

Regression No.	Coefficient				R^2
VIII	Y	Y^2	P_1	P_3	
	0.137	0.118	0.279	0.255	0.952
	($\pm$.064)	($\pm$.013)	($\pm$.224)	($\pm$.054)	

Figures in parentheses are the standard errors of the coefficients.

constant returns to scale, it now appears that they are increasing.[11] In addition, all the coefficients in both analyses are of the right sign, and the results based on Model D yield results of plausible magnitude for the elasticity of output with respect to capital as compared with the elasticities with respect to labor and fuel. Analyses of covariance, comparing regressions VII and I with regressions VIII and V, yield F-ratios of 1.631 and 9.457, respectively; both are highly significant, with 141 and 140 degrees of freedom. A comparison of regression VII with regression III yields an F-ratio of 1.032, which, though not significant, does suggest that neutral variations in returns to scale of the form used are indistinguishable from non-neutral. Hence the hypothesis of neutral variations in returns to scale may be accepted both on economic grounds and on grounds of simplicity.

---

[11] Using the variance-covariance matrix for the coefficients in (14) or (15), one could easily compute, for a given y, a conditional standard error for $1/r$, which could then be used to test whether $1/r$ were significantly less than one (i.e., whether the finding of increasing returns was statistically significant). Unfortunately, the regression program used did not print out the inverse of the moment matrix, so this test could not be made. But there is little doubt, in view of the extremely small standard errors of the estimated α and β, that such a test would have shown the increasing returns found to be statistically significant.

TABLE 8

RETURNS TO SCALE AND ELASTICITIES OF OUTPUT WITH RESPECT TO VARIOUS INPUTS DERIVED
FROM RESULTS PRESENTED IN TABLE 7 FOR 145 FIRMS IN 1955

Regression VII (Model C)

Group	Returns to Scale[a]	Elasticity of Output with Respect to[a]		
		Labor	Capital	Fuel
A	2.92	1.45	0.18	1.29
B	2.24	1.12	0.14	0.98
C	1.97	0.98	0.12	0.87
D	1.84	0.92	0.11	0.81
E	1.69	0.84	0.10	0.75

Regression VIII (Model D)

Group	Returns to Scale[a]	Elasticity of Output with Respect to[a]		
		Labor	Capital	Fuel
A	3.03	0.85	1.41	0.77
B	2.30	0.64	1.07	0.59
C	2.01	0.56	0.94	0.51
D	1.88	0.52	0.88	0.48
E	1.72	0.48	0.80	0.44

[a] Evaluated at the median output for each group.

3. Conclusions and Prospects

The major substantive conclusions of this paper are that

1. There is evidence of a marked degree of increasing returns to scale at the firm level; but the degree of returns to scale varies inversely with output and is considerably less, especially for large firms, than that previously estimated for individual plants.

2. Variation in returns to scale may well be neutral in character; i.e., although the scale of operation affects the degree of returns to scale, it may

not affect the marginal rates of substitution between different factors of production for given factor ratios.

These substantive conclusions derive from two conclusions of methodological interest:

1. The appropriate model at the firm level is a statistical cost function which includes factor prices and which is uniquely related to the underlying production function.

2. At the firm level it is appropriate to assume a production function that allows substitution among factors of production. When a statistical cost function based on a generalized Cobb-Douglas production function is fitted to cross-section data on individual firms, there is evidence of such substitution possibilities.

Inadequacies in the estimation of capital costs and prices and in the treatment of transmission suggest, however, that a less aggregative approach is called for. On a less aggregative level, it may be possible to produce more adequate measures of capital and to introduce transmission explicitly. A simple model of optimal behavior on the part of the firm may then allow us to combine this information in a way that will yield more meaningful results on returns to scale at the firm level.

APPENDIX A

A Relation Between Returns to Scale at the Plant Level and at the Firm Level for an Electric Utility

Consider a firm that produces x_i units in each of n identical plants. If plants and demand are uniformly distributed, all plants will produce identical outputs, so that the total output produced will be nx, where x is the common value. Under these circumstances, a general formula that has been developed by electrical engineers to express transmission losses [8] reduces to

(A.1)
$$y = bn^2x^2 ,$$

where y is the aggregate loss of power. That is, with uniformly distributed demand and identical plants, transmission losses are proportional to the square of total output.

If z is delivered power, we have

(A.2)
$$z = nx - y = nx - bn^2x^2 .$$

Let $c(x)$ be the cost of producing x units in one plant. Production costs of the nx units are thus $nc(x)$. And let $t = T(n, x)$ be the cost of maintaining a network with n plants, each of which produces x units. We may expect that

t increases with x, $\partial T/\partial x > 0$, since larger outputs require more and heavier wires and more and larger transformers. However, t may or may not increase with n. It is likely to decrease with n if the expense of operating and maintaining long transmission lines is large relative to the cost of a number of short lines, and likely to increase if the converse is true.

The total cost of delivering an amount z of power $\Gamma(z)$ is the sum of production costs of a larger amount of power and transmission costs:

$$(A.3) \qquad \Gamma(z) = nc(x) + T(n, x) .$$

Suppose that the firm chooses the number and size of its plants in order to minimize $\Gamma(z)$ for any given z. The values of n and x that minimize $\Gamma(z)$ subject to (A.2) are given by solving

$$(A.4) \qquad c(x) + \frac{\partial T}{\partial n} - x\lambda\mu = 0 ,$$

$$(A.5) \qquad nc'(x) + \frac{\partial T}{\partial x} - n\lambda\mu = 0 ,$$

$$(A.6) \qquad z - (nx - bn^2x^2) = 0 ,$$

where

$$\mu = 1 - 2bnx$$

$$(A.7) \qquad = \frac{z - y}{nx} .$$

The degree of returns to scale at the plant level, $p(x)$, may be defined as the reciprocal of the elasticity of production costs with respect to output:

$$(A.8) \qquad p(x) = \frac{c(x)}{xc'(x)} .$$

It follows from (A.4), (A.5), and (A.8) that

$$(A.9) \qquad p(x) = 1 + \frac{t}{(nx)c'(x)} (e_x - e_n) ,$$

where

$$e_x = \frac{x}{t} \frac{\partial T}{\partial x} , \quad e_n = \frac{n}{t} \frac{\partial T}{\partial n} .$$

Since nx, t and $c'(x)$ are positive, it follows that returns to scale are greater or less than one, according to whether the elasticity of transmission costs with respect to output exceeds or falls short of the elasticity with respect to number of plants. If transmission costs decrease with a larger number of plants, then under the particular assumptions made here, the firm will operate plants in the region of increasing returns to scale. It may nonetheless operate as a whole in the region of decreasing returns to scale.

Let $P(z)$ be the degree of returns to scale for the firm as a whole when it delivers a supply of z units to its customers:

$$(A.10) \qquad P(z) = \frac{\Gamma(z)}{z\Gamma'(z)}.$$

It is well known that the Lagrangian multiplier λ is equal to marginal cost; hence, from (A.5),

$$(A.11) \qquad \Gamma'(z) = \lambda = \frac{1}{n\mu}\left[nc'(x) + \frac{\partial T}{\partial x} \right].$$

Substituting for $\Gamma'(z)$ from (A.11), μ from (A.7), and $\Gamma(z)$ from (A.3), we obtain the following expression for $P(z)$:

$$(A.12) \qquad P(z) = \frac{\Gamma(z)}{z} \cdot \frac{n(z-y)}{nx[nc'(x) + \partial T/\partial x]}$$

$$= \left(1 - \frac{y}{z}\right) \frac{nc(x) + t}{n[xc'(x)] + x(\partial T/\partial x)}.$$

By definition,

$$p(x) = \frac{c(x)}{xc'(x)},$$

hence

$$(A.13) \qquad P(z) = p(x)\left(1 - \frac{y}{z}\right) \frac{nc(x) + t}{nc(x) + [p(x)e_x]t}.$$

Neglecting the last term in the product on the right-hand side of (A.13) for the moment, we see that returns to scale at the firm level will typically be less than at the plant level, solely because of transmission losses; how much less depends on the ratio of losses to the quantity of power actually delivered. The final term in the product is a more complicated matter: If there are increasing returns to scale and if the costs of transmission increase rapidly with the average load (i.e., $e_x > 1$), then it is clear that the tendency toward diminishing returns at the level of the individual firm will be reinforced. It is perfectly possible under these circumstances that firms will operate individual plants in the range of increasing returns to scale and yet, considered as a unit, be well within the range of decreasing returns to scale.

Although this argument rests on a number of extreme simplifying assumptions, it nonetheless may provide an explanation for the divergent views and findings concerning the nature of returns to scale in electricity supply. Davidson [3] and Houthakker [9], for example, hold that there are diminishing returns to scale, while much of the empirical evidence and many other writers support the contrary view. The existing empirical evidence, however, refers to individual plants, not firms, and many writers in the public-utility field may have plants rather than firms in mind.

APPENDIX B

The Data Used in the Statistical Analyses

Estimation of equation (7) from cross-section data on individual firms in the electric power industry requires that we obtain data on production costs, total physical output, and the prices paid for fuel, capital, and labor. Data on various categories of cost are relatively easy to come by, although there are difficulties in deriving an appropriate measure of capital costs. Price data are more difficult to come by, in general, and conceptual as well as practical difficulties are involved in formulating an appropriate measure of the "price" of capital. Such problems are, in fact, the *raisons d'être* for Model B, which permits us to ignore capital prices altogether.

A cross section of 145 firms in 44 states in the year 1955 was used in the analyses. The firms used in the analysis are listed in Appendix C. Selection of firms was made primarily on the basis of data availability. The various series used in the analyses were derived as follows.

B.1. Production Costs

Data on expenditures for labor and fuel used in steam plants for electric power generation are available by firm in [6], but the capital costs of production had to be estimated. This was done by taking interest and depreciation charges on the firm's entire production plant and multiplying by the ratio of the value of steam plant to total plant as carried on the firm's books. Among the shortcomings of this approach, three are worthy of special note:

(a) For many well-known reasons, depreciation and interest charges do not reflect capital costs as defined in some economically meaningful way. Furthermore, depreciation practices vary from firm to firm (there are about four basic methods in use by electric utilities), and such variation introduces a noncomparability of unknown extent.

(b) The method of allocation used to derive our series assumes that steam and hydraulic plants depreciate at the same rate, which is clearly not the case.

(c) Because of their dependence on past prices of utility plant, the use of depreciation and interest charges raises serious questions about the relevant measure of the price of capital. The use of a current figure is clearly inappropriate, but unless we are prepared to introduce the same magnitude on both sides of the equation, it is difficult to see how else the problem can be handled.

B.2. Output

Total output produced by steam plant in kilowatt hours during the entire year 1955 may be obtained from [6]. This was the series used, despite the fact that the peak load aspect of output is thereby neglected. Since the distribution of output among residential, commercial, and industrial users varies from firm to firm, characteristics of the peak will also vary and this in turn will affect our estimate of returns to scale if correlated with the level of output.

B.3. Wage Rates

At the time this study was undertaken, I was unaware of the existence of data on payroll and employment by plant contained in [5]; hence, inferior information was used to obtain this series. Average hourly earnings of utility workers (including gas and transportation) were available for 19 states from Bureau of Labor Statistics files. A mail survey was made of the State Unemployment Compensation Commissions in the remaining 29 states. All replied, but only ten were able to supply data. A regression of the average hourly earnings of utility workers on those for all manufacturing was used to estimate the former for states for which it was unavailable. The resulting state figures were then associated with utilities having the bulk of their operations in each state. In only one case, Northern States Power, were operations so evenly divided among several states that the procedure could not be applied. In this case an average of the Minnesota and Wisconsin rates was employed.

B.4. Price of Capital

As indicated, many practical and conceptual difficulties were associated with this series. Be that as it may, what was done was as follows: First, an estimate of the current long-term rate at which the firm could borrow was obtained by taking the current yield on the firm's most recently issued long-term bonds (obtained from Moody's Investment Manual). These were mainly 30-year obligations, and in all cases had 20 or more years to maturity. This rate was in turn multiplied by the Handy-Whitman Index of Electric Utility Construction Costs for the region in which the firm had the bulk of its operations [4, p. 69]. Two shortcomings worth special mention are:

(a) The neglect of the possibility of equity financing by the method.
(b) The fact that the Handy-Whitman Index includes the construction costs of hydraulic installations.

B.5. Price of Fuel

Since coal, oil, or natural gas may be burned to produce the steam required for steam electric generation, and since many plants are set up to use more than one type of fuel, prices were taken on a per-Btu basis. These were available by state from [4, p. 49], and the state figures were assigned to individual utilities in the same manner as wage rates.

APPENDIX C

Names of Firms and Corresponding Costs, Output, Wage Rate, Fuel Price, and Capital Price in 1955

Firms used in the analysis are listed here in order of ascending output (measured in billions of kilowatt-hours). They are divided into 5 groups containing 29 observations each. These appear on pp. 193–197 following.

(References appear on p. 198, following this Appendix.)

Group A	Production Costs (million $)	Output (billion kwh)	Wage Rate ($/hr)	Fuel Price (¢/million Btu)	Capital Price (index)
1. California Pacific Utilities Co.	0.082	002	2.09	17.9	183
2. Brockton Edison Co.	0.661	003	2.05	35.1	174
3. Essex Country Elec. Co.	0.990	004	2.05	35.1	171
4. The Montana Power Co.	0.315	004	1.83	32.2	166
5. Upper Peninsula Power Co.	0.197	005	2.12	28.6	233
6. Alpena Power Co.	0.098	009	2.12	28.6	195
7. Blackstone Valley Gas and Elec. Co.	0.949	011	1.98	35.5	206
8. Lawrence Electric Co.	0.675	013	2.05	35.1	150
9. Wisconsin-Michigan Power Co.	0.525	013	2.19	29.1	155
10. Cheyenne Light, Fuel and Power Co.	0.501	022	1.72	15.0	188
11. Portland General Elec. Co.	1.194	025	2.09	17.9	170
12. New Hampshire Elec. Co.	0.670	025	1.68	39.7	167
13. Southern Utah Power Co.	0.349	035	1.81	22.6	213
14. Mt. Carmel Public Utility Co.	0.423	039	2.30	23.6	164
15. Bangor Hydro-elec. Co.	0.501	043	1.75	42.8	170
16. Community Public Service Co.	0.550	063	1.76	10.3	161
17. New Port Elec. Corp.	0.795	068	1.98	35.5	210
18. Mississippi Valley Public Service Co.	0.664	081	2.29	28.5	158
19. Superior Water Light and Power Co.	0.705	084	2.19	29.1	156
20. Maine Public Service Co.	0.903	073	1.75	42.8	176
21. Housatonic Public Service Co.	1.504	099	2.20	36.2	170
22. Northwestern Public Service Co.	1.615	101	1.66	33.4	192
23. Missouri Utilities Co.	1.127	119	1.92	22.5	164
24. The Western Colorado Power Co.	0.718	120	1.77	21.3	175
25. Pacific Power and Light Co.	2.414	122	2.09	17.9	180
26. Green Mountain Power Co.	1.130	130	1.82	38.9	176
27. The Central Kansas Power Co.	0.992	138	1.80	20.2	202
28. Arkansas Missouri Power Co.	1.554	149	1.92	22.5	227
29. Northern Virginia Power Co.	1.225	196	1.92	29.1	186

Group B	Production Costs (million $)	Output (billion kwh)	Wage Rate ($/hr)	Fuel Price (¢/million Btu)	Capital Price (index)
1. Lake Superior District Power Co.	1.565	197	2.19	29.1	183
2. Missouri Public Service Co.	1.936	209	1.92	22.5	169
3. Montana-Dakota Utilities Co.	3.154	214	1.52	27.5	168
4. Missouri Power and Light Co.	2.599	220	1.92	22.5	164
5. The Connecticut Power Co.	3.298	234	2.20	36.2	164
6. The United Gas Improvements Co.	2.441	235	2.11	24.4	170
7. St. Joseph Light and Power Co.	2.031	253	1.92	22.5	158
8. Worcester County Elec. Co.	4.666	279	2.05	35.1	177
9. Black Hills Power and Light Co.	1.834	290	1.66	33.4	195
10. Western Light and Telephone Co. Inc.	2.072	290	1.80	20.2	176
11. Southern Colorado Power Co.	2.039	295	1.77	21.3	188
12. Iowa Southern Utilities Co.	3.398	299	1.70	26.9	187
13. Cambridge Elec. Light Co.	3.083	324	2.05	35.1	152
14. Northern States Power Co.	2.344	333	2.19	29.1	157
15. The Tucson Gas, Elec., Light and Power Co.	2.382	338	1.85	24.6	163
16. Madison Gas and Elec. Co.	2.657	353	2.19	29.1	143
17. Central Louisiana Elec. Co.	1.705	353	2.13	10.7	167
18. Savannah Elec. and Power Co.	3.230	416	1.54	26.2	217
19. Otter Tail Power Co.	5.049	420	1.52	27.5	144
20. The Eastern Shore Public Service Co. of Maryland	3.814	456	2.09	30.0	178
21. Central Maine Power Co.	4.580	484	1.75	42.8	176
22. Central Illinois Elec. and Gas Co.	4.358	516	2.30	23.6	167
23. New Bedford Gas and Edison Light Co.	4.714	550	2.05	35.1	158
24. New Jersey Power and Light Co.	4.357	563	2.32	31.9	162
25. Rockland Light and Power Co.	3.919	566	2.31	33.5	198
26. The Empire District Elec. Co.	3.442	592	1.92	22.5	164
27. Western Massachusetts Elec. Co.	4.898	671	2.05	35.1	164
28. El Paso Elec. Co.	3.584	696	1.76	10.3	161
29. Interstate Power Co.	5.535	719	1.70	26.9	174

Group C	Production Costs (million $)	Output (billion kwh)	Wage Rate ($/hr)	Fuel Price (¢/million Btu)	Capital Price (index)
1. Southern Indiana Gas and Elec. Co.	4.406	742	2.04	20.7	157
2. California Elec. Power Co.	4.289	795	2.24	26.5	185
3. Iowa Public Service Co.	6.731	800	1.70	26.9	157
4. Public Service Co. of New Hampshire	6.895	808	1.68	39.7	203
5. Minnesota Power and Light Co.	5.112	811	2.29	28.5	178
6. Gulf Power Co.	5.141	855	2.00	34.3	183
7. Central Hudson Gas and Elec. Corp.	5.720	860	2.31	33.5	168
8. Mississippi Power Co.	4.691	909	1.45	17.6	196
9. Iowa-Illinois Gas and Elec. Co.	6.832	913	1.70	26.9	166
10. West Texas Utilities Co.	4.813	924	1.76	10.3	172
11. Iowa Elec. Light and Power Co.	6.754	984	1.70	26.9	158
12. The Potomac Edison Co.	5.127	991	2.09	30.0	174
13. South Carolina Elec. and Gas Co.	6.388	1000	1.55	28.2	225
14. Pennsylvania Power Co.	4.509	1098	2.11	24.4	168
15. Montana Elec. Co.	7.185	1109	2.05	35.1	177
16. Central Illinois Light Co.	6.800	1118	2.30	23.6	161
17. Wisconsin Public Service Corp.	7.743	1122	2.19	29.1	162
18. Northern Indiana Public Service Co.	7.968	1137	2.04	20.7	158
19. Rochester Gas and Elec. Corp.	8.858	1156	2.31	33.5	176
20. Iowa Power and Light Co.	8.588	1166	1.70	26.9	183
21. New England Power Co.	6.449	1170	2.05	35.1	166
22. Wisconsin Power and Light Co.	8.488	1215	2.19	29.1	164
23. Tampa Elec. Co.	8.877	1279	2.00	34.3	207
24. Atlantic City Elec. Co.	10.274	1291	2.32	31.9	175
25. South Carolina Generating Co.	6.024	1290	1.55	28.2	225
26. Delaware Power and Light Co.	8.258	1331	2.13	30.0	178
27. The United Illuminating Co.	13.376	1373	2.20	36.2	157
28. The Hartford Elec. Light Co.	10.690	1420	2.20	36.2	138
29. Arizona Public Service Co.	8.308	1474	1.85	24.6	163

Group D	Production Costs (million $)	Output (billion kwh)	Wage Rate ($/hr)	Fuel Price (¢/million Btu)	Capital Price (index)
1. Southwestern Gas and Elec. Co.	6.082	1497	1.76	10.3	168
2. The Kansas Power and Light Co.	9.284	1545	1.80	20.2	158
3. Jersey Central Power and Light Co.	10.879	1649	2.32	31.9	177
4. Kansas Gas and Elec. Co.	8.477	1668	1.80	20.2	170
5. Louisiana Power and Light Co.	6.877	1782	2.13	10.7	183
6. The Narragansett Elec. Co.	15.106	1831	1.98	35.5	162
7. Central Power and Light Co.	8.031	1833	1.76	10.3	177
8. Mississippi Power and Light Co.	8.082	1838	1.45	17.6	196
9. San Diego Gas and Elec. Co.	10.866	1787	2.24	26.5	164
10. Public Service Co. of Oklahoma	8.596	1918	1.69	12.9	158
11. Utah Power and Light Co.	8.673	1930	1.81	22.6	157
12. Metropolitan Edison Co.	15.437	2028	2.11	24.4	163
13. Dallas Power and Light Co.	8.211	2057	1.76	10.3	161
14. Public Service Co. of Colorado	11.982	2084	1.77	21.3	156
15. Florida Power Corp.	16.674	2226	2.00	34.3	217
16. Central Illinois Public Service Co.	12.620	2304	2.30	23.6	161
17. Indianapolis Power and Light Co.	12.905	2341	2.04	20.7	183
18. Oklahoma Gas and Elec. Co.	11.615	2353	1.69	12.9	167
19. Texas Power and Light Co.	9.321	2367	1.76	10.3	161
20. Chicago District Elec. Generating Corp.	12.962	2451	2.04	20.7	163
21. The Connecticut Light and Power Co.	16.932	2457	2.20	36.2	170
22. Gulf States Utilities Co.	9.648	2507	1.76	10.3	174
23. New York State Elec. and Gas Corp.	18.350	2530	2.31	33.5	197
24. Kansas City Power and Light Co.	17.333	2576	1.92	22.5	162
25. Southwestern Public Service Co.	12.015	2607	1.76	10.3	155
26. Texas Elec. Service Co.	11.320	2870	1.76	10.3	167
27. Long Island Lighting Co.	22.337	2993	2.31	33.5	176
28. Illinois Power Co.	19.035	3202	2.30	23.6	170
29. Monongahela Power Co.	12.205	3286	1.61	17.8	183

Group E	Production Costs (million $)	Output (billion kwh)	Wage Rate ($/hr)	Fuel Price (¢/million Btu)	Capital Price (index)
1. Carolina Power and Light Co.	17.078	3312	1.68	28.8	190
2. Baltimore Gas and Elec. Co.	25.528	3498	2.09	30.0	170
3. Potomac Elec. Power Co.	24.021	3538	2.09	30.0	176
4. Boston Edison Co.	32.197	3794	2.05	35.1	159
5. Northern State Power Co.	26.652	3841	2.29	28.5	157
6. West Pennsylvania Power Co.	20.164	4014	2.11	24.4	161
7. Arkansas Power and Light Co.	14.132	4217	1.53	18.1	172
8. Pennsylvania Elec. Co.	21.410	4305	2.11	24.4	203
9. Public Service Co. of Indiana Inc.	23.244	4494	2.04	20.7	167
10. Wisconsin Elec. Power Co.	29.845	4764	2.19	29.1	195
11. Virginia Elec. Power Co.	32.318	5277	1.92	29.1	161
12. Indiana and Michigan Elec. Co.	21.988	5283	2.04	20.7	159
13. Pennsylvania Power and Light Co.	35.229	5668	2.11	24.4	177
14. Houston Lighting and Power Co.	17.467	5681	1.76	10.3	157
15. Alabama Power Co.	22.828	5819	1.79	18.5	196
16. Duquesne Light Co.	33.154	6000	2.11	24.4	183
17. Georgia Power Co.	32.228	6119	1.54	26.2	189
18. Union Elec. Co. of Missouri	34.168	6136	1.92	22.5	160
19. Consumers Power Co.	40.594	7193	2.12	28.6	162
20. Appalachian Elec. Power Co.	33.354	7886	1.61	17.8	178
21. Public Service Elec. and Gas Co.	64.542	8419	2.32	31.9	199
22. Southern California Edison Co.	41.238	8642	2.24	26.5	182
23. Niagara Mohawk Power Corp.	47.993	8787	2.31	33.5	190
24. Philadelphia Elec. Co.	69.878	9484	2.11	24.4	165
25. Duke Power Co.	44.894	9956	1.68	28.8	203
26. Pacific Gas and Elec. Co.	67.120	11477	2.24	26.5	151
27. The Detroit Edison Co. and Subsidiaries	73.050	11796	2.12	28.6	148
28. Consolidated Edison Co. of N.Y. Inc.	139.422	14359	2.31	33.5	212
29. Commonwealth Edison Co.	119.939	16719	2.30	23.6	162

REFERENCES

[1] ARROW, K. J., B. MINHAS, H. CHENERY, and R. SOLOW, Capital-Labor Substitution and Economic Efficiency, Memo. C-11 (Revised) Project for Quant.
Res. in Econ. Dev., Stanford Univ. (August 1960).

[2] CHENERY, H. B., Overcapacity and the Acceleration Principle, *Econometrica*,
20 (January 1952), 1-28.

[3] DAVIDSON, R. K., *Price Discrimination in Selling Gas and Electricity*. Baltimore:
Johns Hopkins Press, 1955.

[4] Edison Electric Institute, *Statistical Bulletin, 1957*. New York, 1958.

[5] Federal Power Commission, *Steam Electric Plants: Construction Cost and
Annual Production Expenses, 1956*. Washington, D. C., 1957.

[6] Federal Power Commission, *Statistics of Electric Utilities in the United States,
1955, Classes A and B Privately Owned Companies*. Washington, D. C., 1956.

[7] FRIEDMAN, M., *A Theory of the Consumption Function* (Gen. Ser. 63). New York:
National Bureau of Economic Research (distr. Princeton Univ. Press), 1957.

[8] GEORGE, E. E., Intrasystem Transmission Losses, *Electr. Eng. (Trans. A.I.E.E.)*,
62 (March 1943), 153-58.

[9] HOUTHAKKER, H. S., Electricity Tariffs in Theory and Practice, *Econ. J.*, **61**
(1951), 1-25.

[10] JOHNSTON, J., *Statistical Cost Analysis*. New York: McGraw-Hill, 1960.

[11] KOMIYA, R., "Technological Progress and the Production Function in the
United States Steam Power Industry" (September 1959), duplicated.

[12] LOMAX, K. S., Cost Curves for Electricity Generation, *Economica*, **19**, new
series (1952), 193-97.

[13] MARSCHAK, J., and W. H. ANDREWS, Random Simultaneous Equations and the
Theory of Production, *Econometrica*, **12** (July-October, 1944), 143-205.

[14] *Business Concentration and Price Policy* (Spec. Conf. Ser. 5). New York:
National Bureau of Economic Research (distr. Princeton Univ. Press), 1955.

[15] NERLOVE, M., "Notes on the Identification and Estimation of Cobb-Douglas
Production Functions" (1958-59), duplicated.

[16] NORDIN, J. A., Note on a Light Plant's Cost Curves, *Econometrica*, **15** (July
1947), 231-35.

[17] SHEPHARD, R. W., *Cost and Production Functions*. Princeton, N.J.: Princeton
Univ. Press, 1953.

[18] SOLOW, R.W., Investment and Technical Progress, in K. J. ARROW, S. KARLIN,
and P. SUPPES (eds.), *Mathematical Methods in the Social Sciences, 1959*.
Stanford: Stanford Univ. Press, 1960, pp. 93-104.

[19] WESTFIELD, F. M., "Static and Dynamic Optimization Problems in the Multi-
Plant Firm with Particular Reference to the Electric Power Industry,"
unpublished Ph.D. dissertation, M.I.T., 1957.

III. Theory and Measurement of Monetary Phenomena

8

Interest Rates and "Portfolio Selection" among Liquid Assets in the U.S.

CARL F. CHRIST, *The Johns Hopkins University*

This paper deals with the behavior of holders of liquid assets in the United States. For the most part, it deals with the portfolio composition, so to speak, of liquid assets as between demand deposits, time deposits, savings and loan association shares, U.S. savings bonds, and Treasury bills held outside banks and Federal agencies. Also, it deals briefly with the Cambridge k. There is an appendix containing the definitions of the variables.

In summary, the results are as follows: First, the inverse of a long-term corporate bond rate explains about three-fourths of the variation in the Cambridge k (defined as the ratio of currency and demand deposits to GNP) over the period since 1892 in the U.S., and the relationship appears quite constant. Second, that same variable does very poorly as an explanation of the ratio of currency plus demand *and time* deposits to GNP. This suggests that there may be shifts from demand deposits to time deposits when interest rates are high, and back again when interest rates are low. The results below are consistent with this.

Third, consider the four ratios of the form $D/(D + X)$, where D is demand deposits adjusted and X is one of the four aggregates of liquid assets listed in the first column of Table 1. Consider also four interest rates r_x, each one being an index of the rate of return on one of the four listed aggregates. When one uses least-squares regressions to explain each of these four ratios in terms of the corresponding interest-rate index and real GNP per capita (denoted by y) for 1934–59 in the U.S., the results are as follows: (a) The four multiple R^2's are 0.96, 0.92, 0.50, and 0.62, respectively. (b) The income elasticities decline from a maximum of about 0.3 in the first case to a minimum of about -0.3 in the last, measured at the points of sample means. (c) The interest elasticities are all negative, as expected, and all are between about -0.23 and -0.45, measured at the

The work underlying this paper was supported by the Center for Advanced Study in the Behavioral Sciences. John Gilbert and his staff rendered computing services. I am indebted, for helpful comments, to K. J. Arrow, G. Becker, R. Dorfman, M. Nerlove, H. Rose, and W. L. Smith. The last two discussed an earlier version of the paper at the meetings of the Econometric Society in St. Louis on December 27, 1960.

points of sample means. (d) All the regression slope coefficients in these four equations are more than three times their standard errors.

TABLE 1

REGRESSIONS EXPLAINING RATIOS OF DEMAND DEPOSITS TO THE SUM OF DEMAND DEPOSITS PLUS OTHER LIQUID ASSETS (X), IN TERMS OF THE RATE OF RETURN ON THOSE LIQUID ASSETS AND REAL GNP PER CAPITA, IN THE U.S., 1934-59

Type of Liquid Asset X in the Dependent Variable $D/(D + X)$ (1)	Regression Coefficients		Elasticity at Sample Mean		R^2	Number of Table Giving More Details
	r_x (2)	y (3)	r_x (4)	y (5)	(6)	(7)
T	-0.08	$+0.09$	-0.23	$+0.31$	0.956	3
$T + SL$	-0.12	$+0.031$	-0.45	$+0.12$	0.925	4
$T + SL + SB$	-0.06	-0.06	-0.27	-0.26	0.50	5
$T + SL + SB + TB$	-0.07	-0.07	-0.32	-0.32	0.62	6

All coefficients here exceed three estimated standard errors.

Variables are defined as follows:

D = demand deposits,
T = time deposits,
SL = savings and loan capital,
SB = U.S. savings bonds,
TB = Treasury bills outside banks and Federal agencies,
y = real GNP per capita in thousands of 1954 dollars,
r_x = rate of return on X, in per cent per year.

Fourth, when the three indexes of interest rates are disaggregated, some of the interest rates acquire positive coefficients, contrary to expectation. This is especially true of the rate of return on savings-and-loan capital.

1. The Cambridge k

Originally, this was intended to be a study of the effect of interest rates on the velocity of circulation, using as a point of departure a paper by H. A. Latané[2]. Latané plotted the inverse of Moody's Aaa bond rate (which I denote by r_L for "long-term rate") on one axis, and on the other axis the Cambridge k, defined as currency and demand deposits divided by GNP, for the years 1919–52. The scatter diagram looks roughly linear with a positive slope. (If the Cambridge k and the inverse of the interest rate are linearly and positively related, then k and the interest rate itself are related by a hyperbola that looks much like the Keynesian liquidity preference curve.) Latané fitted two straight lines to these data, one including all the years from 1919 to 1952, and one omitting 1932, 1933, 1942, 1946, and 1947 because, he said, "they were not considered representative." Even without omitting these years, the inverse of the long-term rate explains 76 per cent of the variation in k. As the years went by, I plotted the new data on Latané's graph, and something happened that is very remarkable in the brief history of econometric equations: the new points were closer to the regression line than the points of the sample period!

My plan was to extend this relationship between $1/r_L$ and k backward and forward in time, and to try to introduce other variables that would both make sense theoretically and help to reduce the unexplained variation. I fitted the same equation by least squares to a longer period, 1892–1959, and obtained almost the same slope (0.72 as against Latané's 0.80),[1] and again the inverted interest rate explained 76 per cent of the variation of k. These results are assembled in Table 2, regressions IIA and IIB. The similarity of the coefficients here is quite remarkable.

Consider what regression IIB (based on the years 1892–1959) would show if it were correct.[2] Regression IIB is, from Table 2,

$$ k = \frac{M}{GNP} = 0.131 + 0.716 \frac{1}{r_L}, $$

where M is the stock of currency and demand deposits. The elasticity of M with respect to r_L is independent of GNP and can be expressed as follows:

$$ \frac{\partial M}{\partial r_L} \frac{r_L}{M} = \frac{-1}{1 + 0.183\,r_L}. $$

Since r_L varied during the period 1892–1959 between about 2.5 per cent and 6.2 per cent, the elasticity varied between about -0.68 and -0.47. With r_L at about 4.3 per cent as it was early in 1961, the elasticity is about -0.56, and the indicated demand for currency and demand deposits is \$149 billion when GNP is \$500 billion a year. Each increase of one-tenth of one percentage point in r_L—e. g., from 4.3 per cent to 4.4 per cent—would then lead to a decline in the demand for currency and demand deposits of about $0.56 \times 0.1/4.3 \times 149$, i.e., about \$2 billion. If the stock of money were

---

[1] The dependent variable was k. A positive disturbance representing a higher k than would ordinarily correspond to the given r_L would be associated with a higher-than-ordinary demand for currency and demand deposits. This would be likely to involve some strain on bank reserves, perhaps after a lag, and hence to be followed by a slight temporary fall in $1/r_L$, cet. par. Hence one might expect the true disturbance in this regression to be negatively correlated with $1/r_L$ in the current or subsequent period. If this effect occurred in the current period, the result would tend to bias the slope downward; i.e., the correct value would be likely to be above the least-squares estimate of 0.72. The same remark applies to Latané's estimated slope of 0.80.

[2] Several of the comments in this paragraph were suggested by W. L. Smith at the Econometric Society meeting on December 27, 1960.

TABLE 2

REGRESSIONS OF THE CAMBRIDGE k (OR k' INCLUDING TIME DEPOSITS) ON THE INVERSE OF THE LONG-TERM INTEREST RATE

Regression No. (1)	Dependent Variable (2)	Regression Coefficients		r^2 (A)	Degrees of Freedom (B)	Wrong Signs in Columns (C)	Period (D)
		1 (3)	$1/r_L$ (4)				
IIA[a]	k	0.100	0.795	0.76	32	none	1919–1952
IIB	k	0.131	0.716 (0.050)	0.76	66	none	1892–1959
IIc	k'	0.353	0.676 (0.14)	0.26	66	none	1892–1959

Notes for Tables 2-6.

Each of the regressions tabulated has a serial number, shown in column 1.

Each regression is linear in the variables.

The dependent variable in each regression is shown in the title of the table (in Table 2 it is in column 2).

The estimated intercepts are shown in column 2 (in column 3 of Table 2).

Columns 2–9 (in Table 2, columns 3 and 4) contain some numbers not in brackets or parentheses, on the first line: these are the estimated slopes. They also contain some numbers in parentheses, on the second line: these are estimated standard deviations of the estimated slopes.

In regressions containing the lagged dependent variable x_0, a transformed equation can be computed from the regression, showing x_0 as a function of expected future values of the other variables. Where such a transformed equation has been computed, it is shown on the next line of the table below the regression from which it came.

The squared multiple correlation coefficient is shown in column A.

The number of degrees of freedom is shown in column B.

If any of the coefficients in an equation turn out to have algebraic sign different from what should be expected, the column numbers in which they appear are noted in column C.

[a] Obtained by Latané.

to remain at $149 billion, then at the higher interest rate of 4.4 per cent it could support a GNP of about $507 billion. Thus each rise of a tenth of a percentage point in r_L with no change in M would be associated with a rise of about $7 billion in GNP under present conditions if regression IIB were correct. This suggests that changes in the velocity of money in response to interest-rate fluctuations may be substantial enough to be of concern to the monetary authorities in their attempts to stabilize the economy. Of course, it must be remembered that regression IIB explains 76 per cent, not all, of the variation in k.

After regression IIʙ, I tried a similar equation, but included time deposits in the money-supply variable and called the resulting ratio k'. The relation becomes very poor indeed, the squared correlation coefficient dropping to 0.26, as shown in Table 2, regression IIc. I also tried using the rate on four- to six-month commercial paper instead of the long-term rate; again the relationship is weaker when both time and demand deposits are included than when demand deposits are used alone, but both relations using the short-term rate were so poor graphically as not to be worth computation.

If the variations in k are indeed due to changes in interest rates, it might be expected that short-term rates would provide a better explanation than long-term rates, since short-term assets are better substitutes for money than are long-term assets. Yet, as stated in the last sentence of the preceding paragraph, the reverse was true. A possible key to this puzzle is the following:[3] Suppose that the demand for real currency and demand deposits depended linearly on real wealth (expressed as capitalized real GNP) and on real GNP itself. Then a long-term rate would be better than a short-term rate for capitalizing GNP. Such an equation would say (letting P denote price level):

$$\frac{M}{P} = \alpha \frac{GNP}{Pr_L} + \beta \frac{GNP}{P} + \gamma .$$

Dividing by GNP/P gives a result similar to regression IIʙ except for a term involving $1/(GNP/P)$:

$$k = \frac{M}{GNP} = \alpha \frac{1}{r_L} + \beta + \gamma \frac{1}{GNP/P} .$$

The residuals of regression IIʙ show no relation, linear or otherwise, with real GNP as judged by a graph, which indicates that the residuals are at most slightly correlated with 1/real GNP, which means that if the interpretation suggested here is adopted, a value of about zero should be assigned to γ in the above equations,[4] making them consistent with regression IIʙ. Both α and β appear from the data to be clearly positive.

Thus far we have not explained why the relationship fits so poorly when time deposits are put into the money stock, and so much better when they are not. It seems plausible that part of the effect of the change in interest rates might be to induce shifts into time deposits when rates are high, and back into demand deposits when rates are low. At this point I put aside

---

[3] This suggestion was made by G. Becker after a draft of the paper was written.

[4] If the residuals from the regression of one variable (k) on another ($1/r_L$) are uncorrelated with a third (1/real GNP), then that third variable will add nothing to R^2 if it be included. Its partial correlation with the first variable holding the second constant will be zero, and its coefficient will not differ significantly from zero.

the problem of explaining variations in the Cambridge k, and turned to the study of the portfolio balance among different kinds of liquid assets.

2. Demand Deposits vs. Time Deposits

Demand and time deposits are substitutes. Theoretical considerations suggest that the division of total deposits between demand and time deposits might be expected to depend on real income per capita and on the interest-rate differential between demand and time deposits.

My income variable is real GNP per capita, denoted by y.

Obtaining appropriate data for the interest differential between demand and time deposits is a difficult problem. It is easy enough to find the average interest rate paid on member bank time deposits since 1927 from Federal Reserve data, and on insured mutual savings bank deposits since 1934 from FDIC data. I have made an index of these two rates since 1934, denoted by r_T, giving 62.5 per cent of the weight to the former because over the period the ratio of time deposits in commercial banks to those in mutual savings banks has been close to 5 to 3.

For demand deposits, the situation is complicated by service charges, and by the prohibition in the thirties of the *payment* of interest on demand deposits. (The *imputation* of interest to be credited against service charges was not prohibited, however.) The relevant interest variable is the marginal rate received by demand depositors. Since the interest prohibition, this marginal rate has been equal to the bank's imputed rate for any account that is active enough to incur a service charge in excess of the imputed interest, and the marginal rate has been zero for any account that is inactive enough so that the imputed interest exceeds the service charge incurred. As far as I know, the rates imputed by banks are not available, except possibly through a survey of individual banks. A casual survey of one bank, my own, indicates that these imputed rates are fairly constant: my bank has been imputing 1.68 per cent for at least ten years, although interest rates in general have risen substantially since 1950. Perhaps a variable indicating the general level of bank service-charge schedules should be included in the equation as well as the interest differential between time and demand deposits; data for this are about as wanting as for the yield on demand deposits. We do know that service charges *paid* (not imputed), taken as a per cent of demand deposits, have been small and almost constant since 1934, except for a slight trend, moving from 0.1 per cent in 1934 to 0.4 per cent in 1959.

In the face of these difficulties, I have simply made the assumption that service charges and the imputed yield on demand deposits have been approximately constant since 1934 and so do not matter, except to affect slightly the constant term in the regressions. Accordingly, I have used as the interest variable the average rate of return on time deposits, r_T.

TABLE 3

REGRESSIONS WITH THE DEPENDENT VARIABLE $D/(D + T)$, I.E., THE RATIO OF DEMAND DEPOSITS TO THE SUM OF DEMAND AND TIME DEPOSITS, 1934–1959

Regression No. (1)	Regression Coefficients				R^2 (A)	Degrees of Freedom (B)	Wrong signs in Columns (C)
	1 (2)	r_T (3)	y (4)	$\left(\dfrac{D}{D + T}\right)_{-1}$ (5)			
IIIA	0.707	−0.0850 (.017)			0.52	24	none
IIIB	0.524	−0.0798 (.0051)	0.0893 (.0059)		0.956	23	none
IIIc	0.208	−0.0264 (.0082)		0.716 (.062)	0.930	23	none
IIIc transformed	0.731	−0.0930					none
IIID	0.552	−0.0843 (.017)	0.0963 (.026)	−0.060 (.21)	0.956	22	5
Simple r^2		(−)0.52	0.50	0.90			

See notes following Table 2.

Regressions IIIA and IIIB of Table 3 show that r_T alone explains about half of the variation in the ratio of demand deposits to total deposits, $D/(D + T)$, and that r_T and y together explain about 96 per cent of the variation. In each case the coefficient of r_T is close to −0.08 and is at least five times its estimated standard error.[5]

---

[5] The dependent variable was $D/(D + T)$. A positive disturbance would be associated with a higher D and/or a lower T than usual for the given values of the independent variables. This would be likely to involve a strain on bank reserves, and hence (possibly after a lag) a monetary tightening and a slight temporary rise in r_T and decline in y. Hence one might expect the true current or lagged disturbances in these equations to be correlated positively with r_T and negatively with y. Since r_T and y are uncorrelated ($r^2 < 0.01$), the estimated coefficient of each is independent of whether the other is present or not. A positive correlation between the disturbance and r_T would lead to an overestimate (algebraically) of the coefficient of r_T, so that the correct coefficient is likely to be further from zero than is −0.08. A negative correlation between the disturbance and y would lead to an underestimate of the coefficient of y, so the correct coefficient is likely to be greater than the estimate 0.09 shown in Tables 1 and 3. Analogous remarks apply to Tables 4, 5, and 6.

Consider the implications of regression IIIB:

$$\frac{D}{D + T} = 0.524 - 0.0798r_T + 0.0893y \,,$$

where y, remember, is real per capita GNP in thousands of 1954 dollars. With r_T at 2.66 per cent and y at 2.42 thousand 1954 dollars,[6] as in 1959, this equation implies that $D/(D + T)$ would be 0.528; the actual 1959 value was 0.526, with $D = \$111$ billion and $T = \$100$ billion. A rise of one-tenth of a percentage point in r_T (e.g., from 2.66 per cent to 2.76 per cent) would lead to a decline in $D/(D + T)$ of 0.1×0.0798 or about 0.008, for given real GNP per capita. Starting with a ratio of 0.526, this would mean a decline to about 0.518. This decline might occur through a decline in D alone, a rise in T alone, or both a decline in D and a rise in T with their total constant, as shown in the following (italics show unchanged 1959 values):

	D	T	$D + T$	$D/(D + T)$
Decline in D	107.5	*100*	207.5	0.518
Rise in T	*111*	103.3	214.3	0.518
Both	109.3	101.7	*211*	0.518

If the response to a rise of a tenth of a percentage point in the interest rate r_T on time deposits took approximately the third form shown above (i.e., a shift from demand to time deposits with no change in their total), the resulting decline in demand deposits would be about \$1.7 billion. Presumably, there would be a slight decline in currency held as well; hence the decline in currency and demand deposits indicated by regression IIIB is of the same order of magnitude as the \$2.0 billion decline indicated by regression IIB above in response to a similar decline of a tenth of a percentage point in the long-term bond rate r_L.[7] Thus the substitution between demand and time deposits revealed by this regression is roughly consistent with the behavior of currency and demand deposits described by regression IIB, as surmised at the end of the preceding section (on the Cambridge k).

Regression IIIc in Table 3 shows that r_T and the lagged value of $D/(D + T)$ together explain about 93 per cent of the variation in $D/(D + T)$, the coefficients being at least three times their standard errors. This equation can be interpreted either as a means of estimating the response of $D/(D + T)$ to an *expected* interest rate, or as a means of estimating the response of the *desired* level of $D/(D + T)$ to the interest rate. In either case, the intercept of the transformed equation is the original intercept divided by 1 minus

---

[6] In thousands of 1959 dollars the 1959 value of y would be $2.42 \times 1.126 = 2.72$.

[7] The two rates r_L and r_T had a simple correlation of 0.96 during 1934-1959, and generally moved together; r_L always exceeded r_T, by amounts varying from 1.20 percent to 1.72 percent; r_L is more sensitive to cycles than is r_T.

the original coefficient of the lagged variable, namely $0.208/(1 - 0.716)$, and the coefficient of the interest variable in the transformed equation is the original interest coefficient divided by the same divisor, namely, $-0.0264/(1 - 0.716)$. The result, shown in the transformed regression IIIc in Table 3, gives an interest coefficient that is again close to -0.08 as in regressions IIIA and IIIB.

Regression IIID shows that if all three of the foregoing explanatory variables are included, the result is essentially the same as if only r_T and y are included: the lagged variable adds nothing to the explanatory power of the two variables r_T and y together, and its coefficient is not significantly different from zero.

3. Demand Deposits vs. Time Deposits and Savings-and-Loan Capital

Savings-and-loan capital is a substitute for deposits. Theoretical considerations suggest that the ratio of demand deposits to the sum of total deposits plus savings-and-loan capital, $D/(D + T + SL)$, might be expected to depend on real income per capita and on the rates of return to time deposits and to savings-and-loan capital, r_{SL} (again it is assumed that the rates of service charges and of interest on demand deposits are constant).

I made an index of r_T and r_{SL}, giving 80 per cent of the weight to r_T because the ratio of time deposits to savings-and-loan capital was about 4 to 1 on the average over the period (it fell from about 5 to 1 in 1934 to about 2 to 1 in 1959). This index is denoted by $r_{T.SL}$. The regressions involving $r_{T.SL}$ are numbers IVA, IVB, IVC, and IVF in Table 4.

Regressions IVA and IVB show that $r_{T.SL}$ alone explains about 88 per cent of the variation of $D/(D + T + SL)$, and $r_{T.SL}$ and y together explain about 92 per cent of the variation. The coefficients of $r_{T.SL}$ in both cases are near -0.12 and are over 13 times their standard errors.

Regression IVC shows that $r_{T.SL}$ and the lagged value of $D/(D + T + SL)$ together explain about 93 per cent of the variation of $D/(D + T + SL)$, the coefficients being at least four times their standard errors. When this equation is transformed as regression IIIc was transformed earlier, the transformed coefficient of the interest variable again becomes approximately -0.12 as in regressions IVA and IVB.

Given that $r_{T.SL}$ is highly and positively correlated with $r_T (r^2 = 0.977)$, one would expect (as Table 1 reports) a more interest-elastic relationship here than in the case of $D/(D + T)$, because in this case shifts into savings-and-loan capital are taken into account, as well as shifts into time deposits.

Regression IVF shows the result of using a crude estimate of permanent real income per capita instead of y, which is real GNP per capita. This crude estimate of permanent real income per capita, called y_p, is obtained for any year simply by multiplying together that year's value of y and the

TABLE 4

Regressions with the Dependent Variable $D/(D+T+SL)$, i.e., the Ratio of Demand Deposits to the Sum of Demand and Time Deposits Plus Savings-and-Loan Shares, 1934–1959

Regression No. (1)	1 (2)	r_T (3)	r_{SL} (4)	$r_{T,SL}$ (5)	y (6)	y_p (7)	$\left(\dfrac{D}{D+T+SL}\right)_{-1}$ (8)	R^2 (A)	Degrees of Freedom (B)	Wrong signs in Columns (C)
IVA	0.754			−0.126 (.0093)				0.88	24	none
IVB	0.683			−0.120 (.0078)	0.0308 (.0087)			0.925	23	none
IVC	0.400			−0.0660 (.016)			0.468 (.11)	0.933	23	none
IVC transformed	0.752			−0.124						none
IVD	0.103	−0.0508 (.012)	0.0282 (.018)				0.791 (.17)	0.946	22	4
IVE	0.229	−0.0967 (.028)	0.0404 (.018)		0.0409 (.022)		0.458 (.24)	0.954	21	4
IVF	0.717			−0.125 (.0089)		0.0199 (.012)		0.90	23	none
IVG	0.121	−0.0417 (.026)	0.0205 (.028)			−0.0099 (.027)	0.809 (.18)	0.947	21	4
Simple r^2	1	(—)0.83	(—)0.71	(—)0.88	0.15	0.03	0.89			

See notes following Table 2.

ratio of personal consumption expenditure to personal disposable income. The assumption is that consumption is a good indicator of permanent disposable income, and that the ratio of permanent to actual income is the same for GNP as for disposable income. As regression IVF shows, y_p adds almost nothing to the explanatory power of $r_{T.SL}$. Also, the coefficient of $r_{T.SL}$ remains at about -0.12 as in regressions IVA, IVB, and IVC.

4. Interlude

If I were to stop at this point, it might appear that these results give a fairly satisfactory picture of the demand for demand deposits relative to time deposits and savings-and-loan capital. The form of the equations seems plausible (though there are other plausible forms, some of which would lend themselves better to a simultaneous analysis of the demand for several kinds of liquid assets as functions of income and the several yields). The signs of the estimated coefficients are in accord with economic theory, the values of the coefficients are several times their standard errors, and the correlations are high ($R^2 > 0.92$ for all the multiple regressions discussed so far). Furthermore, the interest elasticities obtained seem fairly well established since they are confirmed by several different regressions.

I have attempted with less success to extend this kind of approach to U.S. savings bonds and Treasury bills, because they too are substitutes for deposits and savings-and-loan capital. And I have tried with still less success to isolate the separate effects of the individual rates of return to the several liquid assets considered. It seems only fair to present the results of these attempts as well, even though the picture they give is not as orderly as the one given thus far.

5. Savings-and-Loan Capital, Continued

Regression IVD is intended to explain $D/(D + T + SL)$ in terms of its own lagged value, and to examine the separate interest rates r_T and r_{SL} rather than their combined index $r_{T.SL}$. The separation raises the correlation slightly, to $R^2 = 0.946$. The coefficient of r_T is negative, as expected, and about four times its standard error. But, surprisingly, the coefficient of r_{SL} is positive and larger than its standard error. This suggests some difficulty with respect to savings-and-loan capital. Similar difficulties arise in other regressions to be described in the following sections. Later a suggestion will be offered as to where the trouble may lie.

Regressions IVE and IVG show the same difficulty: positive coefficients for r_{SL}. These two regressions differ in that one uses real GNP per capita, y, and the other uses the crude permanent real income per capita variable, y_p. The variable y_p adds nothing to the explanatory power of the lagged

TABLE 5

REGRESSIONS WITH THE DEPENDENT VARIABLE $D/(D + T + SL + SB)$, I.E., THE RATIO OF DEMAND DEPOSITS TO THE SUM OF DEMAND AND TIME DEPOSITS PLUS SAVINGS-AND-LOAN SHARES PLUS U.S. SAVINGS BONDS, 1934–1959

Regression No. (1)	Regression Coefficients							R^2 (A)	Degrees of Freedom (B)	Wrong signs in Columns (C)
	1 (2)	r_T (3)	r_{SL} (4)	r_{SB} (5)	$r_{T,SL,SB}$ (6)	y (7)	$\left(\dfrac{D}{D+\cdots+SB}\right)_{-1}$ (8)			
V$_A$	0.529				−0.0544 (.020)			0.24	24	none
V$_B$	0.652				−0.0605 (.017)	−0.0571 (.016)		0.50	23	none
V$_C$	−0.022				0.0128 (.012)		0.993 (.11)	0.83	23	6
V$_D$	0.071	−0.197 (.028)	0.159 (.020)	0.0416 (.047)		0.0479 (.026)		0.88	21	4,5
V$_E$	0.068	−0.0736 (.045)	0.0638 (.035)	0.0134 (.043)		0.0022 (.025)	0.578 (.18)	0.921	20	4,5
Simple r^2		(—)0.30	0.01	(—)0.48	(—)0.24	(—)0.21	0.82			

See notes following Table 2.

variable and the two interest rates, and its presence renders the other coefficients fuzzy. Because of its performance here and in regression IVf mentioned earlier, y_p was dropped from further consideration.

6. U.S. Savings Bonds

U.S. savings bonds are a substitute for deposits and savings-and-loan capital. This was particularly true during World War II, when the spirit and pressures of patriotism might have been expected to shift liquid assets from other forms into savings bonds, or war bonds as they were then called. Therefore, one might hope that if $D + T + SL$ is expanded to include savings bonds, denoted by SB, the resulting total might behave even more regularly *vis-à-vis* demand deposits than does $D + T + SL$. Accordingly, I estimated several equations designed to explain the behavior of $D/(D + T + SL + SB)$, in terms of y and interest rate variables.

The yield of savings bonds is not easy to describe by means of a single number, for it is in fact a schedule depending on how long the investor holds the bond before redeeming it: the yield is zero or very low if he cashes the bond within a few months or years, and rises to its maximum if he holds until maturity. I constructed an index of these various yields, using as weights the proportions of bonds sold in a base year that were cashed in each of the succeeding years; the index is denoted by r_{SB}. More details of its construction are given in the Appendix. I then constructed an index of the average return on time deposits, savings-and-loan capital, and savings bonds, denoted by $r_{T.SL.SB}$ and equal to $0.8r_{T.SL} + 0.2r_{SB}$. These weights correspond to the fact that the ratio of $T + SL$ to SB averaged about 4 to 1 during 1935–59. But the variation was large: the ratio began from infinity in 1934, fell to about 1 in 1945, and rose again to about 3 by 1959.

Regressions Va and Vb in Table 5 show that $r_{T.SL.SB}$ alone explains only 24 per cent of the variation in $D/(D + T + SL + SB)$, while $r_{T.SL.SB}$ and y together explain 50 per cent. In both cases the coefficients of $r_{T.SL.SB}$ are close to -0.06 and are about three times their standard errors.

The income coefficient in Vb is -0.06, and is more than three times its standard error. The negative sign suggests that savings bonds have a higher income elasticity of demand than the other liquid assets that we have been considering.

When $r_{T.SL.SB}$ and the lagged value of the dependent variable are used together, in regression Vc, R^2 rises to 0.83, but the coefficient of $r_{T.SL.SB}$ becomes positive (though only weakly so). Hence this equation is unreliable, and no transformed version of it was computed.

In regression Vd the index of interest rates is replaced by the three separate interest rates r_T, r_{SL}, and r_{SB}. These variables and income y explain about 88 per cent of the variation in $D/(D + T + SL + SB)$, which is much better than the 50 per cent explained by $r_{T.SL.SB}$ and y. Thus

TABLE 6

REGRESSIONS WITH THE DEPENDENT VARIABLE $D/(D + T + SL + SB + TB)$, I.E., THE RATIO OF DEMAND DEPOSITS TO THE SUM OF DEMAND AND TIME DEPOSITS PLUS SAVINGS-AND-LOAN SHARES PLUS U.S. SAVINGS BONDS PLUS TREASURY BILLS OUTSIDE BANKS AND INSURANCE COMPANIES, 1934-1959

Regression No. (1)	Regression Coefficients								R^2 (A)	Degrees of Freedom (B)	Wrong signs in Columns (C)
	1 (2)	r_T (3)	r_{SL} (4)	r_{SB} (5)	r_{TB} (6)	$r_{T.SL.SB.TB}$ (7)	y (8)	$\left(\dfrac{D}{D+\cdots+TB}\right)_{-1}$ (9)			
VIA	0.550					−0.0723 (.021)			0.34	24	none
VIB	0.679					−0.0717 (.016)	−0.0668 (.016)		0.62	23	none
VIC	−0.043					0.0127 (.013)		1.042 (.11)	0.87	23	7,9[a]
VID	0.089	−0.193 (.036)	0.155 (.024)	0.0397 (.052)	−0.0079 (.010)		0.042 (.030)		0.90	20	4,5
Simple r^2						(−)0.34	(−)0.28	0.86			

See notes following Table 2.

[a] In column 9, regression VIc the coefficient should be between 0 and 1 if it is to be interpreted as a coefficient of expectation or of adjustment. See text.

there is independent variation among the three separate interest rates. (See Table 7.) But, as with the ratio $D/(D + T + SL)$, only r_T among the interest rates has a negative coefficient as expected; r_{SL} and r_{SB} have positive coefficients. The coefficient of income is positive again, but only weakly so. The same remarks apply to regression VE, which includes the lagged value of the dependent variable as well as y and the three interest rates. These two equations are unreliable.

7. Treasury Bills

Particularly in recent years, with the yield of Treasury bills high enough to compete with the yields of time deposits and savings-and-loan capital and savings bonds, Treasury bills are a substitute for these other liquid assets, at least for large holders of liquid assets. Accordingly, I tried several equations designed to explain the behavior of $D/(D + T + SL + SB + TB)$, where TB denotes the amount of Treasury bills held by the private non-banking sector (actually, insurance-company holdings were excluded too; they are negligible).

The rate on Treasury bills, r_{TB}, is the average yield on new issues of 90-day bills. I made an index of $r_{T.SL.SB}$ and r_{TB}, denoted by $r_{T.SL.SB.TB}$, with 7 per cent of the weight assigned to r_{TB}, since the ratio of $T + SL + SB$ to TB averaged about 13 to 1 over the period, though it had a trend from about 60 in 1934 to about 8 in 1959.

Regressions VIA and VIB in Table 6 show that $r_{T.SL.SB.TB}$ alone explains about 34 per cent of the variation in $D/(D + T + SL + SB + TB)$, and that this interest rate and income y together explain about 62 per cent of the variation. In both cases the coefficients of the interest variable are close to -0.07 and are more than three times their standard errors.

The income coefficient in VIB is negative (-0.067) like that in the case where savings bonds are included but not Treasury bills, and is more than four times its standard error. The implication is that Treasury bills have a higher income elasticity of demand than the other liquid assets we have been considering.

When $r_{T.SL.SB.TB}$ and the lagged value of the dependent variable are used together, in regression VIc, the result is very much like that in case Vc where savings bonds are included but not Treasury bills: the correlation rises (to $R^2 = 0.87$), but the coefficient of the interest variable becomes (weakly) positive. This equation is unreliable.

In regression VID the index of interest rates is replaced by the four separate rates r_T, r_{SL}, r_{SB}, and r_{TB}. These four rates and y together explain 90 per cent of the variation of $D/(D + T + SL + SB + TB)$. The coefficient of r_T is strongly negative, as usual. The coefficients of r_{SL} and r_{SB} are positive, contrary to expectation, the former strongly so and the latter weakly so, as in the case of $D + T + SL + SB$. The coefficient of

r_{TB} is weakly negative. The coefficient of income is positive again, but only weakly. This equation is unreliable.

Table 7 gives simple correlations among all the independent variables used in Tables 3–6, except for the lagged values of the dependent variables.

TABLE 7

SIMPLE CORRELATION COEFFICIENTS AMONG INDEPENDENT VARIABLES IN TABLES 3–6 (AND r_L),
1934-1959

r_L	r_T	r_{SL}	r_{SB}	r_{TB}	$r_{T.SL}$	$r_{T.SL.SB}$	$r_{T.SL.SB.TB}$	y	y_p	
1.000	0.965	0.73	0.69	0.52	0.959	0.964	0.964	−0.09	0.02	r_L
	1.000	0.74	0.74	0.53	0.988	0.996	0.995	−0.07	0.09	r_T
		1.000	0.17	−0.10	0.83	0.78	0.70	−0.64	−0.56	r_{SL}
			1.000	0.86	0.64	0.72	0.78	0.57	0.68	r_{SB}
				1.000	0.42	0.49	0.60	0.70	0.82	r_{TB}
					1.000	0.995	0.975	−0.20	−0.06	$r_{T.SL}$
						1.000	0.991	−0.11	0.04	$r_{T.SL.SB}$
							1.000	0.01	0.16	$r_{T.SL.SB.TB}$
								1.000	0.931	y
									1.000	y_p

8. Time Deposits vs. Savings-and-Loan Capital

Tables 3–6 appear to account fairly well for the demand for demand deposits relative to the other liquid assets considered, except that, as noted, the individual rates of return to savings-and-loan capital and to savings bonds do not perform as expected. What if one uses the same approach to try to explain the ratio of time deposits to time deposits plus savings-and-loan capital, $T/(T + SL)$, by means of the difference between the return to savings-and-loan capital and the interest rate on time deposits, $r_{SL} - r_T$? I have done no calculations, but a graph of these two variables indicates the following: From 1934 to 1947, the ratio $T/(T + SL)$ was almost constant, varying only between 0.83 and 0.86, while the interest differential fell from about 2 per cent to about 1.3 per cent. Then from 1947 to 1959, while the interest differential fell fairly steadily to about 1 per cent, the ratio $T/(T + SL)$ *also fell* from about 0.84 to about 0.65, in a fairly linear fashion on the graph. Thus the interest differential appeared to have no influence (or else an almost perfectly counteracted influence) from 1934 to 1947, and since then savings and loan capital has grown faster than time deposits, even though the rate-of-return advantage enjoyed by savings-and-loan capital has been dwindling. It is this behavior which I think may be at the bottom of the unexpected positive coefficients of r_{SL} in Tables 4–6.

What can explain this apparent perverse interest-response of time deposits relative to savings-and-loan capital? Between 1934 and 1959 there may have been an improvement in the quality of savings-and-loan capital relative to time deposits as seen by investors. The substantial advertising campaigns of the savings-and-loan associations in the postwar years may have had this effect. So may their lengthening record of safety. The Federal Savings and Loan Insurance Corporation has probably played a role here, even though in effect it merely insures savings-and-loan capital against ultimate loss, not against illiquidity, as contrasted with the Federal Deposit Insurance Corporation, which insures bank deposits against both illiquidity and loss.

9. Further Problems

This brief study raises more questions than it answers. Some of the interesting ones are as follows. What is the relationship of currency to the other liquid assets considered in Tables 3–6?[8] Can one explain the *stocks* of various liquid assets held, rather than (or in addition to) their ratios to each other? Would it be fruitful to separate liquid-asset holdings of households and use disposable income rather than GNP to try to explain them and similarly to treat other groups of asset-holders separately? (Flow of funds data are promising here.) Can one get data to pursue the study prior to 1934 when the FDIC began to publish extensive and useful data? Can one do a better job with U.S. savings bonds, especially during the war, and also with Treasury bills? Can more light be shed on the puzzle of the relation between time deposits and savings-and-loan capital? Can a useful complete model be made incorporating supply as well as demand conditions for liquid assets?

APPENDIX

Definitions of Variables

Note: All stocks of assets are in billions of dollars as of June 30, and rates of interest are in per cent per year, unless otherwise noted below.

C = currency outside banks.

D = demand deposits adjusted, excluding Treasury deposits.

T = time deposits in commercial and mutual savings banks, excluding Treasury deposits.

---

[8] Phillip Cagan [1] is very helpful here. He finds that the ratio of currency to the sum of currency plus demand and time deposits in commercial banks is well explained for 1919–1955 in the U.S. by three variables: expected real income per capita, expected rate of return on deposits net of losses, and the average personal income tax rate.

SL = share capital in savings-and-loan associations, December 31.

SB = U.S. savings bonds outstanding, at redemption value.

TB = Treasury bills held by investors other than Federal agencies, banks, and insurance companies (insurance company holdings are negligible).

r_L = long-term interest rate (Moody's Aaa corporate bond rate, extrapolated before 1919 via Macauley's railroad bond yield index).

r_T = average rate of interest on time deposits (estimated as 0.625 times the rate on member commercial bank deposits plus 0.375 times the rate on insured mutual savings bank deposits).

r_{SL} = average rate of return on share capital in savings-and-loan associations belonging to the Federal Home Loan Bank system (extrapolated before 1944 via the rate on Federal savings and loan associations).

r_{SB} = average rate of interest on U.S. savings bonds, series A–D and E (the rates for holding up to $\frac{1}{2}$ year and up to 1 year were averaged simply; the rates for holding up to $1\frac{1}{2}$ years and up to 2 years were averaged simply; and so on; then a *weighted* average of these rates for holding up to 1 year, up to 2 years, and so on, was constructed. The weights were the proportions of E bonds bought in 1946 that were cashed within 1 year, within 2 years, and so on).

r_{TB} = average interest rate on new issues of 90-day Treasury bills.

$r_{T.SL} = 0.8r_T + 0.2r_{SL}$.

$r_{T.SL.SB} = 0.64r_T + 0.16r_{SL} + 0.2r_{SB}$.

$r_{T.SL.SB.TB} = 0.5952r_T + 0.1488r_{SL} + 0.186r_{SB} + 0.07r_{TB}$.

GNP = gross national product, billions of current dollars per year.

$k = (C + D)/\text{GNP}$.

$k' = (C + D + T)/\text{GNP}$.

y = real GNP per capita, in thousands of 1954 dollars per capita per year.

References

[1] CAGAN, PHILLIP, The Demand for Currency Relative to the Total Money Supply, *J. Polit. Econ.*, LXVI (1958), 303-28.

[2] LATANÉ, HENRY ALLEN, Cash Balances and the Interest Rate—A Pragmatic Approach, *Rev. Econ. Stat.*, 36 (1954), 456-60.

9

The Dynamics of Inflation in Chile

ARNOLD C. HARBERGER, *University of Chicago*

Chile provides a promising ground for the study of inflation, for a number of reasons. Its history of inflation is long, and for practical purposes continuous. Its rate of inflation has varied greatly over time, permitting the testing of theories in which not only the level of prices but also their rate of change plays a role. Its data are relatively good. And, finally, the Chilean economy has achieved a level of development sufficiently high that one can at least entertain the hope that some of the principal inferences derived from a study of inflation there would be applicable to "modern" economies in general. Chile has well-developed financial institutions, a fairly large industrial sector (manufacturing accounts for some 20 per cent of the national income), and virtually no "non-monetary" sector (agriculture accounts for only around 15 per cent of the national income, and consists mainly of commercial rather than subsistence farming).

Chile's inflation began well before the turn of the century, but for the most part was contained within "moderate" limits until the 1930's. By 1929 the wholesale price index (1913 = 100) stood at 193, but by 1947 it had reached 1300, and by 1958 it had gone to over 32,000. It is difficult to date precisely the "takeoff" into inflation of major proportions. In the 1930's the price level slightly more than doubled, with years of rather substantial inflation being interspersed with years of stability or slight deflation. From 1940 onward, the inflation has been effectively continuous, with occasional month-to-month declines in the price level, but with no decline over a period as long as a year.

I have chosen as the period of this study the 20-year span from 1939 through 1958. During this period the wholesale price index and the cost-of-living index both increased over 80 fold. The annual rate of inflation of wholesale prices ranged from 2 per cent in 1943 to 83 per cent in 1955; and that of consumer prices ranged from 7 per cent in 1939 to 71 per cent in 1954.

There can be no doubt that monetary factors played a dominant role in Chile's inflation. During the period covered by this study, the money

I wish to express my indebtedness to Mr. Yoram Barzel for his aid in supervising the computations made for this study, and for the many valuable discussions we had along the way.

supply rose about 100 fold. As real income about doubled during these 20 years, income velocity rose by some 60 per cent. It seems highly plausible to regard this rise in velocity as the reaction of the Chilean public to the increase in the rate of inflation from the earlier to the later part of the period covered. The cost of holding cash balances was closely approximated in Chile by the rate at which the purchasing power of money deteriorated, and it is only reasonable that the ratio of cash holdings to income should decline as this cost increases. We thus have a broad picture of massive increases in the quantity of money leading to substantial inflation of prices, and of this inflation being reinforced by a rather limited "flight from cash" on the part of the public.

1. Scope and Objectives of the Study

In this paper I try to explore in some detail the mechanism by which the Chilean inflation was generated. Hypotheses about this mechanism abound, and opinions are strong and sometimes vehemently expressed. This study was motivated by the belief that only by hard empirical work and close examination of the evidence, can we resolve such conflicts of view as those regarding the Chilean inflation.

This study takes as its task the explanation of movements in the rate of inflation itself (rather than the level of prices). It deals with both annual and quarterly rates of inflation, and with both the consumer and the wholesale price indexes, together with their main components. It seeks to discover the dynamic process by which monetary expansion has its effects upon the level of prices, to ascertain the role of past acceleration of inflation upon the current rate of price rise, and to clarify somewhat the role that wage changes played in the Chilean inflationary process. In the remainder of this section, I shall elaborate upon this brief statement of scope and objectives, discuss the considerations which led to certain key decisions on the design of the study, and introduce the variables used in the econometric work that follows.

1.1. Choice of the Rate of Price Change as the Variable to Be Explained. A study of the Chilean inflation might take as the variable to be explained the level of prices, the level of real cash balances, the rate of change of the price level, or perhaps still others. If the price level is taken as the variable to be explained, even a very crude approach yields quite good results: the coefficient of determination between the quantity of money and the level of either consumer or wholesale prices for the period of this study is 0.99. But the goodness of fit of this relationship is largely determined by the strong upward trends in both of the variables considered; almost any two Chilean series expressed in nominal money units would have a similarly high correlation.

Choosing the level of real cash balances as the variable to be explained provides the investigator with somewhat more of a challenge; here the common upward trend of the money and price-level variables is eliminated by deflating one by the other. John Deaver, in an unpublished study [1], has attempted to explain variations in real-cash balances in Chile. He used as explanatory variables real income per capita and the "expected" rate of inflation, the latter variable being defined as a weighted average of past rates of inflation, with the weights attached to the rates of inflation of past years declining exponentially as the years considered became more remote from the year for which cash balances were being explained. Using these two explanatory variables, Deaver was able to explain 85 per cent of the variation in per capita real cash balances over the period 1932–55, and 94 per cent for the period 1935–55.

This paper will focus on the rate of inflation as the variable to be explained. I make this choice partly because of the challenge it presents. Crude applications of simple theories do not provide such successful explanations when they are applied to variations in the rate of inflation as they do when the level of prices is taken as the dependent variable. Concurrent changes in the money supply explain less than two-thirds of the variation in the annual rate of inflation, and less than a third of the variation in the quarterly rate of inflation of consumer or wholesale prices. Changes in wages do no better. There is thus ample room for improving upon the simplest of explanations. My second reason for making this choice is that the rate of inflation is itself an important variable in policy decisions. Measurements of the effects of other variables (both those beyond and those under the control of policy makers) on the rate of inflation are thus potentially useful as aids in the formulation of policy.

1.2. Use of Quarterly as well as Annual Data.

During the period of this study the annual rate of price rise showed a generally upward trend all the way to 1954–55, and an abatement thereafter. Though the pattern is not a smooth one, the serial correlation is substantial. This leads one to worry whether some explanatory variables might not achieve "statistical significance" merely because their broad movements are similar in shape to those of the rate of inflation, rather than because of any systematic relationship. The use of quarterly data does not eliminate the problems caused by serial correlation in the dependent variable, but it serves to reduce them substantially, for the time path of the quarterly rate of inflation is much less smooth than that of the annual rate of inflation. There is a great deal of within-the-year variation in the rate of inflation (apart from seasonal factors), which would operate to reduce substantially the explanatory power of variables that simply had broad movements similar to those of the annual rate of inflation.

Apart from the above "statistical" motivation for using quarterly data, there is the natural urge, in a study of dynamic movements, to have an explanation which applies to short spans of time as well as to long ones. One would hope that the general picture of the dynamics of inflation which emerges from the use of quarterly data would be similar to that resulting from the use of annual data. Dissimilarities would be danger signals, suggesting the need for further investigation.

1.3. Allowance for the Effects of Past Changes in Money Supply upon the Current Rate of Price Change. It is perfectly obvious that the effects of increases in money supply upon the price level do not occur instantaneously. The path by which such effects take place through time is of interest not only from a scientific point of view, but also from the standpoint of the policy-maker. If the money supply has been increasing at the rate of, say, 25 per cent per annum, and prices at something like the same rate, even a complete halting of the printing presses may not have a substantial effect on the rate of price rise for some time (if the lags between money-supply changes and price changes are long), but may on the other hand bring price rises to a halt within 2 or 3 months (if the lags are short).

One way of capturing the lag pattern by which money-supply changes affect the price level is by introducing money-supply changes with different lags as explanatory variables for the rate of inflation. Thus, if P_t represents the percentage change in the price level during the year t, and M_t represents the percentage change in the money supply during the same year, and M_{t-1} the percentage change in money supply during the previous year, and so on, we may write

$$(1) \qquad P_t = a_0 + a_1 M_t + a_2 M_{t-1} + a_3 M_{t-2} + \cdots .$$

It is to be expected that at some point the introduction of further lagged increases in money supply will no longer add to the explanation of variation in P_t. This point was reached, for both the consumer price index and the wholesale price index, when M_{t-1} was included; the addition of M_{t-2} as an explanatory variable proved useless. Thus, in the annual regressions reported here, M_t and M_{t-1} appear as money-supply variables. A further check on whether these variables actually include all the relevant lag effects is to see whether the sum of their coefficients falls substantially short of the expected level. General equilibrium theory tells us to expect, in a truly *ceteris paribus* situation, that a 1 per cent per annum rise in the quantity of money will produce a 1 per cent per annum rise in the general price level: this would mean the coefficients of M_t and M_{t-1} adding up to 1.0. A regression of the logarithm of the general price level on the logarithms of money supply and real income for the period of this study yields an estimated elasticity of prices with respect to money supply equal to 1.1. The question of choosing between the "theoretical" norm of 1.0

and the "empirical" norm of 1.1 will be begged here, because the sum of the coefficients of M_t and M_{t-1} is not significantly different from either number for either the wholesale or the consumer price index.

For a given sum of the coefficients of M_t and M_{t-1}, the speed or sluggishness of the response of prices to changes in the money supply will be reflected in the ratio of these coefficients. When two different price indexes are compared, however, this ratio is not an unambiguous indicator of speed or sluggishness of response, for the sums of the coefficients of M_t and M_{t-1} need not be the same for the two indexes being compared. Thus, of two indexes, the one with the lower ratio of a_1 to a_2 might nonetheless have a higher a_1, indicating greater current price response to changes in the money supply than the second index. The ambiguity boils down to a question of which of several reasonable measures of speed or sluggishness of response we choose to adopt. In this paper I shall arbitrarily adopt the ratio measure, and say that one price is less sluggish than another if a greater fraction of its total response to a change in the money supply comes in the "current" period.

Measuring the lagged responses of prices to changes in money supply on the basis of quarterly data presented more troublesome problems than those encountered with the annual data. To explain the price change of quarter t on the basis of a succession of money-supply changes representing quarters t, $t - 1$, $t - 2$, and so on would require perhaps six or eight separate money-supply variables, in addition to the other explanatory variables used in this study. This would impose computational burdens beyond the resources available for the study, to say nothing of the problems of multicollinearity that would probably arise when it was attempted to introduce six or seven or eight versions of the same basic series, each lagged one observation behind the next, as separate independent variables.

I proceeded on a step-by-step basis. First I introduced the current quarterly change in money supply, and the same variable lagged one quarter, as variables to explain the current quarter's change in consumer and in wholesale prices. The coefficients of these two money-supply variables turned out to be approximately equal,[1] justifying their amalgamation into a single variable M'_t representing the percentage change in the money supply in the six months prior to the end of the quarter t. As the second step, I introduced M'_{t-2} side-by-side with M'_t in order to explain P'_t, the percentage change in prices during quarter t. Here for the two main (consumer and wholesale) price indexes the coefficient of M'_{t-2} averaged

---

[1] The statement that the coefficients of current and lagged quarterly changes in money supply were equal does not deny that current changes operate more powerfully on prices than do lagged changes. In fact, this is the proper conclusion to draw, for all of last quarter's changes in money supply have the opportunity to influence prices during the whole of the current quarter, while only those current money supply changes which took place at the very beginning of this quarter have the same chance.

slightly less than half that of M'_t. As the third step, I took the liberty of assuming that the same pattern of declining influence would apply to still earlier increases in the money supply. I constructed a variable $D'_t = 0.59M'_{t-2} + 0.28M'_{t-4} + 0.13M'_{t-6}$, which was a weighted average of six-month percentage increases in the quantity of money, with the weight of each successively more remote increase being slightly less than half that of its less remote neighbor. Using M'_t and D'_t, I obtained better explanations of the variations in the quarterly rate of inflation than had emerged from the use of M'_t and M'_{t-2} alone.

I thus settled for a sort of compromise between the possible extremes of estimating distinct coefficients for many separate money variables, on the one hand, and imposing a complete time path by which changes in money supply would influence prices, on the other. The relative weights applying to increases in money supply in the current and the immediately preceding quarter were imposed, though after some experimentation, in constructing M'_t. The relative weights applying to increases in the money supply in the period between 6 and 24 months before the end of the current quarter were also imposed, here without direct experimentation, in constructing D'_t. But the data were left, in each case, to decide the relative importance of M'_t and D'_t in explaining the variations in P'_t. This procedure leaves, I believe, ample scope for the main differences in the speeds of response of different prices to reveal themselves in the results of regressions, while avoiding the worst problems of collinearity, which would come from trying to estimate the pattern of lagged response in much greater detail.[2]

The use of weights that add up to 1.0 in constructing D'_t from M'_{t-2}, M'_{t-4}, and M'_{t-6} gives D'_t, like M'_t, the dimension of a 6-month percentage change in the quantity of money. However, since P'_t is defined as a quarterly percentage change in prices, the sum of the coefficients of D'_t and M'_t is "expected" to be not around 1.0 or 1.1, but only half of this magnitude. (If the money supply were to increase at 10 per cent per six months at a steady pace, we would expect the price level to increase at 10 per cent per six months, which is 5 per cent per quarter.) Similarly, if the quarterly regression for a particular price variable is to tell the same story as the annual regression for that price variable, the sum of the coefficients of M'_t and D'_t in the quarterly regression should equal half of the

---

[2] At a later stage of the study, long after the choice of D'_t was settled upon, I obtained access to electronic computing equipment and experimented with the simultaneous introduction of four separate money-change variables: M'_t, M'_{t-2}, M'_{t-4}, and M'_{t-6}, covering the same 24-month span as is covered by M'_t and D'_t. The results were favorable to the original choice of D'_t. Using the four separate variables yielded only slight improvement in explanatory power (usually none after adjustment for degrees of freedom), but resulted in substantial evidence of multicollinearity—erratic behavior and high standard errors of the individual money-change coefficients.

sum of the coefficients of M_t and M_{t-1} in the annual regression. This test for consistency will be applied when the empirical results are examined.

1.4. Disaggregation of the General Price Indexes into Their Components. It probably is unnecessary to try to justify exploring the mechanism by which inflation strikes different components of a general price index. There is every reason to expect that some prices will be more sluggish than others in responding to general inflationary forces, and to discern these differential responses is surely a proper part of a study of the dynamics of inflation. Moreover, it is often quite revealing in other respects to "break open," so to speak, a regression explaining movements in a general price index into "subregressions" explaining movements in the component indexes. One is startled, at times, when a coefficient that looks perfectly plausible in an aggregate regression turns out to "come from" an implausible component. And hypotheses that appear to stand up rather well to tests involving the general price level are often shattered when one proceeds to the components.

In this study four distinct components of the consumer price index were treated separately: food, clothing, house rent, and miscellaneous prices. The wholesale price index was broken down into import price and domestic price components, and of the latter the agricultural and industrial price components (though not the mineral component) were given separate treatment.

1.5. Allowance for Effects of Past Acceleration of Inflation upon the Current Rate of Price Change. The role the interest rate plays in traditional liquidity-preference formulations of the demand for money is as a cost of holding money for a period; i.e., as a yield from alternative uses of funds that is foregone when cash is held. In Chile, during the bulk of the period covered in this study, the interest rate did not measure the cost of holding cash. Interest rates on bank loans were subject to legal control, and generally were kept at levels substantially below the rate of price inflation, so that the rates actually paid by borrowers were typically negative in real terms. The cost of holding cash for a typical holder can, in these circumstances, be better measured by the deterioration in the purchasing power of money (the rate of inflation).[3]

At the beginning of this paper the rise (of some 60 per cent) in the income

---

[3] It would be still better to use the rate of inflation *plus* the real rate of return that the cash-holder might expect to get from investment in non-monetary assets. But the expected real rate of return on non-monetary assets would surely vary among cash-holders, and would not be available as a statistical series in any case. It is unlikely, however, that the expected real rate of return on alternative assets varied very much over the period of this study, in comparison with the drastic movements of the rate of inflation, so that *movements* in the rate of inflation are likely to reflect *movements* in cost of holding cash quite accurately.

velocity of circulation over the period of this study was attributed to the increased cost of holding cash. Deaver's success in explaining variations in real-cash balances on the basis of changes in the expected cost of holding cash confirms this attribution.

How do these considerations apply in a study that focuses upon explaining variations in the rate of inflation? A simple transformation of the traditional liquidity-preference function permits us to express the price level as a function of the quantity of money, the level of real income, and the expected cost of holding cash. Taking first differences in this function, we can express the rate of change of prices as a function of the rate of change of the quantity of money, the rate of change of real income, and the *rate of change of the expected cost of holding cash*. A high expected cost of holding cash will not in itself induce prices to rise in a particular period, if people have already adjusted their cash balances to the levels dictated by this fact. It is when the expected cost of holding cash is *rising* that people will try to lower their real cash balances, thereby tending to increase the upward pressure on prices.

The variable I have chosen to represent the rate of change in the expected cost of holding cash is the difference between the rate of inflation in the past year and the rate of inflation in the year before that. Since the effect being measured is one that presumably affects people's over-all decisions on how much cash to hold, there is no reason why the cost of holding cash cannot be measured in the same way, whether one is trying to explain movements in rents or movements in food prices. Accordingly, the rate of inflation used for any year in constructing this variable was taken to be the mean of the rates of rise of the wholesale and consumer price indexes for that year.

For convenience of reference, I shall call the variable just defined the "acceleration" variable. In the "annual" regressions, it is labeled A_t. In explaining the change of prices in year t, A_t represents the rate of inflation of year $t - 1$, minus the rate of inflation of year $t - 2$. In the "quarterly" regressions, the acceleration variable is labeled A'_t. In explaining the change of prices in quarter t, A'_t represents the rate of inflation in the year ending just prior to the start of quarter t minus the rate of inflation in the year before that. In this way A'_t is kept entirely free of seasonal distortions.

It should be noted at this point that both A_t and A'_t are bound to be poor representations of the rate of change in the expected cost of holding cash. Perhaps it would have been worthwhile to follow Deaver's procedure of constructing refined weighted averages of past price changes, and then taking first differences in these averages. I decided against this refinement, partly because the most recent changes in the rate of inflation would in any event receive heaviest weight in a "refined" acceleration variable, partly because of the computational costs entailed in arriving at an appropriate weighting procedure, partly because A_t and A'_t are more easily understandable by nonprofessionals than more complicated weighted averages, and partly because of a suspicion that even after great refinement the acceleration variable might not prove very useful in explaining variations in the annual or quarterly rates of change of prices. To elaborate on the last reason, I felt that it was one thing to expect that average real-cash balances would be lower in a period of high inflation than in a period of low inflation, and quite another to expect that the processes by which people adapted their expectations to past experience and by which they adjusted their behavior to changes in expectations were sufficiently regular for changes in any measure of the cost of holding cash to have significant explanatory power for variations in annual or quarterly rates of inflation. The chances of even a highly refined acceleration variable not "working" seemed too great to warrant large investments in refinement. On the other hand, there was a strong likelihood that if the processes involved were sufficiently regular for a refined acceleration variable to work well, crude variables like A_t and A'_t would also give a reasonably creditable performance.

1.6. Allowance for the Effects of Wage Changes on the Rate of Inflation. The role of wages in the inflationary process has been the subject of heated controversy in Chile. As elsewhere, one issue has been whether wages simply responded passively to inflationary forces that were essentially monetary in origin, or whether they played a more active role in the process. An extreme "monetarist" would hold that wages were indeed passive, and that once monetary factors had been adequately taken into account, wage variables would not improve the explanation of movements in the rate of inflation. At the other extreme, we have the position that wages are the principal factor explaining the rate of inflation, and that once their effect has been taken into account monetary variables will not improve the explanation of the inflationary process. The unsophisticated version of this extreme view, holding that monetary factors play no role in inflation, need not be considered here. The sophisticated version would hold that the velocity of circulation was "elastic" within rather wide limits, and would vary to allow prices to adjust to wage changes even if the money supply did not change. So long as the money supply did not get completely "out of line" with wages, monetary variables would not be able to add to the explanation given by wages of the course of prices.

Between these two extremes is what I would call the neo-orthodox position. This position, while accepting the orthodox view that wages would be passive in an ideally functioning, rapidly adjusting, competitive labor market, would deny that actual labor markets generally possess these properties. In Chile, at least, the labor market is fragmented, with many intersectoral distortions, and slow to adjust. Moreover, the government's wage policy has operated to give wages a special degree of "autonomy." During the whole of the period under investigation, there existed in Chile a sort of minimum wage, called the *sueldo vital*. This was the minimum salary paid by the government to white-collar workers in its employ. It was revised upward annually, usually during the first two or three months. of each year. The setting of the *sueldo vital* was largely the result of political negotiations among the parties in Congress, and most observers agree that once a certain percentage increase in the *sueldo vital* was determined, wage contracts in the industrial sector of the economy were adjusted to at least match this percentage increase. Though the *sueldo vital* usually remained constant for a year once it had been set, private wage contracts were under no such restriction, and private wages did tend to drift upward during each year in response to the pressures of the labor market and collective bargaining. But normally their upward drift was slow, so that when a new *sueldo vital* was set in the subsequent year, industrial wages took a discontinuous jump upward, increasing by roughly enough to match the percentage increase determined by the government.

Under these circumstances, it is clear that wage movements could have played an active role in the inflationary process. Autonomous wage rises could lead to price rises even in the absence of increases in the quantity of money, but the neo-orthodox position would hold that if the monetary authorities failed to allow the money supply to increase sufficiently to "finance" a wage rise, unemployment would grow and activity slacken even in the face of a rising price level. In this sort of situation, wages would be able to add somewhat to the explanation given by monetary factors movements in the rate of inflation. On the other hand, if the monetary authorities always increased the money supply by enough (or more than enough) to assure full employment at the new wage level, there would be no strong reason to expect that wages would *add* significantly to a monetary explanation of inflation. Even though the wage rises were an autonomous force producing the inflation, they would in this case have their effects on prices by way of monetary expansion.

In reality, one would expect that in 20 years of Chilean inflationary history there would have been occasions when autonomous wage changes were "financed" by monetary expansion, other occasions when autonomous wage changes were not so financed, and still other occasions when the forces of monetary expansion operated without any significant stimulus from wage movements. Regression analysis is not suited to sorting out incidents into these different classes, but it can give some indications of their relative importance, and can surely distinguish between the extreme positions that deny the explanatory power of either wage changes or monetary changes, once the other is taken into account.

The variable we shall use to represent wage changes (labeled W_t in the annual regressions, and W'_t in the quarterly regressions) is the percentage change in the *sueldo vital* at its latest annual adjustment. Thus, to explain the rise of prices during 1951, we would use the percentage change in the *sueldo vital* from January 1950 to January 1951, and in the quarterly regressions this same change in the *sueldo vital* would be used as an explanatory variable for the price rises that occurred in the first, second, third, and fourth quarters of 1951.[4]

1.7. Allowance for the Effects of Income Changes.
Variations in real income play such an important role in all versions of monetary theory that no discussion of their inclusion as an explanatory variable is necessary. However, some practical problems arose in connection with the income variable to be used in this study, and they do require comment.

The national income data for Chile are available only on an annual basis. This was not a very satisfactory situation for the purposes of this study. Even the annual regressions were concerned with price movements from one December to the next, and the rate of income change within this period could be only imperfectly reflected in the rate of change between one annual average income and the next. The problem was still worse when it came to the quarterly regressions; here it appeared essential to have some way of spreading the observed changes in annual average national income among the separate quarters.

My first attempt was to build up a synthetic monthly income series on the basis of the regression of annual changes in national income on changes in the annual average values of some series (industrial production, electricity output, mining output, and rail traffic) that were also available on a monthly basis. The effort was frustrated by the poor fit ($R^2 = 0.10$) of the basic multiple regression. I then decided to obtain quarterly changes in national income by performing a smoothing operation on the available annual income data. From the smoothed income series I constructed the quarterly income-change variable Y'_t, representing the percentage change in real income from quarter $t - 1$ to quarter t, and the annual income-change variable Y_t, representing the percentage change in real income from the fourth quarter of year $t - 1$ to the fourth quarter of year t.[5]

---

[4] This variable has the possible disadvantage of failing to capture the upward drift of private-sector wages during the periods between the annual adjustments of the *sueldo vital*, but this failing cannot be avoided, owing to the lack of a monthly or quarterly series on private-sector wages. On the other hand, it has the great advantages of being the most clearly "autonomous" of any possible Chilean wage series, and of having substantial and precisely timed movements.

[5] The method of smoothing was as follows: First, changes in the annual average values of national income were expressed as algebraic functions of the unknown quarter-to-quarter changes Q_t. Then the variance of the Q_t was minimized, subject to the constraints that the series generated be consistent with each of the known year-to-year changes in annual average income. This procedure, which was quite laborious, strikes me now as perhaps an excessive refinement, but some sort of smoothing was clearly called for and this one had the virtue of being "objective." Even so, rates of income change had to be assumed on the basis of other data for the year 1939, since the official income series begins in 1940. To save others from going through the same labors again, the series for Y_t and Y'_t are reproduced in Appendix 2 of this paper.

2. Empirical Results

This section presents the results of the empirical part of this study. These are contained in Tables II–V, but to aid in the reading of those tables, I first present in equation form the results obtained by using the rate of increase of the consumer price index as the dependent variable, and recapitulate the definitions of the independent variables. The results found for the consumer price index using annual data are summarized in equations (2.1)–(2.3).

$$(2.1) \quad P_t = -1.05 - 1.05Y_t + 0.80M_t + 0.34M_{t-1} \qquad (R^2 = 0.84),$$

$$\qquad\qquad (7.13) \quad\; (.31) \qquad (.17) \qquad\;\; (.16)$$

$$(2.2) \quad P_t = -0.32 - 0.91Y_t + 0.74M_t + 0.34M_{t-1} + 0.20A_t \quad (R^2 = 0.87),$$

$$\qquad\qquad (9.23) \quad\, (.31) \qquad (.16) \qquad\;\; (.15) \qquad\;\; (.12)$$

$$(2.3) \quad P_t = -1.15 - 0.89Y_t + 0.70M_t + 0.29M_{t-1} + 0.16A_t + 0.13W_t$$

$$\qquad\qquad (9.56) \quad\, (.32) \qquad (.18) \qquad\;\; (.18) \qquad\;\; (.14) \qquad (.22)$$

$$\qquad\qquad\qquad\qquad\qquad\qquad\qquad\qquad\qquad\qquad\qquad\qquad (R^2 = 0.87).$$

Here P_t = percentage change in the price level from December of year $t - 1$ to December of year t,

Y_t = percentage change in real income from the fourth quarter of year $t - 1$ to the fourth quarter of year t,

M_t = percentage change in the money supply from December 31 of year $t - 1$ to December 31 of year t,

M_{t-1} = percentage change in the money supply from December 31 of year $t - 2$ to December 31 of year $t - 1$,

A_t = percentage change in price level during year $t - 1$ minus percentage change in price level during year $t - 2$,

W_t = percentage change in the *sueldo vital* from the first quarter of year $t - 1$ to the first quarter of year t.

The explanatory power of these equations is rather good, and the results appear reasonable. The constant terms (indicating what would happen to the price level if real income, money stock, and the like remained unchanged) are not significantly different from zero. The coefficients of the change in income are not significantly different from -1, indicating that a one per cent rise in real income, other things being equal, causes a fall of about one per cent in the price level. The coefficients of both the current and the lagged change in the money stock are statistically significant, and their sum is not significantly different from $+1$, indicating that a one per cent increase in the quantity of money causes a rise of close to one per cent in the price level, other things equal. When, in equation (2.2), the acceleration of prices (A_t) is added as an explanatory variable, its coefficient turns out to be marginally significant at the 5 per cent level. When, however, the change in wages is also added, the coefficient of A_t loses significance, while W_t itself adds nothing to the explanation of the rate of inflation of consumer prices.

Broadly similar results are obtained when quarterly data are used.

$$(2.4) \quad P'_t = S'_t - 0.63Y'_t + 0.32M'_t + 0.27D'_t \qquad\qquad (R^2 = 0.52),$$
$$ (.22) \qquad (.09) \qquad (.10)$$

$$(2.5) \quad P'_t = S'_t - 0.49Y'_t + 0.33M'_t + 0.26D'_t + 0.05A'_t \qquad (R^2 = 0.54),$$
$$ (.24) \qquad (.09) \qquad (.10) \qquad (.03)$$

$$(2.6) \quad P'_t = S'_t - 0.49Y'_t + 0.31M'_t + 0.21D'_t + 0.04A'_t + 0.04W'_t \quad (R^2 = 0.54).$$
$$ (.24) \qquad (.10) \qquad (.13) \qquad (.03) \qquad (.06)$$

Here P'_t = percentage change in price level within each quarter (e.g., from December 1951 to March 1952),

Y'_t = percentage change in real income from the past to the current quarter (e.g., from the fourth quarter of 1951 to the first quarter of 1952),

M'_t = percentage change in the money supply in the six months ending with the end of quarter t (e.g., from September 30, 1951 to March 31, 1952),

D'_t = a distributed-lag weighted average of the three past values of $M'_t = 0.59M'_{t-2} + 0.28M'_{t-4} + 0.31M'_{t-6}$ (e.g., a weighted average of the percentage increases in the money stock from March 31, 1951 to September 30, 1951; from September 30, 1950 to March 31, 1951; and from March 31, 1950 to September 30, 1950),

A'_t = percentage change in the general price level in the year ending at the beginning of the current quarter minus percentage change in the general price level in the year before that (e.g., percentage change of general price index from December 1950 to December 1951 minus percentage change of general price index from December 1949 to December 1950),

W'_t = percentage change in the *sueldo vital* at its most recent annual adjustment (e.g., that taking place in January 1952),

S'_t = a seasonal constant.

In each of equations (2.4)–(2.6), the sum of the coefficients of M'_t and D'_t is not significantly different from 0.5, once again supporting the view that a one per cent increase in the stock of money tends ultimately to produce, other things being equal, about a one per cent rise in prices. The coefficients of Y_t' are negative in sign, indicating that increases in real income tend, other things being equal, to reduce the rate of inflation. These coefficients are, however, significantly smaller than unity in absolute value, and accordingly do not correspond to the conclusion drawn from the annual data that a one per cent increase in real income leads to a one per cent fall in the price level.[6] As was the case with the annual data, the acceleration variable was marginally significant when it was added to the money and income variables as an explanatory factor for the rate of inflation. But when wage changes were also introduced as an explanatory variable, the coefficients of both wage changes and the acceleration of prices once again turned out to be statistically insignificant.

The coefficients of determination obtained in equations (2.4)–(2.6) appear rather low in comparison with those obtained in (2.1)–(2.3). This apparent reduction in explanatory power is in a sense illusory, for the dependent variables are different in the two sets of regressions. One way to put the two sets of regressions on a comparable basis is to sum the residuals obtained for the four quarters of each year in each quarterly regression. The resulting sum gives the error of the quarterly regression in predicting the annual rate of inflation, and can be compared with the error of the corresponding annual regression in predicting the same thing. In the cases in which the rate of change of the consumer price index is the dependent variable, the variances (about zero) of the two series of errors are almost identical, indicating that the quarterly regressions do just about as well as the annual regressions in predicting the annual rate of inflation. In the cases (presented below) in which the rate of change of the wholesale price index is the dependent variable, the quarterly regressions do much better than the annual regressions in predicting the annual rate of inflation, the variance of the "annual" residuals from the quarterly regressions here being only about two-thirds of the variance of the residuals directly computed from the annual regressions.

The seasonal constants, S_t', were estimated by introducing into each of the quarterly regressions a set of dummy variables, each having the value of one in a certain quarter of each year and zero in all other quarters.

---

[6] This apparent difference may be the result of the relatively greater error in estimating quarter-to-quarter changes in income than in estimating income changes over a whole year; it may also have arisen because the impact of income changes on the price level is distributed through time in a fashion analogous to that already considered for changes in the money supply. I did not consider it wise to attempt to estimate a distributed lag pattern for the effects of income changes on the price level, because the series for quarterly income changes was in any event "artificially" constructed on the basis of annual income data; the method by which this was done was too crude to warrant placing confidence in measures obtained for the separate effects of different lagged changes in income.

The estimated seasonal pattern was essentially the same in each of the regressions (2.4)–(2.6), implying a seasonal fall of prices of $2\frac{2}{3}$ per cent in spring and $1\frac{1}{3}$ per cent in summer, and a seasonal rise of $\frac{1}{2}$ per cent in fall and of $3\frac{1}{2}$ per cent in winter. This is precisely the sort of pattern one

TABLE 1

ANNUAL REGRESSIONS FOR CONSUMER PRICE INDEX AND ITS COMPONENTS

Dependent Variable	Constant Term	Coefficient					R^2
		Y_t	M_t	M_{t-1}	A_t	W_t	
Consumer Price Index	−1.05 (7.13)	−1.05 (.31)	0.80 (.17)	0.34 (.16)			0.84
	−0.32 (9.23)	−0.91 (.31)	0.74 (.16)	0.34 (.15)	0.20 (.12)		0.87
	−1.15 (9.56)	−0.89 (.32)	0.70 (.18)	0.29 (.18)	0.16 (.14)	0.13 (.22)	0.87
Food Prices	−0.66 (11.47)	−1.37 (.50)	1.01 (.27)	0.15 (.25)			0.72
	0.45 (14.98)	−1.16 (.50)	0.92 (.26)	0.15 (.24)	0.30 (.19)		0.76
	0.10 (15.69)	−1.15 (.52)	0.91 (.30) .	0.13 (.29)	0.29 (.23)	0.06 (.37)	0.76
Clothing Prices	0.65 (15.70)	−0.98 (.68)	1.16 (.37)	0.02 (.35)			0.55
	1.08 (22.00)	−0.89 (.73)	1.12 (.39)	0.02 (.36)	0.12 (.28)		0.56
	−0.78 (22.83)	−0.85 (.75)	1.03 (.45)	−0.10 (.42)	0.04 (.33)	0.28 (.54)	0.57
House Rents	4.23 (12.18)	0.00 (.53)	−0.06 (.29)	0.61 (.27)			0.30
	2.82 (15.29)	−0.27 (.51)	−0.04 (.27)	0.60 (.25)	−0.39 (.20)		0.45
	−0.46 (14.98)	−0.19 (.49)	−0.13 (.29)	0.40 (.28)	−0.54 (.22)	0.50 (.35)	0.52
Miscellaneous Prices	−3.01 (14.51)	−1.07 (.63)	1.19 (.34)	0.01 (.32)			0.61
	−3.30 (20.40)	−1.12 (.68)	1.21 (.36)	−0.01 (.33)	−0.08 (.26)		0.61
	−6.05 (20.86)	−1.05 (.69)	1.07 (.40)	−0.16 (.39)	−0.20 (.30)	0.42 (.49)	0.63

Figures in parentheses are standard errors of the coefficients directly above them.

TABLE 2

QUARTERLY REGRESSIONS FOR CONSUMER PRICE INDEX AND ITS COMPONENTS

Dependent Variable	Coefficient					R^2
	Y'_t	M'_t	D'_t	A'_t	W'_t	
Consumer Price Index	−0.63	0.32	0.27			0.52
	(.22)	(.09)	(.10)			
	−0.49	0.33	0.26	0.05		0.54
	(.24)	(.09)	(.10)	(.03)		
	−0.49	0.31	0.21	0.04	0.04	0.54
	(.24)	(.10)	(.13)	(.03)	(.06)	
Food Prices	−0.74	0.30	0.28			0.41
	(.34)	(.14)	(.16)			
	−0.69	0.31	0.28	0.02		0.41
	(.36)	(.14)	(.16)	(.05)		
	−0.69	0.26	0.18	0.00	0.07	0.42
	(.36)	(.15)	(.20)	(.05)	(.08)	
Clothing Prices	−0.83	0.45	0.13			0.37
	(.30)	(.13)	(.14)			
	−0.67	0.46	0.11	0.06		0.38
	(.32)	(.13)	(.14)	(.04)		
	−0.67	0.46	0.11	0.06	0.00	0.38
	(.32)	(.13)	(.18)	(.05)	0.08	
House Rents	−0.19	−0.33	0.98			0.30
	(.45)	(.19)	(.21)			
	−0.25	−0.33	0.98	−0.03		0.30
	(.49)	(.19)	(.22)	(.07)		
	−0.25	−0.43	0.76	−0.06	0.17	0.32
	(.48)	(.20)	(.26)	(.07)	(.11)	
Miscellaneous Prices	−0.26	−0.01	0.66			0.31
	(.34)	(.14)	(.16)			
	−0.20	0.01	0.65	0.02		0.31
	(.37)	(.14)	(.16)	(.05)		
	−0.20	−0.01	0.61	0.02	0.03	0.31
	(.37)	(.15)	(.20)	(.06)	(.09)	

would expect on the basis of the agricultural cycle in Chile and constitutes a positive check on the plausibility of the results. In addition to the seasonal pattern given above, an over-all constant term was estimated. This constant was small in magnitude (−0.9), and not significantly different from zero, indicating that the independent variables appearing in

TABLE 3

ANNUAL REGRESSIONS FOR WHOLESALE PRICE INDEX AND ITS COMPONENTS

Dependent Variable	Constant Term	Coefficient					R^2
		Y_t	M_t	M_{t-1}	A_t	W_t	
Wholesale Price Index	−2.30 (10.83)	−0.85 (.47)	0.79 (.25)	0.37 (.24)			0.68
	−1.62 (14.79)	−0.72 (.49)	0.73 (.26)	0.37 (.24)	0.19 (.19)		0.70
	−6.64 (12.78)	−0.59 (.42)	0.47 (.24)	0.06 (.24)	−0.04 (.19)	0.77 (.30)	0.80
Import Prices	−1.41 (17.97)	−0.80 (.78)	0.48 (.42)	0.73 (.40)			0.46
	−1.22 (25.31)	−0.76 (.84)	0.47 (.44)	0.73 (.41)	0.06 (.32)		0.46
	−7.06 (24.48)	−0.61 (.81)	0.16 (.47)	0.37 (.46)	−0.21 (.35)	0.90 (.57)	0.54
Domestic Goods Prices	−3.68 (10.97)	−0.71 (.48)	0.90 (.26)	0.25 (.24)			0.67
	−2.83 (14.73)	−0.55 (.49)	0.84 (.26)	0.25 (.24)	0.23 (.19)		0.70
	−6.56 (14.00)	−0.45 (.46)	0.65 (.27)	0.02 (.26)	0.06 (.20)	0.57 (.33)	0.75
Agricultural Prices	−0.76 (14.04)	−0.54 (.61)	0.90 (.33)	0.12 (.30)			0.49
	0.61 (18.36)	−0.29 (.61)	0.80 (.32)	0.12 (.30)	0.37 (.24)		0.57
	−2.81 (18.31)	−0.20 (.60)	0.63 (.35)	−0.09 (.34)	0.21 (.27)	0.52 (.43)	0.61
Industrial Prices	−6.76 (12.30)	−0.67 (.54)	0.94 (.29)	0.32 (.27)			0.65
	−6.23 (17.11)	−0.57 (.57)	0.90 (.30)	0.32 (.28)	0.14 (.22)		0.66
	−10.54 (16.28)	−0.46 (.54)	0.68 (.31)	0.06 (.30)	0.05 (.24)	0.66 (.38)	0.72

the equations can fully account for the mean rate of inflation observed in Chile over the period considered.[7]

---

[7] In the actual estimation of the equations, three seasonal dummy variables were introduced, and a regular constant term was also estimated. If we call K the regular constant term, and b_1, b_2, and b_3 the coefficients of the three seasonal dummy variables, we see that the intercept of the estimated equation is $K + b_1$ in the first quarter, $K + b_2$ in the second, $K + b_3$ in the

TABLE 4

QUARTERLY REGRESSIONS FOR WHOLESALE PRICE INDEX AND ITS COMPONENTS

Dependent Variable	Coefficient					R^2
	Y'_t	M'_t	D'_t	A'_t	W'_t	
Wholesale Price Index	−0.56 (.20)	0.37 (.08)	0.19 (.09)			0.51
	−0.44 (.21)	0.37 (.08)	0.17 (.09)	0.05 (.03)		0.53
	−0.43 (.20)	0.28 (.08)	−0.03 (.11)	−0.01 (.03)	0.15 (.05)	0.59
Import Prices	−0.46 (.31)	0.46 (.13)	0.10 (.14)			0.29
	−0.41 (.33)	0.46 (.13)	0.10 (.15)	0.02 (.05)		0.29
	−0.40 (.31)	0.32 (.13)	−0.21 (.17)	−0.03 (.05)	0.23 (.07)	0.38
Domestic Goods Prices	−0.62 (.19)	0.29 (.08)	0.27 (.09)			0.56
	−0.47 (.20)	0.29 (.08)	0.25 (.09)	0.06 (.03)		0.58
	−0.46 (.20)	0.24 (.08)	0.14 (.11)	0.04 (.03)	0.08 (.05)	0.60
Agricultural Prices	−0.68 (.33)	0.39 (.14)	0.07 (.16)			0.47
	−0.54 (.36)	0.39 (.14)	0.06 (.16)	0.06 (.05)		0.48
	−0.53 (.35)	0.32 (.15)	−0.10 (.19)	0.03 (.05)	0.11 (.08)	0.50
Industrial Prices	−0.54 (.20)	0.30 (.09)	0.30 (.10)			0.47
	−0.40 (.21)	0.31 (.08)	0.28 (.09)	0.06 (.03)		0.49
	−0.40 (.21)	0.27 (.09)	0.20 (.12)	0.04 (.03)	0.06 (.05)	0.50

The presentation of the more detailed results in Tables 1–4 follows precisely the pattern established above. The annual regressions given in

third, and K in the fourth quarter. The over-all constant referred to in the text is the mean of these four intercepts, and the seasonal pattern is obtained by taking the deviation of each season's intercept from this mean.

Tables 1 and 3 follow the pattern of equations (2.1)–(2.3). The quarterly regressions given in Tables 2 and 4 follow the pattern of equations (2.4)–(2.6). The results for the consumer price index are reproduced as parts of Tables 1 and 2 to facilitate comparison. As in the cases of equations (2.4)–(2.6), the constant terms and seasonal patterns are not presented explicitly. Suffice it to say that the agricultural cycle was the dominant seasonal force: clothing and industrial prices, for example, show no seasonal pattern at all, while retail food prices and wholesale agricultural prices show a seasonal rise of around 10 per cent going from summer to winter. This 10 per cent seasonal rise in agricultural prices is reflected in a $3\frac{1}{3}$ per cent seasonal rise in the wholesale price index and in a 4 per cent seasonal rise in its domestic price component.

3. Discussion of the Results

In this section I propose to bring out the salient features of the results just presented. The discussion will be on a topical basis, and will assess the results of Tables 1–4 as they bear on each of a series of questions.

3.1. Goodness of Fit. The annual regressions succeed in explaining over $\frac{4}{5}$ of the variation in the annual rate of inflation of consumer prices, and nearly as high a fraction of that of wholesale prices. The quarterly regressions explain more than half the variations in the quarterly rate of increase of both major indexes. The explanations of variations in the component indexes are not as good as those for the general indexes (except for the domestic goods component of the wholesale price index), but are invariably statistically significant at the 5 per cent level. The poorest performances are those of house rents, import prices, and miscellaneous prices.

3.2. The Coefficients of Income Change. These are, as expected, uniformly negative, and in the annual regressions only the coefficient of house rents on income change is significantly different from -1. Those for the wholesale price components are, however, all below unity in absolute value, and several are not significantly different from either zero or -1. The coefficients of income change almost invariably fall in magnitude as we move from the annual regressions to the quarterly regressions, but in a number of cases (the clothing price component of the consumer price index, and all components of the wholesale price index), their level of significance is higher in the quarterly than in the annual regressions. The fact that there are four times as many observations in the quarterly regressions makes it possible to rationalize this improvement in statistical significance while at the same time attributing the fall in magnitude of the income coefficients to the presumedly greater relative importance of the "error component" in the quarterly income-change variable than in its annual counterpart.

Considering the way in which the income variable was constructed, its performance in these regressions seems to me to be remarkably good.

3.3. The Sum of the Coefficients of Change in Money Supply.
I shall here consider the results obtained only in the first two regressions of each set of three; the results from the third regression will be dealt with when the effects of the wage variable are discussed.

In all the annual regressions except that for house rents, the sum of the coefficients of M_t and M_{t-1} exceeds unity by modest amounts. There is reason, therefore, to believe that these lags capture the full effect of money-supply increases on prices, and that inclusion of further lags is unnecessary. Moreover, in all the quarterly regressions except that for house rents, the sum of the coefficients of M'_t and D'_t is almost precisely half of the sum of the coefficients of M_t and M_{t-1} in the corresponding annual regressions. The quarterly regressions tell the same story as the annual regressions, at least in this one respect, and we can thus regard M'_t and D'_t as incorporating the relevant lagged increases in money supply.

3.4. The Speed of Adjustment of Prices to Changes in Money Supply.
The house-rent regressions present a series of puzzles. The outstanding feature of both the annual and quarterly house-rent regressions is the dominant importance of *lagged* increases in money supply in determining rent changes. This can be rationalized in two ways, which are not mutually inconsistent. On the one hand, rent controls were in effect in Chile for much of the period studied, and though in fact they appear to have been widely evaded, there is reason to believe that the index tended to report rents at their controlled levels. It is hard otherwise to explain the fact that during years of rapid inflation of other prices, the rent index often remained constant to the last digit for 10 or 12 months running. The second explanation is the practice in Chile of having annual (and sometimes longer) rental contracts. This practice would itself lead to a tendency for rents to lag behind other prices in responding to inflationary forces, and of course when rent controls were in effect their upward adjustments would tend to come only after a still greater lag.

Some of the other anomalies of the house-rent regression, notably the failure of short-term income changes to produce a significant effect on house rents, and the low explanatory power of the regressions themselves, seem less odd in the light of the above considerations. Nor am I greatly disturbed by the small and statistically insignificant negative coefficient applying to M_t in the annual regression; it seems plausible that current monetary movements should be irrelevant for a very sluggish series. But the coefficient of M'_t in the quarterly regression is not so small, and is on the borderline of statistical significance; the fact that it has a negative sign remains puzzling.

The sluggishness of house rents is the major factor contributing to the significance of M_{t-1} as an explanatory variable for changes in the consumer price index, but this does not mean that, except for house rents, consumer prices adjust almost instantaneously. In the quarterly regressions the coefficient of D'_t was significant for every component of the consumer price index except clothing prices. Judging from the ratios of the coefficients of current and lagged changes in money supply, clothing prices appear to adjust more rapidly than food prices, and food prices more rapidly than house rents. The fact that food prices are more sluggish than clothing prices may be partly explained by the fact that price controls existed for parts of the period under review on some (though by no means all) food commodities. It is interesting in this regard to note that the agricultural price component of the wholesale price index does not appear to be nearly as sluggish as the food price component of the consumer price index (compare especially the quarterly regressions), for wholesale prices were generally free of control for the entire period.

Industrial prices appear, in both the annual and the quarterly regressions, to be far more sluggish than agricultural prices. This is in accord with *a priori* expectations, as are the other results, except those for the "miscellaneous" prices component of the consumer price index and for the import price component of the wholesale price index.

In both these cases the relative sizes of the coefficients of current and lagged changes in money shift drastically as one moves from the annual to the quarterly regressions. One is prone to conclude that the annual and the quarterly regressions are here telling very different stories, but such is not the case. When four 6-month changes in money supply M'_t, M'_{t-2}, M'_{t-4}, and M'_{t-6} are introduced as separate explanatory variables for quarterly price changes, M'_{t-2} turns out to carry virtually all the explanatory power for miscellaneous prices. This change in money supply is "part of" the current change in money supply, M_t, in the annual regressions, and part of the lagged change in money supply, D'_t, in the quarterly regressions. Thus we need not puzzle about the consistency of D'_t carrying the bulk of the explanatory power in the quarterly regressions while M_t does so in the annual regressions for the "miscellaneous" component of the consumer price index. But the economic reason why increases in the quantity of money between 12 and 6 months ago should be so overwhelmingly important for the current change in this category of prices remains obscure.

In the case of import prices, the introduction of four separate money-supply changes reveals quite different results. The coefficients of M'_t, M'_{t-4}, and M'_{t-6} are all substantial and positive, that of M'_t being the largest, but the coefficient of M'_{t-2} is also substantial in size, statistically significant, and *negative*! In the annual regressions M'_{t-2} combines with M'_t to form the "current" money-change variable, M_t; in this case its negative impact works to reduce the size (and significance level) of the current-money coefficient.

In the quarterly regressions M'_{t-2} combines with M'_{t-4} and M'_{t-6} to form D'_t ; in this case it works to reduce the size and significance level of the lagged-money coefficient. So here, once again, we need not worry about the consistency of the quarterly and annual results, but only about the plausibility of the story they tell. The importance of M'_{t-4} and M'_{t-6} does not puzzle me. Import prices varied largely, during this period, in response to variations in exchange rates, and one can detect a clear tendency for exchange-rate adjustments to lag behind internal price inflation. (This lag appears even for periods when the exchange rate was nominally freely fluctuating, for the Central Bank has tended in Chile to intervene in the free market to prevent the exchange rate from rising until forced by depletion of its reserves to allow the rate to rise.) This tendency for the exchange rate (or rates) to lag behind internal inflation renders plausible the positive and significant coefficients of M'_{t-4} and M'_{t-6}. I'm afraid, however, that I cannot provide a similarly plausible explanation for the apparent negative influence of M'_{t-2}.

3.5. The Coefficients of Price Acceleration. One's reaction to the performance of the acceleration variable depends in part on what one expected of it in the first place, and in part on one's interpretation of (or reaction to) the results of including changes in wages in the regressions. When the wage variable is included in the regressions, the coefficient of the acceleration variable is in no case statistically significant at the 5 per cent level. On the other hand, when wages are not introduced, the coefficient of acceleration is clearly significant for industrial and domestic goods prices (quarterly) and for the consumer price index (annual), and is at or near the margin of significance for the wholesale price index (quarterly), agricultural prices (annually and quarterly), domestic goods prices (annually), consumer prices (quarterly), food prices (annually), and clothing prices (quarterly). The reason that there is some question about the introduction of the wage variable is that—at least in the case of the consumer price index and its principal components—the wage variable, while taking explanatory power away from the acceleration variable, does not become statistically significant itself. Also (as will become clear in the next subsection), even in the case of the wholesale price index, where the wage variable is statistically significant, the source of the significance is sufficiently puzzling that one may fairly inquire into what happens when the variable is omitted entirely.

One conclusion holds regardless of our position regarding the wage variable: "acceleration" is not a powerful explainer of variations in the rate of inflation. On the other hand, one might be be reasonably pleased with the performance of the acceleration variable if one were curious to see whether the relationship between changes in the cost of holding cash and changes in the level of real-cash balances were sufficiently precise and regularly timed for changes in the past rate of acceleration of prices to have any perceptible relationship to variations in the annual or quarterly rate of inflation. Even when wages are introduced, the acceleration coefficient has the right sign and a not-implausible magnitude both for consumer prices and for the wholesale prices of domestic goods; and when wages are not introduced, the pattern of results is still more consistent, as well as having greater statistical significance.

If the measured effect of the acceleration variable is "real," the magnitude of its coefficient surely has interesting policy implications. It says, for example, that if prices in 1960 were stable, as against an inflation of 30 per cent in 1959, the *ceteris paribus* working of the acceleration effect would lead to a deflation of about 1.5 per cent in the first quarter of 1961 and of about 6 per cent over the year.

A special word must be said about the curious working of the acceleration variable in the case of house rents. Here it is significant at the 5 per cent level in the annual regressions, its explanatory power is not significantly hurt by the introduction of the wage variable, and its coefficient is *negative*! The explanation is that in this case the acceleration variable is acting as a proxy for still more remote lagged increases in the quantity of money. The house-rent regression was the only one in which the addition of M_{t-2} proved significant, and when M_{t-2} was introduced simultaneously with A_t the coefficient of A_t became insignificant.[8] Thus the curious behavior of the acceleration coefficient in the house-rent regressions is simply another reflection of the extreme sluggishness of response of this component of the consumer price index.

3.6. The Effects of Wages on Prices: Extreme Hypotheses Confronted.

The extreme hypotheses presented in Section 1, one denying any true explanatory power to wage changes, and the other denying any true explanatory power to money-supply changes, may in a sense be straw men, though it is indeed possible to find citations in which various writers at least appear to be espousing one or the other extreme position. But it is nonetheless instructive to begin a survey of the results of introducing wage changes into the regressions of Tables 1–4 with a confrontation of the two extreme views.

In a very real sense, both extreme hypotheses fail. The purely "monetary" hypothesis, which denies any explanatory power to wage changes once

---

[8] The way in which A_t can serve as a proxy for M_{t-2} is interesting: A_t represents $(P_{t-1} - P_{t-2})$, where the P's refer to general price-level changes. The P's in turn are reasonably well correlated with the contemporaneous M's, so that $(P_{t-1} - P_{t-2})$ might be expressed as $(M_{t-1} - M_{t-2})$ plus a (perhaps random) residual. If the residual U is really random, we would have

$$P_t = a_0 + \ldots + a_3 M_{t-1} + a_4(M_{t-1} - M_{t-2}) + a_4 U \ldots.$$

The "true" coefficient of M_{t-1} would be $(a_3 + a_4)$, and that of M_{t-2} would be $-a_4$. Since the estimated a_4 is in fact negative, the "implied" coefficient for M_{t-2} is positive.

monetary factors are properly taken into account, would predict that *no* wage coefficient would be significant. In fact the coefficients of wages are significant for wholesale prices, import prices, and domestic goods prices in the quarterly regressions, and for these plus industrial prices in the annual regressions.

The extreme "anti-monetary" hypothesis fares even worse, for in every case at least one monetary variable remains statistically significant at the 5 per cent level after the introduction of wages.[9]

One can reframe the hypotheses into a somewhat less extreme form, with the monetarists saying that monetary variables alone will explain more of the variation in the rate of inflation than wage variables alone, and with the "anti-monetarists" saying the reverse. In this case, treating the income variable as "neutral," the competition boils down to a test of partial correlation coefficients (the relevant partial r^2 for the monetary variables being the percentage reduction in the unexplained variance which results when they are added as a group). This test is won handily by the monetary hypothesis in all cases except import prices (both quarterly and annual) and wholesale prices (annual). The battle is something of a stand-off in the case of industrial prices (annual).

The "victory" of the wage hypothesis in the case of wholesale prices is a Pyrrhic one, however, for it has its principal source in the wrong place. The wholesale price index is composed of domestic goods prices and import prices; of these two components, theories of wage inflation would predict that wages would have a much more important influence on the former. Indeed, it is difficult to imagine a *causal* mechanism whereby wage changes would in fact have a greater impact on import prices than on domestic prices.

It is possible, however, to find a plausible explanation for the high partial correlation of wage changes with import prices. One of the reasons for the Central Bank's actions against rising exchange rates, even when the rate is nominally freely fluctuating, is a fear (which seems to be perennial in governmental circles in Chile) of public resentment against the effects of rising exchange rates on certain components of the cost of living (particularly sugar, kerosene, wheat, and a tea-like leaf called *yerba maté*).[10] This

---

[9] In the case of house rents the "monetary" variable that remains significant is A_t for the annual regression presented in Table I, but if M_{t-2} is substituted for A_t, both M_{t-1} and M_{t-2} remain significant in the presence of W_t. Lest readers regard it as possibly "unfair" to the wage hypothesis that I have included lagged values of the change in money supply, but not of the change in wages, let me state that adding the wage variable lagged one year produces no change in the above conclusions. The coefficient of the lagged-wage change is not itself significant and it does not deprive the monetary variables of their significance, or add to the significance of the unlagged-wage variable.

[10] It is difficult to ascertain the reasons for the strength of this fear. The effects of devaluation on the cost of living are not nearly so pervasive as the effects of other actions (especially

resentment can be somewhat reduced or assuaged if the government takes the step of devaluation at a time when the public is enjoying the "glow" of a recent or concurrent wage rise.

Some support is given to this interpretation by the magnitudes of the coefficients of wages in the import price regressions. It appears that a one per cent per annum rise in the *sueldo vital* "caused" nearly a one per cent per annum (or nearly a 0.25 per cent per "average" quarter) rise in the import price level. This is the sort of magnitude that one might expect to result if the government regarded both the *sueldo vital* and the exchange rate as policy variables, and tended to accompany or follow adjustments in the *sueldo vital* with roughly similar percentage changes in the exchange rate. The hypothesis is further supported by the fact that when separate "quarterly" regressions are run for each of the four quarters, the bulk of the effect of the wage variable on import prices turns out to occur in the first and second quarters of the year, that is, simultaneous with or immediately after the annual changes in the *sueldo vital*.[11]

3.7. The Role of Wage Changes in the Chilean Inflation: A Possible Interpretation.

The obvious response to the approach taken above is to inquire why monetary and wage hypotheses should be asked to compete in such a way that one excludes the other, when in fact the simultaneous operation of both types of forces is possible. As was indicated in Section 1, autonomous wage changes can be expected to influence prices, even in the absence of changes in the money supply; and they may, moreover, be the "cause" of decisions to increase the money supply, and thus affect prices via monetary variables. In this section I shall accordingly try to give a "non-partisan" interpretation of the evidence of Tables 1–4, assessing as

---

monetary expansion) taken by the Central Bank, and one does not observe the same reluctance to take these other steps. The best explanation that I can find for the particular reluctance to devalue is that when a devaluation occurs, there is a rather immediate and direct rise in the prices of imported products which is attributed in the public mind to the specific action of devaluation. It is easier for popular opinion to "blame" the government for these price rises than for the general inflationary rise of prices, for which the proximate targets of resentment are the retailers, middlemen, and the like, whom the public sees as the ones who actually raise their prices.

[11] The value of 0.23 of the coefficient of W'_t in the regression of Table 4 is thus a bit misleading; it is, in effect, an average of high coefficients in the first two quarters and low coefficients in the last two quarters of the year. Readers may also wonder why the exchange rate has not been introduced explicitly as a variable to explain import price movements. The fact is that for a good share of the period, Chile maintained multiple-exchange systems of varying complexity, and her exchange-rate policy often changed in ways that were much more complicated than simple devaluation (e.g., changing the different rates in the multiple-exchange setup by different percentages). Under these circumstances, and given the fact that year-to-year and quarter-to-quarter changes in the foreign currency price of imports were of minor magnitude, variations in the import price level become the best available measure of changes in the average effective exchange rate.

well as I can the roles wage changes and monetary changes played in the Chilean inflation.

In a sense, I have already begun this assessment in the above discussion of import prices. The "mechanism" discussed there seems to me to be by far the most plausible interpretation of the high correlation between wage changes and import prices. I would interpret the near-significance of wage changes in explaining variations in agricultural prices in much the same way. For most of the period under consideration, Chile has been a net importer of wheat and meat, which of course are also locally produced in large quantities. A variety of special policies (e.g., special exchange rates, government-subsidized imports) have been pursued, from time to time, with respect to these commodities. These policies have operated to reduce the correlation between imported food prices and the "average" exchange rate (measured here by the general level of import prices). Moreover, wheat and meat are only two among many components of the agricultural price index, and the others are not typically influenced by exchange-rate policy. It thus seems quite reasonable that movements in the agricultural price index should show some association with wage changes, but not nearly so strong an association as between import prices generally and wage changes, and such association as does exist would be indirect, with wage changes really functioning as a proxy for exchange-rate movements.

A somewhat similar explanation applies to the house-rent component of the consumer price index. Here the association between wage changes and movements in rents appears to stem from the fact that the levels at which rents were controlled tended to be adjusted in some rough harmony with adjustments in the *sueldo vital*. The plausible reason for this association is, once again, the easier public acceptance of a bitter pill when accompanied or immediately preceded by a sweet one.

Neither in the case of agricultural prices nor in the case of house rents can any plausibility be attached to a "wage-push" interpretation of the partial correlation between price and wage movements. In the case of house rents one can for all practical purposes say that they contain no wage component. In the case of agricultural prices, not only is it true that agricultural wages have not followed the *sueldo vital* with nearly the precision of industrial wages (being often mainly "in kind" and also, for practical purposes, uninfluenced by the sort of union pressure that tends to keep industrial wages in line with the *sueldo vital*), but also any association the *sueldo vital* might have had with agricultural wages would have its influence on prices only via the response of agricultural supply to the changed price of labor, and then presumably only after a crop year. The association between the *sueldo vital* and agricultural prices via exchange rate policy is much more immediate and direct.

Only in the case of industrial prices can a "wage-push" interpretation of the partial correlation between wages and prices be seriously advanced.

And even here there is the possibility that industrial firms used the rise in the *sueldo vital* as a propitious excuse for making price changes they might have made in any event. (Industry in Chile is typically monopolistic or oligopolistic, and firms, like government, may find it convenient to pass bitter pills to the public in conjunction with sweet ones, or at least to try to pass part of the "blame" for price rises on to others [government and/or unions]).

Although wage-push arguments thus have only limited scope for explaining the observed partial correlations between wage changes and price movements, they may have greater applicability. The simple correlation between the wage change occurring at the beginning of year t and the change in money supply during the year t is 0.66, and this suggests that wage changes may have been one of the important factors influencing monetary policy decisions. It is also worth noting that the simple correlation between the wage change at the beginning of year t and the money-supply change during year $t - 1$ is also 0.66. These correlations lend a great deal of credibility to the idea of an inflationary spiral, in which the monetary policy of one year influenced the wage decisions taken at the beginning of the next, and where these wage decisions in turn had their influence upon subsequent monetary policy. The correlations also reflect the rather substantial degree of multicollinearity existing among the independent variables in the third equation of each set.

The presence of this degree of multicollinearity suggests a final experiment. Having already inquired into the degree to which the data give evidence of a statistically separable effect of wage changes on price movements, we may now inquire into the interaction between wage changes and monetary movements in the Chilean inflation. The experiment I propose is the following: Assume a hypothetical period in which money-supply and wages are regularly increasing at the rate of 10 per cent per year. In such a period the individual effects of wage changes and money-supply changes on the price level would be statistically inseparable. Our regressions are not based on such a period, but they can be asked to predict how prices would behave in these hypothetical circumstances. In particular, the question can be asked whether the rates of price rise predicted by those regressions that include the wage variable differ substantially from those predicted by the regressions that exclude the wage variable. The results of this experiment are presented in Table 5. Particularly for the quarterly regressions, but even for the annual ones, there is a striking correspondence between the "predicted" rates of price change coming from the three different equations in each set.[12] One cannot escape the conclusion that for the type of parallel upward drift of the independent variables that we have assumed for this experiment, the three sets of regressions tell pretty much the same story.

---

[12] This correspondence was first pointed out to me by Yoram Barzel.

These results suggest that one of the major roles of the wage variable was indeed as a "transmitter" of inflation from one period to the next, responding to the monetary expansion of the past period and inducing monetary expansion in the subsequent period. The wage variable does not

TABLE 5

PREDICTED RESPONSE OF PRICES (ANNUAL RATE OF RISE) TO A HYPOTHETICAL STEADY INCREASE IN MONEY SUPPLY AND WAGES AT 10 PER CENT PER YEAR

Dependent Variable	From Annual Regressions			From Quarterly Regressions		
	First Re-gression in Set (1)	Second Re-gression in Set (2)	Third Re-gression in Set (3)	First Re-gression in Set (4)	Second Re-gression in Set (5)	Third Re-gression in Set (6)
Consumer Prices	11.4	10.8	11.2	11.8	11.8	12.0
Food Prices	11.6	10.7	11.0	11.6	11.8	11.6
Clothing Prices	11.8	11.4	12.1	11.6	11.4	11.4
House Rents	5.5	5.6	7.7	13.0	13.0	13.4
Miscellaneous Prices	12.0	12.0	13.3	13.0	13.2	13.6
Wholesale Prices	11.6	11.0	13.0	11.2	10.8	11.0
Import Prices	12.1	12.0	14.3	11.2	11.2	11.4
Domestic Prices	11.5	10.9	12.4	11.2	10.8	10.8
Agricultural Prices	10.2	9.2	10.6	9.2	9.0	8.8
Industrial Prices	12.6	12.2	14.0	12.0	11.8	11.8

Col. (1) = (sum of the coefficients of M_t and M_{t-1} in first regression in each set) $\times$ 10.[a]

Col. (2) = (sum of the coefficients of M_t and M_{t-1} in second regression in each set) $\times$ 10.

Col. (3) = (sum of the coefficients of M_t, M_{t-1}, and W_t in the third regression in each set) $\times$ 10.

Col. (4) = (sum of the coefficients of M'_t and D'_t in first regression in each set) $\times$ 20.[b]

Col. (5) = (sum of the coefficients of M'_t and D'_t in second regression in each set) $\times$ 20.

Col. (6) = (sum of the coefficients of M'_t and D'_t, plus twice[c] the coefficient of W'_t, in third regression in each set) $\times$ 20.

[a] The sums of the coefficients in the annual regressions are multiplied by 10, because a 10 per cent rate of increase in each of the independent variables M_t, M_{t-1}, and W_t is assumed.

[b] The sums of the coefficients of M'_t and D'_t are multiplied by 20, because M'_t and D'_t are in units of 6-month changes, while the dependent variable is in units of 3-month changes. Multiplication by 2 is necessary to give the dependent variable the same time dimension as M'_t and D'_t, and once this is done, multiplication by 10 is necessary to get the predicted effect of a 10 per cent increase in M'_t and D'_t.

[c] Twice the coefficient of W'_t is taken because this variable is expressed on an annual basis. If we were to express it on a semi-annual basis, each observation would be half as large, and the estimated coefficients would be twice as large as they emerged in our regressions. Once W'_t is thus adjusted to a semi-annual basis, it has the same time dimensions as M'_t and D'_t, and their coefficients can be added together. The subsequent multiplication by 20 is for the reason indicated in note b above.

significantly alter the predictions in the hypothetical situation of Table 5, and in this sense one does not "need" it. Likewise, in the cases of the consumer price index and the component indexes not dealt with separately above, the wage variable does not add significantly to the variation in the rate of inflation explained by monetary factors; in this sense too, and for these cases, one does not "need" it. But none of this denies that if wage changes had tended in the period to be unaccompanied by monetary expansion, prices would nonetheless have responded. Nor does it deny that prior wage rises were an important factor in inducing monetary expansions during the period. It only says that during this period monetary expansions were typically great enough to "finance" prior wage changes, and that on top of this, monetary expansions had independent variations, which also influenced the price level in much the same way as if they had been accompanied by wage changes.

The view that wages played an important transmitting role is supported by the high correlations (mentioned above) between wage changes and subsequent monetary expansions, and between wage changes and prior monetary expansions. It is also noteworthy that the simple relationships between wage changes and subsequent price changes are exceedingly good ($r^2 = 0.58$ for the consumer price index and 0.70 for the wholesale price index, annual data). It is easy to explain how these high simple correlations are turned into much smaller (in the case of wholesale prices) or practically zero (in the case of consumer prices) partial correlations when the money supply variables are introduced, *if* one assigns to wages the dual role of reflecting past monetary changes and inducing later ones. But I find it difficult to explain it in any other way.

Finally, for those who feel strongly that the wage changes in Chile did play a powerful role, and who wonder how monetary factors can have operated so strongly to "erode," in multiple regression, the high simple correlation between wage changes and prices, an answer of sorts can be given. There are good grounds to believe that if monetary policy had been frequently "tight" in Chile, in the sense of the Central Bank failing by substantial margins to "finance" current or recent increases in the *sueldo vital*, and if when monetary policy was not tight in this sense, it operated rather precisely to "finance" recent wage rises, the wage variable would have "outperformed" the monetary variables in multiple regressions explaining the rate of inflation. The wage variable would be able to explain the rate of inflation both when monetary policy failed to finance the wage rise, and when monetary policy did finance the wage rise. Thus a monetary policy that was generally tight, that yielded at times but not always to wage pressures, and that strongly resisted "overfinancing" a wage rise would tend to produce a high partial correlation between wage changes and the rate of inflation. On the other hand, a monetary policy that was generally easy, that tended to finance wage rises even in its tighter periods and to overfinance them by varying degrees in its looser periods, would tend to produce the sort of results we have observed for Chile, the typically higher partial correlations between monetary variables and the rate of inflation than between wage changes and the rate of inflation.

Chile's monetary policy during the period of this study surely fits the latter description more closely than the former. Indeed, for the bulk of the period, an easy-money policy was virtually forced upon the Central Bank by law. The Central Bank was required to buy any obligations offered to it by the government; as the agent of the government in foreign-exchange matters, it was required to buy and sell foreign exchange at the rates in force at the time; and finally, it was required to rediscount all eligible commercial paper offered to it by the commercial banks at a discount rate fixed by law at a level that was generally well below the rate of inflation. These provisions, particularly the last, precluded the Central Bank from exercising the "normal" means of control over its portfolio and over the size of its note and deposit liabilities, which formed the base of the Chilean money supply. It is difficult to see how in these circumstances the Central Bank could have followed a policy of general restraint, yielding, when it yielded, only to just finance (but not to overfinance) recent wage rises. Indeed, these restrictions on Central Bank policy seem almost designed to produce a hyperinflation, and might well have done so but for special measures.[13] Hence it really should not be surprising that during the period of this study money-supply changes tended more often to outstrip than to lag behind wage changes, and that wages played much more a transmitting than an initiating role in the Chilean inflation.

APPENDIX NOTES

1. The principal source of data for this study was the *Boletín Mensual* of the Banco Central de Chile. This contains the basic data both on prices and on the money supply. The series used for money supply was that for *total del dinero circulante*. This series includes demand deposits (except interbank deposits) but not time deposits. The money-supply series underwent a slight conceptual change during the period of this study, and the price indexes also underwent revisions. In these cases there was

---

[13] The special measures that prevented this outcome were quantitative limits on the expansion of bank credit. Commercial banks were sometimes permitted to expand their loans at $1\frac{1}{2}$ per cent per month, sometimes at $2\frac{1}{2}$ per cent per month, and so on. These limits by themselves were invariably generous enough to permit substantial inflation, and actually, exceptions to the limits were made so often that loans usually expanded by considerably more than the limits would have dictated. Nonetheless, the existence of the limits did effectively prevent the public from obtaining all the loans it desired at the controlled rate of interest, and thus prevented the inflation from getting completely out of hand.

invariably a period of overlap between the "old" and the "new" series, for which two separate annual or quarterly percentage changes could be computed. For the periods of overlap, this study used the mean of these two changes. The *sueldo vital* series is that applying to Santiago (there are regional differences in the *sueldo vital*), and also appears in the *Boletín Mensual*.

2. The basic national income series used was real national income, expressed in pesos of 1950, from *Cuentas Nacionales de Chile*, published by the Corporación de Fomento de la Producción, and from the continuation of this series in mimeographed documents. The procedure for estimating quarter-to-quarter changes in national income was as follows: Let Y_2 be the known change in average annual income from year 1 to year 2, Q_2 be the (unknown) change in quarterly national income from quarter 1 to quarter 2, Q_3 be the same from quarter 2 to quarter 3, and so on. Then it can be shown that $Y_2 = Q_2 + 2Q_3 + 3Q_4 + 4Q_5 + 3Q_6 + 2Q_7 + Q_8$. Y_3, the known change in average annual national income from year 2 to year 3,

TABLE A-1

NATIONAL INCOME VARIABLES Y_t AND Y'_t (% CHANGES)

	Y_t (percentage change in real income from 4th quarter of year $t-1$ to 4th quarter of year t)	Y'_t (percentage change in real income from quarter $t-1$ to quarter t)			
		1st Quarter	2d Quarter	3d Quarter	4th Quarter
1940	7.68	1.00[a]	1.55	2.20	2.85
1941	3.93	3.50	1.84	0.19	−1.46
1942	−0.29	−3.11	−1.05	0.79	3.08
1943	13.31	5.12	3.99	2.84	1.69
1944	3.44	0.54	0.77	1.01	1.24
1945	8.80	1.48	1.98	2.49	2.99
1946	−2.24	3.50	0.78	−1.94	−4.66
1947	−8.27	−7.38	−3.84	0.01	3.26
1948	14.77	6.81	4.78	2.74	0.71
1949	1.15	−1.32	−0.24	0.83	1.91
1950	7.03	2.98	1.88	2.64	−0.34
1951	4.05	−1.45	0.10	1.66	3.21
1952	15.12	4.76	4.19	3.62	3.04
1953	−0.29	2.31	0.80	−0.87	−2.54
1954	−8.29	−4.22	−2.76	−1.30	0.16
1955	3.59	1.62	1.13	0.64	0.15
1956	0.43	−0.36	−0.04	0.26	0.57
1957	3.44	0.87	0.87	0.87	0.87
1958	3.54	0.87	0.88	0.89	0.90

[a] Independently estimated.

is similarly equal to $Q_6 + 2Q_7 + 3Q_8 + 4Q_9 + 3Q_{10} + 2Q_{11} + Q_{12}$. In this way the known annual changes can be expressed in terms of the unknown quarterly changes. There result from the annual national income data from 1940-58, eighteen Lagrangean constraints of the above form, subject to all of which the expression $\Sigma_i (Q_i - \bar{Q})^2$ was minimized. The resulting series is given in Table A-1.

3. No statistical tests for serial correlation of residuals were made, but the plotted residuals were examined for evidence of serial correlation. There was no apparent serial correlation in any of the residual series.

REFERENCE

[1] DEAVER, JOHN V., "The Chilean Inflation and the Demand for Money," unpublished Ph.D. thesis, Univ. of Chicago, 1960.

IV. Econometric Methodology

10

Tests Based on the Movements in and the Comovements between m-Dependent Time Series

LEO A. GOODMAN, *University of Chicago*

1. Introduction and Summary

Tests of the existence of correlation between the movements in two time series, which eliminate at least the primary effects of trends in the series, will be presented in this article. These tests are modifications and generalizations of a test for correlation proposed by Moore and Wallis [14] and of tests proposed by Goodman [8] and by Goodman and Grunfeld [9]. A test of the existence of trend in a time series will also be presented here. This test is a generalization of a test for trend proposed by Cox and Stuart [2].

The tests presented here can be applied to certain kinds of time series that are m-dependent. A time series $X = \{X_1, X_2, \cdots, X_{n+1}\}$ is defined as m-dependent if $(X_1, X_2, \cdots, X_i)$ and $(X_j, X_{j+1}, \cdots, X_{n+1})$ are independent whenever $j > i + m$ (see [13]). For an m-dependent time series, any two observations X_i and X_j will be independent whenever $j > i + m$. Two examples of m-dependent time series are the following: (I) if the $X_1, X_2, \cdots, X_{n+1}$ are mutually independent, then X is zero-dependent; (II) if X is a process of moving averages of the form $X_i = \Sigma_{j=0}^{m} \alpha_j \xi_{i-j}$, where the ξ_i are (unobserved) mutually independent random variables $(i = 0, \pm 1, \pm 2, \cdots)$ (see [1, 20]), then X is m-dependent. Other examples of m-dependent time series could be presented here, but this will not be necessary.

The earlier papers by Moore and Wallis [14], Goodman and Grunfeld [8, 9], and Cox and Stuart [2] present tests that can be applied to certain kinds of time series that are zero-dependent. (The case where the series of

In writing a paper for this volume dedicated to the memory of Yehuda Grunfeld, I set for myself the task of trying to answer some questions that arose in a natural way from some of his methodological and empirical inquiries (e.g., [12]) and from his joint work with me [9]. This paper owes much to his earlier work.

Part of this research was carried out at Columbia University, under sponsorship of the Office of Naval Research (Contract Number NOnr-266(33), Project Number NR 042-034), while the author was a Visiting Professor of Mathematical Statistics and Sociology there; and part at the Department of Statistics, University of Chicago, under sponsorship of the Logistics and Mathematical Statistics Branch, Office of Naval Research. For their helpful comments, the author is indebted to Jacob Mincer and W. Allen Wallis.

first differences are zero-dependent is also discussed in [14].) For times series that are not zero-dependent but that are m-dependent for some $m > 0$, these tests require modification. The purpose of the present paper is to present simple modifications of these tests that can be applied to certain kinds of m-dependent ($m \geq 0$) time series of long duration.

It is often the case that observed time series are not zero-dependent. The earlier papers discussed tests for zero-dependent time series partly because mathematical results were more readily available for this special case; i.e., the case of mutually independent random variables. The earlier authors were of course aware of the fact that the observed time series, to which tests appropriate for zero-dependent series were applied, might actually not be zero-dependent. For example, Cox and Stuart [2], in discussing their test for trend, point out that "positive serial correlation among the observations would increase the chance of a significant answer even in the absence of a trend"; i.e., a significant answer obtained by an application of their test for trend to a (serially correlated) time series might be due to the presence of serial correlation rather than to the presence of a trend. The modification of their test presented in this article does not have this disadvantage.

Moore and Wallis [14] point out that some of the techniques presented in their paper are "restricted in scope by the fact that in many time series problems neither the hypothesis of sequential randomness in observations nor that of sequential randomness in the differences is tenable." The modifications of their test presented herein are not so restricted in scope.

To apply the tests presented here, it is not necessary to know the specific value of m that describes the order of dependence of the observed time series. The value of m could be zero or any positive integer. The magnitude of m should, however, be small relative to the duration of the observed time series. The tests presented here under the assumption that the value of m is specified will actually be suitable even if the true value of m is less than that specified. Thus, even if there is doubt concerning the true value of m for a particular m-dependent time series, it will still be possible to apply these tests. For time series that are not m-dependent for any value of m (e.g., where X_j and X_i are not independent for any $i < j$), the methods presented herein are not to be recommended.

If time series X is m_1-dependent and time series Y is m_2-dependent, where m_1 and m_2 may have different values, then the definition of m-dependence given above implies that both series are η-dependent, where $\eta = \max [m_1, m_2]$. The tests of the existence of correlation between the movements in X and Y presented herein under the assumption that both X and Y are m-dependent can be applied by taking $m = \eta$. If we denote $\min [m_1, m_2]$ by μ, the statistic appropriate for testing the existence of correlation between the movements in X and Y, in the case where X and Y are η-dependent, will converge in probability (under the null hypothesis when X and Y are η-dependent) to the statistic appropriate in the case where both X and Y are μ-dependent. The test statistic appropriate where both X and Y are μ-dependent can be used (instead of the test statistic appropriate when X and Y are η-dependent) even if the order of dependence of X or Y is greater than μ. Thus the test presented in [9], which was justified there in the case where both X and Y are zero-dependent, can also be justified in the case where one of the m-dependent series is not zero-dependent but the other one is.

The tests presented in the earlier papers were based upon the signs of the $X_j - X_i$ for $j > i$, $i = 1, 2, \cdots$. In [9] and [14], $j = i + 1$, $i = 1$, $2, \cdots, n$; in [8], $j = i + k$, $i = 1, 2, \cdots, n + 1 - k$ (k is a fixed positive integer); in [2], other pairs of i and j were used [e.g., $j = i + 2(n + 1)/3$, $i = 1, 2, \cdots, (n + 1)/3$]. If the sign of the difference $X_j - X_i$ is positive, then the "total movement" in X between time i and j is positive. Most of the tests presented in this paper will also be based on the signs of the differences (i.e., the signs of the movements) in the time series. Moore and Wallis [14] have pointed out that "in certain types of data the signs of differences are more accurate than the magnitudes of either the observations or the differences.... With economic measures of the kind for which index numbers are ordinarily used, it may be certain that a change has been in a given direction (e.g., when all components of the index change in the same way), questionable how much the change has been (because of ambiguities in the weighting system), and meaningless to state an absolute standing." For these types of data and for data available only in ordinal form, the methods presented herein may be particularly well suited.

It was not necessary, in the earlier studies, to assume that the distributions from which the observations had come had a specific form (e.g., it was not necessary to assume that the observations were normal variates) in order to derive the distribution of the appropriate test statistics. The tests presented there were distribution-free. It was, however, assumed in these papers that the observations were mutually independent and that the distribution from which they had come was continuous. To derive the asymptotic distribution of the test statistics presented herein, the assumptions made will be somewhat more general.

The calculations required to perform the tests presented in the earlier papers and those presented herein are rather simple. Although the modified tests presented here require more calculations than the earlier tests, these calculations remain simple.

Let $X = \{X_1, X_2, \cdots, X_{n+1}\}$ and $Y = \{Y_1, Y_2, \cdots, Y_{n+1}\}$ be two different observed time series of equal duration. Let $X_{i+1} - X_i = W_i$ and $Y_{i+1} - Y_i = Z_i$ ($i = 1, 2, \cdots, n$). We shall, for convenience, assume that the W_i and Z_i have continuous distributions. Let $U_i = 1$ if $W_i > 0$, and $U_i = 0$ if $W_i < 0$. Let $V_i = 1$ if $Z_i > 0$, and $V_i = 0$ if $Z_i < 0$. If $U_i = 1$, then a positive movement in X occurred between times i and $i + 1$; if

$V_i = 1$, then a positive movement in Y occurred between times i and $i + 1$; if $U_i = V_i = 1$, then a positive comovement occurred; if $U_i = V_i = 0$, then a negative comovement occurred; if $U_i = 0$, $V_i = 1$ or if $U_i = 1$, $V_i = 0$, then a contramovement took place. (The term "comovement" used here is adopted from an earlier work by Friedman [5]. It was also used by Grunfeld [12]. The term "contramovement" is adopted from Goodman and Grunfeld [9].) The observed distribution of the n pairs (U_i, V_i) (for $i = 1, 2, \cdots, n$) can be summarized in the following 2×2 cross-classification table:

U_t \ V_t	1	0
1	a	b
0	c	d

The number of positive comovements in the two time series is a; the number of negative comovements is d; the number of comovements is $a + d$; the number of contramovements is $b + c$; the number of positive movements in X is $a + b$; the number of positive movements in Y is $a + c$.

The usual test of independence in a 2×2 cross-classification table (see, e.g., [17, pp. 65–72]) corresponds to a test of whether a differs significantly from its estimated espected value, $A = (a + b)(a + c)/n$, under the null hypothesis of independence. It tests whether $a - A = \Delta$ differs significantly from zero, using the fact that the estimated variance of Δ is $s^2 = [(a + b)(c + d)(a + c)(b + d)/n^3]$ under the null hypothesis. Moore and Wallis [14] have suggested that the usual 2×2 table test, applied to the table given above, could be used as a test of the existence of correlation between the movements in X and Y, which would eliminate at least the primary effects of trends in the series. They pointed out that this test is appropriate "for the case of randomly arranged [signs of the] first differences" in X and in Y. In the case where X and Y are purely random processes (i.e., zero-dependent stationary time series), they noted [14] that the signs of the first differences in the series would have a negative serial correlation, and that if the 2×2 table test, which was justified by them when the signs of the first differences are randomly arranged, leads to acceptance of the hypothesis that correlation is absent, then it surely would lead to acceptance of this hypothesis if the "null hypothesis of random observations were used; but nothing more can be said definitely until the sampling distribution [of Δ] appropriate to the assumption of random observations is known." The problem raised in [14] led to the derivation by Goodman and Grunfeld [9] of the sampling distribution of Δ for purely random processes of long duration and also for a certain kind of generalization of such time series. (They showed in [9] that the usual estimate, s^2, of the variance of Δ required modification.) For these time series, a simple test of whether Δ differed significantly from zero was obtained.

The test proposed in [9] is appropriate when the X and Y are zero-dependent and the series $U = \{U_1, U_2, \cdots, U_n\}$ and $V = \{V_1, V_2, \cdots, V_n\}$ are stationary. For such time series, this test is a test of the existence of correlation between the movements in X and Y, taking into account (a) the time trends that may exist in X and in Y, and (b) the serial correlation between the signs of the first differences of zero-dependent time series. [The Moore-Wallis test takes into account (a) but not (b), and a related test by Stuart [18] takes into account (b) but not (a).] When X and Y are m-dependent ($m > 0$), the test in [9] does not fully take into account the serial correlation between the signs of the first differences. The test presented herein will take into account both (a) and the serial correlation between the signs of the first differences of m-dependent time series.

Tests of the existence of correlation between the movements in X and Y based on $\Delta = a - A$ compare the observed number, a, of positive comovements, given in the above 2×2 table, with its estimated expected value, A, when the null hypothesis of independence is true. Since A is based on $(a + b)/n$ and $(a + c)/n$, which are measures of an aspect of the "trend" in X and Y, respectively, tests based on Δ test whether the observed number of positive comovements can be "explained" by the trends in X and in Y alone. If we denote the estimated expected values of b, c, d, in the above 2×2 table, by

$$B = \frac{(a + b)(b + d)}{n}, \qquad C = \frac{(a + c)(c + d)}{n}, \qquad D = \frac{(c + d)(b + d)}{n},$$

respectively, we see that

$$a - A = d - D = B - b = C - c = \frac{(a + d) - (A + D)}{2} = \frac{(B + C) - (b + c)}{2}$$

$$= \frac{[(a + d) - (b + c)] - \{[(a + b) - (c + d)][(a + c) - (b + d)]\}/n}{4}$$

$$= \frac{ad - bc}{n}.$$

Thus, a test of whether Δ differs significantly from zero is also a test of whether the number of comovements $(a + d)$, the number of contramovements $(b + c)$, and the difference between the number of comovements and contramovements $([a + d] - [b + c])$ differ from their respective estimated expected values. It is a test of whether the observed values of $(a + d)$, $(b + c)$, $([a + d] - [b + c])$ can be "explained" by the trends in X and Y alone.

The statistic Δ/n is the observed covariance between U_i and V_i. For certain types of data of the kind referred to in [14], where the U_i (and V_i) are more accurate than the W_i (and Z_i), tests based on the observed covariance between U_i and V_i are to be preferred to tests based on the observed covariance between W_i and Z_i. The methods used here to obtain a test based on the observed covariance between U_i and V_i can be modified in a straightforward fashion to obtain a similar test based on the observed covariance between W_i and Z_i. The latter test will also be presented here. Tests based on the rank covariance (or the rank correlation) between W_i and Z_i could also be obtained. Which test should be used in a particular situation will depend upon the type of data available, on the accurancy of the U_i and V_i as compared with the W_i and Z_i, and on the particular null and alternate hypotheses under consideration. For example, if the W_i and Z_i form zero-dependent stationary normal series, the usual test of the null hypothesis that the correlation between two normal variates is zero should be applied to the (W_i, Z_i) (see, e.g., [3]). In some situations, tests based on the rank correlation between the W_i and Z_i will recommend themselves (see, e.g., related remarks in [4]); in other kinds of situations, discussed earlier, tests based on the (U_i, V_i) will be more appropriate.

Under the null hypothesis that the U_i and V_i (or the W_i and Z_i) are independent, the covariance between U_i and V_i (or between W_i and Z_i) will be zero. It will sometimes be of interest to test the null hypothesis that this covariance is some specified value other than zero. For certain kinds of m-dependent time series, methods of testing such hypotheses, of estimating the magnitude of this covariance (i.e., the covariance between U_i and V_i or that between W_i and Z_i), and of obtaining confidence intervals for this covariance, will be presented below. These methods require more computation than the methods referred to earlier.

The U_i and V_i (or the W_i and Z_i) are based on the differences $X_j - X_i$ and $Y_j - Y_i$ for $j = i + 1$. In other words, movement is here defined in terms of the difference in the time series at successive time points. The results obtained in this case can be generalized to the case where movement is defined in terms of the difference in the time series at time points k units apart, where k is a fixed positive integer. These generalizations are presented in Section 3.

The methods used to derive tests of the existence of correlation between the movements in m-dependent time series can also be used to derive tests of the existence of trend in such series. We present such a test in Section 4. Other tests for trend could also be readily derived.

Most of the tests presented here are based on a dichotomous classification of the movements in X (and in Y) indicating whether they were positive or negative. Some of the results presented herein can be modified in a straightforward fashion for situations in which other fixed methods of classification into two or more classes based on the magnitude of the movements are used. The cross-classification table describing the joint distribution of the classified movements in X and in Y can be analyzed in ways other than those discussed here. For example, the problem of measuring the extent of the correlation between the movements in X and Y can be considered, in part, a problem in the measurement of association for this cross-classification table. For a discussion of the latter problem, see [10, 11] and the literature cited there. The choice of a method of analysis will depend on the purpose of the investigation.

2. Tests Based on $a - A$

We shall use the same notation as in the preceding section. We assume throughout that X and Y are m-dependent ($m \geqq 0$). Thus $U = \{U_1, U_2, \cdots, U_n\}$ and $V = \{V_1, V_2, \cdots, V_n\}$ are $(m + 1)$-dependent. For simplicity, we assume also that U and V are stationary. (This assumption implies that trends in X and Y will be, in a certain sense, either constant or nonexistent; some of the results presented here will hold under more general conditions, but we shall not go into these details in this paper; see [13].) For such series, we shall now present a test of the hypothesis that U and V are independent.

Since the U and V series are $(m + 1)$-dependent, we know that the cov $\{U_i, U_{i+t}\} = \epsilon_t$ and cov $\{V_i, V_{i+t}\} = \phi_t$ will be zero for $t > m + 1$. To estimate ϵ_t and ϕ_t for $t \leqq m + 1$, we first compute $g_t = \sum_{i=1}^{n-t} U_i U_{i+t}$ and $h_t = \sum_{i=1}^{n-t} V_i V_{i+t}$ for $t = 1, 2, \cdots, m + 1$. The statistic g_t is the observed number of pairs of time points, t units apart, where there were positive movements in X (at both time points in the pair); h_t is the observed number of pairs of time points, t units part, where there were positive movements in Y. These quantities can also be obtained from 2×2 tables of the following form describing the observed distribution of the $(n - t)$ pairs (U_i, U_{i+t}) and (V_i, V_{i+t}) for $i = 1, 2, \cdots, n - t$:

U_i \ U_{i+t}	1	0
1		
0		

V_i \ V_{i+t}	1	0
1		
0		

The entry in the upper-left cell of the first table will be g_t, and the entry in the corresponding cell of the second table will be h_t. [Note that the usual 2×2 table test of independence applied to the pairs (U_i, U_{i+1}) and to the pairs (V_i, V_{i+1}) has been suggested [6, 7] as a test of the hypothesis of randomness in the U series and in the V series, respectively (the hypothesis that these series are zero-dependent).] Having computed g_t and h_t, we obtain the following consistent estimators of ϵ_t and ϕ_t:

(2.1)
$$\hat{\epsilon}_t = \frac{g_t}{(n-t)} - \left[\frac{(a+b)}{n}\right]^2$$

and

(2.2)
$$\hat{\phi}_t = \frac{h_t}{(n-t)} - \left[\frac{(a+c)}{n}\right]^2.$$

Writing

(2.3)
$$s^2 = \frac{(a+b)(c+d)(a+c)(b+d)}{n^3}$$

and

(2.4)
$$\tilde{s}^2 = s^2 + 2n \sum_{t=1}^{m+1} \hat{\epsilon}_t \hat{\phi}_t,$$

we shall prove in the Appendix that when U and V are independent the asymptotic distribution $(n \to \infty)$ of

(2.5)
$$\frac{(a-A)}{\tilde{s}}$$

will be normal with zero mean and unit variance. The statistic (2.5) can therefore be used to test whether U and V are independent.

The test proposed in [14] did not include the term $2n \sum_{t=1}^{m+1} \hat{\epsilon}_t \hat{\phi}_t$ in the variance computation; i.e., s^2 was used rather than $\tilde{s}^2$. The test proposed in [9] included the term $2n \hat{\epsilon}_1 \hat{\phi}_1$ but not $2n \sum_{t=2}^{m+1} \hat{\epsilon}_t \hat{\phi}_t$.

If time series X is m_1-dependent and time series Y is m_2-dependent, then $\epsilon_t = 0$ for $t > m_1 + 1$, $\phi_t = 0$ for $t > m_2 + 1$, and $\epsilon_t \phi_t = 0$ for $t > \mu + 1$, where $\mu = \min[m_1, m_2]$. It follows from this that (2.4) can be replaced by

(2.6)
$$\tilde{s}^2 = s^2 + 2n \sum_{t=1}^{\mu+1} \hat{\epsilon}_t \hat{\phi}_t,$$

in the computation of (2.5). In particular, tests appropriate for the case in which X and Y are zero-dependent will also be appropriate for the case in which one of these m-dependent series is not zero-dependent and the other one is. It can also be seen that the test appropriate for the case in which both U and V are zero-dependent (obtained by replacing $\tilde{s}^2$ by s^2) will be appropriate also for the case in which one of these m-dependent series is not zero-dependent and the other one is.

If X is m_1-dependent and Y is m_2-dependent, then X and Y are m-dependent, where $m = \max[m_1, m_2]$. In what follows we take $m = \max[m_1, m_2]$.

The test described above was based on the U_i and V_i. A similar test could be based on the W_i and Z_i. Assuming that $W = \{W_1, W_2, \cdots, W_n\}$ and $Z = \{Z_1, Z_2, \cdots, Z_n\}$ form stationary series, the covariances $\text{cov}\{W_i, W_{i+t}\} = \epsilon_t^*$ and $\text{cov}\{Z_i, Z_{i+t}\} = \phi_t^*$ can be estimated consistently by

$$(2.7) \qquad \hat{\epsilon}_t^* = \frac{g_t^*}{(n-t)} - \bar{W}^2,$$

$$(2.8) \qquad \hat{\phi}_2^* = \frac{h_t^*}{(n-t)} - \bar{Z}^2,$$

where

$$g_t^* = \sum_{i=1}^{n-t} W_i W_{i+t}, \quad h_t^* = \sum_{i=1}^{n-t} Z_i Z_{i+t}, \quad \bar{W} = \sum_{i=1}^{n} \frac{W_i}{n}, \quad \bar{Z} = \sum_{i=1}^{n} \frac{Z_i}{n}$$

$$(t = 1, 2, \cdots, m+1).$$

If we write

$$(2.9) \qquad s_W^2 = \sum_{i=1}^{n} \frac{(W_i - \bar{W})^2}{(n-1)},$$

$$(2.10) \qquad s_Z^2 = \sum_{i=1}^{n} \frac{(Z_i - \bar{Z})^2}{(n-1)},$$

$$(2.11) \qquad s^{*2} = s_W^2 s_Z^2 n,$$

$$(2.12) \qquad \tilde{s}^{*2} = s^{*2} + 2n \sum_{t=1}^{m+1} \hat{\epsilon}_t^* \hat{\phi}_t^*,$$

it follows from the results in the Appendix that when W and Z are independent the asymptotic distribution $(n \to \infty)$ of

$$(2.13) \qquad \frac{\sum_{i=1}^{n} W_i Z_i - n\bar{W}\bar{Z}}{\tilde{s}^*}$$

will be normal with zero mean and unit variance. (To apply the Hoeffding-Robbins form of the central limit theorem [13], we assume here that the third absolute moments of W_i and Z_i are finite.) The statistic (2.13) can therefore be used to test whether W and Z are independent. Once again, the statistic (2.12) can be replaced by

$$(2.14) \qquad \tilde{s}^{*2} = s^{*2} + 2n \sum_{t=1}^{\mu+1} \hat{\epsilon}_t^* \hat{\phi}_t^*$$

in the computation of (2.13).

The preceding asymptotic results were derived under the null hypothesis that W and Z (or U and V) were independent. We shall now consider the case in which W and Z need not be independent. Let θ^* denote the covariance between W_i and Z_i. Under the null hypothesis considered in the preceding paragraph, $\theta^* = 0$. We shall assume that the $W_i Z_i$ form an $(m + 1)$-dependent stationary series; this will follow as a consequence, in the case in which W and Z are independent, of the fact that the W and Z are $(m + 1)$-dependent stationary series. The statistic

$$(2.15) \qquad \theta^* = \sum_{i=1}^{n} \frac{W_i Z_i}{n} - \overline{W}\overline{Z}$$

is a consistent estimator of θ^*. Writing

$$(2.16) \qquad \hat{\psi}_t^* = \sum_{i=1}^{n-t} \frac{(W_i - \overline{W})(W_{i+t} - \overline{W})(Z_i - \overline{Z})(Z_{i+t} - \overline{Z})}{(n - t)} - \hat{\theta}^{*2}$$

$$(t = 0, 1, 2, \cdots, m + 1)$$

and

$$(2.17) \qquad \hat{s}^{*2} = n\left(\hat{\psi}_0^* + 2\sum_{t=1}^{m+1} \hat{\psi}_t^*\right).$$

it follows from the results in the Appendix that the asymptotic distribution $(n \to \infty)$ of

$$(2.18) \qquad \frac{(\hat{\theta}^* - \theta^*)n}{\hat{s}^*}$$

will be normal with zero mean and unit variance. The statistic (2.18) can therefore be used to obtain approximate confidence intervals for θ^* and to test the hypothesis that θ^* is some specified value, say θ_0^*. When the null hypothesis is that W_i and Z_i are independent, then $\theta_0^* = 0$ and the value of $\hat{s}^*$ can be replaced by $\tilde{s}^*$.

Let θ denote the covariance between U_i and V_i. A method analogous to that presented in the preceding paragraph could be used to estimate θ, obtain approximate confidence intervals for θ, and test hypotheses concerning θ. The details are given in the Appendix. When the null hypothesis is that $\theta = 0$, the test presented at the beginning of this section will be simpler to apply than will the test corresponding to the one presented in the preceding paragraph.

3. Tests Based on $a_k - A_k$

We now present a generalization of the tests described in the preceding section. It is also a generalization of the tests described by Goodman in [8].

Let $X_{i+k} - X_i = W_{ik}$ and $Y_{i+k} - Y_i = Z_{ik}$ for $i = 1, 2, \cdots, n + 1 - k$, where k is a fixed integer. We shall for convenience assume that the W_{ik} and Z_{ik} have continuous distributions. Let $U_{ik} = 1$ if $W_{ik} > 0$, and $U_{ik} = 0$ if $W_{ik} < 0$. Let $V_{ik} = 1$ if $Z_{ik} > 0$, and $V_{ik} = 1$ if $Z_{ik} < 0$. The observed distribution of the $n + 1 - k$ pairs (U_{ik}, V_{ik}), for $i = 1, 2, \cdots, n + 1 - k$, can be summarized in the following 2×2 cross-classification table:

U_{ik} \ V_{ik}	1	0
1	a_k	b_k
0	c_k	d_k

For $k = 1$, we have $a_k = a$, $b_k = b$, $c_k = c$, $d_k = d$. For $k \geq 1$ the definitions of a_k, b_k, c_k, d_k are analogous to those of a, b, c, d, where now "movement" is defined by considering pairs of time points k units apart, rather than pairs of successive time points.

The existence of correlation between movements in X and Y can be tested by applying to the above table a modification of the usual test of independence in a 2×2 table. This test, which eliminates at least the primary effects of trends in the series, would determine whether a_k differed significantly from its estimated expected value,

$$A_k = \frac{(a_k + b_k)(a_k + c_k)}{n + 1 - k},$$

under the null hypothesis of independence.

Let $U^{(k)} = \{U_{1k}, U_{2k}, \cdots, U_{n+1-k,k}\}$, $V^{(k)} = \{V_{1k}, V_{2k}, \cdots, V_{n+1-k,k}\}$. If we assume that X and Y are m-dependent, then $U^{(k)}$ and $V^{(k)}$ will be $(m + k)$-dependent. For simplicity, we also assume that $U^{(k)}$ and $V^{(k)}$ are stationary. Let $g_{tk} = \sum_{i=1}^{n+1-k-t} U_{ik}U_{i+t,k}$ and $h_{tk} = \sum_{i=1}^{n+1-k-t} V_{ik}V_{i+t,k}$. Writing

$$(3.1) \qquad \hat{\epsilon}_{tk} = \frac{g_{tk}}{n + 1 - k - t} - \left(\frac{a_k + b_k}{n + 1 - k}\right)^2,$$

$$(3.2) \qquad \hat{\phi}_{tk} = \frac{h_{tk}}{n + 1 - k - t} - \left(\frac{a_k + c_k}{n + 1 - k}\right)^2,$$

$$(3.3) \qquad s_k^2 = \frac{(a_k + b_k)(c_k + d_k)(a_k + c_k)(b_k + d_k)}{(n + 1 - k)^3},$$

$$(3.4) \qquad \tilde{s}_k^2 = s_k^2 + 2(n + 1 - k)\sum_{t=1}^{m+k} \hat{\epsilon}_{tk}\hat{\phi}_{tk},$$

we shall prove in the Appendix that when $U^{(k)}$ and $V^{(k)}$ are independent, the asymptotic distribution $(n \to \infty)$ of

$$(3.5) \qquad\qquad \frac{a_k - A_k}{\tilde{s}_k}$$

is normal with zero mean and unit variance. The statistic (3.5) can therefore be used to test whether $U^{(k)}$ and $V^{(k)}$ are independent.

The test proposed in [8] was also based on the $a_k - A_k$, but that test was derived under the assumption that $m = 0$. In this special case, the serial covariance, ϵ_{tk}, between U_{ik} and $U_{i+t,k}$ is zero for $t < k$; the serial covariance, ϕ_{tk}, between V_{ik} and $V_{i+t,k}$ is zero for $t < k$. Thus, when $m = 0$, the variance formula (3.4) can be replaced by

$$(3.6) \qquad\qquad \tilde{s}_k^2 = s_k^2 + 2(n - k + 1)\hat{\epsilon}_{kk}\hat{\phi}_{kk} ,.$$

which corresponds to the variance formula given in [8].

The test in Section 2 based on the (U_i , V_i) is a special case of the test given in this section based on (U_{ik} , V_{ik}). Similarly, a test analogous to the one based on (U_{ik} , V_{ik}), but based instead on the (W_{ik} , Z_{ik}), could be presented, and would be a direct generalization of the test in the Section 2 based on the (W_i , Z_i). If we write θ_k (or θ_k^*) for the covariance between U_{ik} and V_{ik} (or between W_{ik} and Z_{ik}), we find that a test analogous to the test in the Section 2 of whether θ (or θ^*) is equal to some specified value (not necessarily zero) could also be obtained. These tests are given in the Appendix.

The tests proposed in this and the preceding section were based, in part, on the observed distribution of the $n + 1 - k$ pairs (U_{ik} , V_{ik}) $(i = 1, 2, \cdots, n + 1 - k)$ or on the pairs (W_{ik} , Z_{ik}), when k is a fixed positive integer. Considering all possible values of k, there are a total of $n(n + 1)/2$ pairs (U_{ik} , V_{ik}). The observed distribution of these $n(n + 1)/2$ pairs (U_{ik} , V_{ik}) can be summarized in a 2×2 table; the usual measure of association computed for this table will be equal to the partial rank correlation coefficient, $\tau_{XY.T}$, between X and Y with time T held constant (see [8], [9]). The situation considered here is, in a sense, a special case of the usual situation where partial rank correlation may be of interest; here the actual observations on the variable to be held constant, T, are the integers $1, 2, \cdots, n + 1$ (or a linear transformation of them). The tests of the existence of correlation (based on the U_{ik} , V_{ik}) presented in this paper are tests based on modified partial rank correlation coefficients where the $(n + 1 - k)$ pairs of (U_{ik} , V_{ik}) are used instead of the total $n(n + 1)/2$ pairs. This follows from the fact that a test of whether $a_k - A_k$ differs significantly from zero is also a test of whether the usual measure of association for the corresponding 2×2 table differs significantly from zero (see [8]).

4. A Test for Trend

For a zero-dependent time series, Cox and Stuart [2] have presented a very simple test for trend that has rather high asymptotic relative efficiency against the alternative hypothesis that the series consists of zero-dependent normal variates having a linear trend. For m-dependent time series ($m > 0$), this test requires modification. A modified test for trend suitable for m-dependent time series will be presented here. The method used to derive this test is similar to that used to derive the tests presented in the preceding sections. This method can be used to derive other tests for trend. Presentation herein of the modification of the Cox-Stuart test will make clear how other tests for zero-dependent series can be modified in order to obtain tests for trend in time series that are m-dependent.

Let $U_i' = 1$ if $X_{2n'+i} - X_i > 0$, and $U_i' = 0$ if $X_{2n'+i} - X_i < 0$, for $i = 1, 2, \cdots, n'$, $n' = (n + 1)/3$, where $(n + 1)$ is divisible by 3. (We assume that $X_{2n'+i} - X_i$ has a continuous distribution.) The test proposed in [2] is based on the fact that $U' = \sum_{i=1}^{n'} U_i'$ will have a binomial distribution with mean $n'/2$ and variance $n'/4$ when X is a zero-dependent stationary time series. A simple sign test of whether U' differs significantly from $n'/2$ can serve as a test for trend in X (see [2]). When X is zero-dependent and stationary, the asymptotic distribution of

$$(4.1) \qquad \frac{U' - \dfrac{n'}{2}}{\sqrt{\dfrac{n'}{4}}}$$

is normal with zero mean and unit variance. This fact also provides us with a simple test for trend for zero-dependent series.

If X is m-dependent, the time series $U' = \{U_1', U_2', \cdots, U_{n'}'\}$ will also be m-dependent (for $n' \geq m$). If the X series is stationary, the U' series will also be stationary. Writing

$$(4.2) \qquad f_t = \sum_{i=1}^{n'-t} U_i' U_{i+t}',$$

$$(4.3) \qquad s_U^2 = n' \left\{ \left[2 \sum_{t=1}^{m} \frac{f_t}{(n'-t)} \right] - \frac{(2m-1)}{4} \right\},$$

we find, using a method of derivation similar to that used in the Appendix, that when X is an m-dependent stationary series the asymptotic distribution ($n \to \infty$) of

$$(4.4) \qquad \frac{U' - \dfrac{n'}{2}}{s_U}$$

is normal with zero mean and unit variance. The statistic (4.4) can therefore be used to test for trend in X. This test is a modification of the sign test in [2], where the variance $n'/4$ is now replaced by (4.3). When n' is large, the term $2 \sum_{t=1}^{m} f_t/(n' - t)$ in (4.3) can be replaced by $2 \sum_{i=1}^{n'-m} e_i/(n' - m)$, where e_i is the number of values of j such that $U'_j = 1$ for $i < j \leq i + m$ when $U'_i = 1$, and $e_i = 0$ when $U'_i = 0$.

APPENDIX

We shall prove here a somewhat more general result than those presented in Sections 2 and 3 herein. The results presented in those sections will then be viewed in terms of this more general result. We shall use here the same terminology as in Section 3. The method of proof presented here can also be used to prove the result presented in Section 4.

We assume that X and Y are m-dependent. Thus $U^{(k)}$ and $V^{(k)}$ are $(m + k)$-dependent. We also assume that $U^{(k)}$ and $V^{(k)}$ are stationary. Let $E\{U_{ik}\} = p_k$ and $E\{V_{ik}\} = r_k$ $(i = 1, 2, \cdots, n + 1 - k)$. Writing $G_{ik} = U_{ik} - p_k$, $H_{ik} = V_{ik} - r_k$, $F_{ik} = G_{ik}H_{ik}$, $Q_{ik} = U_{ik}V_{ik}$, we see that

(A.1) $$\bar{Q} - \bar{U}\bar{V} = \bar{F} - \bar{G}\bar{H}.$$

where $\bar{Q} = \sum_{i=1}^{n+1-k} Q_{ik}/(n + 1 - k)$, and $\bar{U}, \bar{V}, \bar{F}, \bar{G}, \bar{H}$ are defined similarly. (Since k is fixed, we shall, for the sake of brevity, omit the subscript k associated with $\bar{Q}, \bar{U}, \bar{V}$, and so on.) We shall assume that the Q_{ik} also form an $(m + k)$-dependent stationary series; this will follow as a consequence—in the case where U_{ik} and V_{ik} are independent—of the fact that $U^{(k)}$ and $V^{(k)}$ are $(m + k)$-dependent and stationary. Let $E\{F_{ik}\} = \theta$. Applying the Hoeffding–Robbins form of the central limit theorem [13], we find that the asymptotic distribution of $(\bar{F} - \theta) \sqrt{n + 1 - k}$ is normal with zero mean and variance

(A.2) $$E\{G_{ik}^2 H_{ik}^2\} + 2 \sum_{t=1}^{m+k} E\{G_{ik}H_{ik}G_{i+t,k}H_{i+t,k}\} - [2(m + k) + 1]\theta^2.$$

Similarly, the asymptotic distribution of $\bar{G} \sqrt{n + 1 - k}$ is normal with zero mean and variance

(A.3) $$E\{G_{ik}^2\} + 2 \sum_{t=1}^{m+k} E\{G_{ik}G_{i+t,k}\}.$$

The asymptotic distribution of $\bar{H} \sqrt{n + 1 - k}$ is normal with zero mean and variance

(A.4) $$E\{H_{ik}^2\} + 2 \sum_{t=1}^{m+k} E\{H_{ik}H_{i+t,k}\}.$$

Since $\bar{G}$ converges in probability to zero, $\bar{G}\bar{H}\sqrt{n+1-k}$ will also converge in probability to zero (see [3, p. 254]). Thus the asymptotic distribution of $(\bar{F} - \bar{G}\bar{H} - \theta)\sqrt{n+1-k}$ is also the asymptotic distribution of $(\bar{F} - \theta)\sqrt{n+1-k}$. We have therefore shown that the asymptotic distribution of $(\bar{Q} - \bar{U}\bar{V} - \theta)\sqrt{n+1-k}$ is normal with mean zero and variance (A.2). Writing

$$\text{(A.5)} \qquad \theta = \bar{Q} - \bar{U}\bar{V},$$

$$\text{(A.6)} \qquad \hat{\psi}_t = \sum_{i=1}^{n+1-k-t} \frac{(U_{ik} - \bar{U})(V_{ik} - \bar{V})(U_{i+t,k} - \bar{U})(V_{i+t,k} - \bar{V})}{n+1-k-t} - \hat{\theta}^2,$$

we see that (A.2) can be estimated consistently by

$$\text{(A.7)} \qquad \hat{\psi}_0 + 2 \sum_{t=1}^{m+k} \hat{\psi}_t,$$

which we denote by $\hat{s}^2/(n+1-k)$. Thus the asymptotic distribution of

$$\text{(A.8)} \qquad \frac{[\bar{Q} - \bar{U}\bar{V} - \theta](n+1-k)}{\hat{s}}$$

will be normal with zero mean and unit variance. A test of the hypothesis that θ is equal to some specified value θ_0 can be based on the asymptotic distribution of (A.8).

The preceding results did not make use of the fact that U_{ik} and V_{ik} take on only the values 0 or 1. The results will therefore apply as well if U_{ik} and V_{ik} are replaced by W_{ik} and Z_{ik}, respectively. (It will be necessary to assume that the third moments of W_{ik} and Z_{ik} are finite in order to apply the Hoeffding–Robbins theorem [13].) We thus have obtained a generalization of the result in Section 2 concerning the asymptotic distribution of (2.18). The result presented there was for the special case in which $k = 1$.

When $U^{(k)}$ and $V^{(k)}$ are independent, then $\theta = 0$, and the variance (A.2) can be replaced by

$$\text{(A.9)} \qquad E\{G_{ik}^2\}E\{H_{ik}^2\} + 2 \sum_{t=1}^{m+k} E\{G_{ik}G_{i+t,k}\}E\{H_{ik}H_{i+t,k}\}.$$

(It should be mentioned that formula (A.9) is similar to, but different from, the usual formula for the variance of the observed correlation between two independent linear autoregressive series; see, e.g., [1, 15, 16].) Writing

$$\text{(A.10)} \qquad \hat{\epsilon}_{tk}^+ = \frac{g_{tk}}{(n+1-k-t)} - \bar{U}^2,$$

$$(A.11) \qquad \hat{\phi}_{tk}^{+} = \frac{h_{tk}}{(n+1-k-t)} - \bar{V}^2 ,$$

$$(A.12) \qquad s_U^2 = \sum_{i=1}^{n+1-k} \frac{(U_{ik} - \bar{U})^2}{n+1-k} ,$$

$$(A.13) \qquad s_V^2 = \sum_{i=1}^{n+1-k} \frac{(V_{ik} - \bar{V})^2}{n+1-k} ,$$

we see that (A.9) can be estimated consistently by

$$(A.14) \qquad s_U^2 s_V^2 + 2 \sum_{t=1}^{m+k} \hat{\epsilon}_{tk}^{+} \hat{\phi}_{tk}^{+} ,$$

which we denote by $\tilde{s}^{+2}/(n+1-k)$. Thus, when $U^{(k)}$ and $V^{(k)}$ are independent, the asymptotic distribution of

$$(A.15) \qquad \frac{(\bar{Q} - \bar{U}\bar{V})(n+1-k)}{\tilde{s}^{+}}$$

will be asymptotically normal with zero mean and unit variance. This result will also apply if U_{ik} and V_{ik} are replaced by W_{ik} and Z_{ik}, respectively. We thus have obtained a generalization of the result in Section 2 concerning the asymptotic distribution of (2.13).

Using the fact that U_{ik} and V_{ik} were defined in Section 3 to take on only the values 0 or 1, we see that $\bar{Q} - \bar{U}\bar{V} = (a_k - A_k)/(n+1-k)$, and that the asymptotic distribution of

$$(A.16) \qquad \frac{(a_k - A_k)}{\tilde{s}_k}$$

[where $\tilde{s}_k$ is given by (3.4)] is normal with zero mean and unit variance.

REFERENCES

[1] BARTLETT, M. S., *An Introduction to Stochastic Processes*. Cambridge: Cambridge Univ. Press, 1960.

[2] COX, D. R., and A. STUART, Some Quick Sign Tests for Trend in Location and Dispersion, *Biometrika*, **42** (1955), 80-95.

[3] CRAMÉR, HARALD, *Mathematical Methods of Statistics*. Princeton, N.J.: Princeton Univ. Press, 1946.

[4] DANIELS, H. E., Rank Correlation and Population Models, *J. Roy. Stat. Soc.*, Ser. B, **12** (1950), 171-81.

[5] FRIEDMAN, MILTON, "An Empirical Study of the Relationship Between Railroad Stock Prices and Railroad Earnings for the Period 1921-1931," Master's Thesis, Department of Economics, Univ. of Chicago, 1933.

[6] GOODMAN, LEO A., Simplified Runs Tests and Likelihood Ratio Tests for Markov Chains, *Biometrika*, **45** (1958), 181-97.

[7] GOODMAN, LEO A., Exact Probabilities and Asymptotic Relationships for some Statistics from *m*-th Order Markov Chains, *Ann. Math. Stat.*, **29** (1958), 476-90.

[8] GOODMAN, LEO A., Partial Tests for Partial Taus, *Biometrika*, **46** (1959), 525-32.

[9] GOODMAN, LEO A., and YEHUDA GRUNFELD, Some Nonparametric Tests for Comovements Between Time Series, *J. Amer. Stat. Assoc.*, **56** (1961), 11-26.

[10] GOODMAN, LEO A., and WILLIAM H. KRUSKAL, Measures of Association for Cross Classifications, *J. Amer. Stat. Assoc.*, **49** (1954), 732-64.

[11] GOODMAN, LEO A., and WILLIAM H. KRUSKAL, Measures of Association for Cross Classifications. II: Further Discussion and References, *J. Amer. Stat. Assoc.*, **54** (1959), 124-63.

[12] GRUNFELD, YEHUDA, *The Determinants of Corporate Investment*, Doctoral Thesis, Department of Economics, Univ. of Chicago, 1958.

[13] HOEFFDING, WASSILY, and HERBERT ROBBINS, The Central Limit Theorem for Dependent Random Variables, *Duke Math. J.*, **15** (1948), 773-80.

[14] MOORE, GEOFFREY H., and W. ALLEN WALLIS, Time Series Significance Tests Based on Signs of Differences, *J. Amer. Stat. Assoc.*, **38** (1943), 153-64.

[15] MORAN, P. A. P., Some Theorems on Time Series. I, *Biometrika*, **34** (1947), 281-91.

[16] ORCUTT, G. H., and S. F. JAMES, Testing the Significance of Correlation Between Time Studies, *Biometrika*, **35** (1948), 397-413.

[17] PEARSON, E. S., and H. O. HARTLEY, *Biometrika Tables for Statisticians*, Vol. 1. Cambridge: Cambridge Univ. Press, 1954.

[18] STUART, ALAN, The Power of Two Difference-sign Tests, *J. Amer. Stat. Assoc.*, **47** (1952), 416-24.

[19] STUART, ALAN, The Asymptotic Relative Efficiencies of Distribution-free Tests of Randomness against Normal Alternatives, *J. Amer. Stat. Assoc.*, **47** (1952), 416-24.

[20] WOLD, HERMAN, *A Study in the Analysis of Stationary Time Series*. Stockholm: Almqvist and Wiksell, 1954.

11

Least-Squares Estimates of Transition Probabilities

LESTER G. TELSER, *University of Chicago*

That successive observations of an economic time series often exhibit dependence is well known. Explicit economic theories including lagged values of endogenous variables are designed to explain this aspect of economic time series. Such theories are applications of Markov processes in the sense that current values of economic variables are assumed to depend on earlier values of the same variables. Although these models are familiar in economics, little use has as yet been made of the classical Markov theory of stochastic processes. Such stochastic processes assume that transitions of "objects" from one state to another are governed by a probabilistic mechanism or structure. My purpose in this paper is to present a simple method of estimating the probability mechanism if only a modest amount of data are available. The conclusion to this paper contains warnings regarding the applicability of the method.

Before discussing the estimation problem, I shall give a few examples of applications of Markov processes to economic problems to help illuminate their nature. Suppose we wish to measure the degree of competition among the firms in some industry. Data are often compiled to show the combined market share of, say, the four leading firms in the industry. One may conclude that competition has lessened if the market share of the four leading firms increases over time. However, such a conclusion is misleading if the same four firms are not among the industry leaders during successive time periods. Suppose we define a state to be a size class, so that there are as many states as size classes. We could then study the transitions of firms from one size class to another. By assuming the existence of probabilities that characterize the propensity of firms to move from one size class to another, we may be led to a number of useful discoveries regarding the life cycle of firms, their size distribution, and the level and intensity of competition in the industry. Central to such a study would be the estimation of the transition probabilities.

One may also apply a Markov process in the study of consumer behavior. Suppose there are r brands in a particular product class and we wish to know

---

I am grateful to Albert Madansky, Leo Goodman, Harry Roberts, and Martin Bailey for helpful comments and criticism. I assume sole responsibility for errors.

whether consumers are more likely to purchase a given brand if they have done so in the recent past. We could classify various sequences of purchases according to the brands involved and estimate the probabilities of transitions of purchases from brand to brand. By measuring the attachment of consumers to brands in this way we could learn much about the extent to which consumers regard as substitutes the various brands and, therefore, about the intensity of competition among the brands. This kind of analysis rests on the estimation of transition probabilities among the brands, which are the "states" of this example.

More formally, we can describe Markov processes or chains as follows: Assume there are r states designated E_i $(i = 1, \cdots, r)$. The probability that state i occurs on trial t is denoted by

$$(1) \qquad P(E_{it}) = m_{it}.$$

If the states occur independently on successive trials, then the probability of some sequence of states is the product of the probabilities of these states. Thus, assuming independence, the probability of the sequence E_i on trial t and E_j on trial $t + 1$ is given by

$$(2) \qquad P(E_{it}, E_{jt+1}) = m_{it}m_{jt+1}.$$

A situation in which states occur independently on successive trials is a special kind of Markov process that we may call a zero-order Markov process. This kind of process is more familiarly known as a Bernoulli process and is a well-known and useful probability model. In a first-order Markov chain the probability of a state on one trial is conditional on which trial preceded it. Thus, if the probability of state j on trial $t + 1$ conditional on state i on trial t is denoted p_{ij}, we have

$$(3) \qquad P(E_{jt+1} \mid E_{it}) = p_{ij}.$$

The absence of t subscripts on p_{ij} indicates that the probability of a transition from i to j is the same for all trials. Hence the probability of the sequence E_i on trial t and E_j on trial $t + 1$ is

$$(4) \qquad P(E_{it}, E_{jt+1}) = m_{it}p_{ij}.$$

This implies, in contrast to (2), that knowledge of which state occurred on trial t affects the expectation of which state occurs on trial $t + 1$. In the zero-order chain described by (2), the expectation on trial $t + 1$ is the same for all possible sequences of events preceding trial $t + 1$. Even if we knew what event materialized on trial t, we should not change our expectation regarding the outcome on trial $t + 1$. The conditional probability of E_j on trial $t + 1$ is the same as the unconditional probability of E_j on trial $t + 1$. A zero-order process requires p_{ij} to be the same for all i. However, in a first-order process, $p_{ij} \neq p_{i'j}$ for $i \neq i'$. Only the event immediately preceding trial $t + 1$ affects the probability on trial $t + 1$ in a first-order process. Second- or higher-order processes allow the transition probabilities to vary according to the outcome of the two or more preceding trials. In general, if the occurrence of a state on trial $t + 1$ depends on which of the r states occurred on the h preceding trials, then we say that the process is h-order.

Some examples may clarify the situation. Suppose a fair coin is tossed, so that the probability of heads is $\frac{1}{2}$, as is, of course, the probability of tails. The transition probabilities, assuming independence, are given below.

		trial $t + 1$	
		E_1 = heads	E_2 = tails
trial t	E_1	$\frac{1}{2}$	$\frac{1}{2}$
	E_2	$\frac{1}{2}$	$\frac{1}{2}$

Given the occurrence of heads on trial t the probability of heads on trial $t + 1$ is $\frac{1}{2}$. Given the occurrence of tails on trial t, the probability of heads on trial $t + 1$ is $\frac{1}{2}$. Thus we see from the table that heads occurs on trial $t + 1$ with the same probability regardless of the outcome on trial t.

If the outcome of coin tossing were described by a first-order Markov process, then the probability of heads on trial $t + 1$ might be $\frac{2}{3}$ if heads occurred on trial t and $\frac{1}{4}$ if tails occurred on trial t. The transition probabilities are as follows:

		trial $t + 1$	
		E_1 = heads	E_2 = tails
trial t	E_1	$\frac{2}{3}$	$\frac{1}{3}$
	E_2	$\frac{1}{4}$	$\frac{3}{4}$

Consider a first-order Markov chain. By a simple proposition in the probability calculus,

$$(5) \qquad P(E_{j,t+1}) = \sum_{i=1}^{r} P(E_{i,t}, E_{jt+1}) .$$

Using equation (4), we obtain

$$(6) \qquad m_{jt+1} = \sum_{i=1}^{r} m_{it} p_{ij} .$$

This is a basic equation of a first-order Markov chain that allows us to calculate the probability of E_j on trial $t + 1$, given the transition probabilities and the probabilities of the E_i on the preceding trial t.

A second basic equation is the following:

$$(7) \qquad \sum_{j=1}^{r} p_{ij} = 1 .$$

This equation says that, given the occurrence of state i on one trial, some one of the r possible states must occur on the next trial. The transition probabilities can be arranged in an $r \times r$ matrix P whose entry in the ith row and jth column is p_{ij} and whose row sums equal one. From this matrix other probabilities may be calculated, such as the probability of a transition from i to j in n steps. The reader is referred to Feller [2] for an excellent discussion of the properties of Markov chains.

One way of estimating the transition probabilities (the p_{ij}) is by the method of maximum likelihood, as shown by Anderson and Goodman [1] and by Goodman [4]. Suppose we have a sample of n objects whose movements from state to state on successive trials are described by a first-order Markov chain that has a transition matrix P. We count the number of times objects moved from state E_i to state E_j, and divide this by the number of occurrences of E_i. This ratio is the maximum-likelihood estimate of p_{ij}. To calculate this ratio, we obviously need to know how many transitions there were from E_i to E_j.

Suppose we do not have information on the number of transitions and all we know is the number of occurrences of E_j on trial t ($t = 1, \cdots, T$). Thus we have sample estimates of m_{it}, but do not have data giving direct counts of the transitions from i to j. Is the prospect for estimating the transition probabilities hopeless in these circumstances? The answer is no. Given estimates of m_{it} ($i = 1, \cdots, r$ and $t = 1, \cdots, T$), it is possible to estimate the p_{ij}, using familiar least-squares techniques.

The clue lies in (6), which relates the assumed observable $m_{j\,t+1}$ to the preceding m_{it}. Since (6) is linear in the unknown p_{ij}, if readings on m_{it} are available for enough trials, then we may estimate p_{ij} by ordinary least squares, regarding (6) as a linear regression of $m_{j\,t+1}$ on the m_{it}.

In the numerical example worked out below, we wish to estimate the probability that buyers of a particular brand of cigarettes will switch to another brand or continue to smoke the given brand. We do not have data available on transitions of smokers from brand to brand. We do know the market shares of the brands. We shall estimate the transition probabilities, given times series on the market shares of the brands.

The least-squares technique was first suggested by Miller [10] and applied by him to some psychological data. It was discovered independently by the author. Errors in Miller's analysis were pointed out by Kao [7] and Goodman [3]. Moreover, Goodman [3] demonstrated the correct procedure for solving Miller's problem. He also showed in [3] that the least-squares estimates had certain desirable properties and he suggested a modified least-squares technique to ensure that the estimates obtained would be admissible. Madansky [8], building on Goodman's results, showed how to improve the asymptotic efficiency of the least-squares estimates by the use of weighted regressions, and he pointed out that the weighted-regression estimates would take about twice as long to compute as the estimates in [3]. Madansky noted that "since we have no idea of the relative decrease in the variances of the [weighted-regression] estimates (as compared with the estimates in [3]), we cannot discuss the trade-off between the doubled computation time and the reduction in variance." Unfortunately, this important practical question must still remain unanswered.

In this paper I propose to translate the least-squares technique, as described in the above literature, into the regression terminology more familiar to economists. In the process the proofs of some propositions in Miller [10] and Madansky [8] can be simplified. Some ambiguities in Madansky's treatment are clarified. Finally, the estimation technique is extended to variable transition probabilities and to second- or higher-order Markov chains. The method of extending the estimation techniques presented here for variable transition probabilities was proposed independently by Goodman [5, pp. 622-24] for a somewhat different situation, in order to extend the methods of estimating certain regression coefficients to the case in which these coefficients are variable. A number of applications of the estimation method can be found [11] and [12].

1. Least-Squares Estimates of the Transition Probabilities of a Zero-Order Markov Process

A zero-order Markov process is one in which events occur on successive trials independently of the occurrences on the preceding trials. Hence

$$(8) \qquad\qquad P(E_{it}) = m_i \qquad (i = 1, \cdots, r),$$

and the probability of a particular sequence is the product of the probabilities of the component events of the sequence. Moreover, the probability of the occurrence of state i is the same for all trials. Since one of the r events must occur on every trial,

$$(9) \qquad\qquad \sum_{i=1}^{r} m_i = 1.$$

The probability model is a multinomial such that there are r possible mutually exclusive events and every event has a probability m_i of occurring on every trial.

Assume that on every trial there can be n realizations of the r states. More simply, there is a sample of size n and the number of realizations of state i on trial t is n_{it}, so that $\Sigma_i n_{it} = n$. Thus n_{it} is the number of individuals sampled who are in state i on trial t. There are T trials in all, so that $t = 1, \cdots, T$. The proportion of individuals in state i on trial t is

(10) $$m_{it} = \frac{n_{it}}{n} .$$

The proportion of the individuals in state i for the whole sequence of trials is

(11) $$\frac{1}{T} \sum_t m_{it} = \frac{\Sigma_t n_{it}}{nT} .$$

Every trial consists of a drawing of n individuals from a multinomial distribution with probabilities m_i $(i = 1, \cdots, r)$. We can think of the same n individuals moving from state to state on successive trials so that the probability of a transition from state j to state i equals the probability of occurrence of state i.

The probabilities m_i are unknown and are to be estimated from the sample proportions m_{it}. Let

(12) $$u_{it} = m_{it} - m_i \qquad (i = 1, \cdots, r) .$$

The variable u_{it} is a random variable that cannot be directly observed because it is the difference between the observed sample proportion m_{it} and the true population probability m_i. The expected value of u_{it} is zero, and u_{it} is independent of m_i. The variance of u_{it} is constant and is given by

(13) $$\text{var } u_{it} = \frac{m_i(1 - m_i)}{n} .$$

Denote the least-squares estimates of m_i by $\hat{m}_i$. These are found by choosing m_i to minimize $\Sigma_t \hat{u}_{it}^2$, subject to the constraint $\Sigma_i \hat{m}_i = 1$, where $\hat{u}_{it} = m_{it} - \hat{m}_i$. Hence we must find $\hat{m}_i$ such that

(14) $$\frac{\partial}{\partial \hat{m}_i} \left[\sum_t \hat{u}_{it}^2 + \lambda \left(\sum_i \hat{m}_i - 1 \right) \right] = 0 ,$$

where λ is a Lagrangian multiplier. Therefore, solving (14) for $\hat{m}_i$, we find

(15) $$\hat{m}_i = \frac{1}{T} \left(\sum_t m_{it} + \frac{\lambda}{2} \right) .$$

However, $\Sigma_i \hat{m}_i = 1$ and $\Sigma_i m_{it} = 1$. Therefore, $\lambda = 0$ and

(16) $$\hat{m}_i = \frac{1}{T} \sum_t m_{it} .$$

This happens also to be the maximum-likelihood estimate of m_i. It is in addition the minimum-variance linear unbiased estimator of m_i. Although the sum of the estimates of m_i is constrained to equal one, the estimate of m_i depends only on the m_{it}. However, the estimates of m_i and m_j are not independent, because

$$(17) \qquad \mathrm{cov}\,(u_{it},\,u_{jt}) = -\frac{m_i m_j}{n} \qquad (i \neq j),$$

since we assume multinomial sampling. Moreover, by the hypothesis of independent trials,

$$(18) \qquad \begin{aligned} \mathrm{cov}\,(u_{it},\,u_{it'}) &= 0 \\ \mathrm{cov}\,(m_{it},\,m_{it'}) &= 0 \end{aligned} \qquad (t \neq t').$$

We see that for a zero-order Markov chain (independent trials) the least-squares estimates of the transition probabilities are simple averages of the sample proportions. The least-squares method in this case comes through with flying colors, since it gives the same estimate as the maximum-likelihood estimates. In the next section we derive the least-square estimates of the transition probabilities for a first-order Markov chain. For a different derivation of these least-squares estimates, the reader is referred to [3].

2. Least-Squares Estimates of First-Order Transition Probabilities

In a first-order Markov chain the fraction in state j on trial t is

$$(19) \qquad m_{jt} = \sum_i m_{i,t-1} p_{ij} + v_{jt} \qquad (j = 1, \cdots, r).$$

In this equation p_{ij} is the probability of a transition from state i to state j [see (3)] and v_{jt} is a random variable with properties to be discussed below. Assume, as in the preceding section, that n individuals move from state to state on successive trials. Let the behavior of these n individuals be governed by the *same* transition probability matrix, and let the moves of an individual be independent of the moves of all the others. Thus "follow the leader," contagion, and the like are ruled out. There are n_{jt} individuals in state j on trial t. The number who change from state i on trial $t-1$ to j on trial t is $n_{ij.t}$. The trial subscripts being understood, we have

$$(20) \qquad n_{.j} = \sum_{i=1}^{r} n_{ij} \quad \text{and} \quad n_{i.} = \sum_{j=1}^{r} n_{ij}.$$

Also

$$(21) \qquad \frac{n_{.j}}{n} = \sum_i \frac{n_{ij}}{n_{i.}} \frac{n_{i.}}{n}.$$

Equation (21) is an identity that is valid regardless of the probability mechanism that is assumed to generate the data. However, equation (19) is not an identity because it assumes a particular probability mechanism, namely, a first-order Markov chain. That is, (21) is merely a definition of $n_{.j}$; whereas (19) has empirical content because the transitions need not be governed by a stable set of transition probabilities of the kind postulated in a first-order Markov chain. Let m_{jt} be the observed proportion of individuals in state j on trial t and m_{it-1} be the observed proportion in state i on $t-1$. Hence $m_{jt} = n_{.j}/n$ and $m_{it-1} = n_{i.}/n$. If $n = 1$, then $m_{jt} = 1$ if the individual occupies state j on trial t, and $m_{jt} = 0$ otherwise. The expected number of transitions from state i on trial $t-1$ to state j on trial t, given that there were $n_{i.}$ individuals in state i on trial $t-1$, is $n_{i.}p_{ij}$. Denote the difference between the actual and expected number by u_{ij}. Thus

$$(22) \qquad u_{ij} = n_{ij} - n_{i.}p_{ij}.$$

Clearly for given $n_{i.}$ the expected value of u_{ij} is zero. By hypothesis,

$$(23) \qquad \sum_i u_{ij} = n_{.j} - \sum_i n_{i.}p_{ij}.$$

Dividing through (23) by n and recalling the definition of m_{jt} and $m_{i.t-1}$, we find

$$(24) \qquad v_{jt} = \frac{1}{n}\sum_i u_{ij}$$

from (19) and (23). It follows that v_{jt} equals the difference between the observed and expected proportion of the individuals in state j on trial t. This implies [see (19)] that Em_{jt} is conditional on the *realized*, not on the *expected* $m_{i.t-1}$. In symbols,

$$(25) \qquad Em_{jt} = \sum_i m_{i.t-1}p_{ij} \quad \text{and} \quad Ev_{jt} = 0 \qquad (j = 1, \cdots, r).$$

The form of equation (19) suggests that we may be able to estimate the p_{ij}, given readings on m_{jt} and m_{it-1} $(i = 1, \cdots, r)$ even if we do not know the actual number of transitions n_{ij}. We can regard (19) as a linear regression of m_{jt} on $m_{i.t-1}$ in which the coefficients of $m_{i.t-1}$, the transition probabilities, are to be estimated by least squares. Such least-squares estimates of the transition probabilities will certainly not be minimum-variance linear unbiased estimates, because the independent variable, $m_{i.t-1}$ are themselves stochastic. To show what properties least-squares estimates of p_{ij} possess, we need to study the behavior of the residuals v_{jt}. In particular, the least-squares estimates of p_{ij} are consistent with respect to T if v_{jt} is uncorrelated with $m_{i,t-1}$ for all i and j. (See Mann and Wald [9]).

Madansky [8] has shown that

(26) $$\text{cov } (v_{jt}, v_{i,t-1}) = 0$$

for all i and j. Hence

(27) $$\text{cov } (v_{jt}, m_{i,t-1} - Em_{i,t-1}) = 0 .$$

But

(28) $$\text{cov } (v_{jt}, Em_{i,t-1}) = 0 ,$$

since $Ev_{jt} = 0$. Therefore

(29) $$\text{cov } (v_{jt}, m_{i,t-1}) = 0$$

for all i. Hence least-squares estimates of p_{ij} are consistent with respect to T. Madansky has also shown that for fixed $T > r$, least-squares estimates are also consistent with respect to n, the sample size. Hence these estimates have at least the desirable property of consistency. We defer discussion of other properties of these estimates and now describe the estimation method.

Least-squares estimates of p_{ij} are obtained by choosing a set of estimates $\hat{p}_{ij}$ to minimize $\Sigma_t \hat{v}_{jt}^2$ subject to the r constraints $\Sigma_j \hat{p}_{ij} = 1$ $(j = 1, \cdots, r)$, where

(30) $$\hat{v}_{jt} = m_{jt} - \sum_i m_{i,t-1} \hat{p}_{ij} .$$

The necessary conditions for a minimum are that

(31) $$\frac{\partial}{\partial \hat{p}_{ij}} \left[\sum_t \hat{v}_{jt}^2 + \sum_i \lambda_i \left(\sum_j \hat{p}_{ij} - 1 \right) \right] = 0 ,$$

λ_i being a Lagrangian multiplier. Since $\partial \hat{v}_{ij}/\partial \hat{p}_{ij} = -m_{i,t-1}$, as is easily verified, we find

(32) $$\sum_t \hat{v}_{jt} m_{i,t-1} - \frac{\lambda_i}{2} = 0 \qquad (i = 1, \cdots, r) .$$

But $\Sigma_i m_{i,t-1} = 1$ and $\Sigma_i \hat{p}_{ji} = 1$. Hence it follows from (30) that

(33) $$\sum_j \hat{v}_{jt} = 1 - \sum_i m_{i,t-1} = 0$$

for all t. Summing (32) with respect to j establishes that $\lambda_i = 0$. This result is important. It means that the prior constraints on the coefficients of

(19) are satisfied automatically by the ordinary least-squares estimates and that the constraints on the coefficients are not binding, a result derived by Goodman [3]. The parameters of the equations can be estimated separately; or more precisely, the equations can be dealt with one at a time. We note, however, that the residuals of the equations are not independent, because they satisfy the linear equation (33).

Since $\lambda_i = 0$, the estimating equations reduce to

$$(34) \qquad \sum_t \hat{v}_{jt} m_{i,t-1} = 0 \qquad (i = 1, \cdots, r).$$

There is a complication, however, because the independent variables $m_{i,t-1}$ $(i = 1, \cdots, r)$ satisfy $\Sigma_i m_{i,t-1} = 1$ for all t. If we wish to use the least-squares estimating equations, one of the variables $m_{i,t-1}$ must be omitted. It does not matter which we omit, because the residual v_{jt} is unaffected. Without loss of generality, let us omit $m_{j,t-1}$ and rewrite (19) as

$$(35) \qquad m_{jt} = p_{jj} + \sum_i (p_{ij} - p_{jj}) m_{i,t-1} + v_{jt} \qquad (i \neq j).$$

Equation (35) can be looked at as an ordinary regression in $r - 1$ independent variables obtained from (19) by replacing $m_{j,t-1}$ with $1 - \Sigma_i m_{i,t-1}$ $(i \neq j)$. Let $a_{ij} = p_{ij} - p_{jj}$. There are r estimating equations: $r - 1$ equations are

$$(36) \qquad \sum_i \hat{a}_{ij} \left[\sum_t (m_{i,t-1} - \bar{m}_{i,t-1}) (m_{k,t-1} - \bar{m}_{k,t-1}) \right]$$
$$= \sum_t (m_{jt} - \bar{m}_{jt}) (m_{k,t-1} - \bar{m}_{k,t-1}) \qquad (k = 1, \cdots, r; \quad k \neq j)$$

and the rth is

$$(37) \qquad \bar{m}_{jt} = \hat{p}_{jj} + \sum_i \hat{a}_{ij} \bar{m}_{i,t-1},$$

where $\bar{m}_{jt} = 1/T \, \Sigma_t m_{jt}$, the sample mean proportion. Given estimates of a_{ij} from (36), we derive the estimate $\hat{p}_{jj}$ from (37) and finally $\hat{p}_{ij} = \hat{a}_{ij} + \hat{p}_{jj}$.

Admissible estimates of the transition probabilities are non-negative and do not exceed one. We have not explicitly incorporated these constraints in our procedure. Although $\Sigma_j \hat{p}_{ij} = 1$, some $\hat{p}_{ij}$ could be inadmissible; i.e., some $\hat{p}_{ij}$ could be negative or could exceed one (see related comments in [3]). Although the consistency property of the estimates assures us that for large samples the chance of obtaining some inadmissible estimates is small, this can happen even if the underlying model is correct. Inadmissible estimates are to be replaced by one or zero (usually the latter), as may be appropriate, and a set of admissible estimates obtained so that $\Sigma_t \hat{v}_{jt}^2$ is smaller than any other set of estimates contained in the admissible set. Goodman [3] discusses methods of handling this problem. Systematic methods of solution in this case are given by the methods of quadratic programming (see Houthakker [6]).

TABLE 1

MARKET SHARES OF CAMEL AND LUCKY STRIKE (1925–1943)[a]

Year	Camel (1)	Lucky Strike (2)	Chesterfield (3)
1925	.5056	.2028	.2916
26	.4879	.1899	.3222
27	.4504	.2236	.3260
28	.4068	.3039	.2893
29	.3637	.3616	.2747
1930	.3365	.4118	.2517
31	.3311	.4425	.2264
32	.2936	.4498	.2566
33	.2794	.4008	.3198
34	.3418	.3301	.3281
1935	.3867	.3013	.3120
36	.4074	.2906	.3020
37	.4084	.2949	.2967
38	.3842	.3195	.2963
39	.3746	.3358	.2896
1940	.3708	.3500	.2792
41	.3579	.3653	.2768
42	.3527	.3851	.2622
43	.3276	.3875	.2849

[a] William H. Nicholls, *Price Policies in the Cigarette Industry.* Nashville, Tenn.: Vanderbilt Univ. Press, 1951.

To illustrate the method, we calculate the transition probabilities for cigarette smokers. Annual data are available from 1925 to 1943 giving sales in billions of cigarettes for the three leading brands of that period, (1) Camel, (2) Lucky Strike, and (3) Chesterfield, the products, respectively, of R. J. Reynolds, American Tobacco, and Liggett and Myers. From these sales figures we obtain the market shares of the total sales of the three brands. (See Table 1.) Let us pretend these figures are obtained from a fixed sample of smokers for whom the probability of a transition from brand i to j is constant over time and given by p_{ij}. Assume further that the same transition matrix describes the behavior of all the smokers. Since there are three brands, we need estimates of nine transition probabilities from the three regression equations like (19). We calculate the sums of cross-products indicated by (36) and obtain the following equations:

Camel:
$$1.7268 \, m_{2,t-1} - 0.4457 \, m_{3,t-1} = -1.1163$$
$$-0.4457 \, m_{2,t-1} + 0.2392 \, m_{3,t-1} = 0.3011$$

Lucky Strike:
$$1.0738 \, m_{1,t-1} + 0.2065 \, m_{3,t-1} = -0.9342$$
$$0.2065 \, m_{1,t-1} + 0.2392 \, m_{3,t-1} = -0.4510$$

Chesterfield:
$$1.0738 \, m_{1,t-1} - 1.2806 \, m_{2,t-1} = 0.1187$$
$$-1.2806 \, m_{1,t-1} + 1.7268 \, m_{2,t-1} = -0.2687$$

We solve these equations for $\hat{a}_{ij}$ and find the following:

Camel: $m_{1t} = 0.5451 - 0.6195 \, m_{2,t-1} + 0.1042 \, m_{3,t-1}$
Lucky Strike: $m_{2t} = 0.9654 - 0.6085 \, m_{1,t-1} - 1.3598 \, m_{3,-t1}$
Chesterfield: $m_{3t} = 0.7465 - 0.6498 \, m_{2,t-1} - 0.6375 \, m_{2,t-1}$

This corresponds to (37), in which the constant terms are $\hat{p}_{jj}$. Using the result $\hat{p}_{ij} = \hat{a}_{ij} + \hat{p}_{jj}$, we finally obtain

	Camel (1)	Lucky Strike (2)	Chesterfield (3)
(1) Camel	0.5451	0.3569	0.0967
(2) Lucky Strike	−0.0744	0.9654	0.1090
(3) Chesterfield	0.6493	−0.3944	0.7465

as the estimates of the transition probabilities above, for which the row sums are one. We see that two of the transition probabilities are negative and, therefore, inadmissible. Hence, in this example, admissible estimates that minimize the residual sums of squares include one of the following mutually exclusive possibilities:

(i) $\hat{p}_{32} = 0$,   (ii) $\hat{p}_{21} = 0$,   (iii) $\hat{p}_{32} = \hat{p}_{21} = 0$.

We may calculate the residual sums of squares for these alternatives and select the one and the associated estimates such that the residual sum of squares is smallest. More elaborate methods are unnecessary in this case, because there are only three alternatives. On the assumption $\hat{p}_{32} = 0$, we find the following transition matrix:

	Camel (1)	Lucky Strike (2)	Chesterfield (3)
(1) Camel	0.7700	0.1333	0.0967
(2) Lucky Strike	0.0118	0.8792	0.1090
(3) Chesterfield	0.2535	0	0.7465

These estimates corresponding to alternative (i) minimize the residual sums of squares and are admissible. We may compare the increase in the residual sums of squares by imposing the additional constraint $\hat{p}_{32} = 0$ with the unconstrained estimates in the following table:

	Total Sums of Squares (A)	Residual Sums of Squares	
		Unconstrained (B)	$\hat{p}_{32} = 0$ (C)
Camel	0.8074	0.0844	0.1329
Lucky Strike	1.4538	0.2721	0.3205
Chesterfield	0.2394	0.1452	0.1452

Column (A) gives the sums of squares on the hypothesis that the probability model is a zero-order Markov chain and that the transition probabilities to a given brand equal the average market share of that brand (see Section 1). Column (B) gives the residual sums of squares on the hypothesis that the probability model is a first-order Markov chain and corresponds to the first transition matrix that contains two inadmissible estimates. Column (C) also assumes a first-order Markov chain and shows the residual sums of squares corresponding to the second admissible transition matrix ($\hat{p}_{32} = 0$). By comparing (C) with (B), we see how much the additional constraint $\hat{p}_{32} = 0$ increases the residual sums of squares. For Chesterfields there is no increase, because the unconstrained estimates are admissible. There is a small increase for the other two brands. There is, of course, a considerable reduction in the residual sums of squares on the hypothesis of a first-order chain (B) or (C), as compared to the zero-order chain hypothesis of column (A).

The transition probabilities measure the propensity of consumers to switch from one cigarette brand to another. The elements in the principal diagonal measure their propensity to repeat the purchase of the various brands. The estimated transition probabilities have the interesting property that the column sums are nearly one (the row sums are one by hypothesis). This implies that the equilibrium market shares of the three brands are nearly equal, i.e., one-third of the market for each. The actual market shares in 1943 were not far from these equilibrium levels (see Table 1). The most implausible aspect of the transition probabilities herein calculated is that $\hat{p}_{31}$ is relatively large, whereas $\hat{p}_{32} = 0$. Although it seems fairly clear that from the viewpoint of predicting market shares one does better by assuming a first-order than a zero-order Markov chain, the annual market share data are insufficient to settle the question of whether a more complicated model would yield still better predictions. Perhaps the most implausible assumption underlying the estimates is that the transition probabilities are constant during the 18-year period studied. Ways of estimating transition probabilities that depend on other variables are discussed in the next section.

The simple least-squares estimates considered here are not efficient, because the variance of v_{jt} is not constant. One can use this to improve the efficiency of the estimates, as we shall see. On the basis of results in Anderson and Goodman [1], Madansky [8] has shown that

$$(38) \qquad Ev_{jt}^2 = \frac{1}{n}\left(Em_{jt} - \sum_i m_{i,t-1}p_{ij}^2\right).$$

Since the variance of v_{jt} is not constant, one can improve the efficiency of the least-squares estimates by weighting the observations appropriately. In this case, because $\operatorname{cov}(v_{jt}, v_{jt'}) = 0$ $(t \neq t')$, the covariance matrix of v_{jt} is diagonal and we can use a simple weighting scheme. Unfortunately, the weights depend on the unknown transition probabilities. Madansky recommends that the estimates be prepared in two stages. First, we estimate p_{ij} by unweighted least squares according to (36) and (37). Given these estimates, we define a new residual

$$(39) \qquad x_{jt} = \frac{v_{jt}}{\sqrt{w_{jt}}},$$

where

$$(40) \qquad w_{jt} = m_{jt} - \sum_i \hat{p}_{ij}^2 m_{i,t-1}.$$

Hence the weights are derived from the ordinary least-squares estimates and, according to Madansky, the estimates on the second round obtained by minimizing Σx_{jt}^2 with respect to p_{ij} will be asymptotically more efficient. In his numerical example the second-round estimates fail to satisfy the prior constraints that $\Sigma_j p_{ij} = 1$, and one of the estimated transition probabilities is negative. The former implies a deficiency of the estimation method, a condition that Madansky seems aware of, although he suggests no systematic method of coping with it. Weighted least-squares estimates applied to this problem cannot satisfy the prior constraints on the transition probabilities unless either w_{jt} is the same for all j, or $v_{jt} = 0$ so that we have in effect an infinite sample.

Since Madansky's numerical example is a two-state process, these assertions are illustrated for this special case, although it is easy to see that they hold for any number of states. In addition, a method of obtaining weighted estimates is easily obtained that satisfies the prior constraint $\Sigma_j p_{ij} = 1$. Suppose, therefore, that

$$(41) \qquad \begin{aligned} m_{1t} &= p_{11}m_{1,t-1} + p_{21}m_{2,t-1} + v_{1t}, \\ m_{2t} &= p_{12}m_{1,t-1} + p_{22}m_{2,t-1} + v_{2t}, \end{aligned}$$

and

$$(42) \qquad \begin{aligned} p_{11} + p_{12} &= 1, \\ p_{21} + p_{22} &= 1. \end{aligned}$$

Denote the *unweighted* least-squares estimates of p_{ij} by $\hat{p}_{ij}$. Hence the weights used in the second stage are

(43)
$$w_{1t} = m_{1t} - \hat{p}_{11}^2 m_{1,t-1} - \hat{p}_{21}^2 m_{2,t-1},$$
$$w_{2t} = m_{2t} - \hat{p}_{12}^2 m_{1,t-1} - \hat{p}_{22}^2 m_{2,t-1}.$$

These should be non-negative because the weights are estimates of the variance of the residuals. On the second round Madansky chooses estimators to minimize $\sum_t x_{jt}^2$ where x_{jt} is defined by (39). If we sum the two equations of (41), we obtain

$$1 = (p_{11} + p_{12})m_{1,t-1} + (p_{21} + p_{22})m_{2,t-1} + v_{1t} + v_{2t}.$$

Since $m_{2,t-1} = 1 - m_{1,t-1}$, we find

$$1 = (p_{21} + p_{22}) + (p_{11} + p_{12} - p_{21} - p_{22})m_{1,t-1} + v_{1t} + v_{2t},$$

an identity for every t. Hence (42) implies that $v_{1t} + v_{2t} = 0$. Moreover, provided $m_{1,t-1}$ does not equal $[1 - (p_{21}+p_{22})] \div [p_{11}+p_{12}-p_{21}-p_{22}]$ for all t, $v_{1t} + v_{2t} = 0$ implies (42). Since $x_{1t}+x_{2t} \neq 0$ unless $v_{1t}=v_{2t}=0$, the sum of the weighted residuals cannot lead to estimates that satisfy (42) for almost all finite samples. Hence almost always for any finite sample the unrestricted weighted least-squares estimates Madansky suggests cannot satisfy the prior constraints (42). The proviso almost always is needed to cover the case in which v_{1t} and v_{2t} might be zero for all t, a most unlikely occurrence in a finite sample. The remedy is, fortunately, simple. We minimize $\sum_j x_{jt}^2$ with respect to the $\hat{p}_{ij}$, subject to the constraints of (41). We are to choose $\hat{p}$'s such that

(44)
$$\sum_t x_{1t}^2 + \lambda_1(\hat{p}_{11} + p_{12} - 1) + \lambda_2(\hat{p}_{21} + p_{22} - 1),$$
$$\sum_t x_{2t}^2 + \lambda_1(\hat{p}_{11} + \hat{p}_{12} - 1) + \lambda_2(\hat{p}_{21} + \hat{p}_{22} - 1)$$

are minimized, λ_1 and λ_2 being Lagrangian multipliers. The estimating equations reduce to

(45)
$$\sum \frac{m_{1t}m_{1,t-1}}{w_{1t}} = -\frac{\lambda_1}{2} + \hat{p}_{11} \sum \frac{m_{1,t-1}^2}{w_{1t}} + \hat{p}_{21} \sum \frac{m_{2,t-1}m_{1,t-1}}{w_{1t}},$$
$$\sum \frac{m_{1t}m_{2,t-1}}{w_{1t}} = -\frac{\lambda_2}{2} + \hat{p}_{11} \sum \frac{m_{1,t-1}m_{2,t-1}}{w_{1t}} + \hat{p}_{21} \sum \frac{m_{2,t-1}^2}{w_{1t}},$$
$$\sum \frac{m_{2t}m_{1,t-1}}{w_{2t}} = -\frac{\lambda_1}{2} + \hat{p}_{12} \sum \frac{m_{1,t-1}^2}{w_{2t}} + \hat{p}_{22} \sum \frac{m_{1,t-1}m_{2,t-1}}{w_{2t}},$$
$$\sum \frac{m_{2t}m_{2,t-1}}{w_{2t}} = -\frac{\lambda_2}{2} + \hat{p}_{12} \sum \frac{m_{1,t-1}m_{2,t-1}}{w_{2t}} + \hat{p}_{22} \sum \frac{m_{2,t-1}^2}{w_{2t}},$$

These four linearly independent equations and the two constraints of (41) are solvable for the six unknowns p_{ij} $(i, j = 1, 2)$ and λ_i $(i = 1, 2)$.

By adding the first two equations of (45), we obtain

$$(46) \qquad \sum \frac{m_{1t}}{w_{1t}} = -\frac{\lambda_1 + \lambda_2}{2} + \hat{p}_{11} \sum \frac{m_{1,t-1}}{w_{1t}} + \hat{p}_{21} \sum \frac{m_{2,t-1}}{w_{1t}},$$

and similarly, by adding the last two equations of (45), we find

$$(47) \qquad \sum \frac{m_{2t}}{w_{2t}} = -\frac{\lambda_1 + \lambda_2}{2} + \hat{p}_{12} \sum \frac{m_{1,t-1}}{w_{2t}} + \hat{p}_{22} \sum \frac{m_{2,t-1}}{w_{2t}}.$$

However,

$$(48) \qquad \begin{aligned} \sum \frac{m_{1t}}{w_{1t}} &= \hat{p}_{11} \sum \frac{m_{1,t-1}}{w_{1t}} + \hat{p}_{21} \sum \frac{m_{2,t-1}}{w_{1t}} + \sum \frac{v_{1t}}{w_{1t}}, \\ \sum \frac{m_{2t}}{w_{2t}} &= \hat{p}_{12} \sum \frac{m_{1,t-1}}{w_{2t}} + \hat{p}_{22} \sum \frac{m_{2,t-1}}{w_{2t}} + \sum \frac{v_{2t}}{w_{2t}}. \end{aligned}$$

It follows that

$$(49) \qquad \sum_t \frac{v_{1t}}{w_{1t}} = -\frac{\lambda_1 + \lambda_2}{2} = \sum_t \frac{v_{2t}}{w_{2t}},$$

and these replace the condition on the unweighted regressions that $\Sigma_j v_{jt} = 0$.

For r states there are r^2 equations of the form given by (45) and r constraining equations like (41). These $r(r + 1)$ equations give a unique set of estimates for the r^2 transition probabilities and the r Lagrangian multipliers λ_i. If the resulting estimates are inadmissible, then quadratic programming methods that take into account the inequalities $0 \leqslant p_{ij} \leqslant 1$ are needed to calculate admissible estimates.

This method was applied to the cigarette data and yielded few admissible estimates of the transition probabilities. Inspection of the weighted cross products revealed that the matrixes to be inverted were nearly singular and were extremely sensitive to rounding errors, even in the fourth decimal place of the weights. Because of this, the weighted estimates in the example cannot be regarded as reliable. Unweighted least-squares estimates require omission of one of the independent variables, because the sum of the independent variables is one [see the discussion in connection with (35)]. However, the weighted estimates do not omit any variable. If the variance of the residuals calculated at the first stage do not differ much from trial to trial, then the procedure for calculating the weighted estimates may lead to the inversion of a nearly singular matrix. This may explain the results in my numerical example, assuming, of course, that the underlying model is correct. Whether the additional computations required for the asymptotically more efficient estimates are worthwhile can best be decided by experience. They were not worthwhile in the numerical example I worked out.

3. Variable Transition Probabilities

Up to this point the transition probabilities are assumed to be constant for the sample period. This allows us to estimate them for data giving the observed sample proportions m_{jt} for a sequence of T trials. There are many cases, however, for which it is more plausible to assume that the transition probabilities do not remain constant. Thus we may be in a position to assert that the transition probabilities are functions of certain variables and that they change when the determining variables change. If the actual transition counts are available—that is, if we can observe n_{ij}— then there are direct tests of the hypothesis that the transition probabilities are constant over time as shown in Anderson and Goodman [1]. In our situation, in which the transition probabilities are estimated indirectly by least squares from readings on m_{jt}, we can also estimate the effect of the determining variables on the transition probabilities indirectly. For example, in the numerical example worked out in the previous section, the probability of transition from one cigarette brand to another may depend on the relative advertising expenditures of the companies. If so, then we are led to estimate the parameters of the relation between the transition probabilities and relative advertising expenditures. We now extend the method of estimation to include the case in which the transition probabilities are functions of certain variables. The extension presented here was also suggested in [5, p. 624] for a somewhat different situation where, there too, the regression coefficients were functions of certain variables.

For simplicity, assume that there are two states. Let α denote the probability of remaining in state one and β the probability of transition from state two to state one. Assume there are two variables that determine these transition probabilities and denote them by z_{1t} and z_{2t}. Hence

(50)
$$\alpha_t = f(z_{1t}, z_{2t}),$$
$$\beta_t = g(z_{1t}, z_{2t}).$$

The t subscripts on α and β remind us that the transition probabilities do not necessarily remain constant from trial to trial, provided the z's vary from trial to trial. If the functional form of f and g is specified, and time series of the transitions $n_{11,t}$ and $n_{21,t}$ are available to us, we may estimate directly the parameters of (50). However, even if we cannot observe the transitions, we may still be in a position to estimate f and g because

(51)
$$m_t = \alpha_t m_{t-1} + \beta_t(1 - m_{t-1}) + v_t,$$
$$1 - m_t = (1 - \alpha_t)m_{t-1} + (1 - \beta_t)(1 - m_{t-1}) - v_t,$$

since by hypothesis the transitions are governed by a first-order Markov chain and m_t, z_{1t}, and z_{2t} are observable. To be more specific, assume that in the neighborhood of the sample averages of z_{1t} and z_{2t}, f and g are approximately linear. Hence (50) becomes

(52)
$$\alpha_t \approx a_0 + a_1 z_{1t} + a_2 z_{2t},$$
$$\beta_t \approx b_0 + b_1 z_{1t} + b_2 z_{2t}.$$

Substituting these in the first equation of (51), we find after collecting terms

(53) $\quad m_t = L_0 + L_1 z_{1t} + L_2 z_{2t} + L_3 m_{t-1} + K_1 m_{t-1} z_{1t} + K_2 m_{t-1} z_{2t} + v_t,$

where the coefficients of (53) are related to those of (52) by

(54)
$$L_0 = b_0, \qquad\qquad\qquad L_2 = b_2,$$
$$L_1 = b_1, \qquad\qquad\qquad L_3 = a_0 - b_0;$$
$$K_1 = a_1 - b_1, \qquad\qquad K_2 = a_2 - b_2.$$

If the coefficients of (53) are estimated by least squares, then from (54) we may derive the parameters of (52) that determine the transition probabilities. (See the related system of equations in [5, p. 624].) Because the residual v_t is defined in the same way as in Section 2, the estimates of the coefficients of (53) are consistent, albeit not asymptotically efficient.

A serious difficulty that may complicate the computation of the least-squares estimates of the coefficients of (53) is multicollinearity among the independent variables because

(55) $\quad m_{t-1} z_{it} - Em_{t-1} Ez_{it} = Em_{t-1}(z_{it} - Ez_{it}) + Ez_{it}(m_{t-1} - Em_{t-1})$
$$+ (z_{it} - Ez_{it})(m_{t-1} - Em_{t-1}).$$

This can be made clearer by rewriting (55) as follows:

(56) $\quad m_{t-1} z_{it} = \Pi_{0i} + \Pi_{1i} m_{t-1} + \Pi_{2i} z_{it} + y_{it} \qquad (i = 1, 2),$

where

(57)
$$\Pi_{0i} = \text{cov}(z_{it}, m_{t-1}) - Ez_{it} Em_{t-1},$$
$$\Pi_{1i} = Ez_{it},$$
$$\Pi_{2i} = Em_{t-1},$$
$$y_{it} = (z_{it} - Ez_{it})(m_{t-1} - Em_{t-1}) - \text{cov}(z_{it}, m_{t-1}).$$

Clearly, from (57), $Ey_{it} = 0$.

In equation (53) we include products like $m_{t-1}z_{it}$, as well as the factors of these products m_{t-1} and z_{it}. It may turn out that because of insufficient variation of z_{it} in the sample period, the product $m_{t-1}z_{it}$ is nearly linear in its factors, so that in (56) y_{it} has a small variation relative to $m_{t-1}z_{it}$. If this is the case, there will be nearly linear dependence between $m_{t-1}z_{it}$, and m_{t-1} and between $m_{t-1}z_{it}$ and z_{it}, as in (56), so that the moment matrix of (53) is nearly singular and one cannot obtain reasonable estimates of the coefficients of (53). One remedy (aside from enlarging the sample period, which may not be feasible) is to substitute y_{it} for $m_{t-1}z_{it}$. That is, instead of using the product term directly in (53) we use that part of the product which takes out some of the effect of $m_{t-1}z_{it}$. From the sample means and covariance we may calculate the Π's as shown in (59). We estimate Ez_{it} by $\bar{z}_i = 1/T \sum_t z_{it}$, and Π_{0i} from the appropriate sample moments. We then use in place of $m_{t-1}z_{it}$ the residual from (56). By so doing, we estimate

$$(58) \qquad m_t = A_0 + A_1 z_{1t} + A_2 z_{2t} + A_3 m_{t-1} + B_1 y_{1t} + B_2 y_{2t} + v_t,$$

in which the coefficients satisfy

$$(59) \qquad \begin{aligned}
&A_0 = b_0 + (a_1 - b_1)\,\hat{\Pi}_{01} + (a_2 - b_2)\,\hat{\Pi}_{02}, \\
&A_1 = b_1 + (a_1 - b_1)\,\hat{\Pi}_{21}, \\
&A_2 = b_2 + (a_2 - b_2)\,\hat{\Pi}_{22}, \\
&A_3 = a_0 - b_0 + (a_1 - b_1)\,\hat{\Pi}_{11} + (a_2 - b_2)\,\hat{\Pi}_{12}, \\
&B_1 = a_1 - b_1, \\
&B_2 = a_2 - b_2.
\end{aligned}$$

(Note that $\hat{\Pi}_{21} = \hat{\Pi}_{22}$.) Hence, given estimates of the coefficients of (58) and the estimates of the Π's in (57) derived from the appropriate sample means and moments, we can solve (59) for the coefficients determining the transition probabilities, the a's and b's of (52). The advantage of estimating (58) instead of (53) is that there is likely to be much less collinearity between y_{it} and the other variables than there is between z_{it} and the same variables.

There are certain aspects of the coefficients of (58) worth noting. At the sample averages of z_{it}, the probability of remaining in state one minus the probability of moving to state one from state two is

$$(60) \qquad \bar{\alpha}_t - \bar{\beta}_t = a_0 - b_0 + (a_1 - b_1)\bar{z}_{it} + (a_2 - b_2)\bar{z}_{2t}.$$

This is just A_3, the coefficient of m_{t-1}. The partial derivative of m_t with respect to $\bar{z}_{it}$ is the coefficient of z_{it}. That is,

$$(61) \qquad \frac{\partial}{\partial \bar{z}_{it}}\,\bar{m}_t = b_i(1 - \bar{m}_{t-1}) + a_i \bar{m}_{t-1} = A_i.$$

since by hypothesis the transitions are governed by a first-order Markov chain and m_t, z_{1t}, and z_{2t} are observable. To be more specific, assume that in the neighborhood of the sample averages of z_{1t} and z_{2t}, f and g are approximately linear. Hence (50) becomes

(52)
$$\alpha_t \approx a_0 + a_1 z_{1t} + a_2 z_{2t},$$
$$\beta_t \approx b_0 + b_1 z_{1t} + b_2 z_{2t}.$$

Substituting these in the first equation of (51), we find after collecting terms

(53) $\quad m_t = L_0 + L_1 z_{1t} + L_2 z_{2t} + L_3 m_{t-1} + K_1 m_{t-1} z_{1t} + K_2 m_{t-1} z_{2t} + v_t,$

where the coefficients of (53) are related to those of (52) by

(54)
$$
\begin{aligned}
& L_0 = b_0, && L_2 = b_2, \\
& L_1 = b_1, && L_3 = a_0 - b_0; \\
& K_1 = a_1 - b_1, && K_2 = a_2 - b_2.
\end{aligned}
$$

If the coefficients of (53) are estimated by least squares, then from (54) we may derive the parameters of (52) that determine the transition probabilities. (See the related system of equations in [5, p. 624].) Because the residual v_t is defined in the same way as in Section 2, the estimates of the coefficients of (53) are consistent, albeit not asymptotically efficient.

A serious difficulty that may complicate the computation of the least-squares estimates of the coefficients of (53) is multicollinearity among the independent variables because

(55) $\quad m_{t-1} z_{it} - E m_{t-1} E z_{it} = E m_{t-1}(z_{it} - E z_{it}) + E z_{it}(m_{t-1} - E m_{t-1})$
$$+ (z_{it} - E z_{it})(m_{t-1} - E m_{t-1}).$$

This can be made clearer by rewriting (55) as follows:

(56) $\quad m_{t-1} z_{it} = \Pi_{0i} + \Pi_{1i} m_{t-1} + \Pi_{2i} z_{it} + y_{it} \qquad (i = 1, 2),$

where

(57)
$$
\begin{aligned}
& \Pi_{0i} = \operatorname{cov}(z_{it}, m_{t-1}) - E z_{it} E m_{t-1}, \\
& \Pi_{1i} = E z_{it}, \\
& \Pi_{2i} = E m_{t-1}, \\
& y_{it} = (z_{it} - E z_{it})(m_{t-1} - E m_{t-1}) - \operatorname{cov}(z_{it}, m_{t-1}).
\end{aligned}
$$

Clearly, from (57), $E y_{it} = 0$.

In equation (53) we include products like $m_{t-1}z_{it}$, as well as the factors of these products m_{t-1} and z_{it}. It may turn out that because of insufficient variation of z_{it} in the sample period, the product $m_{t-1}z_{it}$ is nearly linear in its factors, so that in (56) y_{it} has a small variation relative to $m_{t-1}z_{it}$. If this is the case, there will be nearly linear dependence between $m_{t-1}z_{it}$, and m_{t-1} and between $m_{t-1}z_{it}$ and z_{it}, as in (56), so that the moment matrix of (53) is nearly singular and one cannot obtain reasonable estimates of the coefficients of (53). One remedy (aside from enlarging the sample period, which may not be feasible) is to substitute y_{it} for $m_{t-1}z_{it}$. That is, instead of using the product term directly in (53) we use that part of the product which takes out some of the effect of $m_{t-1}z_{it}$. From the sample means and covariance we may calculate the Π's as shown in (59). We estimate Ez_{it} by $\bar{z}_i = 1/T \sum_t z_{it}$, and Π_{0i} from the appropriate sample moments. We then use in place of $m_{t-1}z_{it}$ the residual from (56). By so doing, we estimate

$$(58) \qquad m_t = A_0 + A_1 z_{1t} + A_2 z_{2t} + A_3 m_{t-1} + B_1 y_{1t} + B_2 y_{2t} + v_t \,,$$

in which the coefficients satisfy

$$(59) \qquad \begin{aligned} A_0 &= b_0 + (a_1 - b_1)\,\hat{\Pi}_{01} + (a_2 - b_2)\,\hat{\Pi}_{02}\,, \\ A_1 &= b_1 + (a_1 - b_1)\,\hat{\Pi}_{21}\,, \\ A_2 &= b_2 + (a_2 - b_2)\,\hat{\Pi}_{22}\,, \\ A_3 &= a_0 - b_0 + (a_1 - b_1)\,\hat{\Pi}_{11} + (a_2 - b_2)\,\hat{\Pi}_{12}\,, \\ B_1 &= a_1 - b_1\,, \\ B_2 &= a_2 - b_2\,. \end{aligned}$$

(Note that $\hat{\Pi}_{21} = \hat{\Pi}_{22}$.) Hence, given estimates of the coefficients of (58) and the estimates of the Π's in (57) derived from the appropriate sample means and moments, we can solve (59) for the coefficients determining the transition probabilities, the a's and b's of (52). The advantage of estimating (58) instead of (53) is that there is likely to be much less collinearity between y_{it} and the other variables than there is between z_{it} and the same variables.

There are certain aspects of the coefficients of (58) worth noting. At the sample averages of z_{it}, the probability of remaining in state one minus the probability of moving to state one from state two is

$$(60) \qquad \bar{\alpha}_t - \bar{\beta}_t = a_0 - b_0 + (a_1 - b_1)\bar{z}_{it} + (a_2 - b_2)\bar{z}_{2t} \,.$$

This is just A_3, the coefficient of m_{t-1}. The partial derivative of m_t with respect to $\bar{z}_{it}$ is the coefficient of z_{it}. That is,

$$(61) \qquad \frac{\partial}{\partial \bar{z}_{it}}\, \bar{m}_t = b_i(1 - \bar{m}_{t-1}) + a_i \bar{m}_{t-1} = A_i \,.$$

Thus the coefficients of (58) have an intuitive interpretation in terms of the dependence of the transition probabilities on the determining variables z_{it}.

These results have implications for the regression that omits the product terms $m_{t-1}z_{it}$ in certain circumstances to be described. Thus, suppose we write

$$(62) \qquad m_t = A'_0 + A'_1 z_{1t} + A'_2 z_{2t} + A'_3 m_{t-1} \, ,$$

which is (53) without the product terms. Now suppose we estimate the coefficients of (56), the Π's, by least squares instead of from (57), using the sample mean of the independent variables and the appropriate sample moments. Denote the least-squares estimates of the Π's by Π^*. If $\Pi^*_{ki} \approx \hat{\Pi}_{ki}$ ($k = 0, 1, 2,\ i = 1, 2$) and z_{jt} is nearly uncorrelated with $z_{it}m_{t-1}\ (i \neq j)$ then the coefficients of (62) are nearly equal to the corresponding coefficients of (58). Even though collinearity may prevent estimation of the coefficients of (53) and of (58), it may still be possible to estimate the first four coefficients of (58) from (62), and these coefficients reveal something about the structure of the process—namely, the partial derivatives of $\bar{m}_t$ with respect to $\bar{z}_{it}$ and $\bar{\alpha}_t - \beta_t$. From the sample data it is possible to check whether even unfavorable collinearity still allows us to draw some conclusions about the structure of the process. Finally, we may note that $B_i = K_i$ [from (58) and (53), respectively] but, of course, the other coefficients of corresponding variables will in general differ.

Although the standard errors of the coefficients of (53) and (58) may be calculated in the usual way from the least-squares formulas, ordinary significance formulas do not apply because we do not know the small sample properties of the estimators.

There are two applications in [11] and [12] of the methods discussed in this section. In the first the transition probabilities among brands are assumed to depend on the relative prices of the brands and in the second they are assumed to depend on relative advertising expenditures. In both applications collinearity turned out to be a serious problem, and some insight into the process could be obtained by application of the indirect methods discussed in this section. It happens that the average repeat-purchase probabilities for brands of cigarettes, when we assume that these depend on relative advertising expenditures, are quite similar to the results given in the numerical example of the preceding section. There we found that the repeat-purchase probabilities for Camel, Lucky Strike, and Chesterfield, respectively, are 0.77, 0.88, and 0.75. Allowing the transition probabilities to depend on relative advertising expenditures, the average repeat-purchase probabilities turned out to be 0.82, 0.74, and 0.75, respectively (see [12]).

4. Extension to Higher-Order Chains

The least-squares method of estimating transition probabilities applies to second- and higher-order chains. We may study the method applicable for a second-order chain, and the extension to higher-order chains becomes apparent. As before, let n_{jt} denote the number of individuals in state j on trial t. Let n_{ijt} be the number who change from i on trial $t-1$ to j on trial t. Define

$$(63) \qquad q_{ijt} = \frac{n_{ijt}}{n_{i,t-1}},$$

that is, the fraction of individuals in state i on trial $t-1$ who move to j on t. Let

$$(64) \qquad p_{kj,i} = \text{probability of a transition to } i \text{ on trial } t \text{ conditional on the occupancy of state } k \text{ on trial } t-2 \text{ and } j \text{ on trial } t-1.$$

The basic equation of a second-order chain [corresponding to (19)] is

$$(65) \qquad m_{it} = \sum_{k,j} q_{kjt} p_{kj,i} + v_{it} \qquad (i, j, k = 1, \cdots, r),$$

in which v_{it} is the residual.

It is clear from the form of (65) that in order to estimate the second-order transition probabilities $p_{kj,i}$ we need readings on m_{it}, as in a first-order chain, and readings on $q_{kj,t}$. The latter data would in fact be required for obtaining maximum-likelihood estimates of the transition probabilities of a first-order chain (see p. 273). Least-squares estimates of $p_{kj,i}$, however, do not require data on transition numbers through triplets of states, although the availability of such data allows us to obtain maximum-likelihood estimates of the second-order transition probabilities. Assuming we did have data on m_{it} and $q_{kj,t}$, we would calculate least-squares estimates of $p_{kj,i}$ in the way made familiar in Section 2.

In general, obtaining least-squares estimates of the transition probabilities of an h-order chain requires as much data as would be necessary for the maximum-likelihood estimates of an $(h-1)$-order chain. Thus if the chain is first-order we needed the maximum-likelihood estimates of the zero-order probabilities, namely, the m_{jt}. For a second-order chain we need the transition counts from i to j. Were these available, we could calculate the maximum-likelihood estimates of the first-order transition probabilities. It is practically difficult to imagine situations in which we would have the transition numbers for making maximum-likelihood estimates of all the transition probabilities up to but not including the h-order ones for $h \geqslant 2$. Therefore, although the least-squares estimates extend in an obvious way to h-order chains and this should be pointed out, I doubt that any investigator would make use of the method for estimating second- or higher-order transition probabilities, because if the data were at hand to calculate the maximum-likelihood estimates of the $(h - 1)$-order probabilities, it seems likely that they would also be available for the h-order probabilities.

5. Conclusions

The least-squares estimates of transition probabilities are most useful for the study of the properties of a first-order Markov chain in situations in which data are not available giving the actual transitions between pairs of states and we only know the proportion of individuals occupying the states for a sequence of trials. In the latter case the least-squares estimates are consistent and can be weighted so that they are also asymptotically efficient. The method can also be extended to situations in which the transition probabilities are assumed to depend on other observable variables in a specified way. There are many situations in which a probability model of the kind discussed in this paper may be an appropriate tool of analysis, and the method discussed here allows us to estimate the transition probabilities even when we do not have the data required for the maximum-likelihood estimates.

A crucial assumption underlying the application of the method is that all of the individuals behave according to the same transition matrix. If this condition is not met, then the behavior of the aggregate may not follow a first-order chain even if every individual follows his own first-order transition probability matrix. Unfortunately, checking this assumption needs even more detailed data than would be required for the maximum-likelihood estimates of the transitions of the aggregate. Indeed, to check this assumption we need data on the individual transitions. Although one can make do with rather gross data for estimating the transition probabilities, it is clearly appropriate to use the more detailed data if possible when, as is typically the case, one is unsure whether the Markov chain is an adequate description of the real process. It is desirable, of course, to accumulate more experience with the estimation methods suggested here when limitations of the data force us to use them.

REFERENCES

[1] ANDERSON, T. W., and LEO A. GOODMAN, Statistical Inference about Markov Chains, *Ann. Math. Stat.*, 28 (1957), 89-110.
[2] FELLER, WILLIAM, *An Introduction to Probability Theory and Its Applications*, Vol. I. New York: John Wiley, 1950, chaps. 15-16.

[3] GOODMAN, LEO A., A Further Note on Miller's "Finite Markov Processes in Psychology," *Psychometrika*, **18** (1953), 245-48.

[4] GOODMAN, LEO A., Simplified Runs Tests and Likelihood Ratio Tests for Markoff Chains, *Biometrika*, **45** (1958), 181-97.

[5] GOODMAN, LEO A., Some Alternatives to Ecological Correlation, *Amer. J. Soc.*, **64** (1959), 610-25.

[6] HOUTHAKKER, H. S., The Capacity Method of Quadratic Programming, *Econometrica*, **28** (1960), 62-87.

[7] KAO, RICHARD C. W., Note on Miller's "Finite Markov Processes in Psychology, *Psychometrika*," **18** (1953), 241-43.

[8] MADANSKY, ALBERT, Least Squares Estimation in Finite Markov Processes, *Psychometrika*, **24** (1959), 137-44.

[9] MANN, H. B., and A. WALD, On the Statistical Treatment of Linear Stochastic Difference Equations, *Econometrica*, **11** (1943), 173-220.

[10] MILLER, GEORGE A., Finite Markov Processes in Psychology, *Psychometrika*, **17** (1952), 149-67.

[11] TELSER, LESTER G., The Demand for Branded Goods as Estimated from Consumer Panel Data, *Rev. Econ. Stat.*, **44** (1962), 300-24.

[12] TELSER, LESTER G., Advertising and Cigarettes, *J. Pol. Econ.*, **70** (1962), 471-99.

12

On the Specification of Multivariate Relations among Survey Data

H. THEIL, *Econometric Institute, Netherlands School of Economics*

In the last fifteen years a considerable development has taken place in the field of surveys among entrepreneurs and consumers and in the application of these surveys to the prediction of future behavior and to the analysis of behavior patterns. In some cases these surveys take the "ordinary" numerical form; i.e., they ask for the percentage change in a particular variable compared with the level of some previous period, or the expected percentage change that will take place in some future period. But in an important class of cases the surveys are more modest and ask only for the sign of the change: increase, no change, decrease. There can be no doubt that the latter procedure suppresses valuable information, so that there must be good reasons for the choice of this particular setup. One reason is elementary and perhaps not too good from a scientific point of view: the survey is simpler and hence cheaper from the organizer's point of view when his questions allow only three possible answers. But there is also a more fundamental reason. The organizer must take account of the respondents' readiness to answer his questions, and it is not unreasonable to suppose that this readiness decreases when the questions asked take a more detailed character. It is then still true that such "three-way surveys" suppress essential information, but insofar as this second reason is indeed relevant, it must be doubted whether more detailed surveys reveal the information suppressed in an adequate manner. It is even conceivable that the details asked require so much time that the respondents are induced to answer carelessly in such a way that the limited information revealed by a three-way survey is more valuable than the corresponding information of a more ambitious survey. Clearly, it is the task of empirical analysis to find out where the optimal degree of detail is located, and I think that at the present time we still know little about this important issue.

But let us take for granted that at present surveys exist which allow for only three possible answers (increase, no change, decrease), and let us consider the problem of how to specify behavioral relations for this kind of data. It is not difficult to see that this is indeed a problem. Behavioral relations in terms of conventional statistical data are intuitively rather simple (although their aggregation and specification problems should not be

293

overlooked); but survey relations in terms of increase, no change, and decrease are fundamentally different simply because they use these different concepts. One way to set up such relations is the completely microeconomic type: one can analyze the association over time between the three change types of a given variable and a given firm on the one hand, and the similar change types of one or two explanatory variables of the same firm on the other hand. Another method is to formulate relations that are somewhat more aggregative. The usual aggregation procedure is in terms of test variates, which are three non-negative numbers (adding up to 1) for any given period, variable, and industry; specifically, the three test variates in January 1960 for the production of the Belgian weaving industry (say) are the fractions of the entrepreneurs of that industry who report an increase, no change, and a decrease, respectively, in their production. These fractions are obtained by weighting the responses of the participating entrepreneurs in proportion to the size of their firms (measured, e.g., by the number of employees or the amount of sales).

Test variates have the practical advantage that they are directly available, at least in certain surveys such as the Munich Business Test.[1] The object of this paper is to explore the specification of behavioral relations for the case in which one dependent variable is described as a function of two or more explanatory variables.[2] Section 1 is devoted to the case of two explanatory variables and Section 2 to the generalization of three and more; Section 3 contains an application.

1. Two Explanatory Variables

1.1. Bivariate Fractions of the Explanatory Variables.
Suppose we wish to describe some dependent variable (to be denoted by ζ) in terms of two explanatory variables, ξ and η. For example, ζ = selling price, ξ = buying price of raw material A, η = buying price of raw material B. The survey supplies us with test variates for these variables in each month, which will be written

$$(1.1) \qquad z = \begin{bmatrix} z^1 \\ z^2 \\ z^3 \end{bmatrix}; \quad x = \begin{bmatrix} x^1 \\ x^2 \\ x^3 \end{bmatrix}; \quad y = \begin{bmatrix} y^1 \\ y^2 \\ y^3 \end{bmatrix},$$

---

[1] The publication of this survey is in graphical form: for each variable in each month and each industry, there is a horizontal bar divided into three (colored) parts in proportion to the test variates (possibly after rounding). For example, if 25 per cent of the entrepreneurs answer increase, 50 per cent no change, and 25 per cent decrease, the bar appears as follows:

red	white	blue
increase	no change	decrease

[2] For the case of one explanatory variable, see [2].

where the superscript 1 refers to the fraction of increases, 2 to no change, and 3 to decrease. The sum of the three test variates is of course equal to 1:

$$(1.2) \qquad \sum_{r=1}^{3} z^r = \sum_{r=1}^{3} x^r = \sum_{r=1}^{3} y^r = 1.$$

The problem is to formulate, on the basis of a sample of observations on the vectors (1.1), a relation that describes the test vector z (or some appropriate combination of its elements) in terms of the other two vectors in such a way that this relation can be regarded as a meaningful approximation to the underlying relation between ζ and ξ, η. For this purpose, it is useful to interpret the test variates x^r, y^r as the marginal totals of the following array of bivariate frequencies:

$$(1.3)$$

$(xy)^{11}$	$(xy)^{12}$	$(xy)^{13}$
$(xy)^{21}$	$(xy)^{22}$	$(xy)^{23}$
$(xy)^{31}$	$(xy)^{32}$	$(xy)^{33}$

where $(xy)^{11}$ stands for the fraction of entrepreneurs who report an increase both in ξ and in η, $(xy)^{12}$ for those who report an increase in ξ but no change in η, and so on. Obviously, we have

$$(1.4) \qquad \sum_{r=1}^{3} (xy)^{rs} = y^s; \qquad \sum_{s=1}^{3} (xy)^{rs} = x^r; \qquad \sum_{r=1}^{3} \sum_{s=1}^{3} (xy)^{rs} = 1.$$

The bivariate frequencies $(xy)^{rs}$ can of course be calculated from the individual replies of the participants, but we will assume here that only their marginal totals are available. Nevertheless, it is appropriate to pay explicit attention to the bivariate frequencies when analyzing the impact of ξ and η on ζ. We shall do so under the assumption that the dependence of ζ on each of these variables is monotonic, in which case it may be assumed without additional loss of generality that the relationship is monotonically increasing; viz., by replacing (if necessary) either ξ or η or both by minus itself, so that the fractions of increases and decreases corresponding to such a variable are then interchanged.

Let us now consider the impact of the bivariate frequencies $(xy)^{rs}$ on the fraction of increases in the dependent variable z^1; and let us do so for one particular survey and only for those participants who answer the questions on all three variables. Then we can distinguish between nine groups of participants, each corresponding to one of the frequencies $(xy)^{rs}$; and for each of these groups, a certain fraction (θ_{rs}, say) will report an increase in the dependent variable, another fraction (θ'_{rs}) no change, still another fraction (θ''_{rs}) a decrease. The sum of these fractions is of course 1:

$$(1.5) \qquad\qquad \theta_{rs} + \theta'_{rs} + \theta''_{rs} = 1 \qquad (r, s = 1, 2, 3),$$

because each participant is supposed to report some kind of change in ζ (including no change). It is also easily verified that the following relations hold between the test variates of ζ and the bivariate fractions of ξ and η:

$$(1.6) \quad z^1 = \sum \sum \theta_{rs}(xy)^{rs}; \quad z^2 = \sum \sum \theta'_{rs}(xy)^{rs}; \quad z^3 = \sum \sum \theta''_{rs}(xy)^{rs},$$

where the summations are all over $r, s = 1, 2, 3$. It is worthwhile to note that the θ's can all be regarded as conditional probabilities. For example, θ''_{32} is the conditional probability of a decrease in ζ under the condition that there is a decrease in ξ and no change in η.

The relations (1.6) are basic to the development that follows. It will be noted that they are not in adequate form, given our desire to describe the vector z in terms of the test variates x^r and y^s rather than the bivariate fractions $(xy)^{rs}$. In fact, it is not difficult to see that this desire is simply a practical necessity. Suppose that we were satisfied with (1.6) as a description of the relation between ζ on the one hand and ξ and η on the other. This would mean, given the restriction (1.5), that we need $2 \times 3^2 = 18$ coefficients to specify this relation. More generally, if we have n explanatory variables instead of two, this number is 2×3^n (as will be clear from Section 2), which increases quite rapidly with n: 54 for $n = 3$, 162 for $n = 4$, and so on. It is clearly out of the question to estimate that number of parameters even if appropriate observations are available. Therefore, our task is to find an adequate aggregation procedure.

1.2. Numerical Discussion of the Conditional Probabilities θ_{rs}.
For our understanding of the problem it is useful to consider a plausible numerical example for the array of coefficients θ_{rs}. Let us do so for the case mentioned in the beginning of Section 1.1 (ζ = selling price, ξ and η = buying prices of A and B, respectively); and let us assume that A is a more important raw material than B, and that there are other factors that affect the selling price ("neglected variables") but are of less importance than the prices of A and B. Consider then θ_{11}, i.e., the group of participants who report increases in both buying prices and also an increase in the selling price, measured as a fraction of all those who report increases in the two buying prices; or alternatively, the conditional probability of raising the selling price, the condition being that both buying prices increase. Now given this condition, it seems reasonable to assume that θ_{11} will be sizable, although presumably not 1, because it may occur from time to time that there are other factors besides raw-material prices which induce the entre-

preneur to keep the selling price constant in spite of the raw-material price rise. Moreover, it is conceivable that the price increases of the raw materials are sufficiently large to be reported as an increase in the survey (rather than as no change),[3] but not sufficiently large to induce the entrepreneur to raise his selling price. So let us take $\theta_{11} = 0.75$.

Next, consider θ_{12} and θ_{21}, which are the conditional probabilities of raising the selling price under the condition that one of the buying prices increases while the other remains constant. Obviously, we should expect to find θ_{12}, $\theta_{21} < \theta_{11}$; also, it is reasonable to take $\theta_{21} < \theta_{12}$, given our assumption that A is a more important raw material than B. We shall therefore take $\theta_{12} = 0.5$, $\theta_{21} = 0.4$. It will be noted that this relative importance has to be defined here in a particular manner: so that the price of A dominates the price of B to the effect that a particular response (increase, no change, decrease) for the A-price has *ceteris paribus* a more important impact on the selling price than the same response for the B-price.

This domination becomes important when we consider θ_{13} and θ_{31}, which are the conditional probabilities of raising the selling price when one of the buying prices increases while the other decreases. The two most important determining factors offset each other in this case, so that one would expect an unchanged selling price to be the result in a rather substantial percentage of all cases. But it is certainly conceivable that from time to time an increase of the important A-price, possibly together with an appropriate combination of neglected factors, leads to an increase of the selling price in spite of the decrease of the B-price. So let us take $\theta_{13} = 0.3$, which is smaller than θ_{12}, as it should be. It is also conceivable that a B-price increase is so large that it overcompensates the A-price decrease and leads to a selling-price raise; but this will occur less frequently. So we take $\theta_{31} = 0.15$.

We proceed to θ_{22}, which occupies a position intermediate to those of θ_{13} and θ_{31}: it is the conditional probability of raising the selling price under the condition that both buying prices remain unchanged according to the survey. Again, we should expect that this situation leads in a substantial fraction of all cases to an unchanged selling price; but it is conceivable that in some cases the selling price is raised, first because of neglected factors, second because the changes in buying prices may be small increases that are reported as no change (because they are so small) but are nevertheless jointly sufficient to induce the entrepreneur to raise his selling price. It seems plausible that θ_{22} should lie somewhere between θ_{13} and θ_{31}, because the dominating character of the A-price should be

---

[3] No change is to be regarded as "approximately no change," or a change that falls in the so-called indifference interval; see [3, p. 106]. The organizers of the Munich Business Test give no indications to the participants of the location of this interval.

expected to reduce the conditional probability of raising the selling price under the no-change condition on both buying prices below the conditional probability when the A-price goes up and the B-price down, while conversely, the former probability should be larger than θ_{31}, which refers to the situation when the price of B moves upward and that of A downward. So we take $\theta_{22} = 0.2$.

Finally, we have θ_{23}, θ_{32}, θ_{33}, which should be expected to be fractions close to zero: they represent the conditional probabilities of raising the selling price under the condition that either one or both of the buying prices decrease (with the understanding that if only one of the buying prices decreases, the other remains unchanged). It seems reasonable to take θ_{23} larger than the other two θ's, because it is the only conditional probability whose condition does not imply that the dominating A-price decreases. We should expect that θ_{33} is the smallest of the three and in fact negligible; since the two most important determining factors both decrease, it seems reasonable to assume that the selling price is lowered in most cases and kept unchanged otherwise. We therefore take $\theta_{23} = 0.1$, $\theta_{32} = 0.05$, $\theta_{33} = 0$.

Summarizing our θ's, we have the following array:

$$(1.7) \qquad [\theta_{rs}] = \begin{bmatrix} 0.75 & 0.50 & 0.30 \\ 0.40 & 0.20 & 0.10 \\ 0.15 & 0.05 & 0 \end{bmatrix},$$

from which we conclude that the θ's in each row decrease from left to right, and in each column from above to below. Conversely, when considering the θ''_{rs}, which are the conditional probabilities of lowering the selling price, we can set up a similar array but should expect that its rows increase from left to right and its columns increase from above to below.

1.3. The Existence of Multivariate Matrix Relations. For the case of one single explanatory variable (ξ, say), I developed earlier [3, p. 199] the so-called matrix approach, which amounts to the specification

$$(1.8) \qquad z = Ax,$$

where $A = [\alpha_{rs}]$ is a 3×3 matrix of reaction coefficients. Thus α_{11} can be regarded as the conditional probability of a ζ-increase under the condition that ξ increases, α_{23} as the conditional probability of no change in ζ when ξ decreases, and so on. We can regard (1.6) as a generalization of this approach for two explanatory variables, but another generalization is

$$(1.9) \qquad z = Ax + By,$$

which will be termed a matrix relation for test vectors of three variables.

An obvious question is under which conditions the specification (1.9) is compatible with (1.6) and whether these conditions can be considered realistic. It is sufficient for this purpose to consider the fraction of ζ-increases, for which (1.9) implies

$$(1.10) \qquad z^1 = \sum_1^3 \alpha_r x^r + \sum_1^3 \beta_r y^r$$

for certain coefficients $\alpha_1, \cdots, \beta_3$. By replacing the x^r and y^r by sums of $(xy)^{rs}$ in accordance with (1.4), we find that (1.10) is compatible with (1.6) if and only if

$$(1.11) \qquad \theta_{rs} = \alpha_r + \beta_s \qquad (r, s = 1, 2, 3) \,;$$

i.e., if the conditional probabilities θ_{rs} can all be written as the sum of two numbers, one of which (α_r) belongs to one explanatory variable only (ξ) and the other (β_s) to the other explanatory variable only (η). To grasp these implications more fully, consider the difference $\theta_{1s} - \theta_{2s}$, which is equal to $\alpha_1 - \alpha_2$ and hence independent of s, according to condition (1.11). Similarly, the difference $\theta_{2s} - \theta_{3s}$ should be independent of s. It is instructive to test these conditions for our numerical case (1.7). This can be done by subtracting the second row of that array from the first, and the third from the second, which gives

$$(1.12) \qquad 0.35, \quad 0.30, \quad 0.20 \quad \text{and} \quad 0.25, \quad 0.15, \quad 0.10 \,,$$

respectively. In the same way, $\theta_{r1} - \theta_{r2}$ and $\theta_{r2} - \theta_{r3}$ should be independent of r, which can be tested by subtracting the second column of (1.7) from the first, and the third from the second:

$$(1.13) \qquad 0.25, \quad 0.20, \quad 0.10 \quad \text{and} \quad 0.20, \quad 0.10, \quad 0.05 \,.$$

Each of the four sets (1.12–1.13) should consist of three equal numbers in order that the test be positive for our numerical case. It is seen that this is not true, and that the three figures have a downward trend in each of the four cases. This is a negative result, which suggests that the matrix specification (1.9) is inapplicable; but we should of course add that this statement is, strictly speaking, only valid for the numerical case (1.7). Even so, it is instructive to consider an alternative approach in relation to the same example.

1.4. The Existence of Multivariate Balance Relations. When we formulated our problem in the second paragraph of Subsection 1.1, we required a relation either for the complete vector z or for some appropriate combination of its elements. Since we have obtained no success with respect to the vector, it may be worthwhile to consider such a combination; and for this purpose the so-called balance is convenient, which can be argued as follows. Let us regard the answers to the survey, for each period and each variable and each industry, as random variables that take the three equidistant values 1, 0, and -1, where 1 stands for increase, 0 for no change, and -1 for decrease, and let us define the frequencies for these values as the corresponding fractions of replies: z^1, z^2, z^3 for the vector z. Then the balance is defined as the mean of the distribution

$$(1.14) \qquad b(z) = z^1 - z^3 \,,$$

i.e., as the excess of the fraction of increases over the fraction of decreases. This balance varies from -1 to 1, and it takes the lower (upper) limit if all participants report decreases (increases). The balance is a simple and convenient measure for the degree to which positive and negative changes dominate among the group of all participants, so that it is worthwhile to see whether this measure for ζ can be described in terms of x and y.[4]

For this purpose we have to specify the array θ''_{rs} in addition to θ_{rs}. Let us start by making the simple assumption that the reaction with respect to decreases is symmetric with that with respect to increases, i.e.,

$$(1.15) \qquad \theta''_{2-r,2-s} = \theta_{2+r,2+s} \qquad (r, s = 0, \pm 1) \,.$$

This implies $\theta''_{33} = \theta_{11}$; in our example the conditional probability of lowering the selling price under the condition that both buying prices decrease is equal to the conditional probability of raising the selling price when both buying prices increase. Similarly, $\theta''_{23} = \theta_{21}$, and so on. For the numerical case (1.7) we then have

$$(1.16) \qquad [\theta''_{rs}] = \begin{bmatrix} 0 & 0.05 & 0.15 \\ 0.10 & 0.20 & 0.40 \\ 0.30 & 0.50 & 0.75 \end{bmatrix} \,.$$

The balance of z is now determined by the bivariate fractions $(xy)^{rs}$ according to

$$(1.17) \qquad b(z) = \sum \sum \bar{\theta}_{rs}(xy)^{rs} \qquad (\bar{\theta}_{rs} = \theta_{rs} - \theta''_{rs}) \,;$$

and for (1.7) and (1.16) we have

$$(1.18) \qquad [\bar{\theta}_{rs}] = \begin{bmatrix} 0.75 & 0.45 & 0.15 \\ 0.30 & 0 & -0.30 \\ -0.15 & -0.45 & -0.75 \end{bmatrix} \,.$$

---

[4] Since the three elements of the vector z add up to 1, two of them describe the vector completely; but the same applies to any pair of independent functions of the three test variates. A convenient pair is the balance and the disconformity index, the latter being the variance of the sign distribution discussed above. Reference is made to [3, chap. 4].

A brief inspection of (1.18) is sufficient to see that $\bar{\theta}_{rs}$ obeys an additive rule of the type (1.11):

(1.19) $\bar{\theta}_{rs} = \bar{\alpha}_r + \bar{\beta}_s$ $\begin{pmatrix} \bar{\alpha}_1 = & 0.45 & \bar{\beta}_1 = & 0.30 \\ \bar{\alpha}_2 = & 0 & \bar{\beta}_2 = & 0 \\ \bar{\alpha}_3 = & -0.45 & \bar{\beta}_3 = & -0.30 \end{pmatrix}.$

Hence

(1.20) $b(z) = 0.45x^1 - 0.45x^3 + 0.3y^1 - 0.3y^3 = 0.45b(x) + 0.3b(y)\,,$

which is a homogeneous linear relation expressing the balance of the dependent variable in those of the explanatory variables.

1.5. Linear and Quadratic Reaction Patterns. The results obtained so far imply that the additive rule (1.11) is necessary and sufficient in order (i) that the fraction of increases of the dependent variable can be described linearly in terms of the six response fractions of the two explanatory variables, (ii) that this condition fails to be satisfied, (iii) that a similar condition should hold in the array $\bar{\theta}_{rs} = \theta_{rs} - \theta''_{rs}$ for the balance of the dependent variable to be described in the same way, and (iv) that this condition is indeed satisfied.

Of course, these conditions have been tested only for our numerical example; we should now consider them more generally. For this purpose it is useful to note that (1.11) implies that the array θ_{rs} represents essentially a linear reaction pattern: if we set up a three-dimensional Cartesian space in which the θ's are measured vertically and $r = 1, 2, 3$ and $s = 1, 2, 3$ along the two horizontal axes ($r = 1$ at a distance α_1 from the origin, $r = 2$ at a distance α_2, and so on), then the resulting nine points are all located on the same flat plane. Now it is to be doubted whether this linearity is a plausible assumption. Consider the transitions from θ_{33} to θ_{32} and from θ_{13} to θ_{12}. It seems rather safe to assume that θ_{33} is negligible (see Subsection 2.2) and θ_{32} somewhat larger but still very small, because they are both conditional probabilities of increase under the condition that at least one of the explanatory variables decreases while the other either remains constant or also decreases. Hence we should generally expect that $\theta_{32} - \theta_{33}$ is a very small positive fraction. Considering the other transition (from θ_{13} to θ_{12}), we note that θ_{13} should be typically larger than the θ's just discussed, because its condition implies that at least one of the explanatory variables increases. The other decreases, however, and we should therefore expect that under this condition we should find a substantial fraction of no-change and also of decrease responses. But if we take θ_{12}, the new condition involves no decrease in either explanatory variable; we should therefore expect far fewer decrease responses and also fewer no-change responses. This implies a relatively sizable addition to the increase responses, so that we should expect that $\theta_{12} - \theta_{13}$ is typically larger than $\theta_{32} - \theta_{33}$. In (1.7) the former difference exceeds the latter fourfold.

The argument of the preceding paragraph (which is admittedly intuitive) is essentially nothing else than a restatement in words of the declining trends that we observed in (1.12)–(1.13). I think it is appropriate to take account of these trends, but this should be done in a way that does not involve too many parameters. The suggestion is to replace the unrealistic linear reaction pattern (1.11) by the following quadratic reaction pattern:

$$(1.21) \qquad \theta_{rs} = \left(A\,\frac{3-r}{2} + B\,\frac{3-s}{2} \right)^2,$$

where A and B are positive real numbers. This reaction pattern is not only quadratic but also of the equidistant type: increase, no change, and decrease are represented as $r, s = 1, 2, 3$, respectively, just as they are represented by $1, 0, -1$ in the distribution from which the balance is derived. The complete array takes then the following form:[5]

$$(1.22) \qquad [\theta_{rs}] = \begin{bmatrix} (A+B)^2 & (A+\frac{1}{2}B)^2 & A^2 \\ (\frac{1}{2}A+B)^2 & \frac{1}{4}(A+B)^2 & \frac{1}{4}A^2 \\ B^2 & \frac{1}{4}B^2 & 0 \end{bmatrix};$$

for example, if $A = 0.52$ and $B = 0.36$, we have

$$(1.23) \qquad \begin{bmatrix} 0.77 & 0.49 & 0.27 \\ 0.38 & 0.19 & 0.07 \\ 0.13 & 0.03 & 0 \end{bmatrix},$$

which is close to the numerical example (1.7), the separate elements differing from the corresponding elements of (1.7) by at most 0.03. It is easily seen that the specification (1.22) shows the desired downward trends: subtracting the second row from the first, we obtain

$$\tfrac{3}{4}A^2 + AB; \qquad \tfrac{3}{4}A^2 + \tfrac{1}{2}AB; \qquad \tfrac{3}{4}A^2;$$

and similarly, by subtracting the third row from the second, we obtain

$$\tfrac{1}{4}A^2 + AB; \qquad \tfrac{1}{4}A^2 + \tfrac{1}{2}AB; \qquad \tfrac{1}{4}A^2.$$

If we assume further that the conditional probabilities of decrease θ_{rs}'' are symmetric with those of increase in accordance with (1.15), this gives

$$(1.24) \qquad [\theta_{rs}''] = \begin{bmatrix} 0 & \frac{1}{4}B^2 & B^2 \\ \frac{1}{4}A^2 & \frac{1}{4}(A+B)^2 & (\frac{1}{2}A+B)^2 \\ A^2 & (A+\frac{1}{2}B)^2 & (A+B)^2 \end{bmatrix};$$

---

[5] Note that we must have $A + B \leqslant 1$ in order that all θ_{rs} be $\leqslant 1$.

and by subtraction we find

$$(1.25) \qquad [\bar{\theta}_{rs}] = \begin{bmatrix} (A+B)^2 & A^2 + AB & A^2 - B^2 \\ AB + B^2 & 0 & -AB - B^2 \\ -A^2 + B^2 & -A^2 - AB & -(A+B)^2 \end{bmatrix},$$

which shows that the $\bar{\theta}_{rs}$ are, under the present quadratic assumptions, subject to the following additive rule:

$$(1.26) \quad \bar{\theta}_{rs} = \alpha(2 - r) + \beta(2 - s) \qquad (\alpha = A^2 + AB, \quad \beta = AB + B^2).$$

Hence we have a homogeneous linear relation in the three balances, just as in the special case considered in Subsection 1.4:

$$(1.27) \qquad\qquad b(z) = \alpha b(x) + \beta b(y),$$

α and β being specified in (1.26). It is easily seen that the ratio α/β is identical to A/B, the sum $\alpha + \beta$ with $(A + B)^2$, and the difference $\alpha - \beta$ with $A^2 - B^2$. When α and β are determined or estimated from observational data, one can infer from these about A and B by using

$$(1.28) \qquad\qquad A = \frac{\alpha}{\sqrt{(\alpha + \beta)}}; \qquad B = \frac{\beta}{\sqrt{(\alpha + \beta)}},$$

where the square roots in the denominators are to be taken with the positive sign.

The conditional probabilities of no change, θ'_{rs}, are found by using (1.5). The result can be written in the form

$$(1.29) \qquad \begin{aligned} \theta'_{22} &= 1 - \tfrac{1}{2}(A + B)^2, \\[1ex] \theta'_{rs} &= \theta'_{22} - \tfrac{1}{2}[A(2 - r) + B(2 - s)]^2, \end{aligned}$$

which shows that the conditional probability of no change in the dependent variable is at its maximum when the condition implies no change in the two explanatory variables, and that this maximum is at least $\tfrac{1}{2}$ [because $(A + B)^2 = \theta_{11} = \theta''_{33} \leqslant 1$]. One should expect that θ'_{11} and θ'_{33} will in most cases be decidedly below the other θ'_{rs}.

1.6. Additive Asymmetry. There is no need to stress that the reaction pattern (1.22), (1.24) is restrictive; this is simply due to our decision to use only two parameters. There are a great many possibilities of generalization, but most of them do not lead to manageable results. However, it is worthwhile to pay explicit attention to the case in which the reaction patterns for positive and negative change are, contrary to (1.15), not symmetric. A very simple method of handling this is to add non-negative constants to the θ_{rs} and θ_{rs}'' of Section 1.4:

(1.30)

$$\theta_{rs} = c + \left(A\,\frac{3-r}{2} + B\,\frac{3-s}{2}\right)^2,$$

$$\theta_{rs}'' = c'' + \left(A\,\frac{r-1}{2} + B\,\frac{s-1}{2}\right)^2.$$

By subtracting we find that (1.26) is now replaced by

(1.31) $\bar{\theta}_{rs} = c - c'' + \alpha(2-r) + \beta(2-s),$

where α and β have the same meaning as in (1.26). The relation in balances is now linear, as before, but no longer homogeneous:

(1.32) $b(z) = \bar{c} + \alpha b(x) + \beta b(y)$ $(\bar{c} = c - c'').$

This approach is simple but rather restrictive; it implies that the probability of raising the dependent variable (and similarly for lowering) consists of two parts, one completely independent of the behavior of the explanatory variables (c, c'') and the other directly related to these variables. However, such an interpretation is not completely unrealistic when the reports of some of the participants are subject to bias.

1.7. Multiplicative Asymmetry. An alternative approach (which may seem somewhat more realistic) is to assume that the quadratic reaction pattern (1.22), (1.24) as such is correct but that the coefficients A and B are different for increase and decrease. This leads to four coefficients as a whole (one set A, B for θ_{rs} and a second for θ_{rs}''), and more generally, to $2n$ coefficients when there are n explanatory variables, which seems too much for practical work. We shall therefore confine ourselves to the case in which the A's and B's for increase and decrease have the same relative difference, i.e., when A and B of (1.22) can be written $A(1+\epsilon)$ and $B(1+\epsilon)$, respectively, while those of (1.24) take the form $A(1-\epsilon)$ and $B(1-\epsilon)$. Hence A and B are now interpreted as the averages of the corresponding parameters for increase and decrease, and ϵ measures the relative deviation from the averages. For example, if $\epsilon > 0$, then there is a systematic tendency to report increase in ζ in excess of decrease in the symmetric situation (obtained by interchanging increase and decrease in the explanatory variables).

Under the assumptions stated, the conditional probabilities θ_{rs} and θ_{rs}'' take the following values:

(1.33)

$$\theta_{rs} = (1+\epsilon)^2 \left(A\,\frac{3-r}{2} + B\,\frac{3-s}{2}\right)^2,$$

$$\theta_{rs}'' = (1-\epsilon)^2 \left(A\,\frac{r-1}{2} + B\,\frac{s-1}{2}\right)^2.$$

By subtracting, we find

(1.34) $\bar{\theta}_{rs} = (1 + \epsilon^2)(A^2 + AB)(2 - r) + (1 + \epsilon^2)(AB + B^2)(2 - s)$
$$+ \epsilon\{(A + B)^2 + [A(2 - r) + B(2 - s)]^2\},$$

which suggests that the balance of z cannot be described in terms of the test variates of x and y (owing to the term in braces that is nonlinear in r and s). However, let us now *add* θ_{rs} and θ''_{rs}. This gives

(1.35) $\theta_{rs} + \theta''_{rs} = \frac{1}{2}(1 + \epsilon^2)\{(A + B)^2 + [A(2 - r) + B(2 - s)]^2\}$
$$+ 2\epsilon[(A^2 + AB)(2 - r) + (AB + B^2)(2 - s)],$$

which is identical to $1 - \theta'_{rs}$ as specified in (1.29) in the case $\epsilon = 0$. From (1.35) we conclude

$$(A + B)^2 + [A(2 - r) + B(2 - s)]^2$$
$$= \frac{2(\theta_{rs} + \theta''_{rs}) - 4\epsilon[(A^2 + AB)(2 - r) + (AB + B^2)(2 - s)]}{1 + \epsilon^2};$$

and on combining this with (1.34), we find

(1.36) $\bar{\theta}_{rs} = \left(1 + \epsilon^2 - \dfrac{4\epsilon^2}{1 + \epsilon^2}\right)[(A^2 + AB)(2 - r) + (AB + B^2)(2 - s)]$
$$+ \frac{2\epsilon}{1 + \epsilon^2}(\theta_{rs} + \theta''_{rs}),$$

which implies

(1.37) $$b(z) = \alpha b(x) + \beta b(y) + \gamma(z^1 + z^3),$$

where

$$\alpha = \left(1 + \epsilon^2 - \frac{4\epsilon^2}{1 + \epsilon^2}\right)(A^2 + AB),$$

(1.38) $$\beta = \left(1 + \epsilon^2 - \frac{4\epsilon^2}{1 + \epsilon^2}\right)(AB + B^2),$$

$$\gamma = \frac{2\epsilon}{1 + \epsilon^2}.$$

The procedure recommended is therefore to use a homogeneous linear relation which expresses the balance of the dependent variable in those of the explanatory variables and in the *sum* of the fractions of increase and decrease of the dependent variable. Given α, β, and γ, we can use (1.38) to find A, B, and ϵ; this will be elaborated in Section 2 for the more general case of n explanatory variables.

2. Three and More Explanatory Variables

The generalization to more explanatory variables is straightforward and even more elegant in several respects. Let us write $\xi_1, \cdots, \xi_n$ for these variables (which are supposed to affect the dependent variable positively), $x_1, \cdots x_n$ for the corresponding test vectors, and η and y for the dependent variable and its test vector, respectively. Further, let us write $\theta_{r_1..r_n}$ for the conditional probability that η increases if the change in ξ_1 is of the r_1-type, that in ξ_2 of the r_2-type, and so on, where $r_i = 1, 2, 3$ stand for increase, no change, and decrease, respectively, as before; and we shall add primes to θ for no change and decrease in the dependent variable as in Section 1. The generalization of the quadratic reaction pattern in the case of symmetry is then

$$(2.1) \qquad \theta_{r_1..r_n} = \left(\sum_{i=1}^{n} A_i \frac{3 - r_i}{2} \right)^2, \quad \theta''_{r_1..r_n} = \left(\sum_{i=1}^{n} A_i \frac{r_i - 1}{2} \right)^2,$$

where the A_i are all positive numbers. By subtraction we find

$$(2.2) \qquad \bar{\theta}_{r_1..r_n} = \theta_{r_1..r_n} - \theta''_{r_1..r_n} = A \sum_{i=1}^{n} A_i(2 - r_i),$$

where

$$(2.3) \qquad A = \sum_{i=1}^{n} A_i \leqslant 1.$$

It follows immediately that the following linear relation holds between the balances:

$$(2.4) \qquad b(y) = \sum_{i=1}^{n} \alpha_i b(x_i) \qquad (\alpha_i = AA_i),$$

and that the A_i can be found from the α's by means of

$$(2.5) \qquad A_i = \alpha_i(\Sigma \alpha_j)^{-1/2},$$

where the square root is taken with positive sign.

The generalization of the symmetric case is thus immediate. When there is additive asymmetry so that each θ is increased by c and each θ'' by c'', the resulting balance equation (2.4) is changed by the addition, on the right-hand side, of the constant term $\bar{c} = c - c''$. This is completely similar to the case treated in Section 1.6. When there is multiplicative asymmetry as in Section 1.7, we replace A_i by $A_i(1 + \epsilon)$ in the θ-definition and by $A_i(1 - \epsilon)$ in the θ''-definition. After subtracting, we find

$$(2.6) \qquad \bar{\theta}_{r_1..r_n} = (1 + \epsilon^2)A \sum_{i=1}^{n} A_i (2 - r_i) + \epsilon \left\{ A^2 + \left[\sum_{i=1}^{n} A_i(2 - r_i) \right]^2 \right\},$$

while addition gives

$$\theta_{r_1..r_n} + \theta''_{r_1..r_n} = \frac{1}{2}(1 + \epsilon^2) \left\{ A^2 + \left[\sum_{i=1}^{n} A_i(2 - r_i) \right]^2 \right\} + 2\epsilon A \sum_{i=1}^{n} A_i(2 - r_i) \, ;$$

and hence, upon combining this with (2.6),

$$(2.7) \quad \bar{\theta}_{r_1..r_n} = \left(1 + \epsilon^2 - \frac{4\epsilon^2}{1 + \epsilon^2}\right) A \sum_{i=1}^{n} A_i(2 - r_i) + \frac{2\epsilon}{1 + \epsilon^2} (\theta_{r_1..r_n} + \theta''_{r_1..r_n}) \, .$$

This leads to

$$(2.8) \qquad\qquad b(y) = \sum_{i=1}^{n} \alpha_i b(x_i) + \gamma(y^1 + y^3) \, ,$$

where

$$(2.9) \qquad \alpha_i = \left(1 + \epsilon^2 - \frac{4\epsilon^2}{1 + \epsilon^2}\right) AA_i \quad \text{and} \quad \gamma = \frac{2\epsilon}{1 + \epsilon^2} \, .$$

Conversely, when the α_i and γ are given, one can determine A_i and ϵ from

$$(2.10) \qquad A_i = Q_1 \alpha_i (\Sigma \alpha_j)^{-1/2} \quad \text{and} \quad \epsilon = \frac{1 - \sqrt{1 - \gamma^2}}{\gamma} \, ,$$

where

$$(2.11) \qquad\qquad Q_1 = \gamma[2(1 - \gamma^2)(1 - \sqrt{1 - \gamma^2})]^{-1/2} \, ,$$

all square roots in (2.10) and (2.11) being taken with the positive sign. Furthermore, if we write

$$(2.12) \qquad\qquad \gamma = \sin \theta \qquad (0 \leqslant \theta \leqslant \tfrac{1}{2}\pi) \, ,$$

we have the following alternative expressions for ϵ and Q_1:

$$(2.13) \qquad\qquad \epsilon = \frac{1 - \cos \theta}{\sin \theta} \quad \text{and} \quad Q_1 = \frac{\tan \theta}{\sqrt{2(1 - \cos \theta)}} \, .$$

3. An Application

3.1. **Production Planning of Shoe Manufacturers.** As an example we shall use one of Thonstad's and Jochems's [4] regression analyses which describe the production plans of about 70 German shoe manufacturers in the three-year period 1956–1958 as a function of relevant expectations and appraisals. The dependent variable is hence planned production and will be denoted by $\bar{P}$. It refers to the following question, which is asked at the end of each month: Do you plan to raise (keep unchanged, lower) the rate of your production in the next month compared with the present? Three explanatory variables will be used:

H. THEIL

(1) Appraisal of the stock of finished goods, to be denoted by F_A. Question: Do you consider the stock of your finished goods (shoes) in the present situation too large (just normal, too small)?

(2) Stock of orders, to be denoted by O. Question: Did your accumulated stock of orders increase (remain the same, decrease) in this month compared with the previous month?

(3) Expected general business conditions in the next half year, to be denoted by $\bar{G}$. Question: Do you expect that conditions in the shoe industry will improve (remain the same, deteriorate) in the next six months?

TABLE 1

ALTERNATIVE REGRESSIONS FOR THE BALANCE OF PLANNED PRODUCTION

Coefficients (and their standard errors)					
$b(F_A)$	$b(O)$	$b(\bar{G})$	$\bar{P}^1 + \bar{P}^3$	1	$\hat{\sigma}$
—0.033(0.10)	0.130(0.05)	0.534(0.11)			0.1227
—0.296(0.09)	0.141(0.04)	0.284(0.10)		0.099(0.02)	0.0907
—0.241(0.08)	0.119(0.04)	0.253(0.10)	0.376(0.07)		0.0880
—0.262(0.09)	0.125(0.04)	0.254(0.10)	0.282(0.19)	0.027(0.05)	0.0890

The time series of observations on these variables are given in the Appendix of this paper. Four alternative least-squares regressions will be considered, in each of which the balance of planned production is the dependent variable and the balances of the above-mentioned three explanatory variables the independent ones.[6] The first regression is confined to these variables. The second allows for additive asymmetry by including a constant term, the third includes $\bar{P}^1 + \bar{P}^3$ as independent variable and hence allows for multiplicative asymmetry. The fourth contains both a constant term and $\bar{P}^1 + \bar{P}^3$, so that it allows for both kinds of asymmetry. The results are gathered in Table 1, which shows (i) that the signs of the point estimates of the coefficients are all in accordance with *a priori* expectations, (ii) that the residual variance ($\hat{\sigma}^2$) is almost twice as large for the first regression compared with the other three, so that it seems reasonable to assume that there is some kind of asymmetry, (iii) that the coefficients of the three explanatory balance series are not particularly sensitive to alternative specifications except when the specification includes neither a constant term nor the variable $\bar{P}^1 + \bar{P}^3$, (iv) that we have a slightly smaller residual variance when $\bar{P}^1 + \bar{P}^3$ is introduced than in case this

---

[6] Note that the usual least-squares setup implies that the multiplicative coefficients are constant (although unknown), whereas in the present case these coefficients are based on conditional probabilities that may fluctuate from month to month. Reference is made to [2] for a discussion of this point.

variable is replaced by a constant term, and (v) that the addition of a constant term in case $\bar{P}^1 + \bar{P}^3$ is already introduced leads to a slightly larger residual variance. The last feature is due to the fact that the reduced number of degrees of freedom overcompensates the reduction of the sum of squares of the estimated disturbances.

The obvious choice is therefore multiplicative asymmetry, for which the point estimates of the third specification of Table 1 give

$$(3.1) \qquad b(\bar{P}) = -0.241b(F_A) + 0.119b(O) + 0.253b(\bar{G}) + 0.376(\bar{P}^1 + \bar{P}^3).$$

Confining ourselves to point estimates, we thus find $\gamma = 0.376$, implying $\epsilon = 0.195$, $\theta = 0.396$, $Q_1 = 1.06$. Also, $\alpha_1 = 0.241$ (after replacing F_A by minus itself), $\alpha_2 = 0.119$, $\alpha_3 = 0.253$; hence, applying (2.10), we find

$$(3.2) \qquad A_1 = 0.33 ; \qquad A_2 = 0.16 ; \qquad A_3 = 0.34 .$$

The complete array of coefficients

$$\theta_{r_1 r_2 r_3} , \quad \theta'_{r_1 r_2 r_3} , \quad \theta''_{r_1 r_2 r_3} ,$$

based on the A_i and ϵ as specified above, is given in Table 2.

TABLE 2

ESTIMATED CONDITIONAL PROBABILITIES
OF INCREASE (θ), NO CHANGE (θ'), AND DECREASE (θ'') FOR PLANNED PRODUCTION

r_3	r_2 1	2	3	r_2 1	2	3	r_2 1	2	3
	$\theta_{1 r_2 r_3}$			$\theta_{2 r_2 r_3}$			$\theta_{3 r_2 r_3}$		
1	0.98	0.80	0.64	0.63	0.49	0.36	0.36	0.25	0.17
2	0.62	0.48	0.35	0.35	0.25	0.16	0.16	0.09	0.04
3	0.34	0.24	0.15	0.15	0.08	0.04	0.04	0.01	0
	$\theta'_{1 r_2 r_3}$			$\theta'_{2 r_2 r_3}$			$\theta'_{3 r_2 r_3}$		
1	0.02	0.19	0.34	0.35	0.47	0.57	0.57	0.64	0.68
2	0.36	0.48	0.58	0.58	0.64	0.68	0.68	0.69	0.68
3	0.58	0.65	0.68	0.68	0.69	0.67	0.67	0.63	0.55
	$\theta''_{1 r_2 r_3}$			$\theta''_{2 r_2 r_3}$			$\theta''_{3 r_2 r_3}$		
1	0	0.00	0.02	0.02	0.04	0.07	0.07	0.11	0.15
2	0.02	0.04	0.07	0.07	0.11	0.16	0.16	0.22	0.28
3	0.08	0.12	0.16	0.17	0.22	0.29	0.29	0.36	0.45

NOTE: r_1 refers to minus the appraisal of stock of finished goods, r_2 to the stock of orders, r_3 to the expected general business conditions in the next six months.

3.2. The Derivation of Asymptotic Standard Errors. It will hardly be necessary to stress that such a large array of coefficients as that of Table 2 must be characterized by specification errors if we force it into a pattern that is determined by only four coefficients $(A_1, A_2, A_3, \epsilon)$. Therefore, if we compute asymptotic standard errors under the assumption that the specification used is correct (as will be done in this section), the result should be regarded as measuring some kind of lower limit to the inaccuracy that must be expected to exist in reality.

Considering (2.10) or (2.13), we observe that the following relation exists between the differentials of ϵ and γ:

$$(3.3) \qquad\qquad d\epsilon = Q_2 d\gamma \,,$$

where

$$(3.4) \qquad Q_2 = \frac{1 - \sqrt{1 - \gamma^2}}{\gamma^2 \sqrt{1 - \gamma^2}} = \frac{1 - \cos\theta}{\sin^2\theta \cos\theta} = \frac{2\epsilon}{\sin 2\theta} \,.$$

Let us now interpret the differentials $d\epsilon$ and $d\gamma$ as sampling errors around the population value. Then, by applying the usual technique of computing asymptotic standard errors [i.e., squaring both sides of (3.3) and taking the expectation],[7] we obtain

$$(3.5) \qquad\qquad \operatorname{var} \epsilon = Q_2^2 \operatorname{var} \gamma \,.$$

For the data of Section 3.1, Q_2 is estimated as 0.560 and var γ as 0.00439, which gives 0.037 for the asymptotic standard error of ϵ.

The standard errors of the A_i are derived in the same way. Consider (2.10) and take differentials on both sides of the A_i-equation:

$$(3.6) \qquad dA_i = \sum_{j=1}^{n} \frac{\partial A_i}{\partial \alpha_j}\, d\alpha_j + \frac{\partial A_i}{\partial Q_1}\, dQ_1 = A_i \left[\frac{d\alpha_i}{\alpha_i} - \tfrac{1}{2} \frac{\Sigma d\alpha_j}{\Sigma \alpha_j} + \frac{dQ_1}{Q_1} \right].$$

The differential dQ_1 can be expressed in $d\gamma$. Using (2.12) and (2.13), we find

$$(3.7) \qquad\qquad dQ_1 = Q_1 Q_3\, d\gamma \,,$$

where

$$(3.8) \qquad\qquad Q_3 = \frac{1}{2 \cos\theta} \left(\frac{4}{\sin 2\theta} - \frac{1}{\epsilon} \right).$$

---

[7] See, e.g., [1, chap. 9].

On combining (3.6) and (3.7), we obtain

$$dA_i = A_i \left[\frac{d\alpha_i}{\alpha_i} - \tfrac{1}{2} \frac{\Sigma d\alpha_j}{\Sigma \alpha_j} + Q_3 \, d\gamma \right],$$

and hence, after squaring and taking the expectation:

$$(3.9) \qquad \text{var } A_i = A_i^2 \left\{ \frac{\text{var } \alpha_i}{\alpha_i^2} + \frac{\Sigma\Sigma \, \text{cov} \, (\alpha_j, \, \alpha_k)}{4(\Sigma \alpha_j)^2} - \frac{\Sigma \, \text{cov} \, (\alpha_i, \, \alpha_j)}{\alpha_i \Sigma \alpha_j} \right.$$
$$\left. + Q_3^2 \, \text{var } \gamma + Q_3 \left[2 \, \frac{\text{cov} \, (\alpha_i, \, \gamma)}{\alpha_i} - \frac{\Sigma \, \text{cov} \, (\alpha_j, \, \gamma)}{\Sigma \alpha_j} \right] \right\}.$$

When we substitute the least-squares estimates of Section 3.1 in the right-hand side of (3.9), we obtain $Q_3 = 0.330$ and the following asymptotic standard errors:

$$(3.10) \qquad s_{A_1} = 0.11, \qquad s_{A_2} = 0.05, \qquad s_{A_3} = 0.12 \, .$$

The analysis can be extended to the standard errors of the conditional probabilities (the θ's), but this is straightforward and not pursued here.

(References appear on p. 313, following the Appendix.)

APPENDIX

TABLE A.1

TEST VARIATES RELATING TO THE GERMAN SHOE INDUSTRY, 1956–58

(ALL MULTIPLIED BY 100)

Month	Planned production*		Appraisal of stocks		Stock of orders		Expected general business conditions[a]	
	$\bar{P}^1$	$\bar{P}^3$	F_A^1	F_A^3	O^1	O^3	$\bar{G}^1$	$\bar{G}^3$
1956, J	18	4	9	2	50	23	7	8
F	17	13	19	5	3	50	18	7
M	17	7	22	8	2	51	17	8
A	10	8	16	2	7	62	25	7
M	11	14	26	2	20	49	25	3
J	18	7	37	2	47	15	27	3
J	17	1	29	2	56	9	17	3
A	19	—	19	4	14	31	14	6
S	6	7	13	6	4	47	10	2
O	3	12	13	12	19	38	14	4
N	8	7	19	9	46	12	12	3
D	18	7	17	14	62	12	16	22
1957, J	17	5	21	10	41	17	15	1
F	16	6	21	7	27	30	17	2
M	11	6	21	25	23	43	26	1
A	32	4	14	28	10	45	33	2
M	36	6	25	32	43	26	40	—
J	45	3	19	26	67	13	31	—
J	25	1	12	29	76	8	28	1
A	35	1	4	33	39	15	26	—
S	30	1	7	41	32	15	25	—
O	34	—	1	38	44	21	31	—
N	24	11	9	37	52	22	11	3
D	35	9	13	29	25	25	6	7
1958, J	21	6	28	6	23	36	7	12
F	8	7	16	7	15	52	1	26
M	2	3	14	14	1	69	3	28
A	3	12	24	10	15	63	12	29
M	9	6	37	2	44	27	7	31
J	12	7	36	2	68	11	4	21
J	11	10	32	1	43	23	3	28
A	4	16	31	1	14	57	5	14
S	5	23	27	7	4	88	12	21
O	6	26	25	5	37	47	9	27
N	8	23	42	2	55	25	6	31
D	15	13	38	3	27	19	7	31

[a] Plans and expectations are dated in the month in which they were formulated. For example, at the end of January 1956, 18 per cent of the participants planned an increase of their production in February and 7 per cent expected at that time an improvement of general business conditions in the shoe industry in the next half year.

REFERENCES

[1] KENDALL, M. G., *The Advanced Theory of Statistics*, 5th ed., Vol. I. London: Griffin, 1952.

[2] KLOEK, T., and D. B. JOCHEMS, *Specification Errors in Bivariate Relations among Business Test Data*. Forthcoming report of the Research Center of CIRET.

[3] THEIL, H., *Economic Forecasts and Policy*, 2d ed. Amsterdam: North-Holland, 1961.

[4] THONSTAD, T., and D. B. JOCHEMS, *The Influence of Entrepreneurial Expectations and Appraisals on Production Planning. An Econometric Study Based on Business Test Data for the German Leather and Shoe Industry*, Report No. 2 of the Research Center of CIRET (1960), to be published in the *Int. Econ. Rev.*

Author Index

315

Subject Index